# THE POWER
## OF YOUR
# INFLUENCE

## STAN TOLER

**HARVEST HOUSE PUBLISHERS**
EUGENE, OREGON

## The Power of Your Influence

Copyright © 2018 Stan Toler
Published by Harvest House Publishers
Eugene, Oregon 97408
www.harvesthousepublishers.com

ISBN: 978-0-7369-7305-2 (pbk.)
ISBN: 978-0-7369-7306-9 (eBook)

Library of Congress Cataloging-in-Publication Data

Names: Toler, Stan, author.
Title: The power of your influence : 11 ways to make a difference in your world / Stan Toler.
Description: Eugene, Oregon : Harvest House Publishers, 2018.
Identifiers: LCCN 2017046610 (print) | LCCN 2017061156 (ebook) | ISBN 9780736973069 (ebook) | ISBN 9780736973052 (pbk.)
Subjects: LCSH: Influence (Psychology)—Religious aspects—Christianity. | Power (Christian theology) | Change—Religious aspects—Christianity.
Classification: LCC BV4597.53.I52 (ebook) | LCC BV4597.53.I52 T65 2018 (print) | DDC 248.4—dc23
LC record available at https://lccn.loc.gov/2017046610

# CONTENTS

Introduction:

# THE POWER TO CHANGE THE FUTURE

*What is leadership? It's an influence
process—any time you are trying to influence
the thinking, behavior, or development of
another, you are engaging in leadership.*

**KEN BLANCHARD**[1]

You're reading this book because you want to change the world. Perhaps you wouldn't state it quite so dramatically, but the reason you picked up a book on the power of influence is that you have a vision for your life—or your family, community, church, or country—that remains unfulfilled. You want something to be different tomorrow than it is today.

Maybe that something is as mundane as having a clean house. You'd like your family or your roommates to pick up after themselves and do the dishes occasionally. You're tired of nagging, and you don't know what to do next.

Or perhaps you are after larger-scale change. You'd like to change the culture in your workplace or see different policies enacted at your school. You may even aspire to end human trafficking or solve the clean-water crisis in a developing country.

Whatever your dream may be, you've probably already discovered two important things: (1) You cannot achieve this alone, and (2) you cannot force others to join you. The only way to bring real, lasting change to your world is to harness the single most powerful attribute that you or any human being possesses: influence.

## METHODS THAT DON'T WORK

When people long for change, they normally begin by trying two things that are equally ineffective. No doubt you've traveled these roads already. The first is to try to change the world by working harder. We might call this the *power-of-one* method.

### The Power-of-One Method

When you see a problem, you say to yourself, "I can do something about this!" And you dive in with all your energy. You notice the trash along the roadside in your neighborhood, so you stop and pick it up. You want your organization to be more effective and efficient, so you stay later to get more done. You want the world to be a better place, so you become a better person.

The power-of-one approach is well illustrated by the often-repeated story of the starfish.[2] According to one variation of the story, a young man is walking along the beach when he notices an older man picking up starfish that have been stranded by the tide and, one by one, throwing them back into the sea. The younger man surveys the beach and sees a countless multitude of helpless creatures on the sand.

"Look at all these starfish," he says to the old man. "There must be thousands of them. What difference do you think you can make saving one starfish at a time?"

The old man nods, then picks up a starfish, throws it back into the water, and says, "It made a great difference for that one."

The story illustrates the impact one individual can have on another, and it's inspiring at that level. Yet many people who apply this philosophy eventually become frustrated and discouraged. They are moved by a great need but quickly become overwhelmed by its scope. Saving one starfish doesn't solve the underlying problem, so they work harder and harder and harder. At the end of the day—or a few weeks, or perhaps a year or two—they become exhausted, crushed by the weight of an endless need. Some professions have developed terms to describe this, like *burnout* and *compassion fatigue*.

Working harder will not eliminate the problems you dream of solving. You will only exhaust yourself in the process. And that brings us to a second, equally futile approach.

### The Power-Up Method

Realizing that the power of one will never be enough, many well-intentioned folks aim to enlist others in achieving the change they hope for. But, as you may have noticed, other people don't always do what we'd like them to do. When they don't, our first resort is often to apply some form of pressure to gain their compliance. We might call this the *power-up* approach.

We discipline our children, sometimes using corporal punishment, to make them behave. We implement policies in the workplace that will compel others to comply. We even pass laws that will force others to behave as we think they should. And those are just the formal uses of the power-up approach. Informally, we may resort to manipulation, social pressure, or even threats and intimidation to make others join us in the wonderful world we are trying to create.

The power-up approach is doomed to fail, however. Though it may be successful in the short term, social scientists have found that punishment is simply ineffective in changing behavior permanently.[3] When the punishment or other external pressure is removed, people immediately revert to their former ways. And there are many occasions when powering up simply backfires, causing others to harden in their resolve.

Perhaps the best recent example of this comes from the Civil Rights Movement. During the early 1960s, civil-rights activists sought to desegregate bus terminals, universities, restrooms, and other public accommodations in accordance with federal law. Those in positions of authority powered up to prevent it. Activists were met with firm, often violent, resistance, including frequent arrests and the use of fire hoses and attack dogs. Those power tactics backfired, however, as activists persevered and continued to take their stand. In time, public sympathy swung in their favor.

Power tactics may bring a temporary change to a given situation, but they never work in the long run. To achieve the changes you envision, nagging, arguing, intimidating, or even legislating will not change the hearts and minds of others. To do that, you need a tool that is far more subtle, powerful, and effective. You need the power of influence.

## A BETTER WAY

On August 28, 1963, Dr. Martin Luther King Jr. stood on the steps of the Lincoln Memorial in Washington, D.C., and addressed a crowd of some 250,000 people. As you may know, King was the leader of a nonviolent resistance movement aimed at securing equal rights for persons regardless of race. Rather than powering up, King's followers powered down, allowing themselves to be arrested and sometimes beaten without fighting back. On that day in Washington, King delivered his now-famous speech "I Have a Dream," in which he said he looked forward to the day when "all of God's children"—no matter their background—could join hands and proclaim they are "free at last!"[4]

These words rallied millions to the cause of civil rights. Without a bullhorn or bullwhip, nor a fire hose nor an attack dog nor a pair of handcuffs, Dr. King moved millions of people to change their minds about a pressing social issue, and thus changed the character of a nation. How did he do it? With the power of influence.

The purpose of this book is to enable you to achieve your dreams by teaching you to leverage that very power. If you are exhausted from trying to bring about change all by yourself, this book is for you. It will equip you to enlist others in pursuing your vision. If you are frustrated and perhaps even feeling foolish or guilty for the ways you've "powered up" on others, trying to force them to see things your way, this book is for you too. It will help you discover the freedom and confidence to simply be yourself, knowing that your life, your character, and the strength of your vision have far more potential to bring change than does any form of physical power or manipulation. And the stakes are high. Living out your faith by mastering the power of influence is one of the most important things you will ever do.

## WHY THIS MATTERS

The power of influence matters so much because without it, you'll be trapped in a cycle of frustration and ineffectiveness. The danger is that you may not achieve the dreams you have for yourself, or you may even find yourself worse off than before. That's what happened at on July 25, 1914. Two days earlier, Baron Giesl von Gieslingen, the ambassador of the Austro-Hungarian Empire to Serbia, handed a note to the Serbian foreign ministry. A Serbian nationalist had assassinated Austrian Archduke Franz Ferdinand and his wife in Sarajevo, Bosnia. In response, the Austro-Hungarians powered up. They insisted the Serbian government comply to certain terms of agreement over the matter.

The Austrians assumed they could easily win with such a power move, but they were wrong. The deadline came and went, and Serbia mobilized its army. Three days later, Austria-Hungary declared war on the Serbs. Other European powers soon joined their allies on either side of the conflict, and World War I had begun, eventually costing more than 17 million lives.

When you resort to power over influence, you can have no idea what the unintended consequences will be. You probably won't start an international war, but using power tactics in your home, your workplace, your church, or your community can have devastating effects. You risk losing relationships, bruising friendships, damaging your marriage, and destroying the very community context you hope to influence.

Gutting it out with the power-of-one approach can be disastrous also. The stress you may accumulate from overworking, over-caring, overcommitting, and overextending yourself can greatly affect your health—both physical and emotional—and your overall well-being.

Perhaps the worst consequence of not understanding the power of your influence is that you may never reach the goals you dream about. Your life, your family, and your community may never change in the ways you envision if you are not able to enlist others to join you through the positive, magnetic, irresistible power of your influence.

## POWER FOR GOOD

Perhaps you've heard the old story about the salt shop. A man walked into a store one day and asked if they sold salt. "Sure," the clerk said, "we've got lots of it. What kind do you need?"

"I'm not sure," the man replied. "Why don't you show me what you have."

Taking the customer by the arm, the clerk led him through the store, where he showed him row after row of table salt. "Is this what you're looking for?" the clerk asked.

"I don't think so," the man replied.

"No worries," said the clerk. "Follow me." He led the customer deeper into the store to show shelves of kosher salt, rock salt, Himalayan salt, sea salt, flaked salt, pickling salt, softener salt, smoked salt, Alaea salt, and fleur de sel.

The customer's eyes went wide with wonder. "Oh my!" he exclaimed. "You really do sell salt, don't you?"

"Not really," the clerk replied. "We hardly sell any at all. But that salt salesman, wow! He really knows how to sell salt."

When you master the power of influence, like the salt salesman, you'll unlock your ability to enlist others in following your lead. Without powering up and without working yourself to death, you'll begin to see the changes you envision. But make no mistake, influence is not mere salesmanship. Influence is the effect we have on others through our words, actions, and attitudes. It is the power of your life, character, and vision, shaping your world for the better. Yet most of us are unaware of the impact we have on others—either positive or negative.

What do you want to accomplish? Take a moment and envision the change you hope for in your family, in your community, or in your world. You're about to learn the lessons that will enable you to make this vision a reality.

## THE ROAD AHEAD

This book will show you how influence works on yourself, those around you, and the world at large. You will discover the tremendous power you have to affect the world for good, along with practical strategies to leverage that influence in order to make positive change.

Part 1 of this book lays a *cognitive foundation* for what follows. You will come to *understand* the nature of influence and how it operates in your life.

Chapter 1 introduces the idea that *influence is the subtle effect you have on others through your words, actions, and attitudes.* Your influence can be sweet and attractive, like the smell of freshly baked cookies, enticing others to follow. Or it can have precisely the opposite effect. Like the first negative comment on social media, your influence may draw others into negative thinking and actions, leaving them worse off than before. You will become aware of the ways you currently influence others and be motivated to use your influence to make positive change.

Chapter 2 defines the *three dimensions of influence*: self, others, and the world. These are not discrete areas, as if influence in one arena were somehow separate from influence in the others. Rather, these three dimensions operate simultaneously. You have the power to influence your own thoughts and behaviors, the attitudes and actions of others, and those at one remove from you (the world). You will understand the dimensions of influence and realize the importance of influencing yourself and your great potential for influencing others.

Part 2 of the book is about crafting your influence. You will learn the nine key sources of your influence and how to produce a greater influence on others.

Chapter 3 describes the *power of your vision*. Vision is your preferred version of the future, a picture of the positive change you are trying to make in yourself and others. A strong, positive vision brings two benefits. First, it acts as a beacon in your life, guiding each choice you make. Second, it attracts others who may have a vague wish for positive change but have no idea how to articulate or pursue it. A person with a strong faith and a vision for the future will influence others. In this chapter, you will be prompted to articulate the positive change you are trying to make and to organize your life around it.

Chapter 4 describes the *power of your thoughts*. Your thoughts determine your influence because they affect everything about you. You cannot hope to influence others positively until you are thinking and living positively yourself. Centering on the age-old wisdom that "as [a man] thinks in his heart, so is he" (Proverbs 23:7 (NKJV)), this chapter describes the incredible power of your thoughts in forming your actions and character. You will learn how to influence your own attitudes and actions by choosing positive patterns of thought.

Chapter 5 describes the *power of your words*. They are the single most powerful means of influence at your disposal. This chapter illustrates the near inevitability that complaining, naysaying, belittling, and other forms of self-fulfilling prophecy will be realized. You will also be shown the tremendous power of positive speech to shape reality, while learning the speech patterns that influence others and gaining practical strategies for harnessing the power of positive speech.

Chapter 6 describes the *power of your example*. Your example is the silent influence you have over others, even when you are not aware of it. By embodying the change you hope to see in the world, you place a seal upon your words, giving them even greater power. In this chapter, you will learn how your example actually influences others, the factors that limit your positive example, and how to cultivate a consistently strong influence through your habits and actions.

Chapter 7 describes the *power of your presence*. Presence is the impact a person makes on others simply by being in the room. Presence is the sum of a number of subtle factors, including demeanor, manner of speech, facial expression, energy level, and behavior. In this chapter, you will come to see the often-underestimated effect of your presence both in person and online, and you will discover strategies for changing "the temperature of the room" simply by being present.

Chapter 8 describes the *power of your encouragement*. Encouragement is a form of positive speech that takes influence to a new level. When you encourage others, you directly influence their thoughts and actions. The results can be astounding. In this chapter, you will discover the explosive power of encouragement and be motivated to practice it consistently in your relationships.

Chapter 9 describes the *power of your generosity*. Generosity is giving to others without expectation or obligation. You can be generous with time, abilities, or resources. Generosity influences others in two ways. First, it establishes leadership by example, showing others the needs or opportunities that are most important. Second, it has a nudge effect, prompting others to be generous also. In this chapter, you will be inspired to become more generous and will be prompted to identify specific ways to practice generosity.

Chapter 10 describes the *power of your commitment*. Commitment is your willingness to stick with a positive vision even when it's difficult to achieve. Strong commitment is highly influential because people respect those who are willing to sacrifice for a goal over the long term. This chapter will provide strong motivation to remain engaged in the process of change over time.

Chapter 11 describes the *power of your sacrifice*. Generosity is sharing from abundance; sacrifice is giving of oneself at a level that risks loss. Sacrifice produces the most powerful influence because it is a demonstration of love. The influence of Gandhi, Dr. Martin Luther King Jr., Billy Graham, Bill Bright, John C. Maxwell, and other great leaders endures precisely because they were willing to put the needs of others ahead of their own. In this chapter, you will be inspired to give the greatest possible gift to others: yourself.

Finally, each chapter concludes with The Key Three: three critical questions for personal reflection. Remember that none of the learning in this book will benefit you if it stays inside your head. To be of use, it must trickle down into your heart and flow out through your words and actions. By reflecting on the ideas communicated here, you will both solidify the learning in your mind and discover practical ways to translate that learning into action.

When we have finished, you will *realize* what influence is, *understand* how it operates in your life and the lives of others, and *be empowered* to extend your influence to make positive change in yourself and in the world around you. What would you like to accomplish today? We're about to begin the journey to achieve that goal.

**THE KEY THREE**

1. State the main reason you're reading this book. What do you hope to achieve by it?

2. Are you more likely to resort to the power-of-one method, the power-up method, or the power of influence? Why?

3. How would you define *influence*?

Part 1

# UNDERSTANDING YOUR INFLUENCE

# THE NATURE OF INFLUENCE

*Our chief want in life is somebody*
*who shall make us do what we can.*

**RALPH WALDO EMERSON**[1]

You've heard it said, "There's one in every crowd." Most of the time when that well-worn descriptor of human behavior is used, it's not good news. It is often applied to someone who stands out because of their negative impact on others. "There's one in every crowd" could be applied to the person who always speaks their mind while others stare at the floor or the sky. It could refer to that one person who forgets to turn off their cell phone at church or who drives slow in the passing lane. It might be said of that one guy who yells "Get in the hole!" at a golf tournament, before the golfer has even taken a swing. It seems that in every place people gather, there's one ill-mannered, boorish, or obnoxious person. We've all experienced the negative power of that one person among many. If we're honest, we would probably admit that we've *been* that person on some occasions. The saying "There's one in every crowd" usually refers to negative influence, the power we all have to affect others in destructive ways.

Negative influence is easy to spot because it makes an immediate impression. It's noticeable. Less noticeable—but just as impactful— is "that one person" who exercises a positive influence. Though we haven't coined a phrase to describe this phenomenon, we have all experienced it. I'm talking about that one person who holds the door open for others, setting a tone for politeness in the workplace. Or it could be the one person who arrives home in a good mood, transforming a hectic day into an enjoyable family dinnertime. Or it could be the one person who lightens the mood with a little humor after receiving bad news. Motivational speaker Zig Ziglar said, "Send out a cheerful, positive greeting, and most of the time you will get back a cheerful, positive greeting. It's also true that if you send out a negative greeting, you will, in most cases, get back a negative greeting."[2] That's precisely true, and it describes the tremendous power of influence in our lives. Though these may seem like mundane examples, they are anything but that.

This chapter will define influence and show you how it operates in your life. You will become more aware of the ways you currently influence others, and you will be motivated to use that influence to make positive change. You can be "that one person" who changes the world for the better. Are you ready to try?

## THE DEFINITION OF INFLUENCE

Influence is the subtle effect you have on others through your words, actions, and attitudes. Your influence can be sweet and attractive, like the smell of freshly baked cookies, enticing others to follow—or it can have precisely the opposite effect. Like the first negative comment on social media, your influence may draw others into negative thinking and actions, leaving them worse off than before. Let me illustrate this concept with an employment experience shared by my friend Lawrence.

When Lawrence was in college, he worked at a shoe store, where he was one of the leading salesmen. "Being one of the best made me a little cocky," he confessed, "so I got a bit lazy with some of the less-desirable aspects of the job." Lawrence gradually quit putting away the "drags," or unsold shoes shown to customers, and stopped pitching in with store-closing tasks like vacuuming the floor and restocking displays. "I even got a bit sassy to the assistant manager," he admitted, referring to the person who was often assigned the evening shift.

Before long, the power of influence kicked in and other employees followed suit. Within a few weeks, the store became a stressful and chaotic place as other employees also refused to cooperate with the managers. "That's when Charlie brought me in for a little chat," Lawrence said.

Charlie was the store manager, a good-natured guy but nevertheless a strong leader. "Charlie sat me down and started asking questions," Lawrence recounted. "He asked how I was doing. Whether I was having any problems at home or at school. If I was upset or in any kind of trouble. I was a bit taken aback because he seemed so interested in me."

When Lawrence admitted that everything in life was fine, Charlie zeroed in on the real problem. "Then you have no excuse for the way you've been acting," he said. "I'd like you to start pitching in with the extra chores, and treat my assistant with more respect." Then came the real power words: "I expect more from you, Lawrence. You're better than this."

*Ouch!* Lawrence thought. "I knew he was right," he said. "To be honest, I had no idea how my bad attitude was affecting others, and I didn't want to be 'that guy.' Charlie motivated me to change."

This is the power of influence in action. Every day, your attitudes, words, and actions are operating on those around you. If you are alive, you have influence. The only question is whether that influence will be positive or negative. Will you be "that one guy" who writes a sarcastic comment on every social media post, poisoning the online atmosphere? Or will you be "that one gal" who, like the shoe store manager, influences others to be the best version of themselves? How will you use your influence?

## ASPECTS OF INFLUENCE

To take control of your influence, you must understand what it is and how it operates. It's a bit like flying an airplane. Flight is a complex process involving the forces of thrust, lift, and drag, not to mention the added impact of the weather and the aerodynamics of the craft. It would be foolish—and dangerous—to hop into a Cessna with no training and expect to fly. Yet anyone can learn to fly, given proper instruction and a little experience. The same is true of exercising influence. You can lead others in positive ways when you understand these key aspects of influence.

### Influence Is Subtle

First, influence is subtle. Though it is the strongest power you possess, it does not always produce an immediate, visible impact. To exert influence is to play the long game, aiming for victory in months or years, or even over a lifetime.

We are conditioned to believe that the effects of exercising power will be immediate, visible, and overwhelming. Possibly that's because we've seen physical power applied that way during wartime. Military terms like *blitzkrieg* and *shock and awe* have made their way into our vocabulary, influencing the way we think about producing change in any area of life, not just the battlefield. We have come to expect immediate results for our efforts.

Living in the digital age probably contributes to this expectation as well. Not that long ago, a computer that took less than five minutes to boot up was considered "fast." We now expect electronic devices to boot on demand and web pages to load instantly. When we press "send," we assume that the other person has already received our text.

Not surprisingly, we bring this expectation of immediate, visible results to our desire for change. We'd like to change a policy at work and see immediate compliance, or explain to our spouse how we feel about an issue and gain instant agreement. When we don't see a direct response to our efforts, we become frustrated. That's when we're tempted to either power up or give up.

Influence, however, does not always produce instant results. Its power is subtle, sometimes almost imperceptible. Yet influence, over the long term, can exert irresistible force. What may begin as a single raindrop of influence can, over time, become an inescapable flood.

In that way, influence is like the power exerted by the moon as compared with the power of the sun. The sun represents direct power. When it shines directly on you, its heat and intensity are impossible to ignore. That's especially true at higher elevations or in places closer to the earth's equator. Stand in direct sunlight in the mountains of Colorado, and your skin will burn in a matter of minutes. Those burning rays will have you putting on a hat or reaching for the sunscreen. Or take a walk in the tropical sun at midday, and you'll very quickly tire from the heat. You'll soon take shelter in the shade until that burning lamp gets a bit lower in the sky.

The sun's power is direct, immediate, and overwhelming. Just what we'd like our influence to be.

In reality, however, our influence is more like the power of the moon. We see the moon far less often because it's visible mostly at night. And the intensity of the moon's glow is only a fraction of the sun's. You can look directly at the moon without shielding your eyes, and nobody ever put on a hat to protect themselves from moon burn.

Yet the moon exerts tremendous power on the earth, moving the tide of vast oceans twice a day. Because the moon is much closer to the earth than is the sun, the moon's gravitational pull is actually greater than that of the massive star. The moon can raise or lower the level of the ocean by several feet, an effect that is amplified closer to shore and in bays or estuaries. In Canada's Bay of Fundy, the tide produces a sea-level change of more than 40 feet. This tidal change is so dramatic that it causes the falls on the Saint John River in New Brunswick to flow backward twice each day!

You could stare at the seashore for hours and not realize that the moon was gently, persistently affecting the level of the ocean. Yet if you didn't move for a long time, you'd get your feet wet.

Just because the influence of the moon is subtle does not mean that it lacks power or effect. The same is true for your influence. You may not see its impact in a day or even a year, but over time your attitudes, words, and actions will produce change in the world around you.

### Influence Is Continual

Few things are more annoying than a dripping faucet. A single drop of water has very little power by itself. You probably wouldn't notice the sound, and 0.05 milliliters of $H_2O$ would evaporate very quickly. Yet one drop of water every few seconds quickly becomes a headache, both psychologically and physically. The sound is enough to drive you crazy, and those single drops combined would be enough to soak through the floor in a matter of hours.

Influence, positive or negative, is similar in that no single instance may be decisive. However, hour by hour, day by day, and year by year, the power of our influence adds up. We influence others constantly, whether we are aware of it or not. But those moments of influence are like single drops of water. It is their aggregate force that produces results.

Think of it this way: anyone can arrive for work in either a good mood or a bad mood. If you enter your workplace a bit snarly one time, few people would probably notice. But show up with a scowl day after day, and you'll begin to disrupt the team. Some will start to avoid you. Others will join in the grumpiness or complaining, and the entire environment will be affected by your negative influence.

In the same way, if you compliment a coworker on her performance once, that kind word will be appreciated but could be easily forgotten. However, if you look for opportunities to praise others for a job well done and frequently offer pats on the back, they'll soon look to you for leadership. Your positive attitude will influence others.

The key thing to remember is that you are *always* influencing others, whether you want to or not. Your life is like a radio transmitter. It is always broadcasting a message, whether it's "I'm bored," or "I'm angry," or "This is stupid"—or something more positive like, "I'm in a good mood," or "You're welcome." Your attitude, words, and actions continually exert their gravitational pull on others.

Think about how you spent the last 24 hours. What did you do? What kind of mood were you in? What were you thinking about? Whom did you see, speak to, interact with? And here's the most vital question: Was your influence on those people positive or negative? Were you more like a dripping faucet or a gentle breeze? You influence others whether you choose to or not, so the best thing is to be intentional about exerting a positive influence.

### Influence Is Dynamic

There's a documentary that goes by the title "You Can't Be Neutral on a Moving Train."[3] The idea is that the train has picked a direction, even if you haven't. It's impossible to stand still on earth while the train is moving; you're going one direction or another. Your influence is like that. It is dynamic, not static. It will affect others in some way, either positively or negatively.

Some people have a stronger influence than do others, of course. Among strong personalities, the wallflower in the group may be overlooked. Your influence may be overshadowed or unnoticed, but it will never be neutral.

Have you ever been selected to participate in a consumer survey or an opinion poll? If so, did you do it? It's possible that you were either too busy or too little interested to share your thoughts. Or perhaps you were miffed at the company, disgruntled about politics, or just didn't want to participate. But here's the thing: even by not responding, you were telling the pollster *something.* The motivation behind your message may have been unclear, but you did deliver a message. You said, "No."

When you come home and don't speak to your spouse, you're not being neutral. You're sending a negative message (or a positive one, if you're allowing them to focus on a task). When you don't raise your hand in class, you're sending a message—perhaps that you're bored, or don't understand, or are shy, or that the instructor hasn't reached you yet. It's impossible to be in any social context and exert no influence whatsoever. Your attitudes, words, and actions—or nonactions—say something.

That doesn't mean you always have to speak, always have to participate, or always have to respond. Of course not. But it does mean you must be aware that your influence—even through the nonverbal vibe you transmit to others—is never zero. It will always be either positive or negative.

Again, review your last 24 hours. Think about the times when you were the least available or the least open to others. What message did that send? Was it something positive, like, "I'm focused on being productive," or "I need sleep," or "Can we do this later?" Or was it a more negative message, like, "You're not important," or "I'm too busy for you," or "I don't want to deal with this"?

Remember that many aspects of your influence are subtle. They can be communicated even by facial expressions and nonverbal clues like a sigh, a groan, or a giggle. What did you communicate to others when you thought you were communicating nothing at all? By asking yourself that question, you are beginning to take control of your influence so you can leverage its possibilities.

## Influence Is Variable

Dwelling on the power of your influence can seem a bit overwhelming. You may be thinking, *I can't do this! There's just so much to wrap my mind around.* It's not uncommon to feel a bit helpless and overwhelmed when contemplating a life change. You may feel it's impossible to develop the level of your influence for a variety of reasons.

One reason is that you may feel a lack of control over your life. Perhaps you have seen yourself as a passive person or you've been surrounded by dominant personalities. When others have exerted control over you, it can be difficult to think of yourself as having the power to change.

As a result, you may have fallen into a pattern of learned helplessness. You may have developed the lifestyle of allowing life to happen around you, passively accepting the outcome of situations or the decisions of others in a fatalistic way.

Third, you may have fallen for the idea that your life cannot be changed. "This is just who I am," you may say. "I'm a failure," or "I'm a weak-willed person," or "I'm a nobody." Your false belief system limits you to thinking that you must accept life as it now is, that no positive change is possible.

None of that is true. It is possible to change your life. You have the freedom to make choices for yourself. Your previous ways of looking at the world, seeing yourself, and interacting with others do not have to determine your future. You have the ability to control how you influence others. Your influence is variable.

If you have fallen into a pattern of thinking negatively and thus projecting a negative attitude to the world, that can change. *You* can change! If you have simply allowed life to happen, accepting whatever comes as if you have no choice, that can be changed too. You can exercise your freedom to make choices, form responses, build new relationships and sever old ones. If you have believed that you are the sum total of your past actions—especially your past mistakes and failures—that can change. Your past does not have to define you. You have the power to define yourself.

Think of the butterfly. These beautiful, delicate creatures are loved by nearly everyone for their colorful wings and airy flight. Of course, they begin life looking—and behaving—very different, as caterpillars. These wiggly worms have 13 body segments, and most are a dull brown color. They inch along the ground and crawl up plant stems, nibbling on organic matter. In order to grow larger, the caterpillar must molt, shedding its own skin four or five times before entering its cocoon. No one unfamiliar with the life cycle of the butterfly would think much of a caterpillar. These lethargic creatures don't show much potential.

Yet before the butterfly emerges from the cocoon, a great transformation has taken place. Fuzzy feelers have been replaced by graceful wings. The dull color has changed to bright orange, yellow, or purple hues. The drab insect that inched along the earth is now capable of gliding above it, some at speeds of up to 30 miles per hour!

Like the caterpillar, you can be transformed from dull to colorful, passive to active. Your influence over others may once have been slight, or it may have been largely negative in the past. No matter. You can influence yourself by changing your thoughts, and you can influence others to follow you through the positive power of your attitudes, words, and actions. Your influence need not remain what it is today. You have the power to change, and by changing, to change the world.

## BE THE ONE

We are living at a time when the power of influence is clearly on display, a time when positive influence is sorely needed. Fake news, social media trolls, and widespread suspicion of others have combined to create a culture of outrage. It seems that each day brings louder shouting, less communicating, and a greater gap between well-meaning folks who happen to hold different opinions. We desperately need more people to realize the tremendous power of influence and to use it in positive ways.

This situation is not unlike one that occurred some 2,500 years ago in the ancient nation of Judah. This nation had wandered far from its roots and become riddled with corruption. God said in Ezekiel 22:29, "The people of the land practice extortion and commit robbery; they oppress the poor and needy and mistreat the foreigner," denying them justice. Verse 30 adds that God looked for someone who would rebuild the nation and "stand...in the gap on behalf of the land" in order to avoid its destruction.[4] But no one was found, and, sadly, the nation was destroyed.

We too are in need of leaders who will "stand in the gap" on behalf of their families, their communities, and even their country. The world seems filled with negative influences, those who degrade society through their negative attitude, careless words, and hostile actions. The stakes have never been higher, and people are desperately searching for positive influencers.

Will you be "that guy" or "that girl" who reverses the tide in your home, workplace, school, or community? Will you harness the subtle, dynamic, irresistible power of your attitude to create positive change? I think you are the one who can say to those around you, "We're better than this." When you lead through the power of your influence, others will follow. I believe in you.

### THE KEY THREE

1. Did any section of this chapter cause you to reflect on your influence in a new light?

2. Be honest with yourself: Is your influence on others currently trending positive or negative?

3. What motivates you to be a positive influence on others?

# THREE DIMENSIONS OF INFLUENCE

*If you want to make an impact, start with yourself.*

**—JOHN C. MAXWELL**[1]

A political election may be the ultimate test of influence. In countries from Andorra to Zimbabwe, Australia to Zambia, candidates periodically vie to be the people's choice for president, prime minister, or other offices at the head of state. It's no easy task to influence the thinking and decision-making of millions, sometimes hundreds of millions, of people.

In a recent presidential election in France, 11 candidates squared off in the first round, each hoping to gain the support of a majority of the country's millions of voters. As you can imagine, each politician faced a serious challenge in getting his or her message to the people. France is a nation of nearly 67 million people covering more than 248,000 square miles. The previous candidate to win a presidential election in France spent more than 20 million euros on the campaign. The barriers of time, travel, and communication are enormous in such an undertaking. How do you multiply your influence in order to reach millions of people in a short time? That's the question each candidate faced.

Jean-Luc Mélenchon, representing one of France's minority parties, knew that he would have to get creative in order to compete for votes. So the 65-year-old politician found a way to multiply his presence while conserving precious campaign funds. Mélenchon appeared live onstage at a rally in Lyon (eastern France), while a holographic image of himself was projected via satellite to crowds in six other cities, including one on the island of La Réunion, a French territory in the Indian Ocean, some 5,600 miles away![2] Critics called it a gimmick, but they simply may have been sorry they didn't think of it first.[3] Using technology, Mélenchon was able to appear live and in 3-D to supporters across the globe. He multiplied his influence—in three dimensions.

While Mélenchon's hologram may have been a new use of technology for swaying voters, three-dimensional influence is nothing new. In fact, to be effective, all influence must be cast in three dimensions: *self*, *others*, and *the world*. In this chapter, you will come to understand the three dimensions of influence and realize the vital importance of maintaining integrity in each one—especially the self.

## INFLUENCE STEW

Influence exists in three dimensions, and they are always interrelated. The first dimension is *self*. To influence others, you must first influence yourself by taking control of your thoughts and attitudes. The second dimension of influence is *others*. This may be what you think of first when hearing the term *influence*. The third dimension of influence is *the world*, or people at a distance from you—those you don't personally interact with. These folks know you by your reputation, your work, or your communications. This widest dimension of influence is what Mélenchon exercised via hologram. He wanted to move the hearts and minds—not to mention the votes—of people who would never know him personally. To do so, he presented, well, himself.

That makes the point that these dimensions are not discrete or separate from one another. They are and must be interconnected. You cannot influence others to have a positive attitude if you do not have one yourself. Though that may sound obvious, it isn't always. And you cannot hope to influence the world if you do not first exert that same influence on those around you. There's no sense trying to persuade the people who don't know you to follow you, when the people who know you best will not. Like the hologram, which presents a whole person in three dimensions, all dimensions of your influence must be in sync, fully integrated with one another.

Another way to think of influence is as a stew. If you were to make a beef stew, for example, you'd probably want these three basic elements: meat, potatoes, and gravy. Those classic ingredients, seasoned with a few spices, would make a delicious meal. And you'd need all three. Meat and potatoes without the gravy wouldn't be a stew. Nor would gravy and meat alone. All three elements must be present to make the stew. But when you eat the stew, where does one ingredient end and another begin? You might take a bite that's mostly meat and another that's mostly potatoes, but the beauty of the stew is that all elements are more or less equally present. That's what gives it the flavor.

Your influence is the same way. It cannot exist without impacting all three dimensions—self, others, world—in similar ways. There's a word to describe those who attempt to exert influence while missing one of these key dimensions: *hypocrite*. If you fail to keep connected and consistent in each of the three dimensions, you will undermine your own influence and, quite possibly, harm your reputation. To be successful in influencing others, which is likely your primary goal, you must maintain the integrity of your influence.

Let's take a look at each of the three dimensions of influence. As we do, consider the ways you must grow in one dimension or another if you are to achieve your goals.

## INFLUENCING YOURSELF

The first dimension in which you exercise influence may seem unlikely. We usually think of influence as something either that we exert over others or that others exert over us. Even the concept of influencing yourself may seem strange, as if you were two or more different people inhabiting the same life. But isn't that what you are?

Freudian psychologists speak of the id, the ego, and the superego as three aspects of the self. The id refers to our baser instincts; the superego to the moralizing, critical-thinking aspect of ourselves; and the ego to the executive function that mediates the two. Ancient religions sometimes refer to the three aspects of self as body, mind, and spirit. The apostle Paul also referred to a divide in the human nature, labeling one part the "old self" and the other the "new self." The first is riddled with selfish desires and prone to repeated failures, and the other is set free by faith in Christ and able to gain self-mastery.[4] Others have comically pictured these aspects of human nature as a devil sitting on one shoulder and an angel on the other, each whispering into our ear to influence us.

Whether or not you have thought of it in such terms before, you've certainly experienced this battle within yourself. One part of you wants to be disciplined, eat properly, and exercise regularly. The other part wants to eat junk food, sit on the couch, and relax. One part of you wants to save money, get out of debt, and live responsibly. The other part of you loves to spend money without counting the cost. No doubt you've won and lost countless such battles with yourself over the years. The term often used to describe this struggle to follow our better nature is *self-discipline*. However, I prefer the term *self-influence*.

Regardless of the terminology we place around this dynamic of self-influence, it is vital for success in every aspect of life, especially in influencing others. Self-influence is not simply a spiritual virtue or a psychological attribute with no bearing on "real life." It is a basic survival skill for beings, and it's the bedrock of influencing others. If you cannot influence yourself to be disciplined, kind, loving, or fair, you can never hope to cultivate that attribute in others. Your own failure in that area will be evident to all, undercutting your influence.

The old saying goes that you cannot take someone to a place you've never been, and, in terms of influence, that's true. You will never cultivate in others the character, mind-set, attitudes, and behaviors you do not display yourself. If you would influence others to follow you, you must first lead yourself. As has often been said, "You must be the change you want to see in the world."

How do you influence yourself? Obviously, this battle for self-mastery is a complicated challenge for human beings. It's written about in some of the most ancient spiritual writings, and it continues to be a subject of debate among psychologists. Many books have been written on the subject, and several of the chapters in this book deal with various aspects of self-mastery. For now, let's begin with the most basic step. To influence yourself, you must choose to take control of your own life.

Does that sound obvious? Believe me, it is not. Many people live with the mistaken idea that they are helpless. Realizing there are many things in life that they cannot control—such as the weather, the economy, the behavior of others, or the past—they conclude that they have no control over anything, including their own thoughts and actions. They become victims to the will of the id, the "old self," or the devil on their shoulder. They lack self-discipline and suffer the consequences of their inaction in the form of ill health, debt, or unhappiness.

If that describes you, I have good news. You *can* change. You may not have the power to change other people, and you certainly can't change the past, but you can change the future, beginning today. You can choose to think positive thoughts. You can choose to react positively in the face of adversity. You can choose to be active rather than passive. And all of that begins with your basic choice to take control of your own life—to influence yourself.

If you have not realized your need to influence yourself, make the choice to do it starting today. Resolve that you will not maintain a victim mind-set, passively accepting the version of yourself that you have created over the years—or that others have influenced you to be. Choose to become the person you hope to influence others to be.

Yes, this will take time. Self-influence is a lifelong endeavor. All the more reason to start today.

## INFLUENCING OTHERS

The second dimension of influence is others, meaning the people with whom you are in direct contact. These are your family members, friends, classmates, coworkers, neighbors, or any person with whom you interact in the course of a day—even store clerks or passersby on the street. Remember, your influence is continual, and it is never neutral. Every day you exert influence on the people you see—or who see you. Following are a few things to keep in mind about your influence on others.

Your influence over others is important because it is the launch pad for your influence on the world. The people who know you the best should trust you the most, so if you cannot influence your loved ones, your friends, and others who have a direct window into your character, your influence will never grow wider. This concept has been a basic tenet of leadership theory for centuries and is even recorded in the Bible. The apostle Paul wrote to a young man named Timothy, giving him advice on appointing leaders in the fledgling churches of the first century. Paul wrote, "If anyone does not know how to manage his own family, how can he take care of God's church?"[5] If the people closest to you don't respect and trust you, it's likely that no one else will either.

This does not mean that every single person you meet must think highly of you if you are to extend your influence. Some of us are surrounded by irrational or dysfunctional people. And everyone has one or two people in their lives with whom they simply don't click. Even the greatest leaders are not able to influence everyone. However, if your good character is not evident to those close to you, generally resulting in trust and respect, your influence on the world will remain limited.

Also, the old adage holds true: you don't get a second chance to make a first impression. Internet entrepreneur and social media guru Gary Vaynerchuk is known for his animated style, and a quote often attributed to the energetic pitchman says, "I influence anybody who is able to get through the chaos of my first impression." Hopefully, lots of people push through that first impression to learn from the bestselling author of *The Thank You Economy*. However, you should not count on others being willing to battle through your bad attitude, complaining, anger, or negativity in order to get to know the "real you." From the looks and gestures you exchange with other drivers on the freeway to the casual words you say to store clerks, your first impression, like scent or shadow, precedes you wherever you go. Get it right, and it will open the door to positive influence. Blow that first impression, and you may permanently lose your opportunity to impact that person.

The tremendous potential of one person's influence over others was evident in the handling of an overbooked flight from Chicago's O'Hare Airport to Louisville, Kentucky. Airline personnel asked whether four passengers on Flight 3411 would be willing to step off the plane and take a later flight. Three people volunteered, but a fourth was involuntarily "bumped" from the flight. The man selected was a 69-year-old physician who not only refused to give up his seat, but also refused to cooperate with airport security personnel who were called to forcibly remove him. Cell phone cameras recorded the scene as the man was literally dragged kicking and screaming from the airplane. Within a short time, the videos were shared on social media and picked up by the mainstream press. The fallout was swift and substantial, as public opinion quickly swung against the airline for what seemed to be heavy-handed tactics. The airline's stock plummeted amid threats of a boycott, doing great damage to the carrier's reputation.[6] The lawsuit filed by the disgruntled passenger turned out to be the least of the airline's problems.

Though that situation was complex and I make no judgment about the persons directly involved, it's obvious that the airline's ability to attract other potential passengers and investors was harmed by a bad interaction with a single customer. The airline's influence on *others* (in this case, a particular person with whom they had direct contact) hampered their influence on *the world* (everyone else).

Carefully cultivate your influence over the people with whom you have contact each day. They are your gateway to reaching the world.

## INFLUENCING THE WORLD

The third dimension of influence is the world: those who are at one remove from you. This includes the people you communicate with on social media but do not personally know; those who read your books or listen to your speeches; the people who buy your products or benefit from the money you donate to various causes. In the electronic age in which we live, this realm of influence could truly include the whole world. Your vision for change may be more modest than that, and you may be thinking primarily of influencing your community, or the people you work with, or perhaps just your family. That's fine. But remember that your influence *will* operate in this wider context whether you wish for it to or not. The world is socially connected, and not just through the Internet. Your reputation, your work, and your legacy may travel far beyond the people you influence day by day.

Your influence in this wider context can be summed up in a single word: *reputation.* Those who don't know you personally may still come to know *about* you. People who work at the same company you do will know whether or not you have a volatile temper long before they meet you face to face, if they ever do. Your selfless acts of kindness or sacrifice may become known to people you will never meet, influencing them to display the same virtues.

Your reputation has great power, partly because it is impersonal. Those who know you—your family and friends—will never believe all the best about you, nor all the worst. They know you well enough to realize that you are not a saint, but they still love you. They can overlook your faults and foibles. They can fill in the blanks with their personal knowledge of your character. Those at one remove, however, have nothing but your reputation to go by. They will fill in the rest with their imagination, for better or worse.

For that reason, you must guard your reputation carefully. It is one of your most precious—and most fragile—assets. Investor Warren Buffett, the Sage of Omaha, said, "It takes twenty years to build a reputation and five minutes to ruin it. If you think about that, you'll do things differently."[7]

Perhaps no one knows that better than Justine Sacco, the public relations executive who became an object of widespread criticism for a single careless remark made on social media. Before boarding a flight from London's Heathrow Airport to Cape Town, South Africa, Sacco tweeted this comment: "Going to Africa. Hope I don't get AIDS. Just kidding. I'm white!"

Justine Sacco had just 170 followers on Twitter. Her comment was likely meant as a jest to those closest to her, never intended for a wider audience. But during the 11-hour intercontinental flight, her tweet traveled also, making its way around the globe. Her comment went viral on social media, reaching far beyond her inner circle of friends and associates. Without intending to, Justine Sacco had influenced the world.

Sacco later said the statement was intended as an ironic comment on white privilege, but while she slept on the plane it was taken literally by thousands of social media users who were quick to voice their outrage. When Sacco turned on her phone upon landing in South Africa, it was flooded with messages. One person she knew from long ago acquaintance wrote, "I'm so sorry to see what's happening." Then another friend called to say, "You're the No. 1 worldwide trend on Twitter right now." Many angry readers had begun to castigate Sacco online and demand her firing, seeming to revel in her humiliation. Her parent company issued a statement saying, "This is an outrageous, offensive comment. Employee in question currently unreachable on an intl flight." Sacco later told a reporter how losing the respect of nearly everyone affected her. "I cried out my body weight in the first 24 hours," she said. "It was incredibly traumatic." And, as the faceless mob had demanded, she was fired from her job.[8]

Your influence over yourself, others, and the world are all connected. The words you say, even inside your own head or to your closest associates, can have a wider impact than you can imagine. As D.L. Moody reportedly once said, take care of your character, and your reputation will take care of itself. Maintain the integrity of your influence in all three dimensions.

## INFLUENCE IN ACTION

The stories just mentioned show the tremendous danger in mismanaging your influence. Yet there is also tremendous potential to affect others for the good when your influence over yourself, others, and the world are in perfect alignment.

On June 12, 1929, a little girl was born to a Jewish couple, Otto and Edith, who were living in Germany. Fearing the coming persecution of Jews under the Nazi regime, Otto moved his family of four to the Netherlands in the late 1930s. But no place in Europe was safe from the Holocaust, and the family was forced into hiding. There, this child, now a girl of 13, spent the next 25 months hidden in the annex of rooms above Otto's office in Amsterdam, kept secret and aided by a few close friends of the family. The girl occupied her time by reading and by writing in her diary.

The girl wrote about all of the things you might expect an adolescent girl to be concerned with. She wrote about her family, the others who were also confined in the annex, and her hopes and dreams for the future. The remarkable thing, however, is how she, still a child, was able to maintain positive thoughts and a confident outlook in what must have been a frightful and depressing situation. Living in virtual captivity, she was able to influence herself to remain cheerful, positive, and hopeful about the future. That attitude had an impact on her family and others who knew her.

In time, however, the family was betrayed to the Nazis. They were arrested and deported to concentration camps. In March of 1945, nine months after her arrest, this young girl, now fifteen years old, died of typhus.

By now you may have guessed that this child was Anne Frank. Her diary, saved during the war by one of the family's helpers, was first published in 1947. Since then, *The Diary of a Young Girl* by Anne Frank has been translated into more than 60 languages.

It has sold more than 30 million copies, making it one of the best-selling books of all time and one of the most widely read books in the world.[9]

Because she was able to influence herself to be positive, kind to others, and hopeful, Anne Frank had tremendous influence over her family and their close friends. And because she was able to influence others, they preserved her words for publication, and Anne Frank has exerted tremendous influence on millions of people around the world.

Of all the words in Anne Frank's diary, perhaps the most moving are these, which should be a grand inspiration to every person who aspires to make a positive change: "I want to go on living even after my death! And therefore, I am grateful to God for giving me this gift, this possibility of developing myself and of writing, of expressing all that is in me."[10] She also said, "How lovely to think that no one need wait a moment, we can start now, start slowly changing the world!"[11] "We all know that 'example is better than precept.' So set a good example, and it won't take long for others to follow."[12]

This is the power of influence in three dimensions. When you influence yourself, you influence others. When you influence others, you reach the world. So what are you waiting for?

**THE KEY THREE**

1. How would you describe the connection between the three levels of influence?

2. In what ways do you need to influence yourself more positively?

3. Who are the people you influence on a daily basis, and what is the result of that influence?

Part 2

# CRAFTING YOUR INFLUENCE

# THE POWER OF YOUR VISION

*All our dreams can come true if we have the courage to pursue them.*

**WALT DISNEY**[1]

If you had been traveling by train from the town of Banbury, England, to London on the morning of April 6, 2015, you'd have been in for a surprise. Passengers on the First Great Western service from that market town along the Oxford Canal had settled in for the 64-mile jaunt to London when crewmembers hopped aboard and put the commuter train in motion. Only instead of heading east, toward London, they drove the train west, toward Swansea. The direction was not a mistake; the crew meant to go to Swansea. That was their assignment. The problem was that they had boarded the wrong train. They had a destination in mind, but they were still headed in the wrong direction.

The crew soon realized their mistake and headed back to Banbury station. Passengers had to catch the next train, causing them to arrive late at their destination. "We are really sorry," said a company spokesman. "Unfortunately the train crew boarded the wrong train."

One person tweeted, "I'd have thought this was page 1 of the Train Driver's Manual." He added good-naturedly, "But then I've made pretty stupid mistakes at work too."[2]

In fact, nearly everyone has made that identical error—setting out in the wrong direction and taking others along for the ride. That's precisely what happens when we exercise influence without vision. We don't know where we're going, and we lead others on the same chase.

Possibly you've been on both sides of this situation, as a driver and a passenger. Perhaps when you were younger, you idolized a friend who you thought was cool. Maybe you adopted their manner of speech and copied their attitudes, only to find that their personality or outlook completely changed within a few months. Though you thought they had it all together, they were really just finding themselves. That's influence without vision.

Or you may have worked for a company that announced a grand, new corporate strategy, only to abandon it within a few weeks. It became clear that the leaders had no firm direction. They exercised influence without vision.

You may have done this yourself, strongly voicing an opinion and urging others to adopt your point of view, only to change your mind. You were able to influence others but did not have a clear vision of the future you wanted to create.

Influence without vision is, at best, a waste of time. At worst, it's a danger to you and your community because it erodes trust, squanders resources, and could lead others to a place they have no desire to be. If it is true that you can't take others to a place you've never been, it's also true that you can't take others to a destination when you don't know where it is. If you hope to have lasting influence, you must have a clear vision.

What happens when you have both vision and influence? Well, just about anything. It is a powerful combination that leads to real change in people's lives and in the world.

A strong, positive vision both guides your life choices and serves as an inviting call to others, attracting them to join you. In this chapter, you will learn how to form, articulate, and communicate the change you hope to make in the world, thus influencing others to join you.

## WHAT VISION IS

First, let's define what vision is. Vision is your preferred version of the future, the positive change you are trying to make in yourself and others. Simply put, your vision is the change you want to see in the world. You've probably seen before-and-after pictures, the photos people take before and after they begin their diet or undertake some renovation project. Laid side by side, these photos make a dramatic illustration of the change that has occurred, whether it's weight loss, home improvement, or new construction. The contrast is often inspiring.

The problem, of course, is that you don't have before-and-after pictures of yourself or your house before you begin the project. All you can see is the now—the problem that exists. You see the weight you want to lose. You see the outdated kitchen appliances or the vacant space.

To get yourself motivated on your own project, you must *envision* a future reality that doesn't yet exist. What we call vision is the "after" photo that exists only in your mind. It's a picture of the reality you're trying to create. To make any worthwhile change in your life, your community, or your world, you must be able to see that preferred future. You must have a mental image of the change you want to make in the world.

Lack of vision is the reason most well-intentioned leaders are not able to produce the change they long for. They may understand that the world is not right, or that something in their personal life, family, or workplace isn't functioning as it should be. But it takes no vision to name the problem. Everyone can see it! It requires no foresight to realize that you are in poor physical condition, or your company is losing money, or the streets in your town are riddled with potholes. Problems are always obvious. What's not so clear is the compelling idea of what *could* be if people are willing to work for change. Stating the problem requires nothing more than good eyesight. To see the future, well, that takes vision.

Let's pause right here and return to the central question of this book: What is the change you hope to make in the world? You may be thinking primarily of the problem and stating your "vision" in those terms. For example, you may say, "I'm overweight," or "I wish I wasn't in debt," or "Our company keeps losing money." Each statement certainly represents a problem in need of a solution, but that is not a vision. A vision is a clear, compelling view of the *future,* not the problems of the present. Examine these statements and see if you notice the difference from the ones above:

- I see myself fit, healthy, and having energy to do the things that matter to me.

- My family is debt free and gives generously to worthy causes.

- My company is thriving and has the capital to enter new markets.

Do you notice the difference? Problem statements are flat and uninspiring. They are often demotivating because they focus attention on what's wrong. While it's vital to face the reality of your situation squarely, no matter how bleak it may seem, you cannot hope to produce change by dwelling on the problems of the present. You must look to the future and see an inspiring, positive, hopeful image of what *will* be. And that brings us to the real value of vision, how it functions in your life and how it translates into influence in the lives of others.

## HOW VISION WORKS

The first function of a strong vision is that it becomes your guide into the future, telling you which direction to take. If you have a clear vision, you'll drive your train in the right direction every time. If you have a smartphone or a GPS, you already know the value of this kind of navigation system. A GPS uses triangulation to tell you two vital pieces of information: where you are and the location of your destination. A global positioning system can calculate your location on the planet within a few feet by measuring the time it takes a signal to travel between a system of satellites and a receiver—the handheld unit you refer to as a GPS.[3] It tells you where you are. In vision terms, that's like stating the problem. But the GPS can tell you something more: the location of your destination. When you know those two things— where you are and where you want to be—you always know which direction to take.

That's the first function of vision in your life. You already know where you are (that is, the problems you face), but vision tells you where you want to be. By comparing the two, you will always have a foolproof guide for making decisions about what to do next. You know which way to travel because you can clearly see where you want to wind up.

Let's translate that into real-world terms using a couple of the examples we've already mentioned. If your vision is to be fit, healthy, and energetic, then you will have clarity about what to do when offered the opportunity to skip your bike ride or have a second slice of pizza for lunch. The answer to both is no. Why? Because you can see your destination, and you know that both of those options are detours away from it.

If your vision is to be debt free, then the questions "Should we buy a new computer on credit?" and "Will we pay more than the minimum on our credit card payment?" both have obvious answers. No, you won't take on further debt, and yes, you will sacrifice to make progress on repayment. The first is a detour away from your destination; the second is a giant step toward it.

That's the power of vision. It gives you a clear picture of where you are in relation to where you want to be. It guides your path into the future.

A second function of vision relates not to you but to others. Just as vision is a GPS to guide your decision making, it is also a beacon, guiding others toward a future they may not have been able to see for themselves.

For centuries, beacons of various types have guided voyagers to their destinations. Signal fires, lighthouses, and, now, electronic signals have given ship captains and pilots a clear indication of the path toward a port, around a shoal, or onto a runway. A beacon tells others, "This way!" And that's precisely what your vision will do for those around you. It will guide them toward a destination they can't clearly see on their own.

Many people long for this sense of direction in their lives but have difficulty articulating a vision for change. Yet when a leader comes along and says, "Here's what's possible for our family" (or company or community or church), others latch on to that signal like a fighter jet locked on to the approach beacon of an aircraft carrier. Though they may not be able to define the vision themselves, they will recognize it when they see it and will be readily influenced by it.

When Dr. Martin Luther King Jr. spoke of a world in which people would "not be judged by the color of their skin but by the content of their character," he articulated a vision that few would have imagined, but multitudes latched onto it.[4] That speech, in part, led to profound changes in American society.

When President John Kennedy stood in front of a joint session of Congress and announced, "I believe that this nation should commit itself to achieving the goal, before this decade is out, of landing a man on the moon and returning him safely to the earth," he excited the imagination of a nation that had never dreamed of such a venture.[5] Yet that bold vision became a shining beacon for a generation, inspiring the nation to meet that goal in just eight years.

This is the power of vision in action. A strong, positive vision acts as a beacon for others, rousing them from apathy, lethargy, and exhaustion, and motivating them to create change.

When you form your vision and begin to share it, your ideas will become a guiding light for others to follow. Your family members, neighbors, and fellow students will be rallied to the dream of a changed world. Who knows? You might even inspire a nation.

## VISION INHIBITORS

If vision is such a natural way to motivate oneself and influence others, why don't more people have a clear, compelling vision of the future? Like most things, creating and sharing a positive vision is easier said than done. The reason is that there are powerful forces at work against anyone who dares to dream and to inspire others with that dream. As a would-be influencer, you must be aware of the factors that inhibit your ability to create and cast a vision. Following are three powerful vision killers. Two of them reside within you, and the third you will encounter in others.

### Fear

Whether we like admitting it or not, most of us are afraid of change. All change, even positive change, brings with it the unknown. The moment you begin to dream of a different reality, you will be confronted with questions about the future. You intuitively realize that creating change in any context will alter the status quo of relationships, economics, and other systems in your life. Though you may never voice these questions aloud, you will begin to wonder about things like these:

- How will standing up for my rights affect my relationships with my siblings?
- If I adopt a healthier lifestyle and my spouse doesn't, how will that affect our marriage?
- Will I lose friends if I change my habits of spending and socializing?
- Will I lose my job if I begin to push for changes at work?

Fear is a natural first reaction to the thought of change. Fear is a vision killer and, therefore, an influence killer. To influence others in a positive direction, you must first face and conquer the fears that reside within you. Vision requires courage.

Are you willing to work for change in your life and in your relationships, even though there are risks involved? Are you more committed to your vision for the future than to the status quo? Have you counted the cost of making changes in your world? You must risk in order to grow.

### Self-Doubt

The second barrier to vision is *self-doubt*. Dreaming about the future is much easier when you're alone at home, envisioning the world as you'd like it to be. Yet as soon as you step outside your door, you're forced to face this simple reality: you are just one person, and the world is an awfully big place. You become keenly aware of your own shortcomings, and you begin to ask questions like these:

- Can I really make my vision reality?
- Was I foolish for thinking things can really change?
- What if I fail?
- Who am I to take on this challenge?

- What if nobody listens to me?
- Am I smart enough, strong enough, or good enough to make this happen?

Self-doubt is the devil on your shoulder, continually whispering into your ear, "You must have been crazy to think this was possible!" Self-doubt is a perfectly normal experience, and, sadly, it stops many would-be influencers in their tracks. Paralyzed by these inner demons, they quietly decide that it's simpler and safer to put their vision on the shelf and accept things the way they are.

To form and share your vision with others, you will need self-confidence. This is not an inflated sense of self that leads you to believe you have no weaknesses and can do things that are beyond your ability. Self-confidence is a proper sense of your own worth that leads you to believe that if others can succeed, you can too. You do have what it takes to be a dreamer, a doer, an influencer. Are you ready to stop listening to the voice of doubt and doom and tune in to the voice of faith, hope, and possibility? Are you willing to believe that you—yes, *you*—can make a positive change in the world? If so, you're ready to influence others.

## Resistance

The third force that works against vision is not internal but external. It is the *resistance* you will meet in others when you begin to exercise influence. All change is initially met with this resistance because all people feel the same feelings of fear and self-doubt when the possibility of change is presented. Every person you meet will be wondering about the same questions that you have faced. However, unlike you, they will have an object for their negative emotions—you. As the one presenting a vision for change, you will become the focus of their negative energy. This resistance may take shape in passivity, hostility, avoidance, undermining, or outright conflict. When that happens, just remember you also had to work through your fears and doubts about this vision. Allow others the opportunity to do that as well, but don't allow their resistance to inhibit your dreams, or the sharing of those dreams with others.

Are you willing to face the pushback of family members, friends, and even total strangers concerning your vision? Then you are ready to become an influencer.

## KEEPING IT SIMPLE

As you form your ideal for a positive future, be careful to articulate that vision in terms that will inspire both you and others. A common mistake among those who seek change is that their vision for the future is too complex to be easily understood. To be influential, your vision must be simple, inspiring, and easy to remember. But you would be surprised at how complex some vision or mission statements are.

Now consider this statement from the Alzheimer's Association: "Our vision: A world without Alzheimer's disease."[6] Or this from Oxfam: "Our vision is a just world without poverty."[7] It's likely that either of those statements could inspire your interest in joining the cause, or at least learning more about it. The most influential statements of vision are clear, concise, specific, and inspiring.

What do you hope to achieve? How do you want to influence others? Consider these statements that articulate some common personal dreams.

- My vision is to lose 30 pounds in one year.
- I will be debt free in two years.
- My dream is a 100 percent graduation rate.
- We can end discrimination in our workplace.

If you cannot state your dream for the future in a single sentence, it may not be clear to others—or even to you. If it takes more than five to ten words, it probably won't be inspiring. But when you can see it clearly, state it briefly, and repeat it easily to others, your positive picture of the future will influence many to join you.

## FROM VISION TO INFLUENCE

Having a positive, inspiring vision for the future is a first step to influencing others. But that vision will have little effect it if is printed on a business card and tucked into a drawer, or posted on a web page that nobody visits. To affect others with your vision, that vision must exert a positive force in your life and in theirs. There are two primary ways that takes place.

## Live It

The first way to influence others with your vision is to *live it*. Your vision must be more than a slogan you repeat from time to time. It must actually influence *you* in the plans you choose, the decisions you make, and the way you live your life. John C. Maxwell said, "Good leaders must communicate vision clearly, creatively, and continually. However, the vision doesn't come alive until the leader models it."[8] Andy Stanley has coined the phrase "wear it" to describe this aspect of leadership. When it comes to creating change in an organization, Stanley says, "It's not enough to believe it. You must be seen doing it."[9]

To be credible in influencing others, you must be committed to enacting the changes you ask them to adopt. If you want others to be more respectful of each other in your home, then you must keep your temper in check and speak with kindness. If you hope to create a workplace in which each person is treated fairly, you must be generous in giving credit to others for their contributions and make room at the table for newcomers. You cannot hope to inspire others to create a world that you are not willing to sacrifice for yourself.

## Repeat It

The second way to influence others with your vision is to *repeat it*. The Rule of Seven is an old marketing principle that holds that a prospect must see or hear a marketing message at least seven times before they will take action on it. That's why, for example, advertisers are willing to place their ads on television, radio, or websites until people are nearly sick of seeing them. The technical term for this is *effective frequency*. This has to do with the number of exposures that are necessary for a person to respond to an advertised message. Beyond that point, the exposure can become wasteful.

So what is the effective frequency of a vision? How many times does a person have to hear that positive idea of the future before they adopt it for themselves? How many times can you repeat your vision to others before they no longer care to hear it?

Many leadership experts would say that there is no effective frequency for vision. In other words, people must hear it constantly in order for it to become part of their thinking. And it is impossible to repeat a vision too often because people easily forget it or become distracted from pursuing it. In practical terms, this means that you must repeat your vision to others as often as you possibly can so that it becomes a natural part of their thinking and doesn't get crowded out by the busyness of life.

What does that look like? It's saying things like, "Remember, we're going to be debt free in two years" every time you make a decision about spending. It's saying to a coworker, "Good job with that project. We're well on our way to being the most innovative company in our industry." It means looking in the mirror every day and repeating the words, "I will be at my goal weight by my birthday," then saying it to your spouse each time you choose a restaurant. To influence others with your vision, it must become part of your vocabulary—and theirs.

When you are tired of talking about the positive change you hope to see in the world, you're just getting started with being an influencer. And when you begin to hear your vision repeated back to you by family members, coworkers, neighbors, and friends, you know that your influence is taking hold. Model your vision with every choice you make, and repeat it to others at every opportunity. As you do so, your influence will begin to grow.

## THE RIGHT TRAIN

Let's return to the train platform in Banbury for a moment. Imagine yourself as a London-bound traveler who was inadvertently hijacked toward Swansea by a conductor who'd boarded the wrong train. You rode along for miles, knowing that you were bound for the wrong destination but unable to do anything about it. How do you suppose that would feel? What emotions would you experience? Frustration? Anger? Helplessness? Resignation? Now imagine your relief the moment the crew realized their error and stopped the train. They were still a long way from Banbury, and an even farther distance from London. But a critical change had been made. Someone had come to see that the train was headed in the wrong direction and had begun to do something about it.

Now that you have a clear vision for the future, you're like the train conductor who has realized the problem and begun to address it. You can't change your destination overnight, but you have already changed your direction. By adopting a positive vision for the future, you have taken the first critical step to changing your world. Even if your destination is still a thousand miles away, it feels much more empowering and hopeful to take one step toward it than to be sitting still or moving the other way.

You're on the right train now. You see a clear picture of a better future for yourself or your family or your workplace or the world. Now that vision can serve as your GPS, guiding your decisions from day to day. And the more often you enact that vision and repeat it to others, the more it will become their beacon, drawing them along with you. You have a clear picture of a preferred future, and that is the first step toward influencing others to follow. Your train is now headed in the right direction, and you are well on your way to changing the world.

### THE KEY THREE

1. State your vision for the future in one sentence.

2. Name one life change you can make right now to act on that vision.

3. Tell one person about your vision and ask them to join you in making it reality.

4

# THE POWER OF
# YOUR THOUGHTS

*For as he thinketh in his heart, so is he.*

**PROVERBS 23:7 (KJV)**

The train had just pulled out of Circular Quay Railway Station in Sydney for a ten-minute run to Central Station, the busiest rail port in New South Wales, Australia, serving some 11 million riders per year. Passengers sat quietly, as commuters often do, some reading and others looking out the window, possibly anxious about whatever events the day might bring.

Just then a railway employee came on the public-address system to make an announcement. Generally, live announcements—as opposed to prerecorded messages—are muffled and difficult to understand. Passengers often tune them out entirely, preferring to focus on their newsfeeds or listening to music through headphones. But on this day, ears perked up all over the train. Passengers who'd had their eyes glued to smartphones or tablets became attentive, listening to the conductor's message.

"Good morning, ladies, gentlemen, and children," the conductor said clearly and cheerfully. "This is the 7:35 a.m. from Penrith to Central, and you'll be pleased to know that we are right on time."

Smiles began to appear on the passengers' faces.

"This means that we'll get you to where you're going in plenty of time," the announcer continued, his voice animated, "and what a lovely morning it is in Sydney today. The sun is shining, temperature is about

53

21 degrees, birds are singing, and all's right with the world. I trust you have a great day wherever you're going. Thanks for catching my train this morning, and I hope to see you again soon. Have a great day!"

The good mood proved to be contagious. By the time the announcement concluded, passengers were not only smiling but had even started connecting with one another. Perfect strangers struck up spontaneous conversations, something almost unheard of on a busy commuter train. Why? Because the cheerful attitude of the friendly conductor had done what a positive attitude will do anywhere in the world, in any context, with any group—it had influenced people to follow.[1]

You have probably experienced something like that before. When a coworker arrives showing visible enthusiasm for the day ahead, the whole team becomes energized. One person's positive attitude can influence an entire workplace. That can be true in a negative sense as well. When a flight is delayed, all it takes is one passenger to begin complaining, and a sour mood will infect the entire cabin.

Attitude is contagious. Like a yawn, it will spread from person to person, affecting the atmosphere of a family, classroom, office, or any other group. Your attitude, for better or worse, will influence those around you.

And here's something you may not know: you have the power to control your attitude through the thoughts you choose to entertain. How you think determines how you feel. How you feel shapes how you act and react in any situation. And your attitude—that is, your thoughts and feelings displayed through behavior—will influence any group you are in. All of that begins with the mind.

If you want to have a positive influence on others, you must have a positive outlook fueled by positive thoughts. If you allow yourself to engage in a negative thought pattern, that will work its way out into your words and actions, even your facial expressions. And that will negatively influence those around you. The ancient wisdom of the Bible rings true: "As [a man] thinks in his heart, so is he" (Proverbs 23:7 NKJV). Your thoughts determine your influence because they affect everything else about you.

In this chapter, you will come to understand why it is so important to take control of your thoughts, fueling your mind with a positive outlook. You'll also learn the seven types of positive thinking that will produce a positive influence. And what's more, you'll discover that, regardless of how negative you may have been in the past, you *can* change your mind and become a positive person. You can influence those around you with joy and hope. It all starts when you take control of your most valuable asset, your mind.

## HOW POSITIVE THINKING CHANGES YOU

For centuries medical professionals have studied the human condition through the lens of disease. That means they have generally paid less attention to healthy people than to the sick, and they have focused their attention on what's wrong with an eye toward making it better. In other words, they've focused on the symptoms and root causes of illness and tried to alleviate or eliminate them. That has also been true in the relatively new medical specialty of psychology. It has been driven largely by the attempt to identify and eliminate mental illness.

However, there is an emerging focus on wellness in the practice of medicine, and that exists within the practice of psychology as well. *Positive psychology* focuses on fostering positive attitudes toward one's experiences, individual traits, and life events with the goal of minimizing destructive thoughts and creating a sense of optimism toward life. Positive psychology examines how ordinary people can become happier and more fulfilled.

Barbara L. Fredrickson, a researcher at the University of Michigan, found that positive thinking is more than just a feel-good exercise; it actually changes the way your brain works. In her experiment, Fredrickson divided her subjects into five groups and showed each group different video clips, each intended to foster a different kind of emotional response. The first group saw clips intended to create feelings of joy; the second, hope; the fourth, fear; and the fifth, anger. The third group was the control group, so they watched videos that were not intended to evoke any emotional response.

Afterward, Fredrickson asked each person to imagine themselves in a situation where they would experience similar emotions to what they'd just seen, and write down what they would do in response. Each person had a piece of paper with 20 blank lines that began with the words, "I would like to. . ."

Here's where it gets interesting. People who saw images that evoked fear or anger wrote down the fewest responses, but those who saw images of joy and contentment recorded many more. Fredrickson concluded that when we experience positive emotions like love, joy, and contentment, we see more possibilities for our lives. Positive emotions actually make you think bigger, while negative emotions limit your sense of possibility. Frederickson proposed that

> positive emotions *broaden* an individual's momentary thought-action repertoire: joy sparks the urge to play, interest sparks the urge to explore, contentment sparks the urge to savour and integrate, and love sparks a recurring cycle of each of these urges within safe, close relationships. The broadened mindsets arising from these positive emotions are contrasted to the narrowed mindsets sparked by many negative emotions (i.e., specific action tendencies, such as attack or flee).[2]

This means that when you dwell on negative thoughts such as complaining, worry, anger, anxiety, and unforgiveness, it shuts down your brain's ability to cope with problems and find solutions. But when you entertain thoughts of hope, love, and joy, you increase your mind's ability to solve problems and create a better future. Positive thinking actually changes your brain.

There's more. Fredrickson also proposed, "Positive emotions promote discovery of novel and creative actions, ideas and social bonds, which in turn *build* that individual's personal resources...These resources function as reserves that can be drawn on later to improve the odds of successful coping and survival."[3] Positive thoughts lead to increased "social bonds," which become a resource for the future. That's a complex way of saying that positive thinking increases your influence with others.

Fredrickson summarized her findings this way:

When positive emotions are in short supply, people get stuck. They lose their degrees of behavioural freedom and become painfully predictable. But when positive emotions are in ample supply, people take off. They become generative, creative, resilient, ripe with possibility and beautifully complex. The broaden-and-build theory conveys how positive emotions move people forward and lift them to the higher ground of optimal well-being.[4]

While it may have taken a psychological study for many to accept these ideas, they have been obvious to positive thinkers for centuries. Positive thinking results in a greater sense of personal well-being—plus, it increases your ability to solve problems, make friends, and influence others. The key to broadening your influence is something you already have: your mind. All you have to do is activate it with positive thoughts.

## HOW YOUR THOUGHTS AFFECT YOUR INFLUENCE

The link between your thoughts and your influence is clear, and it's confirmed by the teaching of the Bible: "A good man brings good things out of the good stored up in his heart, and an evil man brings evil things out of the evil stored up in his heart. For the mouth speaks what the heart is full of."[5] What you harbor in your heart (or mind) eventually finds its way out into your words and actions. The face you present to the world—literally, the expression on your face—is a reflection of the thoughts within you. So it's not at all surprising that positive thoughts produce positive influence and vice versa. Let's explore that concept a bit, beginning with the effect of negative thinking.

Negative thinking adversely affects your influence in a number of ways. First, your negative thoughts become a *self-fulfilling prophecy*. That simply means that when you think negative thoughts about yourself or your situation, they are likely to come true. When you think you will fail, you are more likely to fail. When you think people won't like you, chances are good that they won't. Why? Because your negative thoughts begin to work themselves out in negative actions. You think you'll fail, so you don't prepare as well. What's the point? You become more nervous because you're expecting to bomb. You're worried about meeting others, so your hands become sweaty and you say very little. You have a worried look on your face. Those factors add up to reduced likeability. Your negative thoughts become a predictor of your negative influence.

Second, negative thinking *turns off others.* The problem with negative thinking is that it won't stay inside your head. It comes out through your teeth in the form of complaints, gossip, sighing, or fault finding. People are seldom willing to follow a naysayer.

Third, negative thinking *limits vision.* As Frederickson's research shows, when you dwell on fear, anger, and other negative feelings, your brain is not as well able to envision possibilities. You can't see what's possible; therefore, you're unable to share a positive vision with others. You don't become an influencer because you have no fresh alternatives to offer.

Finally, negative thinking results in *discouragement.* Negative thinkers ultimately become stuck where they are, unable to see a better future or move toward it. Their dour attitude is unattractive to others, so they lose whatever influence they may have had.

The good news, of course, is that positive thinking expands influence in the opposite direction. When you are a positive thinker, your positive thoughts become self-fulfilling prophecies that work in your favor. While that doesn't guarantee success, it improves the odds that you will influence others. When you have a positive attitude, you produce positive speech, demeanor, and facial expressions. You become the bright light in the room that everyone is drawn to, giving you an opportunity to influence them with your ideas. And you see possibilities. Positive thinking is like a shot of adrenaline for the brain, kicking it into high gear. It enables you to envision a better future—which is precisely the point at which you can influence others.

If you want to expand your influence, expand your mind. Fuel it with positive thoughts. Doing so will literally change your brain, making you better able to envision the future and enlist others to help you in creating it. How do you do that? Let's examine the kinds of positive thoughts that increase your influence over others.

## SEVEN TYPES OF POSITIVE THINKING

We generally lump all types of positive thought under that one umbrella term—*positive thinking*. By doing so, we reduce a highly complex way of looking at the world to a simplistic metaphor: seeing the glass as either half-empty or half-full. Though *possibility thinking* is important—and we'll talk more about it shortly—positive thought includes much more than your first response to a situation. It is an outlook that affects virtually every aspect of your inner life. Following are seven types of positive thinking that will produce a dramatic change in your attitude and actions. Let's examine each one in order to understand the way it increases your influence over others.

### 1. Optimism

Optimism is often used as a catchall term for positive thinking, but let's explore what the word really means. The term can be traced to the philosopher Gottfried Wilhelm Leibniz, who concluded that the world in which we live is the "best (optimum) among all possible worlds."[6] In the best possible world, the best possible circumstances must exist and everything must be getting better rather than worse. So, classic optimism is usually seen as a naïve, unrealistic notion about the goodness of the world and the virtuous nature of human beings. But this is not at all what we mean by optimism as a form of positive thinking.

Of course, we know that evil exists in the world, so optimism is not a simplistic belief that all of life's circumstances are somehow good. Neither does optimism require a belief that the world is always getting better. We know from history that great evils have taken place again and again in the form of war, disease, and natural disaster. What we mean by optimism is the hopeful thought that better possibilities do exist and that they are in fact *more likely* to occur than negative ones. The optimist believes that, all things being equal, it'll probably all work out for the best. And usually it does.

For example, when the stock market takes a downturn, as it often does, one risk is that it will lead to a great crash, producing a world-wide economic depression in which millions are unemployed and people are left homeless and begging for food. That could happen. But an optimist knows that it probably won't, and doesn't spend time worrying about it. She believes that, while things may be more difficult for a time, she probably won't lose her job or house, and things will work out fine in the end. An optimist knows that when he is delayed by an accident on the freeway, it's possible that he'll miss the sales opportunity—but that's unlikely. More likely is that the client will understand that traffic can be unpredictable and will offer another chance to make the pitch.

Optimists think about what's most likely to happen rather than focusing on the less likely—and more frightful—things that probably won't come to pass. Therefore, optimists seldom waste brainpower on anxiety, worry, or gloomy thoughts about the future. That frees their minds to engage in creative possibilities and problem solving.

Optimists are more likely to influence others because optimism is a form of thought leadership. People are naturally drawn to positive thoughts and wish to avoid negative ones—even if they may be thinking them. As you give voice to the real probability that there are better days ahead, despite the current circumstances, others will listen to you. Remember, optimism does not mean dismissing problems or being unwilling to face challenges squarely. This is not a form of denial. It's a determination to focus on the best possible outcomes, then work to make them reality.

If you want to influence others, practice optimistic thinking. Don't allow your mind to dwell on frightening but remote possibilities. Spend your brainpower on the more likely, more positive outcomes of a situation. That positive thinking will draw others to you.

## 2. Humility

Humility may seem like an unlikely aspect of positive thinking, but the most positive thinkers are truly humble. What I mean by that is that they have a correct view of themselves. They see themselves accurately, neither thinking too much nor too little of their own worth and ability. That accurate understanding of themselves produces a high level of self-acceptance, which is an attractive character trait.

Interestingly, a very important aspect of positive thinking is to avoid thinking too highly of yourself. In the field of psychology, it has long been observed that most people tend to overestimate their own ability and undervalue the contributions of others. This bias was first noted by researchers David Dunning and Justin Kruger and is known as the Dunning-Kruger Effect. The pair found this odd phenomenon in their research. People who are not good at a certain task—like singing, for example—tend to overestimate their ability. In other words, they think they can sing really well when they can't. You've probably stood in church next to someone with a Dunning-Kruger bias. They belt out every song as if they were a great talent when they can barely carry a tune. The corollary to this effect is that people who have a high level of ability often underestimate themselves, thinking they're less talented than they really are.[7] You've probably encountered people like that too. Though they may be the most talented member of your team, they are reluctant to volunteer, saying, "Someone else can probably do it better." They're not kidding; they really believe that.

Another interesting phenomenon is that we often attribute our own success to internal factors—such as our intelligence, ability, charm, or personality—and attribute our failures to external factors: luck, the weather, or the misdealing of others. So when we succeed, it's because we're great, and when we fail, it's because we're unlucky. However, we're likely to reverse those categories for others. When they succeed, it's because of luck, and when they fail, it's because they're somehow inferior.

Humility is the antidote to this. Simply put, humility is the ability to see yourself accurately, neither inflating your own ability nor undervaluing your contribution—and seeing others in that same, honest way. Both errors (inflating a sense of ability or undervaluing contributions) often stem from an inadequate level of self-esteem. Those who inflate their ability and look askance at others often fear being seen as inferior to others. And those who undervalue themselves often fear rejection. The humble person has a proper sense of self-esteem, and therefore does not look to others for a sense of well-being. He or she can honestly say, "You know, I'm just not a good singer and I'm not afraid to admit that; maybe someone else should sing the solo," or "Yes,

I really am best qualified for this task, so I'll take it on." Humility is not thinking poorly of yourself, but seeing yourself honestly and accurately. And that's a very positive attitude.

Humble people are influential because their ego needs are very low. They are unjealous of the abilities and successes of others; they're never looking for "ego strokes" for the contributions they make; and they are not afraid to give praise or thanks to others. As a result, they are seen as trustworthy.

To grow in humility, spend some time examining yourself. Candidly appraise your strengths and weaknesses. Don't be afraid of this exercise. Welcome the opportunity to know yourself better. Accept who you are. Determine how you will change and grow. When you have done so, you will actually feel more positive about yourself and be less dependent on the need for external praise.

### 3. Abundance

When you have a good idea at work, do you tend to keep it quiet until you can act on it, thereby reserving the credit for yourself? Or do you share the idea with others at the first opportunity? When your coworker forgets her lunch, do you make a mental note to eat at your desk because you've only brought one sandwich? Or do you volunteer to share with her, knowing that the meal was barely enough to feed one, let alone two?

These real-world choices illustrate the difference between a *scarcity mind-set* and *abundance thinking*. The first set of reactions in each example illustrate a scarcity mind-set. This thinking is based on the idea that there is a limited amount of good in the world, barely enough to go around. It results in a desire to hoard everything from food to money to good ideas, keeping them to yourself in an effort to ensure that you have what you need. Scarcity thinking produces anxiety and worry about the future.

Abundance thinking is based on the opposite notion: seeing good as an infinite supply, something we can create at will. Abundance thinkers believe that "there's always more where that came from." As a result, they're willing to give away good ideas, share food, loan money (or give it away), and welcome others. They believe they'll have another good idea tomorrow, and that someone else will share with them when they are in need.

Though this may sound like folly, it's actually taught in the Bible. Jesus said, "Give, and it will be given to you. A good measure, pressed down, shaken together and running over, will be poured into your lap. For with the measure you use, it will be measured to you."[8] Abundance thinkers have found that this dictum is generally true. Sure, you'll meet stingy people once in a while. But when you share with others, they generally share with you too. Abundance thinking is not mere wishful thinking. It's built into the fabric of the universe.

Abundance thinkers are able to multiply their influence over others for several reasons. They are generous with others, and generosity is always rewarded. They are not threatened by apparent shortages of resources, and their worry-free minds are better able to find solutions. They are willing to include others who bring an unequal supply of resources or ability.

If you tend to see things from a scarcity point of view, it will at first be challenging to adopt an abundance mentality. When you feel yourself slipping into stinginess and hoarding, practice saying to yourself, "There's always more where that came from." You'll be amazed at how consistently that turns out to be true.

### 4. Openness

Positive thinkers are open-minded. That does not mean, as is sometimes thought, that they are willing to accept every new idea or that they have no firm convictions. Open-minded people do indeed hold firm ideas, but they are willing to change those ideas based on new information. Closed-minded people feel threatened by new information because they fear change. They have determined that they know all there is to know about business, parenting, marriage, politics, and life in general. Their worldview is a closed system, impenetrable even by facts and logic.

While open-minded people have firm ideas about how to operate their business, they do not write it off to luck or questionable business practices when they see a competitor succeeding ahead of them. They are eager to learn something new about themselves or their industry. Open-minded people also have firm convictions about politics. Since they know what they believe, they are not threatened by hearing what others believe. They are open to conversation and not distressed by new ideas or new information.

Open-minded people multiply their influence because they are open not just to new data, but also to new people. They are welcoming, attentive, and unruffled by new experiences. Because they have the self-confidence to listen and learn, they gain the respect of others, and their opinions take on even greater weight.

To become more open-minded, simply ask yourself this question when your mind wants to close against new information, new ideas, or new people: "What am I afraid of?" In nearly every case you'll find that there is no reason to fear the simple act of listening to what others have to say.

### 5. Possibility

The late pastor and author Robert Schuller coined the term *possibility thinking* to describe another aspect of positive thought. In contrast to those who see only negative outcomes—the "glass half-empty" thinkers—Schuller wrote, "The possibility thinkers perceptively probe every problem, proposal, and opportunity to discover the positive aspects present in almost every human situation. They are people—just like you—who when faced with a mountain do not quit. They keep on striving until they climb over, find a pass through, tunnel underneath—or simply stay and turn their mountain into a gold mine."[9]

Possibility thinking looks at every situation with this question in mind: "What good can I find in this?" This sort of thinking is exemplified in the line from George Bernard Shaw, famously quoted by Robert F. Kennedy, "Some people see things as they are and say why? I dream things that never were and say, why not?"[10] Possibility thinkers are convinced that a good outcome is possible no matter how difficult the situation may be. This goes beyond optimism—the idea that the worst possible result is unlikely—to probe for a positive outcome when disaster seems certain.

I love the joke about two boys who were twins, one a natural possibility thinker and the other a die-hard pessimist. The boys' parents noticed the difference in their temperaments and took them to a psychologist for evaluation. The doctor observed them and concluded that he could change their outlook and, therefore, their behavior.

The psychologist placed the pessimistic child in a room filled with all the toys any boy could want. He put the possibility thinker in a room filled with horse manure. "That should adjust their attitudes," he stated confidently. A video camera placed in each room allowed the doctor and parents to observe both children.

Contrary to all expectations, the pessimistic child continued to have a dour attitude, complaining that he had nobody to play with. Surrounded by all the good things in life, he continued to see the world in a negative light. Then the psychologist and parents looked in on the other child. They were amazed to find him digging through the manure. The psychologist ran into the room and asked what on earth the boy was doing. He said, "With all this manure, there's got to be a pony in there somewhere!"

Possibility thinkers are always influencers because people are always looking for fresh possibilities. Even negative thinkers long for a better world. They're just convinced no positive change is possible. If you can show others realistic prospects they have not yet seen, even confirmed pessimists will rally to your side. Everyone wants to believe in possibilities. Some are simply too tired, too worn down, and too defeated to imagine them for themselves.

## 6. Big Picture

The idea that positive thinkers are detached from reality is a standard criticism. Some would argue that positive thinkers go through life, seeing the blue skies ahead but never noticing the storm clouds on the horizon. All they can see is the forest, never the trees or the danger lurking among them. Positive thinkers simply aren't paying attention to the details, so the objection goes.

However, research indicates that people who are less concerned with details are actually happier and better able to function. A granular focus can actually interfere with our ability to do life. One researcher noted that people in a depressed mood are more likely to notice small changes in a person's facial expression and interpret them negatively, while happy people seem to overlook slight facial cues.[11] In other words, focusing on the trees to the point of being nitpicky can tend toward negative thinking and make you less effective. Positive-thinking people are more able to step back and see the forest. Granular thinking may be important from time to time, but big-picture thinking is essential to maintain a positive outlook and, therefore, to cast influence.

Do you tend to be a detail-oriented person or a big-picture thinker? There's nothing wrong with either, but you must be aware if your tendency is to focus on the minute details of a situation, as that can lead to paralysis. It's good to have some emotional intelligence, interpreting the social cues in a group of people. However, if you're constantly wondering, "What did she mean by that?" or "Why didn't he look up when I walked in?" you'll be paralyzed by anxiety.

It's okay to be the one asking about funding and budgets and how to make a project financially viable. But if you're always analyzing spreadsheets, you likely won't be inspired by the grand aims of the venture; you won't see what's possible.

Step back and look at the big picture. Be okay with not knowing every single detail. Trust others to do their job—whether in your home, workplace, or community—and shed the anxiety that inevitably comes with your desire for control. Even a detail thinker can look up at the sky occasionally. You don't have to count every star to be breathless at the sight of the heavens.

Big-picture thinkers are always more influential than those who see only the fine details. The abilities to envision a grand sweep of change and tolerate a bit of uncertainty are essential to leading others into the future. Yes, you must occasionally ask the hard questions about how all of this will work. But don't be afraid to think big.

## 7. Responsibility

A final aspect of positive thinking has to do with the freedom to make choices for yourself. Positive thinkers have a strong sense of *responsibility.* They believe that they have both the ability and the responsibility to take ownership of their own lives. They understand that they can and must think and act for themselves.

While that may sound obvious, it is anything but that to many people. Those with a negative outlook have been conditioned, sometimes by years of failure, to believe that they cannot improve their lives. They see themselves as victims, helpless at the hands of fate—or circumstances, or the economy, or giant corporations, or their family, or some other external force. Sadly, many come to have this victim mentality after years of abuse by others. Now they feel unable to move forward in life, even though their circumstances may have changed. They are not actors but reactors in their own lives.

I know that condition very well. I recall the pain, sadness, and frustration I felt at just 11 years of age when my father was killed in an industrial accident. Not well off to begin with, our working-class family was plunged into poverty. I carried a deep anger and a negative outlook well into my teenage years.

Fortunately, my college roommate, John C. Maxwell, and I were exposed to one of the great positive thinkers in the country during my freshman year of college. We attended a rally to hear Dr. Norman Vincent Peale, who had just authored the landmark book *The Power of Positive Thinking,* and other great motivators, including Zig Ziglar, Earl Nightingale, and W. Clement Stone. That rally marked the beginning of a profound change in me, for it was there that I discovered the incredible power of one's attitude upon behavior, happiness, future prospects, relationships—everything in life. It was the start of my life as a positive thinker, taking responsibility for my own choices.

Further, it was in a college chapel session two weeks later that I realized how positive thinking is fueled by faith. Immediately after hearing Roy S. Nicholson speak, I wrote these words in the front of my Bible: "A positive mental attitude without a positive faith will result in positive failure."

If you feel hopeless and helpless about your circumstances, I urge you to accept this fundamental truth: you have the power, with God's help, to choose your thoughts, your attitude, and your purpose in life.

While there may be circumstances around you that you cannot change, you can change the most important factor in your happiness. You can choose to take responsibility for your life.

If you struggle with a sense of helplessness about your future, practice repeating these twin truths to yourself: "I am responsible," and "I can." You are indeed responsible—not for what happens to you or around you, but for choosing your attitude and actions in response. That is something only you can do. Never surrender that power to another. You may not have the ability to change other people or to change certain circumstances in your life, but you can choose positive thoughts. You can choose to make changes in your own life. You can choose a different future than the one that has been handed to you.

People who exhibit and continually practice an inner strength are influencers because they have a strong sense of will and purpose, and that is always attractive to others. Those with a victim mind-set will remain stuck in life, unable to influence themselves or others. But those who understand that they are responsible to make their own choices will influence others to come along with them.

## YOU CAN THINK POSITIVELY

For some, the prospect of adopting a positive mind-set is daunting. After years, or perhaps a lifetime, negative thought patterns become ingrained in the mind and emotions. You may think it's impossible to change your thoughts. But you can.

Begin by recognizing the negative thought patterns that have become part of your life. Notice when you are responding with pessimism, a scarcity mind-set, closed mindedness, or a victim mentality. Don't become discouraged or frustrated with yourself. Simply notice which types of negative thinking affect you most. Then you will know the areas in which you need to change.

Believe in yourself. Realize that you do have the ability and responsibility to take charge of your own mind. God created you as unique and gifted. Do not doubt that you can do this. Though it may take some time, you can become a positive thinker.

Seek accountability from a trusted friend or family member. Ask them to gently remind you of your resolve to be a positive thinker, and have them point out the instances when you slip into negativity. Share your journey with them and celebrate your success together.

And be persistent. When you recognize negative thinking within yourself, displace those thoughts and replace them with positive ones. Realize that you will have setbacks, but you will grow over time to become a positive thinker. Keep your goal in mind and do not become discouraged. You can do this!

Regardless of how negative your thinking may have been in the past, you can change. You can become a person whose thoughts and actions are characterized by optimism, humility, abundance, openness, possibility, magnitude, and responsibility. You can become a positive person. And when you do, you will influence those around you to be positive too. Remember, it all starts when you take control of your most valuable asset, your mind.

## THE KEY THREE

1. Review the seven types of positive thinking and determine the ones in which you need to grow.

2. Name three practical steps you can take to become more positive in your thinking.

3. Enlist an accountability partner who will help you on your journey to become a positive thinker.

# THE POWER OF YOUR WORDS

*Words are a form of action, capable of influencing change.*

**—INGRID BENGIS**[1]

A blind man sits on a city street. Beside him is a sign that reads "I'm blind, please help." All around him people are making their way through the streets, some laughing and chatting, others bored and distracted. Few notice the man, and only occasionally does anyone respond to his message. One or two people toss a small coin in his direction, which he eagerly gathers up and drops into a tin can by his side. Despite his pitiable condition and request for aid, almost no one notices or cares.

A well-dressed young woman happens by. She too walks past the man, then stops. She returns to regard the blind man and his circumstances. Without a word, she takes up his tattered cardboard sign, turns it over, and writes something on the other side. The blind man, aware that someone is nearby, reaches out to touch her stylish shoes. The woman replaces the sign and walks away.

Within moments passersby begin to notice the blind man. Most of them reach into their pockets to offer help. Coins now shower down about the man, who eagerly scoops them up, filling his tin can with money.

Sometime later, the young woman returns and stands before the man, smiling in approval. Sensing her presence, the man reaches out, feeling the same shoes as before. "What did you do to my sign?" he asks.

Kneeling down, the woman places a hand on his shoulder and says kindly, "I wrote the same, but different words." As she walks away, we see the sign as the woman recreated it:

"It's a beautiful day and I can't see it."[2]

This fictional story, conveyed in a brief video titled "The Power of Words," became an internet sensation for good reason. It shows the amazing power of words to influence the thoughts and actions of others. If you hope to influence others with your vision for the future, your positive thoughts must be translated into positive words. Your words have the power to change the world.

Words are the single most potent means of influence at your disposal. In this chapter, you will discover the incredible power contained within the simple words you speak every day. You'll learn how negative words undermine your influence in the world, and you'll find out how to use positive speech to deepen your impact on those around you.

## WHY WORDS HAVE POWER

Words have great power in our lives because they shape how we perceive reality. Words do not have the power to create reality, but they do change how we understand it, and therefore how we feel about it and what we do about it. Words are the key to belief, and belief unlocks action.

For example, when you meet someone for the first time, a single word of introduction has the power to shape how you feel about that person and, therefore, how you respond to them. Have you ever met someone whom you'd heard described as untrustworthy, narcissistic, shallow, or uninteresting? What was your first reaction to them? Likely you were looking for signs to confirm the judgment you'd been given. Even if that description was untrue, it probably took a long time to dispel the notion. One negative word shaped your perception of the individual, making it nearly impossible to see their better qualities. In the same way, when you meet someone who is described as likable, friendly, or funny, you're almost certain to be receptive to them and give them the benefit of the doubt.

Words are the filter that reality must pass through to get into your brain. As such, they have tremendous power to shape how you think, feel, and behave.

It's no surprise, then, that politicians, activists, and marketers vie to define the terms surrounding any idea or product. When passing a law, it makes a huge difference whether the public perceives it as a "job killer" or a "deficit reducer." And we are much more likely to buy a product that is presented in terms of its benefits—chic, cutting edge, elegant, excellent—rather than its drawbacks—expensive, unnecessary, unproven.

Words have even greater power when applied to people. You've heard the old saying, "Sticks and stones may break my bones but names will never harm me." That adage focuses on the first part of our understanding of words: they do not create reality. A rock thrown in your direction may literally reshape a part of your anatomy, but a name, label, insult, or other word cannot affect your physical well-being; it can't change reality.

That's a nice thought, and it may help some folk to let insults roll off their backs. Yet anyone who has been on the receiving end of name calling or trolling will tell you that words applied to your spirit have the same effect as words applied to any other thing. The words cannot change your objective reality, but they can shape how you perceive yourself. Negative words really can cause psychological damage.

When you speak words, either positive or negative, they influence those around you to accept your view of reality. When you disparage an idea, others will think less of it, regardless of whether it is true or false. When you praise a product, others will be more inclined to try it, regardless of its objective benefits. In that sense, your words have tremendous power. They are a potent means of exercising influence over those around you.

To use your words as a means of influence, it's important to understand various kinds of speech—both positive and negative—and how they impact your ability to influence others. We'll begin by examining several forms of negative speech that you must learn to recognize and avoid.

## NEGATIVE SPEECH THAT KILLS INFLUENCE

Most forms of negative speech are merely negative thinking expressed in words. They are your negative thoughts and formulations cast as the most rudimentary form of action—talking. Negative speech undermines your ability to influence others in two ways.

First, negative speech is always hostile either to a person or an idea. While it is legitimate and often helpful to offer a negative opinion—saying that something isn't true, for example, or that an idea is infeasible—negative speech often goes beyond that. It can become a kind of attack, often subtle, against another person. So negative speech is an influence killer because it sets you in opposition to the very people you might want to influence.

A second reason negative speech undermines influence is because speaking negatively easily becomes a habit, making you appear to others as a negative person. While it might be true that negative influence is still influence, it certainly is not the influence you want to exert on others. The hope you have for the world is positive. You want others to accept your vision for a better future in your family, workplace, or community. Negative speech may make you a destroyer, but it will never make you a builder.

To influence others in a positive direction, you must offer a hopeful, positive alternative to their current perception of reality—not simply undermine the way they currently think. Let's see how negativity kills your influence in these common forms of negative speech.

### Complaining

Complaining is voicing displeasure over circumstances, particularly about things that are beyond your control. We are all tempted to complain about things (or people) whom we don't like. You cannot change the weather, so you complain that it's raining when you'd like to be out. You can't clear up a traffic jam, so you sit on the freeway and complain about being stuck. You cannot change the behavior of coworkers, so you voice a gripe to them and others.

Complaining feels good but is entirely counterproductive. It seems like a positive thing to do because it gets your frustration off your chest, relieving the annoyance temporarily. And it can be a bonding experience. When you complain, others will join you, making your aggravation a shared event.

The effects are short lived, however, and voicing complaints nearly always produces two negative effects in your life. First, it makes you feel worse in the long run by reinforcing the idea that you are helpless. Complaining about the rain does nothing to construct a positive plan for the day. It just makes you feel trapped in the house. Complaining about a coworker does nothing to address the problem. It merely makes you feel stuck in a situation you can't control. Far from improving your outlook, complaining actually makes you feel more frustrated.

Second, complaining reduces your ability to lead others in finding positive solutions. For one thing, you are far less likely to look for solutions when you trap yourself in a loop of negative thinking. Remember how negative thinking affects the brain. When you complain, you are far less likely to be able to think creatively and come up with solutions. Not only that, but complaining also casts you in a negative role among your peers. Family members, coworkers, and online friends may find humor in your complaints and even join you for a while, but they are unlikely to see you as a leader. Your ability to influence them in a positive direction will be severely compromised by your penchant for complaining.

### Expressing Outrage

Outrage is a useful emotion when confronted with something truly outrageous. We do right to be outraged by genocide or the abuse of children or racial discrimination. However, the outrage that we most often hear expressed, especially on social media or other online forums, is something closer to the self-righteous condemnation of others. Outrage over gross evil is perfectly legitimate and necessary. But loudly condemning others for their mistakes, missteps, or errors in judgment while ignoring our own shortcomings is one of the most virulent forms of negative speech today.

As Jesus once said, it's the height of hypocrisy to take a speck of sawdust out of another person's eye when you have a two-by-four lodged in your own.[3] When you express rank indignation or outrage over what should be forgivable offenses, you undermine your influence by making yourself appear hypocritical. As with complaining, it's easy to aggregate a group of followers who are similarly indignant. But if you want to extend your influence, reserve your outrage for the truly outrageous. Be known as a person who is tolerant and fair minded.

## Naysaying

Naysaying is devaluing an idea without giving it full consideration. You will hear it nearly anytime a change is proposed at work, school, church, or any other social structure. The two most popular statements of naysayers are "That'll never work" and "We've never done it that way before," with honorable mention going to "We tried that once and got nowhere."

Naysayers purport to be good leaders because, in their minds, they're trying to save everyone time. What they *think* they're saying is "Trust me, I have this one figured out." What people actually hear, however, is "You're not smart enough to think this through," which is a terribly negative message to give to others. Most often, what naysayers would say if they were being totally honest is something more like this: "I'm so afraid of change that I'm not even willing to consider what you're proposing."

Naysayers may be successful in winning an argument or controlling the decision making of a group, but that is a far cry from influence. Real influence is guiding people to a positive outcome that you have envisioned, not simply blocking others from implementing their ideas.

## Criticizing

Criticizing is demeaning a person or idea without constructive intent. This is not the same as constructive advice, sometimes called constructive criticism (more on that later). What is meant here by criticism is tearing others down with no intention of building them up.

It's easy to be critical because other people—including you and me—have plenty of faults. We all make mistakes, do things imperfectly, overreact occasionally, and get wrong ideas. Almost everyone can see the faults and foibles in another person, so being critical is the easiest thing in the world to do. And it feels good. For some reason, we always feel as if we stand a little taller when we're standing on the rubble of another person's work, ideas, or reputation.

We don't, of course. And criticism is entirely detrimental to our ability to influence others. When you become known as a critic, people will look to you only when they want to hear the worst about a person, idea, or situation. But since they realize that your judgments are always negative, they will never trust you to provide the way forward.

### Gossiping

Gossiping is criticizing someone who is not present. Gossiping may also be defined as repeating negative information about a person—whether true or untrue—without a definite need to do so. Privately warning a friend who is considering a business deal that the other party once swindled you is not gossip. The information is true and you have a definite need to share it privately. However, telling a group of friends that another person's marriage is breaking apart—so you've heard—is gossiping. The information may indeed be true, but when shared with no positive intent and to a wider circle than necessary, it becomes gossip. Gossip usually begins with the words, "I heard that . . ."

Nearly all negative information that cannot be verified may be considered gossip, regardless of the forum in which it is shared. By that definition, much of the news we read via social media might be considered gossip. To avoid gossiping, ask yourself these three questions:

1. Do I know for sure that this is true?

2. Do I have a constructive and compelling reason for repeating this information?

3. Am I sharing this information with the minimum number of people required to satisfy my reason for sharing?

If the answer to any of the three questions is no, sharing it with even one person is likely a form of gossip.

Gossiping, like complaining, is negative influence. It influences others *not* to trust, accept, or welcome another person, initiative, or idea. A person with a reputation for gossiping is generally considered untrustworthy, even by those who give ear to the gossip. Therefore, those who gossip are seldom able to influence others in positive ways. To protect your influence over others, avoid gossiping.

## Trolling

Trolling is a new form of negative speech unique to online communication. It is faultfinding and gossiping in online media, particularly social media. Trolling is purposely destructive speech, often aimed directly toward another person. Trolls say negative—often hostile or nasty—things to or about others with no other purpose than to tear down their ideas or shame them.

Trolling is easy to do because of the relative distance that the internet provides (online versus face to face) and the shared outrage of a group or tribe. Sarcastic comments left on a blog, belittling jokes passed along through social media, and "gotcha" tweets and Facebook posts are all examples of trolling.

Trolls have great power to destroy but none to cast vision, influence positively, or provide leadership. If you hope to influence others, you cannot begin that leadership with sarcasm, mockery, or insults. To lead positively, communicate positively.

## Spinning

The concept of *spin* has entered our vocabulary through politics, where a politician's surrogates or other pundits will amplify a speaker's remarks in order to "spin" them in a different direction. While it is legitimate to clarify a speaker's intention, the term *spin* has come to mean shading or distorting the truth by providing an alternative view of reality.

It isn't just politicians who spin the facts. A struggling business may spin their situation to a creditor by saying that they are "positioning themselves for success." A deceitful spouse may spin their behavior as "misremembering" what happened.

This old joke about a political candidate reveals the absurdity of trying to spin the truth. The politician said, "Half of my constituents are for this issue, and the other half of my constituents are against it. I want to make it absolutely clear to all that I am 100 percent behind my constituents!"

Most people are uncomfortable with telling outright lies, but untruthfulness comes in many lesser forms—such as exaggerating, omitting important facts, and making misleading statements. People who spin the truth seldom have influence outside their tribe. In other words, the only people they influence are those who already believe their ideas. If you want to cast wide influence, tell the truth, without embellishment, in all situations.

## POSITIVE SPEECH THAT SHAPES INFLUENCE

Negative speech is an influence killer, but positive speech enhances reputation and builds influence. When you become a positive thinker, those positive thoughts will seep out through your words. As they do, you'll become known as a person who is affirming, open to others, and brimming with good ideas. You'll become an influencer. Here are several kinds of positive speech that will establish you as an influencer of others. While some are the direct opposites of the negative speech we just examined, many are unique forms of positive communication. Master these, and others will listen to you.

### Making Positive Observations

Making positive observations is simply pointing out what's good, right, or hopeful in a situation. It is the opposite of complaining, which voices the negatives. Positive observations inspire hope and opportunity by identifying what's possible in any given situation. Rather than making you feel dour and helpless, positive observations build your spirit and create new possibilities.

For example, if it's raining on the day you planned to play golf, one reaction would be to complain about the weather, making you feel miserable and trapped. A positive observation could be to mention that it's a perfect day for reorganizing the basement.

When you're stuck in traffic, you can complain about the

inconvenience, making you and your companions tense and anxious, or you might observe that it's a great opportunity to finish your conversation or listen to an interesting podcast.

Making positive observations begins with asking the question, "What does this make possible?" when confronting a frustrating circumstance. If you think about it, there is nearly always some new opportunity hidden within a disappointment. Those who make positive observations are natural influencers, and their enthusiasm for new ideas gains them respect.

## Complimenting

A compliment is a positive observation addressed to a person. It points out something good, right, or pleasing about them. It's the opposite of an insult. Notice, however, that there is an important difference between compliments and flattery. Flattery is false or inflated praise given for the purpose of influencing another person. You might flatter a person about their appearance, hoping they'll accept your invitation to dinner. Or you might flatter your boss's management ability, hoping she'll promote you or give you a raise. Flattery is always a bit exaggerated and always calculated for some ulterior purpose.

In contrast, compliments are honest, often spontaneous, and always free of charge. You compliment a coworker on his performance because you're honestly impressed. You compliment your spouse on their appearance because it is pleasing to you. You praise a child's growth or learning because you have a genuine desire to see them grow. A compliment must be sincere, and it must be offered without the hope of gaining something in return.

There is a saying that goes something like this: "Show me a man who doesn't like praise, and I'll show you a man who doesn't like anything." Those who are liberal with compliments are natural influencers because people crave honest praise about themselves. People have a difficult time seeing themselves accurately, and truthful, positive feedback is always welcome. But most people do have enough self-awareness to spot flattery. They know when they're being played, and they come to resent it. Those who give honest compliments are sought out and valued.

Be generous with complimenting others. It costs you nothing to observe the best in another person, and it gains trust, furthers relationships, and builds influence.

### Giving Constructive Advice

Constructive advice is feedback or instruction given for the purpose of helping another person change, learn, or succeed. While some call this constructive criticism, I prefer the more positive term *advice*, because the word *criticism* has come to have an entirely negative connotation.

Constructive advice is easy to formulate but challenging to deliver well. Other people's gaps in learning or ability are always plain to see, so it's often very easy to understand where they need to grow. However, people are naturally defensive about themselves and their shortcomings, so advice in any form is often unwelcome. Following are some things to remember when giving constructive advice.

First, *the receiver must be open to it.* Avoid offering unsolicited advice, no matter how noble your motivation may be. Wait for the person to ask for your opinion, or gently offer to share your expertise. If there is no permission to share your advice, it will be unwelcome, and it will likely undermine your ability to influence the person further.

Second, *remember that hearing about your own failings, shortcomings, or need for improvement is difficult.* Be gentle, and always point your advice in a positive direction. I like to use the "sandwich method," placing constructive advice between two compliments. Here's an example: "Wow, I'm really impressed by how well you prepared for that presentation. Great job! Here is one idea that might help you deliver the material with greater impact. Again, I'm so impressed by the depth of information you shared." Hearing what they've done right always makes people more receptive to hearing how they could improve. And you can use this method in any setting, including with spouses, children, or neighbors.

Third, *check your motivation.* If your true desire is to vent irritation about a person's failings rather than to help them grow as a person, don't attempt to offer constructive advice. This is about the other person's growth and learning, not your frustration. Be sure that you're motivated by a genuine concern for others.

When given properly, constructive advice is a powerful form of positive speech. When you focus on others with the intention of helping them, it builds trust, respect, and influence.

### Vision Casting

Vision casting is sharing your picture of the future with others in a way that inspires them to join you in creating it. This goes beyond making positive observations or finding the silver lining in a frustrating situation. Vision casting is defining a clear, positive vision for the future that excites the imagination of others and unlocks their motivation.

Many people confuse vision casting with goal setting, but the two are entirely different. Goals are specific, measurable, and time bound. They tell you exactly what you want to do next, and, in most contexts, you simply have to announce them, gain agreement, and then follow up to ensure they're achieved. "Paint the deck railing by the end of this month" is an example of a goal concerning home improvement.

Vision is different. It is a broad picture of an outcome, not a specific road map to achieving it. While a goal is a flat description of an achievement, a vision is an inspiring picture of the future. A vision for home improvement might be "to create an inviting, comfortable space for our family and friends."

Also, a goal can be created, posted, and reviewed occasionally to ensure progress. A vision must dwell within the mind, inspiring motivation nearly every day. A goal may be reviewed monthly or quarterly. A vision must be repeated over and over again until it becomes hardwired into one's thinking.

So vision casting must be done continually, especially in informal situations. Goals are announced at the annual meeting; vision is reinforced in casual conversation. Goals are placed on a spreadsheet; vision becomes part of your email signature. Goals often engender a sense of responsibility; vision creates possibility.

When you repeat your vision frequently, positively, and hopefully, you inspire others to join you in making it reality. In that sense, vision casting is the foundational form of influence. It is the positive speech that most directly affects the thoughts and actions of others.

### Truth Telling

Truth telling is being honest in any given situation. It is the perfect blend of tact and candor, saying what is true in a helpful manner that neither conceals, withholds, nor harms others. It is the opposite of spinning, which presents a distorted or self-serving view of reality.

Providing correct information is an important part of truth telling, obviously. But as we saw with the discussion on spinning, it is possible to use or omit factual information in a way that misleads others. Honesty goes beyond factual accuracy to give a true presentation of reality. When you have 17,421 subscribers to your blog, you could spin that number by saying that you have "some 20,000 daily readers." Or you could, more truthfully, say that "about 17,000 people receive my posts by email." If you are 20 minutes late for an appointment, you could, perhaps accurately, state that you got held up by an accident on the highway. Or, knowing that the accident caused only a 10-minute delay, you might more honestly say, "I'm sorry I kept you waiting."

It's important to remember, however, that being honest is not a license for being rude. Some people confuse the two, dishing out truthful but insensitive comments with the disclaimer, "I'm just the sort of person who speaks their mind," or, "I tell the truth, and I don't care if you don't like it." Truth and tact are not mutually exclusive. While candid confrontation is sometimes necessary, it is nearly always possible to be honest and kind at the same time.

Here is the simple truth that those who get caught in the "spin zone" seem to forget: people find complete honesty refreshing, and they respect those who practice it. An ancient proverb holds that "an honest answer is like a kiss on the lips."[4] How true that is. In a world too often characterized by dishonesty and manipulation, it is pleasing to find an honest soul. That's why truthful people are always influential. When people realize that you are more committed to telling the truth than to protecting your ego or agenda, they will trust and respect you all the more.

## *Apologizing*

An apology is an admission of truth regarding one's own failure, combined with a willingness to make amends. It is one of the rarest forms of positive speech because it requires deep humility. An apology requires a voluntary exposure of one's fault and places oneself at the mercy of another. It is risky and threatening, which is why so many people avoid apologizing.

As alternatives to offering an apology, we often resort to defensive tactics such as ignoring, rationalizing, or blaming. We may pretend that we've done nothing wrong or that no breach in a relationship has occurred. "Problem? What problem?" we say, refusing to acknowledge what happened. Or we may invent reasons why our behavior was necessary or why we are not truly at fault. We say things like, "It's not my fault; I was really tired," or "How was I supposed to know the project was due yesterday?" Worse, we may blame others, even the person we've wronged. We may throw around accusations such as, "She started it," or "If you had been on time, none of this would have happened." Such tactics only make the situation worse. They deepen the rifts in our relationships with others and undermine our influence.

To apologize is simply to admit the truth and offer to make amends. "I'm sorry I said that. I was in the wrong, and I'd like to make it up to you." "I didn't see the car parked there, and that was careless of me. I'm sorry about that, and I'm going to notify my insurance company right away."

When you are at fault in any situation, you gain respect and credibility by admitting the truth. Apart from being the right thing to do—which it always is when you are in the wrong—apologizing builds your influence over others because they come to see that you are truthful, even about yourself.

## START THE CYCLE

If you still doubt the power of positive words, consider this letter, which appeared some years ago in an advice column in the *Chicago Tribune*.

In August of 1991, I was told I had brain cancer and my chances of living another five years were at best 50-50. When word of this leaked to my friends, two of them began a letter- and card-writing campaign. All the pilots employed by our airline got involved.

The response was overwhelming. I received stacks of cards and letters every day. The doctors and nurses also let me know they were interested in my recovery and gave me a lot of T.L.C. The all-female team in the radiation department where I took my treatment deserves special mention for its perpetual smiles and supportive attitude. My pilot buddies collected enough money to send me and my family to Disney World for a beautiful vacation.

Surrounded by all that love, I couldn't help but get better. I am now classified as a cancer survivor, and the support of my friends continues to this day. I am convinced that "friend therapy" can be a big factor in recovery.

To all those incredible people who helped me in my time of need, I say thank you and may God bless you.

Robert Berry, Shreveport, La.

Columnist Ann Landers responded: "While I am not suggesting that positive thinking can cure cancer, there is a great deal of evidence that the immune system does respond to what goes on in the brain. Thanks for a real upper. I'm sure you've spread a lot of joy today."[5]

Your words can have a dramatic, positive effect on those around you. Though your words may not have the power to cure cancer, your encouragement will speed and support the recovery of those afflicted. Your words cannot single-handedly transform the entire internet, but your gentleness and honesty can be a beacon of hope to those mired in manipulation and negativity. Your words cannot change reality, but they can inspire those around you to change it for themselves.

Positive thoughts beget positive words. And your positive words can reframe a negative situation, encourage a dispirited person, and point to a positive future. Your words do indeed have power. Use them well.

· · · · · · · · · · · · · · · · · · **THE KEY THREE** · · · · · · · · · · · · · · · · · ·

1. Take mental inventory of your speech patterns for the past 24 hours. Note your use of both positive and negative words, and identify the trigger moments for each.

2. Name one form of negative speech you intend to eliminate, and one form of positive speech you intend to cultivate.

3. Choose one person in your home, school, or workplace and ask them to hold you accountable to use your words in a positive manner.

# THE POWER OF YOUR EXAMPLE

*If you would convince a man that he does wrong,
do right. But do not care to convince him. Men
will believe what they see. Let them see.*

**HENRY DAVID THOREAU**[1]

According to legend, a monk named Brother Leo was known for his incomparable leadership at a particular monastery in France. The holy man was regarded as such a great leader that his reputation spread all over Europe. Other monks would make pilgrimages to France to learn from this extraordinary man. On one occasion, a group of monks set out to visit Brother Leo, but on the way they began to argue over who was responsible for doing the group's chores.

On the third day of their journey they met another monk on his way to the same monastery, and he joined their group. This monk never argued about chores and did them willingly. When the others would bicker about whose turn it was to cook or clean up, he would simply get up and do the task himself. After several days, the others began to follow this patient monk's example, and the bickering came to an end.

At last they reached their destination, and the traveling monks announced the purpose of their visit. "We would like to meet Brother Leo," they told the man who greeted them.

"But our brother is among you!" the man replied, pointing to the patient monk who had joined them on their journey.

Your example is the silent influence you have over others, even when you are not aware of it. People observe what you do to an even greater degree than they heed your words. Positive thoughts produce positive words, and both should produce positive behavior in you. That consistent example—embodying the change you want to see in the world—will place a seal upon your words, giving them even greater power.

In this chapter, we will review the basic truth that actions speak louder than words. We will then dig deeper on that concept to understand how your example actually influences others. And finally, we will explore the factors that limit your positive example and discover how you can cultivate a consistently strong influence through your habits and actions.

## WHY YOUR EXAMPLE MATTERS

Do your actions have any bearing on your influence, or are results the only thing that matters? As incredible as it may seem, our culture is engaged in a debate right now about that very question. What was once accepted as a bedrock principle of leadership—"character counts"—is now being dismissed as a quaint archaism. In politics, business, and even the church, it appears that we are more and more willing to tolerate those who say one thing and do another, so long as they are able to bring about the outcome we hope for.

Yet it is a grave mistake for anyone to think they can escape the character question for long. High-profile leaders, entertainers, or athletes may be given more grace in this area while they are in their prime. But a fickle public will quickly indict those character flaws when the heroes stop winning, making money, or producing hits. For ordinary folks like you and me, character always has been and always will be an essential component of influence. People follow those whom they trust, and nothing builds trust better than a good example. Here are four reasons your positive example is essential to influencing others.

### 1. Your example sets the tone that others will follow.

As in the story of Brother Leo, example exerts a silent, powerful influence over others. When the example is consistent, people will naturally begin to align themselves with it. This is true of many behaviors, even in humorous ways. When you smile, people will smile back. When you laugh, others will join you in laughing. And a yawn is one of the most contagious of all human behaviors. It's possible that you had to stifle the urge to yawn after simply reading the word. Scientists now believe that yawning is contagious because of our innate desire to bond with others through shared experience. The urge is so powerful that one study found that even dogs will join in more than 70 percent of the time.[2] Your example matters because people who are close to you will have a natural tendency to copy your behavior, whether good or bad. Your actions influence others to follow.

## 2. Your example models what you are trying to accomplish.

Example is a great, natural teaching tool. As the old saying goes, "A picture is worth a thousand words." Brother Leo could have lectured the monks about volunteerism or having a gentle spirit, but his example communicated those traits more effectively than any speech could have done. When you greet customers with a smile and welcome, others will see how to offer good service. When you load the dishwasher properly, others will understand how to get the dishes cleaner. When you show up for work on time and quit at a reasonable hour, other people learn how to structure a daily routine. Another adage puts it this way: "Tell me and I will forget. Show me and I will remember."

## 3. Your example raises others' sights, helping them see what's possible for themselves and the world.

I've never been a great golfer, but I enjoy a round from time to time. Years ago, when I was learning to play, I thought the game was impossible. I simply could not hit the ball straight down the fairway; my slice was legendary. I was ready to give up the game altogether. Then one day I saw the club pro at our local course step up to the first tee. He stretched briefly, teed the ball, then let his club come to rest just behind it. In a flash, he drew back the club and unleashed the quickest, most powerful stroke I'd ever seen, turning his body into a veritable corkscrew with his follow through. With a satisfying *thwack*, the ball erupted from the tee and flew high, straight, and long, coming to rest well over 250 yards down the middle of the fairway.

"So *that's* how it's done," I said to myself. Though I've never achieved that level of mastery, that single shot gave me a new perspective on the game of golf. I began to see what was possible and resolved to keep trying.

Your example can have that same influence over others in whatever arena you're working. When you forgive someone who has wronged you, others will see it's possible to forgive. When you resist gossip, profanity, or other forms of negative speech, others will see they can too. When you achieve financial freedom by avoiding debt and investing money, your example becomes a beacon for others to follow. Many people simply don't know (or can't make themselves believe) that a different life is possible for them. Your example can raise their sights and give them hope.

### 4. Your example keeps you involved in your own vision.

It is frightfully easy to make resolutions for yourself, your family, or others, and never follow through on them. You've experienced this, no doubt, when starting a budget, determining to get in better physical shape, or resolving, "This year, we're going to plant a garden!" That's easy to say in February, but by May your attention may have turned to other things.

When you set a positive example for others, you keep yourself engaged in the work you're trying to accomplish. In fact, you influence yourself. When you are mindful to put your cell phone down when behind the wheel, you show your kids something important about safe driving—and you also reinforce your own desire to protect your family. When you take a walk at lunchtime rather than heading straight back to your desk, you set an example of physical fitness for others to follow—and you also reinforce your own desire to have an active lifestyle. Your positive example benefits others, to be sure. But it benefits you even more.

Setting a good example is easier said than done, however. Even those with good intentions occasionally find themselves influencing others in the wrong direction by their actions (or inaction). Let's talk about some example killers and how to avoid them.

## EXAMPLE KILLERS

A saying attributed to famed investor Warren Buffett holds that "it takes twenty years to build a reputation and five minutes to ruin it."[3] The same could be said of your good example—and the influence that goes with it. Past instances of this sort of failure are all too easy to recall. Everyone can remember a case of a politician whose example of public service was negated by self-serving financial dealings, or a religious leader whose moral example was contradicted by scandal. When such things happen, the damage often extends well beyond the incident at hand. Skeptical onlookers may in the future gaze askance at any examples of altruism or decency, figuring that nobody is able to "practice what they preach."

The lesson here is that you can be your own worst enemy in the area of displaying a positive example. When you contradict your own good words and intentions through thoughtless, foolish, or selfish actions, the damage to your influence can be irreparable. That makes it essential to understand the three most common example killers. When you understand them and how they can creep into your life, you'll be able to avoid them, preserving the influence of your good example.

### Hypocrisy

The first example killer is *hypocrisy*. Hypocrisy is giving the appearance of having a virtuous character or point of view that you don't really possess. Everyone abhors hypocrisy, but it's relatively easy to slip into because we all aspire to ideals that we have not yet fully achieved. You value truthfulness, so you may loudly, and genuinely, decry dishonesty in others. Yet when you come under pressure, you are tempted to exaggerate, report false numbers, or tell a "white lie." Few people set out to be hypocrites, but most of us end up behaving hypocritically at some point in our lives.

Hypocrisy is toxic to influence precisely because people are so finely attuned to it. Honest mistakes are easy to overlook, but when someone appears to be dealing falsely by pretending to be something they're not, it arouses deep anger. Even a hint of hypocrisy will be harmful to your influence.

To avoid hypocrisy, you must do more than meet the minimum standard of integrity or truthfulness. You must set an example of good character. Don't simply recall facts to the best of your ability. Ensure that you communicate an accurate understanding of the truth, without embellishment or omission. Don't simply report your expenses accurately; give the benefit of the doubt to your employer by not claiming any expense that might push the boundaries of the company's policy. Practice what you preach. Treat others as you'd like to be treated. Go out of your way to avoid the appearance of being hypocritical. The higher your integrity, the greater your influence. A single drop of hypocrisy can taint your example for years to come.

### Inconsistency

The second example killer is *inconsistency*. In terms of your example, inconsistency is setting a good example at some times but not others. It is a lack of constancy or dependability in modeling your vision for the world.

Setting an inconsistent example merely frustrates others because they come to think they can't count on you. You may be the first one to the team meeting one day, brimming with good ideas and full of enthusiasm. That attitude and action set a good example, and others may begin to look to you as a leader. But when you show up tired and irritable the next week, eyes glued to your phone and grunting one-word answers, they will quickly conclude that you're not serious about making an impact. The next time you try to rally the troops, no one will listen. They'll believe that you don't mean it or won't follow through.

Consistency is vitally important in influencing anyone—from coworkers, to family members, to neighbors and friends. When they see you behave the same way all the time, regardless of the circumstances, your example will be highly influential.

### Arrogance

The third example killer is *arrogance*. Arrogance is a feeling of superiority that reveals itself through a prideful or condescending attitude. Arrogance can be real or imagined. In other words, it doesn't matter whether you actually *feel* superior to others or not; when people perceive that you do, it will undermine your example. Nobody likes to be looked down upon, so people will not respond to an arrogant person regardless of whether or not they set a positive example in other ways.

When you are setting a good example and you know it, it can be difficult to avoid feeling self-righteous or superior. You may have observed this in others, or perhaps felt the tendency yourself. When you begin to take control of your health by exercising properly and eating wholesome foods, it can be tempting to be judgmental of those who still reach for the Twinkies and plop down on the couch. When you are diligent in getting enough sleep so you can arrive for class or work refreshed and ready to go, it's tempting to roll your eyes at those who shuffle in five minutes late, unprepared for the day. Ironically, it is your own good example that makes it possible for you to feel arrogance—which undermines your example!

To combat the tendency to be arrogant or judgmental, remember a couple of things: First, the people whom you are tempted to judge are the very ones you are trying to influence. Rather than focusing on their poor habits, think about the needs they face and how much it would help them to adopt better habits, as you've done. Think about how their behavior hurts them, not how it affects you. When you do, you'll feel compassionate toward others, not judgmental. Second, remember that you too have weaknesses and blind spots. A good dose of humility is a great cure for arrogance. Though you may set a good example in some areas, there are probably others in which you need more discipline. Each of us is a work in progress, so respond to others with kindness. The same standard you use in dealing with them will likely be used on you someday. Opt for gentleness every time.

Don't allow an attitude of superiority to creep into your heart, regardless of how much progress you have made. Remember that you struggled to get where you are. Avoid pointing to yourself as a good example. Never hold up others as a bad example. Let your actions speak louder than your words, and others will see that you have something good to offer them.

## EXAMPLE BUILDERS

Hypocrisy, inconsistency, and arrogance are influence killers. They undermine your good example, destroying whatever positive influence your silent actions might otherwise have had. It's also true that there are example builders. Obviously, integrity, consistency, and humility—the direct opposites of influence killers—help to build your good example. Beyond these, however, here are a couple of practices you can incorporate into your life to strengthen your ability of setting a positive example.

### State Your Motivation

Poor motivation is the primary cause of inconsistent performance. If you are setting an inconsistent example, it's not necessarily because you lack discipline. It's more likely that you yourself are unconvinced of the importance of what you're doing. That lack of conviction makes it all too easy for your attention to be drawn elsewhere, or for you to back off when discipline is required. But when you are convinced tomorrow's meeting is important, you'll turn off the TV and get to bed early. When you are fully committed to getting out of debt, you'll pass up impulse purchases at the checkout counter.

To solidify your good example, check your motivation. Refer to your vision—the change you'd like to see in yourself, your family, or the world around you. Remind yourself why this matters so much. Keep those thoughts in your mind by reviewing them daily. When you do this, the sine wave of up-and-down behavior will flatten into a steady pattern of achievement.

### Create Strong Habits

Habits are like the operating system of the mind: the thoughts, attitudes, and actions that drive daily life. Many people are unaware of their own negative patterns and how those patterns sabotage achievement and happiness. However, when you create strong, positive habits, you set yourself up for success. Your positive example becomes automatic because it stems from actions you no longer think about taking.

To understand how habits become automatic, requiring no thought, consider something you do every single day. Regardless of whether or not you think of yourself as a highly structured person, you probably have some daily habits such as brushing your teeth, feeding the dog, or locking the door before you go to bed. Now, think for a minute: Did you do that yesterday? Do you remember brushing your teeth? Are you sure you fed the dog? Can you be positive that you locked the door? Probably not. It's likely you have no recollection of doing those things because you do them without making a conscious choice. They have become automatic.

When you automate positive behaviors by making them habits, you improve your lifestyle and make it more likely that you will create a positive example in your personal life, work, education, or anything you do. Following are a few positive habits you might consider adopting.

### Bedtime and Waking Routines

Consider adopting a standard bedtime. When you go to bed at the same time each day, you're more likely to wake up fresh and well rested, thus better able to navigate your day. You'll be more likely to keep a positive attitude, work energetically, and set a good example in all you do.

Also, create habitual routines around going to bed and waking, involving things like shutting down your computer, brushing your teeth, praying and meditating, arranging clothes for the next day, packing a lunch, and stretching or exercising. These routines will help you sleep more soundly and start your day with greater energy.

### Work Startup and Shutdown Routines

Many people become inconsistent in their work performance—or in setting a positive example in the workplace—because they begin their day 15 minutes behind schedule and never catch up. One reason for this is they lack consistent workday routines. Arriving for work at the same time every day, avoiding checking social media when your computer starts up, working from a preplanned agenda, and doing routine tasks in a given order will help you dive into work in a relaxed, confident manner.

It also helps to end work with a shutdown ritual, rather than walking out of the office with your inbox full and the message light blinking on your phone. Establish a routine that closes out one day's business and lays the groundwork for tomorrow. That'll help you move through each day with confidence and control, setting a good example for others.

## Physical Habits

Proper diet and exercise are much touted because of their value to one's appearance. We all want to look good. But good health habits help you set an example as well. When you appear fit and energetic, people are more apt to follow your lead. And being healthier results in having more energy, accomplishing more, and having improved discipline in other areas of life.

Establish strong habits around healthy eating, physical flexibility, strength, and aerobic fitness. This is more than simply starting the latest fad diet or joining a gym. It is creating habits around nutrition and fitness that add up to a healthier, more active lifestyle. Your physical disciplines will enhance your ability to set a good example in attitude, work ethic, productivity, and other areas as well.

## Mental and Spiritual Habits

It's been said that there are no weak people, only weak minds. If that is true, then establishing intellectual and spiritual habits will strengthen other areas of your life and assist you in setting a positive example. For me, those habits include reading for at least an hour a day, plus daily time for prayer and Scripture study. Your habits may differ, but don't neglect this area of your life. When life gets hectic, it's very difficult to "find time" for activities like reading, studying, deep thought, or meditation. That's why you must do them habitually, just like eating or bathing. Make your personal-growth habits a regular feature of your life.

The numbers vary from one expert to another, but it's said that it can take anywhere from three to six weeks to establish a habit. After that, it's yours for life. Take a few minutes to think about the habits you'd like to add to your daily or weekly routine, and which you would like to drop. Chances are good that you have one or two bad habits that infringe on your ability to set a good example. Habits like binge eating or drinking, excessive television watching or social media use, or frivolous spending actually work against your desire to influence others with your silent example. The sooner you eliminate them, the better.

## BEING REAL

When you have a strong motivation to influence change and establish healthy routines in your life, you are likely to set a positive example. Seeing your passion and self-discipline, others will be drawn to you and begin to adopt your behaviors, just as the monks did in the legend about Brother Leo. Remember, though, that influence killers abound. You can easily sabotage your good example through hypocrisy, inconsistency, or arrogance.

That reminds me of a joke Melvin Maxwell told me about a man who went to the zoo in search of work. This man was willing to clean cages, feed animals, or do just about anything.

When the manager saw that the man was stockily built, he said, "I do have one job you might do. Our gorilla died last week, and we don't have a replacement. We do have a gorilla suit though. I'll hire you to wear the suit and impersonate the gorilla until his replacement arrives."

"I'll do it," the man said.

The next day, he arrived for work and was fitted with the suit. All morning long, he stomped around the gorilla enclosure, beating his chest, shaking the bars, and swinging on vines in front of the crowd. The audience loved it. But the man got so excited that he swung too high and landed himself over the fence in the lion enclosure.

Immediately, a large male lion strode toward the man in the gorilla suit. Realizing that any move on his part would give away the deception, he tried to keep his mouth shut. But as the lion approached, fear overwhelmed him and he cried out, "Help!"

Just then, he heard the lion speak as well. "Shh!" he whispered. "Keep your mouth shut or you'll get us both fired!"

Far too many people cruise through life pretending to be something they are not. Though they may be successful in gaining attention for a while, that influence will be short lived. It is difficult to keep up the pretense for long, and their true character inevitably comes forth in their words and actions. You simply cannot fake a good example.

However, when your motivation is genuine and your discipline is strong, your positive actions can become a source of inspiration and encouragement to the people around you. You can change the world without saying a word through the power of your good example.

## THE KEY THREE

1. State your motivation for change. Say out loud why it matters so much to you that you influence others in the area you have chosen.

2. Name one bad habit you would like to eliminate from your life in order to strengthen your example.

3. Name one good habit that you will acquire to reinforce the example you hope to provide.

# THE POWER OF
# YOUR PRESENCE

*The further you go in life, the more you realize what
you're going to leave this earth. It's not going to
be, "It was a great platform. It was great to win the
Super Bowl," but really and truly what you're going
to leave on this earth is the influence on others.*

**JOE GIBBS**[1]

I believe in the power of presence," said Debbie Hall, a psychologist in San Diego's Naval Medical Center and a volunteer for the Disaster Mental Health Team of her local Red Cross chapter. Hall discovered a powerful lesson on the power of presence while working in the wake of Hurricane Katrina. She said, "I and several other Red Cross volunteers met a group of evacuees.... We were there, as mental health professionals, to offer 'psychological first aid.' Despite all the training in how to 'debrief,' to educate about stress reactions and to screen for those needing therapy, I was struck again by the simple healing power of presence. Even as we walked in the gate to the shelter, we were greeted with an ardent burst of gratitude from the first person we encountered. I felt appreciated, but vaguely guilty, because I hadn't really done anything yet."[2]

The response Hall received is not unusual from victims of disaster or trauma. My good friend Jo Anne Lyon, founder of the aid organization World Hope International, encountered the same phenomenon when visiting West Africa at the height of Sierra Leone's civil war. She described that experience in her book *The Ultimate Blessing*, in which she discusses meeting an elderly refugee:

She was a small woman, and very frail. Her son told me that she was one hundred years of age, and I had no doubt of it. Family members had carried her for miles through the rugged bush country of Sierra Leone to the safety of a refugee camp in Kalia, Guinea. She was hunched over and walked only with assistance. Leaning on her son's arm, she approached me slowly as if to speak. Her voice was weak. I leaned down and listened as she whispered hoarsely, "Thank you. Thank you for being here. I thought we had been forgotten."[3]

In both these cases, the responses these women received weren't offered because they had brought extraordinary help, gifts of cash, a supply of medicine, or any other tangible benefit. They just showed up. They were present. And that simple fact produced a great blessing and an overwhelming sense of gratitude in the beleaguered people they met.

The effect of your presence is real and important, even in ordinary life. It isn't just disaster victims who need the presence of others. We are all communal beings, and it's important for us to be in the company of others. That makes your presence one of the greatest gifts you can give to another person, and one of the key elements of your influence in the world.

Woody Allen is noted as saying, "Showing up is 80 percent of life."[4] You can make a tremendous difference in the lives of others by being there. Beyond the things you say or do, your presence is the impact you have on others simply by being in the room. It is the sum of a number of subtle factors, including demeanor, manner of speech, facial expression, energy level, and behavior—but the most important aspect of your presence is simply being there.

In this chapter, you will come to see the often-underestimated effect of your presence on others, and you will discover strategies for changing "the temperature of the room" just by walking into it. You will learn how being who you are, right where you are, is one of the subtlest, most powerful ways to influence others.

## WHAT PRESENCE IS

Your presence is tangible in the sense that you are a real, flesh-and-blood person who takes up physical space. You have a material presence wherever you go. But the concept of presence goes well beyond the cubic inches you occupy. Your presence is the intangible effect you have on others merely by being there. In that sense, presence is difficult to define. But you know it when you see it or, perhaps more accurately, when you feel it. Your presence is like a fragrance that precedes you into a space, having a subtle effect on those whom you contact and lingering after you are gone. Your presence changes how people feel and respond in any given situation.

If that sounds a bit vague, it may help to think of your favorite movie actor. Powerful performers like Tom Cruise, Nicole Kidman, Denzel Washington, and Angelina Jolie can electrify a scene just by walking onto the set. Love them or hate them, most people cannot help but watch them. They dominate the attention of the audience, often without saying a word.

While we may not be movie stars, we too have presence. We all communicate something when we walk into a room—and sometimes when we leave it. The simple fact of being present says something to others, as does the fact of being absent. Beyond that, our expressions, energy, eye contact, posture, and many other silent signals communicate to those around us, even when we appear to be doing nothing at all.

Presence may seem a bit like *example*, which we looked at in the previous chapter, but it is quite different. Your example is set by the positive things you do to provide a model, instruction, or motivation for others. Your presence, on the other hand, is not your actions or words. It is *you*, who you are and how you comport yourself in a given situation. This comparison chart may help clarify the difference between example and presence.

| Example Says... | Presence Says... |
|---|---|
| "Here's what I'm doing." | "Here I am." |
| "Follow me." | "Be with me." |
| "This is how it's done." | "This is who I am." |
| "Let me show you." | "I'm here for you." |

When you take an action that models good behavior for others, you're using the power of your example. When you simply choose to be yourself in a social context, you're exercising presence.

The power of presence is strong and meaningful, though it is indirect. Your words, especially your persuasive words, exert a direct influence on others. Your example is a less direct form of influence, but it still produces a result. People will follow your example and do what you do. But your presence influences others by enhancing their admiration and respect for you personally. It sets a mood or tone for the interactions that follow.

While it may sound calculating or manipulative to talk about the value of your presence in influencing others, it's actually a very meaningful and important part of your relationship with them. Medical and spiritual caregivers have long understood the tremendous importance of presence for healing and growth. When a nurse visits someone's bedside and places a hand on the patient's shoulder, it is an act of presence. That simple human contact also makes the patient more willing to follow the nurse's instructions, speeding recovery. Visiting a funeral home to comfort a widow is also an act of presence, even if no words are exchanged. Just being in the room is important. Presence is what makes it possible for the minister to later speak words that promote forgiveness, healing, and recovery.

If you want to lead people in the moment, like a military commander, use words. If you want to influence people to change short-term behavior, add the power of your example. But if you sincerely hope to gain the trust of others so that you can influence them over a lifetime, you must be present with them.

## CREATING A POSITIVE PRESENCE

How do you create a positive presence? Do you simply show up when invited, and possibly smile more? Given that presence is an intangible quality that flows from your unique personality, outlook, and characteristics, is it even possible to alter your presence? What if your presence has a negative effect on others? Can you change that?

The elements of presence are difficult to pin down, but it is possible both to identify them and to change them in yourself. With a bit of thought and intentionality, you can exert a positive influence on others through your presence, even if you've had a negative effect in the past. Following are several elements of presence, along with some guidelines for improving the effect of your presence.

## Self-Awareness

The first element of presence is self-awareness. You must be aware that you do in fact have a presence, and you must become aware of how that presence affects others. Most people are totally unaware of the fact that they affect others by being in a room, nor do they understand what that effect is. To exert a positive influence on others, you must give attention to both.

"Who, me?" That's the typical response you will hear when you point out the effect of a person's presence. For example, when a team member is sullen and silent, moodily sucking the life out of a meeting by refusing to comment or make eye contact, they will nearly always express surprise when challenged. "But I wasn't doing anything!" they'll protest. And they'll be right. However, it's possible to exert a negative presence with few or no overt actions. Though the person may be unaware of their presence, others will be acutely aware of how that person's demeanor affects the team.

Likewise, when you compliment a student on being a leader in the classroom, they may be taken off guard. They simply don't realize that being cheerful, being on time, making eye contact, and smiling all exert a powerful influence on those around them.

Everyone has a presence, though some may have a stronger presence than others. You may have a family member, friend, or coworker who dominates every social setting without really trying. When they smile, everyone else does too. When they decide to skip a meeting, most team members also fail to show. Others have a less intense effect on others. They may be overlooked at first, and they likely feel that nobody would notice if they were there or not. Not so. Each of us has some effect on others through the simple act of being present or absent and through the demeanor with which we present ourselves.

It's helpful to think of presence as a fragrance. When you wear perfume or cologne, you probably can't smell it, but others can. It's the same with foul odors. If you've been working in the barn all day, you can no longer smell the manure. But show up for dinner without changing your clothes, and the whole family will remind you: "Ew! Take a shower!"

So the first step to improving your presence is to be aware that you have one. Every day, wherever you go, you exert some influence on every person you meet. And remember, presence can be positive or negative. Some people make others uneasy by their presence, while some put others at ease. Some exude tension; some bring a sense of calm. Some appear weary and disorganized, while some bring a sense of energy and confidence.

What is your effect on others? Is it positive or negative?

That's a key question to ask yourself about presence. To continue the fragrance analogy, just like you can't smell yourself, how will you know what your presence is like? How do others perceive you? Here are a couple of ways to find out.

### 1. Observe how others respond to you when you are present.

Do all eyes focus on you when you enter a room? When a decision must be made, do people stop and look toward you? If so, you likely have a very strong presence. If not, don't be self-conscious. There are no bonus points for having a strong presence—only for having a *positive* one. If people are less likely to respond to you in a social setting, it probably means that you have a milder presence, and that's fine.

### 2. Ask one or two people whom you trust.

This may be challenging, and you must be prepared to receive what you hear without becoming defensive. You might ask questions like, "Do you think I tend to warm up a room when I enter, or shut it down?" Or, "On a scale of one to ten, how would you say I affect the people around me, if one is completely negative and ten is completely positive?" You might ask a couple of follow-up questions to help you understand the response.

Regardless of your starting point, you can make your presence more positive. Exploring the following aspects of presence will help you sort that out.

## A Focus on Others

Having just stated that the first element of improving your presence is to be self-aware, the next element may seem to be a contradiction. However, to increase the impact of your presence, you must forget about yourself and focus on others. Remember, your influence is not about you. Your purpose is to improve your home, workplace, community, or other social context by making positive change. And to do that, you must be focused on the needs of other people, not yourself.

One of the key factors that contributes to a negative presence is self-centeredness. When people are selfish—either in general, or when they are simply self-absorbed in a given moment—they suck attention away from others. Even when they are silent, their sullenness communicates loudly, "I'm not happy!" or "I'm not getting what I need!" Being late, not giving attention to others, failing to make eye contact, not listening, appearing to be bored or distracted: all these things communicate that you feel you are more important than other people, and that's a terribly negative impression to give. It deflates the mood at a dinner table or in a classroom, conference room, or living room.

On the other hand, when you are able to put your needs aside temporarily and focus on other people, you communicate just the opposite. You show them through your presence that they are important, you are with them, and you are fully engaged in whatever is happening. You do that, first of all, by being present in the first place. You also communicate a positive presence by simple behaviors like being on time, listening, taking part in what's happening, making eye contact, and smiling. Notice what others are doing and saying. Respond when appropriate. Don't follow every remark in a conversation with a comment about yourself. Ask questions. Be interested in other people and what they need.

When you enter a hospital room, a quiet presence is essential. In a business meeting, an alert, engaged demeanor is appropriate. In every social context, ask yourself, "What's happening here? What do others need? How can I take part?" When you focus on others rather than yourself, you will create a positive presence that will be most welcome.

### Intentional Presence or Absence

Imagine yourself in this situation: A coworker's grandmother passes away. You know your coworker well enough to know her grandmother was very important in her life, but you never met the woman yourself. You have a casual but growing relationship with your coworker, though you don't know anyone else in her family. She mentions that visiting hours at the funeral home will be tomorrow evening. You wonder, "Should I go?"

That question exposes the next aspect of presence, which is to be intentionally present—or absent—when appropriate. The difficulty, of course, is that it's sometimes hard to know which is best. Though there is no infallible guide for making such decisions, you should consider being present when

- your presence is expected by social convention;
- it is required by your school, employer, or other organization to which you belong, even if it is inconvenient for you; or
- being there would bring cheer or comfort, even though it's not required or expected.

Being present shows respect and demonstrates your willingness to put others first. A weekly team meeting may be boring, and you can certainly ask your employer to alter the meeting or excuse you. But it's disrespectful to others to simply not show up. And attending your neighbor's graduation may not be expected or required, but doing so could be a nice way to signal your concern and interest in the relationship.

Remember that presence alone is a powerful communicator. The simple act of attending a meeting, visiting a nursing home, showing up at a Little League game, or dropping by an open house is a positive, respectful sign that says, "You matter." Your presence is a gift: the gift of yourself. That gift is nearly always an honor to receive.

When you choose to be present, be intentional—not just in the choice to be there, but in how you comport yourself throughout the event. Be on time. Dress appropriately. Engage with those who are present. Don't duck out early without good reason. Wherever you are, be all there.

Likewise, be intentionally absent when appropriate. There are some occasions when your presence is not needed, would not be entirely welcome, or might hinder whatever is taking place. It may be more appropriate to stay away in such cases. For example, consider not being present when

- your presence would create awkward tension, even if you might have a right to attend;
- your absence might allow others to grow by letting them have a chance to lead or make decisions; or
- your absence may not be noted, but attending would place a burden on you or your family.

You may have a strong interest in the outcome of a decision, but if allowing others to make it could strengthen their leadership, you may want to skip the meeting. While you could attend your friend's open house, they might not have a strong interest in whether you are there or not. Taking the evening off to rest could be a wiser choice. Remember that in either case, your focus should be on others. Within the limits of your own energy and resources, ask, "How can I help others by being present?" and "Will my absence be positive, negative, or neutral in its effect on others?"

### Presentation and Demeanor

I once led a small group in which two of the attendees exerted an equally strong—and opposite—influence by their presence. One man—I'll call him Jake—was usually a few minutes late for our meetings. He generally came straight from work at a small business he owned, and he often seemed a bit harried and wore a pained expression. Whatever he'd experienced that day stuck to his face like glue, and his demeanor was stressed and anxious. Jake was about six foot two, and as our meeting progressed he would frequently sit forward a bit with his head hung low until someone would venture to ask, "Jake, what's up? You seem a little off tonight." With that prompting, Jake would unburden his mind about a run-in with a vendor, a near miss he'd had in traffic, or a long list of the problems his industry was facing.

The other man—I'll call him Robert—was a retired fellow and a widower. Though he lived on a fixed income, he always managed to dress well. Generally, Robert arrived a few minutes ahead of our group meeting and helped me set up chairs. He often stayed a few minutes afterward as well, chatting with the other attendees. Robert was no more than five foot six, yet he sat comfortably erect with one leg casually crossed over the other. He was a quiet man, and never the first to speak when a discussion started. When Robert did offer an opinion, it was in a calm tone that aimed to bring consensus.

Both men vividly illustrate the next aspect of presence, which is personal presentation and demeanor. By arriving late, wearing disheveled work clothes, and communicating through his facial expression and posture that something was amiss, Jake often derailed our meetings just as they were getting started. He generally swung the group in a negative direction even before saying a word. Robert, on the other hand, managed to exert a positive influence on the group simply by being in the room. His dress, demeanor, and comportment were appropriate and inviting, and he always set a positive tone.

Because your presence is basically you and everything about you, all aspects of your personal presentation can affect your influence in this area. Here are a few things to pay special attention to as you consider the way your presence works on others.

## Dress

Everyone has a personal style, whether it's cool and casual, dressed and pressed, or a little bit of grunge. The way you dress reveals something about you, and no one style is inherently better than another. Your style does communicate something, however, and it's important to remember that not all modes of dress are appropriate for all occasions. Attending a formal reception in shorts and flip-flops will certainly communicate that you are comfortable and approachable, but it may also communicate a lack of respect for the guest of honor. Wearing casual dress slacks and loafers to a beach party may show that you are a tidy, orderly person, but it may also indicate that you have little interest in participating in the event.

With a few exceptions (for example, when black tie is requested, or where there is an office dress code), there are no firm rules about how we dress. Just keep in mind that the way you present yourself in terms of clothing and hygiene is part of your overall presence. Be yourself, of course, but think about others as well, and how your appearance will affect your interactions with them.

### Comportment

Comportment is your manner of bearing, such as your demeanor, posture, facial expressions, and so forth. It is how you look and the vibe you give off to those around you. It's easy to tell when someone, like Jake in my small group, is out of sorts. You can see it in their facial expression, their slouch, the listless way in which they walk, and in semi-verbal clues such as sighs or yawns. The act of walking into a room initiates your presence. The way you comport yourself establishes what that presence will be.

Remember that your presence—in fact, every aspect of your influence—is an inherently social phenomenon. You are present *with others*. Things like appearing sullen, slouching, resting your head in your hands, and staring out the window may come naturally to you, but they may also communicate to others "You don't matter," or "I'd rather be somewhere else."

Be fully present wherever you choose to be. It is your choice, after all. Take responsibility for that choice by presenting yourself in a pleasant and appropriate way. Smile. Be attentive. Remain alert. Focus your attention on others or the matter at hand. Communicate through your facial expression, posture, and attentiveness that you are engaged with the people you've chosen to spend time with.

## Manners

Manners are generally accepted rules for polite social behavior. These are things like remaining silent while others are speaking and silencing your cell phone in a movie theater. Like many other aspects of presence, your manners are invisible to you but plain as day to everyone else. Our culture prizes individualism to such a degree that the very concept of manners may seem obsolete. However, when a client insists on checking social media accounts during your presentation, or a neighbor plays loud music late at night, you quickly realize that the subtle ways we show either respect or contempt for others really do matter.

To create a positive presence, give attention to these casual, habitual actions that can either make or break your influence:

- Stand when someone enters the room.
- When you are a guest, remain standing until invited to sit.
- Greet people when introduced, and introduce others.
- Make eye contact with the person to whom you are speaking.
- Avoid taking calls or checking messages on your phone during meetings or conversations.
- Say "thank you" when offered anything, even if you decline the offer.
- Invite others to be served ahead of yourself.
- Greet everyone you meet with a smile.
- Avoid gratuitous criticism of others.
- Don't repeat unflattering things about another person, even if they're true.
- Don't tailgate.
- Be on time.
- When entering a building, hold the door open for the next person.

- Don't talk with food in your mouth.
- Silence your cell phone in public places.
- Discipline your own children diligently and other people's children not at all.
- Speak pleasantly to waiters and clerks, even when they make mistakes.
- Don't use foul language in public.
- Don't offer your opinion unless asked.
- Say little about your own achievements.
- Don't talk too much.

Displaying good manners really boils down to treating others as you would like to be treated.[5] Do that, and your presence will likely be sweet and welcome. Your influence will surely grow.

### Online Persona

We have been speaking of presence in terms of in-person contact with others—and for many of us, that's the primary way we leave our footprints on the world. However, through social media accounts, blogs, comments, and of course emails, each of us also creates an online presence that has the same potential to enhance or degrade our influence. We are present with people in a virtual realm every day, and those interactions can be even more powerful and long lasting than those created through our physical presence.

Also, we may create an online persona, perhaps unintentionally, that is very different from our physical presence. This happens for two reasons.

1. WE FILTER OUR ONLINE IMAGE BY CAREFULLY SELECTING THE ITEMS WE POST, ESPECIALLY PHOTOS, TO MAKE US APPEAR IN THE BEST POSSIBLE LIGHT.

To read some people's social media feeds, you might think they were the happiest, wealthiest, thinnest, most exciting folk who ever lived! Their online interactions show only the most positive aspects of their lives, and only the most flattering angles of themselves.

Without intending to, we can create an inflated or unrealistically positive persona in the online sphere. That kind of presence can actually undermine your influence by making you seem false or unapproachable. Everybody has problems, after all.

## 2. We don't always filter the things we say to or about others online.

The distance and quasi anonymity of the internet make it all too easy to say things online that we would likely never say in real life. We may be more direct, more prone to insult someone or express outrage, and more liable to repeat questionable information than we would be among a group of neighbors or friends. Without meaning to, we can create an online presence that is cynical, angry, judgmental, or just plain negative.

Treat your online presence in the same way you do your in-person existence. Realize that you do have a presence in the digital world, examine whether it is positive or negative, and take steps to project a winsome nature to those you meet online. Be present in the places where your presence is welcome and expected. Remain absent in the places where your presence might be detrimental to others. Without being false or hypocritical, let your demeanor communicate warmth through positive interactions, compliments, and helpful comments. Remember that humor doesn't always come across as well online as it does in person. Be careful when making jokes lest they be taken as insults. Be polite. Use good manners.

Your digital footprint can magnify your actual presence and extend it to places you could never otherwise go. That offers tremendous potential for extending your influence. It also carries with it the danger of easily damaging your influence through carelessness. Let your online image match your physical presence in warmth and positivity, and your influence will grow accordingly.

## FOR OTHERS

Simply by being who you are, right where you are, you can have an impact on others. Being present with them and just being yourself offers a gift of respect and dignity. That's just as true in a corporate boardroom as it is in a refugee camp. People are blessed by your intentional presence, which disposes them to respect you and accept your influence in their lives.

It's important to remember, however, that the act of presence must be done for others, not for ourselves. We must be self-aware in order to be intentionally present, but we must also set aside our needs in order to focus on others.

Author Barry Corey observed this principle in action one day in Fullerton, California. Corey was going for a run in the city when he noticed two men ahead of him on the sidewalk. Based on their appearanace, Corey judged them to be homeless men and quickly jogged around them. One of the men had, in his hand, a bag from a fast-food eatery.

Just then, the taller man called out, "Hey, Barry."

Corey turned around to see a man he knew, a university professor who was a national expert in his field.

"What are you doing here at this time of day?" Corey asked. The professor tried to avoid answering directly, but Barry pressed for a response. Finally, the latter came clean.

"My friend and I every so often go to McDonald's early in the morning and buy a bag of Egg McMuffins. Then we walk around the city streets to find drifters, and we have breakfast with them."[6]

How incredible that a man of this stature would get up early to simply spend time sharing a meal with homeless people. This man's presence affected the life of at least one homeless man, and his example has influenced countless others—including you and me.

This is the power of presence, and that power is available to you every day. It simply involves being with others for their benefit and not yours. Though you should not offer your presence in the hope of a reward, when you invest yourself in others, that gift is returned in intangible ways. It is an investment in the future.

**· · · · · · · · · · · · · · · · THE KEY THREE** · · · · · · · · · · · · · · ·

1. Consider your presence both in person and online. Determine whether it is currently positive or negative.

2. Name two key areas mentioned in this chapter in which you might improve your presence.

3. Name one person or group of people with whom you will be intentionally present this week.

# THE POWER OF YOUR ENCOURAGEMENT

*When you're kind to others, you help yourself;*
*when you're cruel to others you hurt yourself.*

**PROVERBS 11:17 (MSG)**

A young woman I'll call Helen was teaching math to junior-high students, which is never an easy task. By the end of the week, the students were feeling the stress of learning a new concept. Their nerves were frayed, and their faces showed frustration. Some were becoming snarky with one another and with Helen.

Realizing that the class would spiral into negativity without some intervention, the young teacher arrived at an idea. She asked the students to take a sheet of paper and write the name of each person in the class. "I told them to think of the nicest thing they could say about each of their classmates and write it down," said Helen. Students took the rest of the hour to finish the assignment, then turned in their papers. "They seemed more relaxed," she observed.

Over the weekend, Helen wrote the name of each student on a sheet of paper and listed the positive comments the other students had made about him or her. The following week, she gave each student their list. Within moments, smiles broke out around the room.

"Really?" one student whispered. "I never knew that meant anything to anyone."

"I didn't know anyone liked me that much!" another student exclaimed.

Helen was satisfied that the assignment had accomplished its purpose by raising everyone's spirits, and she never mentioned it again.

A number of years later, Helen attended the funeral of one of those students, a bright young man who was killed while serving his country in wartime. The church was packed with the friends of this young man, "Mark," including many former classmates. Afterward, Helen attended a gathering at Mark's parents' home, along with many of her former students. Mark's parents approached Helen and said, "We want to show you something. Mark was carrying this when he was killed." With that, his father produced a paper from a wallet. It was the list of what Mark's classmates had written about him.

"Thank you so much for doing that," Mark's mother said. "As you can see, Mark treasured it."

Some of the former classmates overheard. One said, "I still have my list. It's in my top desk drawer at home." Another said, "I have mine, too. It's in my diary." "I put mine in our wedding album," said another. "I bet we all saved them," a fourth student chimed in. "I carry mine with me at all times."

"That's when I finally sat down and cried," Helen says. "The lesson my former students taught me that day became a standard in every class I taught for the rest of my teaching career."[1]

This story illustrates two basic truths about encouragement: The first is that everyone needs it—craves it, in fact—and treasures it. The second is that you may never realize the tremendous power your encouraging words will have on another human soul. When you encourage others, you unleash a positive power that will far outlive the few moments it takes to speak the words. Your encouragement can change a person's life forever.

Encouragement is a particular form of positive speech that takes your influence to a new level. When you encourage others, you directly affect their thoughts about themselves, their situation, and their future. The results can be astounding. In this chapter, you will discover the explosive power of encouragement and be motivated to practice it consistently in all your relationships.

## HOW ENCOURAGEMENT WORKS

Encouragement is hopeful affirmation offered to another person, particularly when they have experienced some form of disappointment, failure, or loss. Encouragement dwells in the middle space between compliments and constructive advice. Without minimizing the reality of one's current situation, it inspires hope for the future.

When someone misses a promotion at work or is denied entry into their preferred university, they will be disappointed. Indeed, they may realize something painful about themselves because of that frustrating experience. However, encouragement does not dwell on that reality but points to a better future: "You'll bounce back from this. I see how determined you are, and I know you're going to succeed."

When a person goes through a divorce, their feelings of rejection, disappointment, or shame may be acute. A word of encouragement helps lift their sights beyond that. "Many people love you, and you are not alone." "You're a strong, confident person, and I know you will get through this."

When you encourage another, you demonstrate sincerity and empathy. When others see that you understand their pain and genuinely care about them, you gain influence in their lives. But please note that this should never be done with the ulterior motive of gaining influence. Encouragement, like a compliment, must be given for another's benefit. We encourage others only because we truly sympathize with their need.

### What Encouragement Is Not

When offering encouragement, it may be tempting to reach for any positive statement in an attempt to lift another's spirits. That's dangerous because even those who are emotionally low have a keen sense of reality. They know when they're being offered platitudes or unrealistically optimistic statements. When encouraging others, you must beware of offering the following three types of false encouragement.

FLATTERY

Flattery is excessive or insincere praise, especially when given for the benefit of the speaker rather than the hearer. When the boss fails to deliver on a big project, it may be tempting to say, "You're still the best boss I've ever had. This company is lucky to have you!" Some of that may be true, but it will ring false if the boss realizes you're only buttering her up in order to gain a promotion, or you're trying to minimize your part in the failure. Don't offer encouragement you don't stand behind. People long to be shown the silver lining in a bad situation, but they resent flattery or condescension.

### Denial of Reality

Encouragement is not a denial of the facts, no matter how bleak they may be. On the contrary, it is an offer of affirmation or hope within the negative circumstance. Telling someone, "Don't worry, it'll all work out," after their mother has been given a terminal diagnosis is not sound encouragement. It's better to offer an encouraging statement that deals fully with the facts at hand: "I'll be with you, and we'll get through this together." When in doubt, it is better to say nothing than to appear unconcerned or out of touch with the reality another person faces.

### False Promises

An offer of help can be a great way to encourage others. It lets them know they're not alone and provides some hope for a solution. However, a false promise can do more harm than good. When a friend has a legal problem, it may be tempting to say, "We'll get to the bottom of this. Justice will be done." Unless you're a lawyer, that's likely a promise you can't keep. And even attorneys avoid promising to control the result of a legal proceeding. You can offer to seek justice, but you can't promise a particular outcome. You can promise to help someone financially, but beware of promising to resolve a person's debts. You can offer help to a sick friend, but you can't promise they'll get well. Desperate people latch on to hope wherever they can find it. Don't make an unwise promise that will lead to further disappointment.

### Why Encouragement Matters

When you've just enjoyed a satisfying meal, it can be difficult to imagine what hunger is like. In the same way, when your circumstances are good, it can be hard to understand why encouragement has such power in a person's life. But encouragement matters for at least three reasons.

## LIFE IS HARD

Life is difficult, and that's true even when there is no obvious crisis in a person's life. We never know the burdens and trials another person may be facing. A popular saying widely misattributed to Plato states, "Be kind, for everyone you meet is fighting a hard battle." As if to prove the veracity of that statement, it was likely written by a man named John Watson (a real person, though, not Sherlock Holmes's friend). A version of the quote appeared in *The British Weekly* in 1897.[2] Perhaps one of Watson's burdens may have been that other people got the credit for his work. How frustrating! Others carry more profound inner burdens, such as the loss of a child, a chronic illness, an unloving spouse, or the pain of an embarrassing failure. Though they may never reveal that struggle, it can remain with them every day, even for a lifetime. That means nearly every person you meet could benefit from a word of encouragement, regardless of how cheerful they may appear. When you make yourself an encourager, you become a welcome and sought-after presence in others' lives.

## EVERYONE NEEDS AFFIRMATION

Encouragement is vital because all human beings want and need affirmation. Sure, there are a few folks who act as if they don't care what others think. And there may even be a tiny minority who are truly unconcerned about the opinions of others. But the vast majority of human beings long to be noticed, valued, and affirmed. Even people with a normal level of self-esteem enjoy—and occasionally need—words of affirmation. When you encourage others, you take on a wonderful, positive role in their lives. Genuine encouragers are much loved and highly respected. They become great influencers.

## DISCOURAGERS ABOUND

Discouragement is a far more common experience than is encouragement. For every positive voice that offers hope, comfort, and affirmation, a person is likely to encounter ten voices that express annoyance, doubt, or frustration. Even if you have a high level of self-esteem, a steady barrage of discouraging talk is bound to affect your spirits. We all need a few positive voices to counterbalance the negative ones we hear throughout the day. Encouragement is like a gentle breeze. You never know exactly when to expect it, but it's refreshing whenever it comes.

Encouragement really works. It produces a marvelous, often instantaneous, positive effect on others. Dale Carnegie observed,

> Tell your child, your spouse, or your employee that he or she is stupid or dumb at a certain thing, has no gift for it, and is doing it all wrong, and you have destroyed almost every incentive to try to improve. But use the opposite technique—be liberal with your encouragement...let the other person know that you have faith in his ability to do it...and he will practice until the dawn comes in at the window in order to excel.[3]

Everyone needs encouragement. When you provide genuine words of affirmation and appreciation, you open a window of hope into a weary soul. You exercise influence of the noblest type, that which is born of deep concern for others.

## HOW TO BE AN ENCOURAGER

Now that you understand what encouragement is and isn't, let's talk about how to become an encourager. For some, this comes naturally. You may be the type of person who is always attuned to the needs of others and liberal with words of affirmation. If so, that's great. These ideas will add to your repertoire of encouragement. Others are less naturally inclined to offer encouragement. They may be less likely to notice when others need affirmation, or have a harder time finding words that offer authentic encouragement rather than false hope. If that describes you, this section will show you when and how to encourage others. Let's begin by learning the occasions when encouragement may be most needed.

## When to Encourage

The first obstacle some people face in becoming an encourager is knowing when to offer a word of affirmation or reassurance. Nobody wants to come off as a false encourager, constantly offering pick-me-ups that are unneeded and perhaps unwelcome. The good news is that, other than during an acute crisis, there really is no wrong time to offer encouragement. When someone has just received a diagnosis or is grieving a recent loss, sharing sorrows may be more welcome than words of cheer. People need some time to absorb the shock of their circumstances and to mourn loss. However, at virtually any other time, encouragement will be welcome. Be especially alert for the following opportunities to encourage others.

### WHEN THEY'RE STRUGGLING

Encourage others whenever you notice they are struggling in life, with health, or in their work, schooling, relationships, finances, or career—to list a few examples. Some of these occasions are obvious and difficult not to notice. When a person experiences a serious illness, injury, divorce, or loss of a loved one, everyone around them is likely to know about it. But remember that many struggles exist below the surface. How are you to know when someone is facing a significant problem in life? More often than not, they'll tell you.

Watch your social media feed, and you'll see lots of people sharing their need for encouragement. They'll mention a problem in their family, an illness, difficulties in their relationships, loneliness, and even boredom. Some of these cries for encouragement may be voiced as complaints, but look deeper. And when you engage in conversation with people at work, school, or church, you'll often hear direct statements of their need, though you may pass over them lightly. When others request prayer, express frustration, voice a fear, or even grumble, they're giving clues to the burdens they carry. Don't miss those calls for encouragement.

### WHEN THEY'RE WORKING HARD

The next time you're at a restaurant, take a moment to observe your server—not just when they're at your table, but as they go about their work. You'll likely see a person who is extremely busy, in almost constant motion, and working hard. Are they unhappy? Probably not. They may love their work and be energized by the dinnertime rush. But expending all that energy is likely to take a toll. Try saying, "Wow, you're working hard and doing a great job," and see how their face brightens. Anyone engaged in a difficult task is a candidate for encouragement, even though they may appear to have everything under control.

Be aware of the effort that others expend in other contexts as well. Notice the energy your spouse puts in to earning a living, parenting, and maintaining your home. See the effort it takes for your children to complete homework, athletic training, or music practice. Observe the concentration and focus of a coworker who is pushing hard to meet a project deadline. Any of them may be like a waiter at a restaurant— not unhappy, but becoming tired, grateful to be affirmed for their hard work. Encourage those who are working hard in any pursuit.

## When They Fail

Failure is not unlike the other kinds of struggles mentioned earlier, but it carries an added feature. Those who fail experience not only a sense of loss, but also a sense of shame or responsibility. That can be true in a business failure, the failure of a project, the loss of a game, a divorce, a bankruptcy, and in countless other situations when the result is not the one hoped for. The sense of personal embarrassment or shame heightens the need for encouragement in the wake of a failure. To make matters worse, a person's pride may hinder them from seeking the community and camaraderie in which encouragement naturally flows. Be alert to those around you who have experienced failure. They are ripe for encouragement.

## Whenever

Remember what we learned earlier in this chapter: everyone you meet is facing a hard battle, though you may not be aware of it. Though they may show no signs, most people have a deep inner struggle, burden, or need that causes them to welcome and even crave the affirmation of others. Don't wait until you discover a specific need. Be an all-purpose encourager. Be willing to affirm others in any and every situation.

## Types of Encouragement

"But I don't know what to say." That may be the most common objection to offering encouragement. Some folk are not apt with words, and they struggle to know what to say to someone who has been through a divorce, lost a loved one, or is facing a personal crisis. Realizing that flattery and false hope are unwelcome, they fear saying anything at all. When you are stuck for words, consider offering encouragement in one of these categories.

### Personal Affirmation

You may not know what to say about a situation, and you certainly can't make predictions about the future. But you can always say something kind about the individual. "I really like you." "You're a good person." "You've been a good daughter." "You have done well." If offered sincerely, any positive statement about another person will be both welcome and encouraging. Everyone wants and needs to be appreciated, regardless of the situation they face. This may be the simplest and easiest type of encouragement to offer because every person has value, and each person can be affirmed for the good within them.

### Acknowledgment of Effort

When I was young, my baseball coach Frank Ramsey understood the power of encouragement as a motivator. While some coaches yelled loudly and berated their players for mistakes, he always found something positive to affirm in a player, even when giving correction. "Great swing! Just remember to keep your feet planted." "You've got a great arm; now we have to work on your control." "Good hustle! We'll get 'em next time." Being acknowledged for what they did right made the players more willing to hear correction and more eager to try again.

When someone has tried and failed, affirm the effort. You're not giving absolution or ignoring their shortcomings. You're simply acknowledging the sweat and struggle they expended. You're pointing to the good they did rather than dwelling on what they failed to do.

## Words of Hope

Hope is what any discouraged person longs for. They're desperate to know if things will be okay and if they have a future. You may not have the answer to their specific questions, but you can offer hope based on eternal truths. The sun actually will come up tomorrow. The world will continue to turn, the seasons will change, and life will go on. Simply being reminded of this can bring hope in the face of disappointment. And in some cases, you may be able to offer even more particular hope based on your knowledge of the situation. While you must avoid minimizing the loss or frustration that a person is experiencing, you can still offer words of hope like these:

- "You're a young person, and I believe you can bounce back from this."
- "In a year from now, your life may be in a very different place."
- "People won't remember your failure so much as that you tried your best."
- "Tomorrow is another day, and we can try again."

Encouragement always looks to the future. Words of hope are encouragement in one of its most powerful forms.

## Presence

There are times when words are hard to come by and unnecessary. Your presence at key times in life is an encouragement all by itself. Visiting a hospital, attending a funeral, stopping by after work, hanging out on a Saturday—each of these gestures may be an encouragement to others regardless of the words exchanged, if any at all.

### Ways to Encourage

Just as there are several types of encouragement, and each may fit slightly better in one situation than another, there are also various ways to offer encouragement. The first way we generally think of is through words of affirmation. We say something encouraging to others. Yet there are other ways, including nonverbal ways, to encourage a person. And even when we use words, there are a variety of ways to deliver them. Let's think about some of the ways in which we might encourage another person.

## Casual Comments

Encouragement often takes the form of words, but those words need not be formal or rehearsed. In fact, the more purposeful we are in crafting words of encouragement, the harder it may be to deliver them with sincerity and authenticity. The most welcome words of encouragement are often delivered off the cuff: "Great job!" "Nice try." "I'm praying for you." Don't wait for a formal occasion to encourage a friend. You can do this in the moment. Offer encouragement right on the spot, as soon as you notice the opportunity. As long as your words are sincere, they need not be well rehearsed.

## Public Praise

Few things are more encouraging than to be singled out in a positive away among family, friends, or peers. When you have the opportunity to encourage someone in front of others, that praise or affirmation will carry double the weight. When a coworker returns to work after an illness, you can publicly welcome her, say how much she has been missed, and express hope for the team's success with her back on the job. When your team has lost a contest, it will hearten each of the players to hear their valiant effort affirmed out loud.

While encouragement regarding sensitive matters must be delivered privately, personal affirmation and acknowledgment of effort can often be delivered in public. Correct privately, praise publicly. Remember that rule, and your words of affirmation will always be welcome.

## Handwritten Notes

A casual word is always helpful, but a handwritten note can become a valued keepsake, delivering encouragement for days or even years to come. Several years ago a woman wrote to an advice columnist to express her appreciation for those who sent notes of encouragement when she faced a devastating life crisis. She said, "When I began to receive notes of comfort and encouragement, I discovered how remarkable the healing power of true friendship can be. Please tell your readers that any show of concern will help. The simple sentence, 'I'm sorry about your trouble,' says it all."

The columnist agreed. She responded, "Many people are inclined not to say anything for fear they will cause embarrassment or open old wounds. Wrong. A word of compassion and encouragement is always appreciated."[4] And when that word of encouragement is written by hand, it may be even more appreciated because of the extra effort required to deliver it.

### ELECTRONIC COMMUNICATION

Electronic media has the tremendous value of immediacy. They make it possible to deliver instant encouragement to nearly anyone within seconds of discovering the need. A text, email, or social media message that says, "Thinking of you" can cut through a person's loneliness and offer hope.

Just remember that the ease of such communications may make them prone to overuse. As with all forms of encouragement, e-messages must be authentic and heartfelt in order to be welcome and effective. Also, because they are so quick and easy to deliver, e-messages may carry less weight than an in-person visit, phone call, or handwritten note. By all means, use electronic communications. But be aware that other channels of affirmation may be needed as well.

### GIFTS

Gifts can be a form of encouragement that is especially useful for those who have difficulty putting their thoughts into words, or on occasions when more overt communications might be intrusive. Interestingly, the act of giving a gift is the real encouragement, more so than the gift itself. Flowers will last only a few days, but the act of sending them delivers a cheerful message that will be long remembered. It says, "I'm thinking of you." A gift of food wordlessly communicates, "I'm here to help." Beyond the words printed on a greeting card, the gift's arrival in the mail will say, "You are important to me." These messages are deeply encouraging and a pleasure to receive.

## Nonverbal Affirmation

There are many other nonverbal ways to encourage another, such as hugs, pats on the back, nods, smiles, high fives, or thumbs-up gestures. These casual signals offer affirmation or demonstrate concern without a word spoken. Remember that any form of touch, such as a hug, requires a good deal of tact and sensitivity in order for it to be welcome and meaningful. When you are alert for them, you'll find opportunities to deliver a smile or high five many times a day. These are great modes of encouragement for "whenever."

## YOUR CHOICE

We each face a choice when it comes to encouraging others. We can be alert to the needs of others, sensitive to their hurts and struggles, and willing to offer support for the challenges they face. Or we can insulate ourselves from their concerns, focusing on our narrow channel of interaction with them as a coworker, neighbor, or classmate, while ignoring their deeper needs. That's the easier choice in some ways. It allows us to maintain a comfortable distance from the sometimes-messy and troubling struggles others face.

Yet when you make the choice to be an encourager, you'll find that something remarkable happens. You gain a network of friends and acquaintances with whom you share life. You receive encouragement as well as give it. You develop relationships that go beyond the surface concerns of chatting about the weather or cooperating on a project. You make friends.

In the end, the choice you make about encouraging others is really a choice about your own character and the type of life you'll lead. Will you close yourself to others, holding them at an emotional arm's length? Or will you dive into life with them, sharing their joys and sorrows, triumphs and failures? Will you be an encourager?

For those who are eager to extend their influence and affect the world in positive ways, that's an easy choice to make.

## THE KEY THREE

1. Consider this question: *Does encouraging others come naturally to me?* If so, why? And if not, why not?

2. Review the types of encouragement and ways to deliver encouragement listed in this chapter. Identify those you think you can most readily use.

3. List three people you know who may be in need of encouragement, and encourage them before the end of the day.

# THE POWER OF YOUR GENEROSITY

*Gain all you can. Save all you can. Give all you can.*

**JOHN WESLEY**[1]

In 1976 a young man named Tom graduated with honors from Claremont McKenna College in California and accepted a position in his family's business back home in Kansas City. Tom worked hard and was soon promoted. In 1981, after automating the company's office network, he was elected president of a division. Later, he coordinated efforts with the US government to create an innovative plan that allowed online access for millions of Americans who deal with the federal government each year, eliminating millions of pages of paperwork. Tom was promoted to president of the entire company in 1989 and named CEO in 1992.[2]

Despite Tom's success in the business world—and the million-dollar annual income that went with it—he felt that something was missing from his life. After a good deal of soul searching, Tom Bloch made an astounding decision. He resigned as CEO of H&R Block, the world's largest tax preparation firm, to take a job teaching math to middle schoolers at St. Francis Xavier, an inner-city parochial school.

You might think the decision to generously give his time and talent to educate young people would have satisfied Tom's need for "more," but his generosity was just getting started. One night while browsing the internet, he noticed that the youth volunteer participation rate in Kansas City was very low. After sharing his concern with his wife,

Mary, the Blochs took action and founded the Youth Service Alliance of Greater Kansas City. That effort is one of several causes the couple has supported through the Thomas M. and Mary S. Bloch Philanthropic Fund.[3] Tom later cofounded University Academy, a public charter school in Kansas City. The school has grown to more than one thousand students, and over the last five years all but two graduates have gone on to attend college, an amazing success rate for an urban school.[4]

Tom's story illustrates the incredible power of generosity to change the world around you. When you give voluntarily to others and without obligation, you unleash a power that can transform their lives—and yours too. In this chapter, you will discover why generosity is such an effective form of influence and a potent agent for change. Like Tom Bloch, you may discover the greater purpose you've been missing in your own life.

## GENEROSITY AND INFLUENCE

Generosity is giving to others without expectation or obligation. You can be generous with time, abilities, resources, and in many other ways, but the key element in each case is giving without an expectation of return. When you hope to receive something back after giving to someone, whether it's interest on a loan or even a favor in return, you're not being generous—you're making an investment. Generosity is a pure contribution. It's a donation made to charity, with or without a tax deduction. It's a favor offered to someone who cannot possibly return it. It's sharing ideas or sales leads or business contacts with someone who needs them, knowing that those assets may be lost to you. Generosity is a gift, plain and simple, and it influences others in three ways.

### 1. Generosity is leadership by example.

Your generosity shows others what is most important to you. When you put your time, energy, money, or other resources into something, your contribution puts a neon sign over that need to say, "This matters!" You draw attention to your highest priorities by generously providing your time, talent, and treasure to them.

## 2. Generosity has a nudge effect, prompting others to be generous also.

You may have noticed that when one person volunteers for a task, others are more likely to join in. The first volunteer helps others overcome their internal resistance. When you share anything, from money to ideas to space at the table, you'll prompt others to join you.

## 3. Generosity builds trust.

When your giving is truly generous, it is done without expectation—a pure sacrifice. As we'll see in a later chapter, sacrifice on the part of a leader is a powerful motivator. When others realize that you are more concerned for their needs—or for the poor, the marginalized, or others who are struggling—than you are for yourself, they will be far more likely to trust your leadership or advice.

Generosity should never be practiced in the hope of reward, yet we can easily recognize the correlation between liberal giving and respect. When you give of yourself, you influence others. When you withhold your resources from others, your influence will diminish. Generosity commands attention.

## SCARCITY VERSUS ABUNDANCE

Generosity does not come easily to everyone. We are all wired to put ourselves first, so the thought of giving away resources, especially money, sets off alarm bells in our subconscious. *How do I know the need is legitimate? What if people take advantage of me? What happens when I run short of money, time, or ideas?*

These questions are quite natural. For one thing, we're trained to be responsible for ourselves, so we believe that we should look after our own needs, and everyone else should do the same. We figure that the world works only if each person pulls their own weight.

Also, most people have at least a little natural suspicion of others. In some of us, that wariness is more acute, to the point that we find it hard to trust people who present themselves as being in need. "What are they hiding?" we may wonder. "Maybe it's their own fault they're in this situation." We can also be skeptical about the results of generosity.

People have been giving to the poor for thousands of years, yet poverty still exists. What difference does our generosity really make?

Finally, we're all just a little bit selfish at heart. We realize that there will be only one certain result of giving our money away: we won't have it anymore!

Nearly all of our objections to generosity can be traced to a single idea. This thought runs like an electric current through all our hesitations to be charitable. It causes us to cling tightly to the things we have and resist sharing with others. This idea is called *scarcity thinking*.

Scarcity thinking is based on the notion that all resources are both finite and in short supply. In this mind-set, everything that exists has a firm limit, and once exhausted it can never be replenished. For example, if I have two dollars and I give one to you, I have become poorer. Money is scarce, and I don't know how I will ever replace the dollar I gave away. If I share my ideas with you, you'll succeed and I won't because good ideas are rare and hard to find. If I volunteer my time for a charitable organization, I'll have less time to do the things that matter to me because there are only 24 hours in a day. That's a snapshot of scarcity thinking.

When we believe that everything we possess is in short supply, we'll resist sharing them with others and possibly never even use them ourselves. Scarcity thinking causes us to withdraw from others and hoard what we have.

But there is another way to look at the world, and it is the polar opposite of scarcity thinking. It's called an *abundance mind-set*. Abundance thinking is based on the belief that nearly everything is plentiful or at least renewable, so there is always more where it came from. While it is true that many things have a firm limit—the hours in a day, for example, or the square footage of a piece of real estate—value is unlimited. We create more of it every day. There is no limit to the number of good ideas your mind can produce. You always have the possibility of earning more money. More food can be grown, more clothing bought, more friends made, and more wealth created. People who think this way are never afraid of running out because they know the things that matter most in life are truly unlimited. Relationships, ideas, friendship, cooperation, contentment, opportunity, and love have no finite boundary.

You may be thinking, "But they're wrong! My wallet has only twenty dollars in it, and when it's gone, it's gone." On one level, of course, you're right. It is possible to run out of money or food or time. Yet abundance thinkers have discovered that a lifestyle of generosity not only provides for their needs, but actually produces better results than does scarcity thinking. Rather than running short of resources, abundance thinkers continually find themselves encountering more. Those who practice generosity find that they receive it in return.

This idea is nothing new. It's confirmed by the wisdom of the Bible, for Jesus said, "Give, and it will be given to you. A good measure, pressed down, shaken together and running over, will be poured into your lap. For with the measure you use, it will be measured to you."[5] The contemporary saying, "What goes around, comes around," expresses a similar idea. Whatever you put forth into the world, you will eventually receive in return. When you are generous, others will be generous with you. When you share ideas, more good ideas will come to you. When you welcome a new person into your circle of friends, you don't lose your place, you gain a new friend. When you share time, money, encouragement, ideas, or resources of any kind, you'll find yourself encountering more of the same—maybe not immediately, but sometime soon. Openhanded people eventually discover that the world opens its hand to them in return.

The opposite is true as well. Scarcity thinking produces scarcity. When you close yourself to others, they close themselves to you. When you hoard your resources, others don't benefit from them, and you may not either. When you refuse to share ideas, you cut yourself off from discussions, contacts, and opportunities. When you offer a closed fist to the world, you're likely to receive bare knuckles in return.

When you give generously, you change the world and yourself in important ways. You meet a need in others, which is always a hopeful and positive thing to do. By sharing, you begin to create your vision for the future.

Generosity also meets a need within you. Like Tom Bloch, you too have a desire for "more" in your life. You want your life to count for something. You may be trying to succeed in your career, master your craft, or even make a lot of money, but deep down you hunger for something more significant. You want meaning, purpose, and value in your life. When you make the choice to be generous, you will discover that purpose. You'll find that when you volunteer your time for others, you don't have less time for yourself; instead, you enjoy your time all the more. When you give money to others, you find greater satisfaction in meeting their needs than in spending on yourself. When you practice hospitality, you don't lose your privacy but gain valued relationships. Generosity is a golden key that unlocks the true treasures of the universe: friendship, purpose, and fulfillment.

## HOW TO BE GENEROUS

When you hear the word *generosity*, you probably think first about money. The term is often used by those asking for a financial contribution. We receive those pitches all the time, pleas to contribute money to a charity, a religious organization, a radio station, or even a panhandler on the street. Indeed, financial giving is the first and most obvious way of practicing generosity, but it is by no means the only one. Think holistically about generosity, and you will quickly realize there are many ways to be generous. We will begin our discussion with finances, but we'll go on to explore seven other ways to be generous toward others.

### Donating Money

Donating money is a primary way to practice generosity because money fills such a variety of needs. It can provide food, shelter, clothing, medical care, labor, or just about any tangible thing. Once you have adopted an abundance mind-set, giving money away is much less intimidating, especially when you are convinced of the need. And giving is even easier to do when you make it part of your financial plan.

Many people designate charitable giving in their budget. Some follow the time-honored practice of the *tithe,* setting aside ten percent of their income for donation to their faith community or other worthy causes. While that may seem like a lot, there are many folks who give even more, offering sizable gifts to worthy causes even beyond their budgeted amount. Remarkably, this practice seems to make the remaining dollars stretch even further, as purposeful giving requires careful budgeting.

Some wonder about the result of their giving, refusing to donate to any cause unless they are convinced the money is being used ethically and is producing tangible results. It is certainly wise to be sure that any organization you contribute to is reputable and well managed, and it is sometimes appropriate to designate the purpose of a donation. But beware of trying to micromanage the use of your contributions. A donation is a gift. When you give it, you surrender control of the funds.

Others wonder about the wisdom of on-the-spot generosity, such as contributions made to an organization soliciting funds outside a shopping center, or handouts given to a person on the street. What if the money is misused? What if a panhandler uses it to buy alcohol or drugs? There is no one-size-fits-all methodology for handling such opportunities. You must let your conscience be your guide. And remember that one of the joys of giving is responding to urgent needs that touch your heart. When you feel prompted to give, do so. Certainly, you'll want to give funds wisely. But don't allow fear or suspicion to prevent you from doing good.

### Spending Time

Your presence is a gift, and spending your time with others or on their behalf is a way of being generous. Time is the most precious resource we have because it represents our very lives. We may not like to think of it, but our days really are numbered. When you spend your time, you are parting with a portion of your life. And time really is money for a great number of people. Anyone whose income is tied to productivity realizes the dollar value of an hour. At the time of this writing, it's currently worth $7.25. For many artists and professionals, an hour of time is worth far more than that.

Spending your time is a gift—and when you think of it that way, it is actually more inviting to be generous in this area. Let's put a nominal value on your time. For the sake of this discussion, we'll say that an hour is worth 20 dollars. So if you volunteer three hours a week to teach literacy, you're not only helping someone learn to read but also contributing perhaps 60 dollars per week to a good cause, including the value of your preparation time and commuting. Over the course of a year, you could easily add more than $3,000 of value to a wonderful organization.

In practice, of course, it costs you less than that to be generous with your time. When you spend 15 minutes on the phone offering wisdom to a friend, you've given a gift that may produce incalculable results. When you spend the afternoon at a wedding, or stay after work to lend a hand to a coworker, or babysit for an evening so a single mom can have a break, you give gifts people crave even more than money: your presence and your friendship. Spending time is a wonderful way of sharing with others.

### Providing Expertise

Some of the time you spend with others will be spent simply being available or doing tasks that anyone could accomplish. But you probably have another resource to provide in the form of skill or expertise in a particular subject area. When you provide that as a service to others, you help them in at least two ways: First, you almost certainly save them money because they would likely have to pay someone else for that capability. Second, you offer freedom and peace of mind because they are likely seeking help in a time of crisis.

An elderly person whose furnace breaks down faces a big problem. On a fixed income, they may be panicked about how to survive the winter. Your donation of expertise as an HVAC technician both saves money and provides tremendous peace of mind.

True, it can be annoying to be constantly solicited for free professional advice or services. School teachers are usually the first ones asked to lead a small group at church. Accountants are always nominated for treasurer of their club or committee. Auto mechanics, doctors, and lawyers get called frequently by friends and acquaintances who want to "pick their brain" for a minute. You'll likely need to set some commonsense limits on the amount of time you spend giving free services. Yet be generous in sharing your expertise. You almost certainly have knowledge, skill, experience, or talents that could benefit someone else. When you freely share with others, you open your hand to the world. The world will open its hand to you in return.

## Offering Ideas and Information

Sometimes scarcity thinking reveals itself in our attitude toward the intangible resources we hold, including ideas. We may hoard ideas and information, especially at work, because doing so brings us a greater sense of security. For example, if you're the only one who knows where all the fire extinguishers are located, or how to balance the books at month's end, or how to prepare the order for an important client, then your place in the company seems more secure.

We may hoard ideas too, fearing that if we give away our best concepts, others will succeed ahead of us. That's classic scarcity thinking applied to knowledge rather than tangible resources.

Your willingness to share ideas and information is a clear signal that you've adopted an abundance mind-set, and it's a key way of being generous with others. Contrary to your intuition, giving these things away actually multiplies both the ideas and your value to others. When you are the only one who understands a process, people feel forced to deal with you. But when you teach them how a complicated system works, they will see you as an expert and begin to seek your counsel. When you hold on to a concept until you have a chance to develop it, you slow the momentum in your department. But when you hand out good ideas like jelly beans, you become the go-to person for creative solutions.

Be generous with your ideas. Share information as widely as you can. Your generosity will be rewarded with influence.

## Sharing Relationships

Relationships are another intangible resource that can be generously shared. As with ideas and information, we may be tempted to hoard our most valuable relationships precisely because they mean so much to us. After all, you don't want to lose a valuable client, and adding another person to your mentoring group would seem to diminish your role in it. But relationships, like ideas, multiply when they are shared. Love, friendship, and camaraderie are infinite resources. There is always room for one more person in your heart, and likely at the dinner table or in your circle of friends.

Never be afraid to make a referral, provide an introduction, or offer an invitation. Connectors—people who have a reputation for bringing others together—are always valued acquaintances. When you are generous in including new people into your circle or introducing acquaintances to one another, both sides will value your friendship all the more. It is true that not every personality fits into every social structure, such as a team or work group or support group. But don't allow fear of a misfit or fear of loss to prevent you from trying. You don't lose a friend when you share that friend with others. You gain more. Connectors are influencers.

### Giving Credit

Credit, meaning affirmation or praise for the things you have done, is yet another intangible you may be tempted to hoard. But it is better when shared.

Everyone likes to be praised, and we all enjoy being noticed or rewarded for our achievements. That can lead us to gather as much acclaim as we can for ourselves and avoid doling out any credit to others. But when you are generous in affirming others, you'll find that the principle of abundance operates in this area as well. The more you praise others, the more likely you are to be affirmed for the things you do. It's not that you should praise others with a mercenary motive. You simply understand that the world rewards generosity.

When you receive recognition or an award for any achievement, share the credit with those who helped you succeed. Be like an Academy Award winner on Oscar night: thank everyone you can think of. They'll be grateful for the notice, and it will build trust and influence.

Be generous in praising others who succeed ahead of you, including other teammates, coworkers, family members, and fellow students—even competitors. They will be grateful for your recognition and will respect your humility. Be willing to forego the credit when your good ideas are attributed to someone else. It'll be an exercise in modesty. And besides, piping in with "But that was my idea!" appears cheap and ungracious. Generous people praise liberally. Be known as a generous person.

## Lending Resources

Lending, donating, or sharing resources is another way to practice generosity. Many of us have more resources than we need at any given moment. For example, there is likely a set of tools in your garage you aren't using just now, and perhaps won't for several weeks or months. You could easily loan them to a friend, saving him or her the expense of a purchase.

Take a mental inventory of your attic, basement, closets, and spare room. What unused items do you see there? A typical home is likely to contain at least a few things that are seldom or never touched, such as a musical instrument, second television set, spare computer, toys, clothing, tools, bicycles, spare dishes, or perhaps even a car. When you share, lend, or donate such items, you meet another person's need out of your excess, the very definition of generosity. Unlike a donation of money, a loaned item will likely be returned, allowing you to be generous over and over with the same resource.

Think for a moment about the needs that may exist within your social network. Some of those needs are likely temporary. Do you have an item that might meet a need for someone else? And what items do you have that you will likely never use again? Could you donate them to an individual or worthy organization?

Make generosity a part of your lifestyle. Don't fear that others will think of your garage contents as their personal inventory. You can easily deal with abusive practices if others take advantage of your kindness. Remember: "Give, and it will be given to you."[6]

## Offering Hospitality

Hospitality is an all-but-forgotten form of generosity in American culture. Though a prized virtue in some other lands, many of us in the

United States have relegated hospitality almost entirely to the industry of hotels, restaurants, and catering. Yet hospitality is so much more than offering someone a place to stay or a meal. It is welcoming strangers into your presence, wherever that may be. It is seeing to the needs of others—including their needs for refreshment and lodging—ahead of your own.

One way of providing hospitality is to host someone for a meal or to provide them a place to stay. Another is to welcome a newcomer into your workplace, school, or other social setting. Remember that any first-timer will have certain needs or questions and may feel out of place. You can be hospitable by offering a new student a tour of the school, by orienting a new employee to office procedures, or by showing a new neighbor the best places to shop. You can also practice hospitality by making sure each person in the breakroom is included in the conversation, or ensuring that nobody gets left behind when a group goes out for lunch.

Offering hospitality is not only a kind thing to do but also a powerful influencer, as my friend Heather discovered. When the administrators of her graduate studies program asked if anyone would temporarily host a newly arriving international student, Heather quickly volunteered—the only one in her program to do so. She and her husband provided accommodations, meals, and transportation to the student while he became oriented to a new country. They also arranged housing for the student and his wife, who would arrive later.

Though this student was from a culture that highly valued hospitality, he was surprised to encounter such generosity—including the use of a car—among Americans. "Heather," he asked in a slightly puzzled tone, "why are you doing this?" That question opened the door to a wonderful conversation about culture, worldview, and faith, and it was the beginning of an ongoing friendship between the two families.

When you share your welcome with others, you gain respect, trust, and influence in their lives.

## SLEEPING WELL

Juan Antonio "Chi Chi" Rodriguez was one of the most colorful characters in the sport of golf during the more than two decades he was a fixture on the PGA circuit. He won eight major tournament titles and went on to play in the Senior PGA Tour. Besides winning, the diminutive Puerto Rican was known for two things: his quick wit and his generous spirit.

As a young boy, Rodriguez worked in the sugar cane fields—his help was needed because there were six children in the family to feed. When the boy realized he could make more money as a caddie at a local golf club, he took a job there and became hooked on the game. As a grown man, after achieving success on the PGA tour, Rodriguez never forgot the struggles of his early life, and he never lost his heart for those in need. Though he had experienced scarcity, he lived by an abundance mind-set. He recalled, "My father would give his dinner to any hungry kids who walked by and then go in the backyard and pick weeds from the yard to eat. Everything I ever had I have shared. If you worry about giving, you will never have enough, of anything."[7]

Years later Rodriguez ran into financial problems. He joked, "I was making $37,000 and spending $100,000 on the poor. But so what? God forget [*sic*] to tell me how to say no." Thankfully, today, he and the Chi Chi Rodriguez Youth Foundation, which he founded in 1979, are doing well.[8] The voluble golfer summed up his approach to life this way: "Takers eat well, but givers sleep well."[9]

Generosity is a lifestyle. When you are generous with others, that liberality is rewarded in trust, respect, and influence. The world repays in kind. Givers receive more. Hoarders receive less. Be a giver, and opportunity will follow you.

Generosity is not a leadership tactic. It is a lifestyle of openness toward others and a freedom in spending your time, talent, and treasure for those in need. When you are generous with others, you'll find meaning in life and a sense of peace that may have eluded you before. As Rodriguez noted, "Givers sleep well."[10]

## THE KEY THREE

1. Survey your attitudes and habits regarding generosity.

Do you tend to have a scarcity mind-set or an attitude of abundance?

2. Name your chief obstacle to practicing generosity, then state what you will do to confront that objection or fear.

3. List three people in your social network who might benefit from your generosity. Choose at least one person to share with today.

# 10

# THE POWER OF
# YOUR COMMITMENT

*Difficulties are just things to overcome, after all.*

**ERNEST SHACKLETON**[1]

The 1968 Olympic Games in Mexico City were memorable for a number of reasons, one being the extreme altitude of the venue. At 7,350 feet above sea level, the altitude had a noticeable effect on the athletes. In sprints and short-distance races, the thinner air allowed for record-shattering performances. However, that same atmosphere caused a hardship for distance runners, who labored to draw every breath. Competitors in the men's marathon, the ultimate test of endurance, suffered the most. When the race began at 3:00 p.m. on October 20, the last day of the track and field competition, 75 athletes representing 41 countries set out from the Plaza de la Constitución on the 26.2-mile course. Only 57 runners would finish the race.

Defending champion Abebe Bikila would have been the favorite, having grown up in Addis Ababa, Ethiopia, which sits at an even higher altitude than Mexico City. But Bikila was handicapped by a stress fracture and was recovering from a recent appendectomy. Attention turned to Mamo Wolde, another Ethiopian who had trained at these same altitudes and competed in both the 1956 and 1964 Olympics. But Belgium's Gaston Roelants held the lead at the 12-mile mark, and Kenya's Naftali Temu edged ahead near mile 16. Meanwhile, 3 runners, including Wolde, were poised for a challenge.

Yet the real drama in the race was unfolding miles behind the lead group. John Stephen Akhwari was one of many competitors who struggled to compete in the thin air of Mexico City. Halfway through the race, Akhwari was among a group of runners vying for position when he was knocked to the pavement. Akhwari suffered a wound to his shoulder, plus the dislocation of his right knee. Incredibly, after receiving medical treatment, the intrepid Tanzanian elected to continue running. Far ahead on the course, Mamo Wolde had indeed taken the lead and gone on to win, a full three minutes ahead of the second-place runner. Meanwhile, John Stephen Akhwari limped on.

More than an hour later, 56 runners had finished the course and 18 more had dropped from the field. The sun had set on Mexico City, and most of the vast crowd had filed out of the stadium. Then word came in that a final runner was about to enter. Television cameras recorded the scene as Akhwari, limping along on his bandaged knee, finally crossed the finish line. He had been running for three hours and twenty-five minutes under grueling conditions and with no prospect of earning a medal. Later, a reporter asked Akhwari why he had continued to run. He replied, "My country didn't send me to Mexico to start the race. They sent me here to finish."[2]

John Stephen Akhwari's story has inspired countless athletes and many others who have faced near-impossible odds. He embodies the concept of commitment. Commitment is a willingness to continue pursuing a goal even when it becomes difficult or costly to achieve.

Those who display a high degree of commitment are highly influential because people respect the willingness to remain steadfast over the long term. In a world where it is easier than ever to quit one endeavor and begin another, those who remain committed to their vision, especially through times of adversity, become strong influencers. In this chapter, you will gain a firm motivation to remain engaged in the process of change despite the obstacles that may come your way. You will learn to harness the power of commitment.

## WHY WE WALK AWAY

Quitting is easy, which is why so many people do it every day. That is not to say that those who abandon a goal—whether it is finishing school, remaining married, or starting a new business—are somehow soft or inferior. On the contrary, most of the people I've known who walked away from some pursuit were wonderful people who tried very hard to succeed. When I say that quitting is easy, I simply mean it's easier to quit than to remain committed to a goal in the face of adversity. Perhaps it would be more accurate to say that commitment is difficult.

And that is why commitment is such a powerful influence on others. We have all faced situations in which we gave our best, so far as we understood it at the time, but came up short. Rather than regroup and try again, we decided the goal was not worth the getting and let it slip away. So when we see a person who has been married for 50 years, or has maintained a successful business, or has finished a college degree, we admire their ability to persevere. We respect their commitment.

Sadly, most people quit just a bit too soon. None of us knows the future, so we cannot see how close we are to success. Those who have remained committed to their goals and achieved them almost always make some version of this statement: "I was on the verge of quitting when I had my big breakthrough," or, "I was ready to throw in the towel but decided to give it one more try; that's when success came." Like marathon runners who typically hit "the wall" around mile twenty, just six miles from the finish, visionaries in pursuit of any goal are likely to face their most discouraging moments when they are on the verge of success.

The reasons people back off on their dreams are complex, and it isn't simply because they lack character. Here are some reasons you may be tempted to abandon your dream too early. To understand them, we'll trace the stages every goal or project must go through to reach success: the launch, the climb, the dip, and the next phase.

### Fear of Failure

Any project or goal typically involves four distinct phases. First is the launch, which includes planning, gathering resources, and making a start. This is the ribbon-cutting for a new business, the wedding ceremony, or the first day of classes in a new degree program. Everyone is excited on these occasions because the venture is fresh and filled with possibility. Whether it's a long van ride to Disney World or the first day of a new job, we all begin a new venture with eagerness. A few people, however, give up on the project right at the start. They abandon the project just at or before the launch. Why? Because they fear failure.

Sensing that it would be better to walk away now than to slog through weeks or years of frustration only to wind up with nothing, they back off at the very beginning. This is the groom who gets "cold feet" before the wedding. Is that caused by a genuine belief the marriage should not take place? Or is it simple fear that causes him to walk away? This is also the investor who pulls out at contract stage, or the homebuyer who walks away at the closing. In such cases, it is likely fear that caused them to abandon the goal: the fear of failure.

### Eagerness Without Commitment

The second phase of any endeavor is the climb. That's when the hard work comes in. When the honeymoon is over—in a marriage or any other venture—discipline is needed in order to make this climb toward the goal. This is when you must stay up late and study for exams, get up early and go to work, or endure the daily grind of dealing with customers, changing diapers, or doing chores. The climb is hard work, and this is where those who were merely eager for the start of a project begin to fall away. Yes, they were eager for the goal. But they were not fully invested in achieving it. Eagerness will only carry you so far.

### Loss of Hope

Many people are able to remain committed through the climb. The climb is hard work, but at least they are making slow and steady progress toward their goal. They can put up with the fatigue and frustrations because it seems that they're getting closer. They have the end in sight. Though it may take years of more work, they can remain committed because they know they're making progress.

Then comes the third stage in the life of any pursuit, which Seth Godin calls "the dip."[3] This stage comes after you've been climbing for a while. As the name implies, the dip is a downturn. Suddenly, everything changes. You start arguing more. You run short of money. You're more tired than you've ever been in your life. Customers complain. Coworkers walk out. Rather than slogging uphill, you find yourself cast down into a deep, dark valley. The goal now seems impossible. You question whether you have the ability to continue.

This moment is when most people abandon their dream. It's not hard work they're afraid of; it's failure. Calculating that the goal is now permanently beyond their resources and capacity to reach it, they choose to step back. Many people quit during this stage because they simply lose faith in the goal.

### Inability to Pivot

Those who do remain committed through the dip generally find that something amazing happens. The hardship they face—the dip—becomes a critical element in their success. During this time of loss and confusion, they realize they must make adjustments in order to keep going.

In business, this may be called a *pivot*. This is when you decide that your snow removal company must become a landscape company if it is to survive. It's when you determine you'll need additional training, or more staff, or a fresh approach to fundraising in order to get your nonprofit off the ground. It's when some couples realize they must accept one another's imperfections and forgive old hurts if they are to enter a new phase in their marriage.

Remarkably, the dip can be a necessary element for success because it forces the hard analysis and creative thinking that are necessary to solve problems. Those who can pivot—meaning they can make changes in themselves, their thinking, and their approach to the goal—can usually remain committed. Those who cannot pivot often fall away during the dip.

### Lack of Personal Reserves

The fourth phase of the venture is, hopefully, the finish. This is the achievement of the goal: success in business, unity in marriage, completion of the degree, change in legislation, the publication of the book, or whatever the goal may be. The term *finish* may be misleading, however, because one goal often leads to another, and the cycle begins again. Successfully raising children leads to an empty nest, which is a new life stage with its own challenges. Success in business leads to the creation of wealth, which must then be properly managed.

Many people achieve their dream only to see it slip away later because they cannot remain committed through the finish of one project and the start of another. Often, the reason is that they lack the personal reserves to keep going. Though they may be creative thinkers, they need the personal discipline to manage their dream through its eventual success. They may become distracted, or lack self-confidence, or grow bored or tired. To remain committed to a goal beyond its completion and into the next phase of development requires a new level of commitment, one that many people are missing.

## HOW TO DEVELOP COMMITMENT

If you have backed off on a goal before, you're not alone. The important thing is to learn from your experience. You really can remain committed far beyond the eagerness that causes you to launch your aspiration: through the difficulties of the long climb, past the inevitable dip, and even beyond the realization of your dream. It helps to understand the four phases of any project or venture. Besides that, here are five simple things you can do to develop your influence and stay committed to your dreams.

### 1. State Your Motivation

One of the most powerful ways to build your staying power on a vision, goal, or project is to clarify from the outset why this matters to you. When you understand your true purpose, you'll be better equipped to move from the initial flush of eagerness to the kind of true commitment that can weather the disappointments that are sure to come. Renowned Danish philosopher Søren Kierkegaard put it this way: "What matters is to find a purpose, to see what it really is that God wills that I shall do; the crucial thing is to find a truth which is truth for me, to find the idea for which I am willing to live and die."[4]

While your current vision for change may be less central to your true life's purpose, the more strongly you feel about your vision—the closer it is to your core values and beliefs—the more fully you'll be able to commit to it. Look for the link between the ways you are trying to influence others and your life's purpose. Write down a statement of your vision *and* why it matters so much to you. This statement is for your eyes only, so it need not be pretty or polished; only clear, concise, and meaningful to you. Establish in your own mind the importance and urgency of your vision, and your commitment will remain strong throughout the life cycle of your dream.

## 2. Recall Your Goal Weekly

Once you have taken the time to write down your vision, stating your motivation for achieving your goal, place that statement where you'll be sure to see it regularly. Don't tuck it in a notebook, slide it into a desk drawer, or allow it to get buried in a file on your computer. Make it your screen saver, tape it to the bathroom mirror, or place it wherever you keep your daily to-do list. It's crucial you see the statement often and review it purposefully at least once a week.

Muhammad Ali was known for his flamboyant style, including the pronouncement of himself as "The Greatest." No one can claim, however, that he was not an outstanding boxer and a great champion. Ali was blessed with amazing natural talents, but that was not the only ingredient in his success. According to a Twitter post, he later recalled, "I hated every minute of training, but I said, 'Don't quit. Suffer now and live the rest of your life as a champion.'"[5] Keeping his purpose squarely before him enabled the "Champ" to endure the long climb of physical training and, I'm sure, the dip of his first-ever career loss to Joe Frazier, a loss he made good in a rematch.

Remind yourself of your purpose frequently. It will solidify your commitment.

## 3. Seek a Support Community

Our culture tends to idolize the lone-wolf character: that strong, independent person who can persevere alone through all odds. That makes for a nice movie hero, but in real life everyone needs a support network in order to face adversity. You'll be far more likely to maintain your commitment if you surround yourself with a community of supporters. These are encouragers, coworkers, and friends who share your commitment to your vision for change.

Don't have a support community? No problem. You can create one simply by asking people to join you. An old proverb holds that "a cord of three strands is not quickly broken."[6] That's another way of saying there is strength in numbers. If you go it alone, your own resolve will carry you only so far. But when you are allied with others who share your vision, it will strengthen your commitment, enabling you to remain steadfast in your aims to the very end.

## 4. Recognize Impossibilities

It's important to say a word here about the difference between obstacles and impossibilities. An obstacle is a hurdle to overcome, a difficulty to work through, a challenge to your commitment that you must face and resolve. Lack of funding is an obstacle. Opposition from key stakeholders is an obstacle. Your own need for rest, learning, or growth are obstacles. With some creative thinking, perseverance, and teamwork, most obstacles can be overcome. Obstacles do not prevent you from reaching your goal; they merely make it more difficult. Obstacles become a test of your commitment, but they should not break your resolve.

Some things, however, are not mere obstacles, but true impossibilities. You may have a dream of becoming president of the United States, and you may influence a number of people to join you in that pursuit. However, if you are not a "natural born citizen," are less than 35 years old, or have not lived in the country for at least 14 years, you can't serve as president. You are constitutionally ineligible. True, you could attempt to amend Article II, Section I, Clause 5 of the US Constitution, but for all intents and purposes, your election is an impossibility.

Some impossibilities arise after you undertake to achieve your vision. You may face some obstacles—such as a lack of funding, physical limitations, or opposition from others—that are so monumental they render your dream an impossibility. Think of John Stephen Akhwari limping toward the finish line of the Olympic marathon. As the very last competitor on the course, still running even after the medals had been awarded, his original goal of winning the race had become an impossibility. What do you do when you face not obstacles, but impossibilities?

In such cases you have two choices. One is to discontinue the pursuit of your goal. In many instances, that is the wisest thing to do. Commitment is not the same as insanity, after all. There is no shame in abandoning a goal that is no longer possible to achieve, or for which the costs have simply become too great.

Sometimes, however, there is merit in remaining committed even in the face of impossible odds. Akhwari's dedication in finishing a race he could not possibly win has been an inspiration to many. Often, political candidates or other advocates for change will continue their campaign even when winning has become an impossibility. Their continued efforts draw attention to the worthiness of their cause.

Whatever your choice, make it with eyes wide open. Understand when your obstacles have become impossibilities. Be realistic about your circumstances. Whether you choose to abandon your vision or to carry on for the sake of principle, do so fully aware of the outcome you face.

## 5. Don't Quit

Notice that even in the face of an impossibility, we do not quit, but rather make the choice to abandon the pursuit of a goal. Is that mere semantics? Not really. Quitting always carries with it the idea of being beaten. It is giving up on something you really want to achieve but simply cannot pay the price to attain. Quitting is always a defeat, which is why those who do so seldom command respect, while valiant "losers" like Akhwari are esteemed for their sacrifice. Soldiers who surrender rather than cause further bloodshed when faced with inevitable defeat are not deserters. We make a distinction between those who quit based on fear and those who make a deliberate choice to discontinue. Don't quit.

## KEEP GOING

Few athletes in recent memory have been both as inspiring and as controversial as Lance Armstrong, the cyclist who was stripped of his seven Tour de France championships for admitting to using performance-enhancing drugs. Regardless of those failings, Armstrong has been a hero to many because of his courageous fight against cancer. He is not only a cancer survivor, but has become a tireless advocate for cancer research. In a book about his comeback to the sport of cycling after treatment for testicular cancer, Armstrong wrote,

> Pain is temporary. It may last a minute, or an hour, or a day, or a year, but eventually it will subside and something else will take its place. If I quit, however, it lasts forever. That surrender, even the smallest act of giving up, stays with me. So when I feel like quitting, I ask myself, which would I rather live with? Facing up to that question, and finding a way to go on, is the real reward.[7]

You face the same question and the same potential for reward. The obstacles you meet in the pursuit of your dream are almost certainly temporary. Will you allow those short-term setbacks or hardships to take your eyes away from your goal, the positive change you hope to make in the world? Or will you face up to that question, finding a way to keep your commitment strong, and going on to see the realization of your dream?

Everyone has backed off on a goal at some time or other, so if you quit when things are difficult few will blame you. You might, however, bring regrets upon yourself that will be difficult to live with later on. If you are able to remain committed to your dream through thick and thin, you will find that something amazing happens. Like Akhwari, limping toward the finish line, you will begin to hear the cheers of those who applaud your commitment. They will respect you more highly and follow you more willingly because they see the strength of your resolve.

Whatever good goal you are pursuing, don't quit. Think of the finish line and remember all the reasons you chose to pursue this change in the world. Become inspired again by your dream for the future, and keep going.

**• • • • • • • • • • • • • • • • THE KEY THREE • • • • • • • • • • • • • • • • • •**

1. Recall the four stages of an endeavor and determine which stage you are in now.

2. What obstacles might you face in achieving your goals? What resources do you have—or can obtain—for overcoming them?

3. Write out your motivation for the change you hope to see in the world. If you have already written this statement, review it now.

11

# THE POWER OF YOUR SACRIFICE

*Each time a man stands up for an ideal, or acts to improve the lot of others, or strikes out against injustice, he sends forth a tiny ripple of hope.*

**ROBERT F. KENNEDY**[1]

My father, William Aaron Toler, was one of the greatest men I've ever known. Though he died when I was just 11 years old, his life was dedicated to serving his family. He began his working life as a coal miner in McDowell County, West Virginia, the most productive coal region in the state but one of the poorest counties in the nation. Dad worked every day in the mines, returning home tired, his face blackened with coal soot. Our tiny home in Baileysville provided just enough shelter for our family of five. Because Dad worked underground all day, he seldom saw daylight, especially during the winter months. Mining is a perilous occupation, and Dad broke his back three times in the mines while laboring to feed our family. More than once I saw him cough up black coal dust into a snow-white handkerchief, a common occurrence among miners of that day.

Realizing that his family's welfare depended on his own health, Dad chose to move our family to Columbus, Ohio, in search of a better life. Things didn't improve immediately though, and he went several months without finding work. Even so, Dad's attitude was always bright. We ate a lot of pinto beans and fried bologna, but we were happy.

Eventually Dad did find a job with a construction company, and we were all elated. I know it felt good to my father to be employed again, and the whole family was excited to have a bit more money for food and occasional treats. Dad was working, Mom was content, and my brothers and I were doing well in our new school. Everything seemed to be back to normal—actually, better than the "normal" we had known up to that point.

Then one Monday morning Dad went to work and never came home. Having escaped the harrowing dangers of the coal mine, he was electrocuted in a tragic on-the-job accident.

I recall many lessons my father taught me during our few years together: the value of hard work, how to save money, the blessings of faith and family, the power of a positive attitude. Yet the most important lesson I learned from Dad was the power of sacrifice.

Dad worked hard at the risk of his own health and life, but he did not do it for himself. His goal was never to enjoy luxuries or to advance his own name. Dad toiled day in and day out to provide for his family and to support our local church. He did it for us. He did it for God. And he never complained. He was cheerful even in the direst circumstances. Why? Dad was hopeful by nature, but it was more than that. He realized that he was the leader in our home and was responsible for our well-being. He would not allow himself to be dispirited because he knew how it would affect the rest of us.

I have been privileged to know many great people during my lifetime. I've had the opportunity to learn from pastors and statesmen, great athletes and powerful business executives—the kind of people who create tremendous impact on the lives of others. Yet I can honestly say that no human being has been a greater influence in my life than my father. That was not because he was wealthy or powerful, highly educated or extremely successful. It was because of the power of his sacrifice on behalf of his family and his faith.

Generosity is sharing from abundance. Sacrifice is giving at a level that risks loss. Generosity results in gratitude, but sacrifice produces devotion. Sacrifice leads to the most powerful influence because it is a demonstration of love. The influence of Mahatma Gandhi, Dr. Martin

Luther King Jr., Bill Bright, and other great leaders endures precisely because they were willing to put the needs of others ahead of their own.

In this chapter, you will learn the power of sacrifice. You will be inspired to give the greatest possible gift to others: yourself.

## SACRIFICES THAT IMPACT OTHERS

Human beings are naturally inclined to put themselves first. Though we all have nobler moments, our first instinct is to place our own wants and needs ahead of others' wants and needs. This is the urge you have to take the largest piece of pie for yourself, to step on the gas when you see another driver approaching the same intersection, or to think, "I wish that was me," when someone else receives an award or recognition. This impulse for self-promotion is one of the most basic aspects of human nature. Though we recognize that it must be held in check, and we may be largely successful at doing so, the impulse never really goes away.

That's why acts of personal sacrifice are so compelling. When we see another person set aside their desire for self-protection, self-promotion, or self-preservation in order to benefit others, we are truly impressed. For example, when we see a video of a man wading into rushing floodwaters to save a child, or when we hear of a person who donates a kidney to a friend or shares their last bit of food, something inside us says, "Wow." We find ourselves hoping that we would do the same in similar circumstances, but we're not sure. Selfless sacrifice is one of the few things that garners universal respect. And that's exactly why it is such a powerful influencer. When others see that you are genuinely more concerned for their well-being than for your own, they will esteem you highly and listen to you closely.

As with the other influence builders mentioned in this book, self-sacrifice is not a mere tool for gaining attention. Faux altruism is usually easy to spot and winds up having the opposite effect. People disrespect those who use the appearance of concern to manipulate their emotions. We should sacrifice for the needs of others because it's the right thing to do, not because we hope to gain from it. At the same time, it's helpful to recognize the ways in which our sacrifice enables us to influence others for the common good. When you place others ahead of yourself in these key areas, you gain a greater ability to influence them for good.

## Surrendering Your Power

The first way we can sacrifice for others is in the area of power, which can be defined in terms of rights, privileges, and control of circumstances. Though you may not feel like a powerful person, each of us has a certain amount of power in all our social contexts. We have rights as citizens. We enjoy privileges based on our family relationships or social status. And we hold some power in our social relationships and employment. Our instinct is to cling to our privileges and power, and to enhance them whenever possible. We are competitive by nature, we vie for promotions, and we are eager to gain special privileges that set us apart from others. So when we go against that urge and voluntarily surrender power on behalf of others, it establishes our leadership and influence.

Nelson Mandela was president of South Africa from 1994 to 1999, but he is perhaps better known as a crusader against apartheid who spent 27 years in prison. At his sentencing in 1964, he faced possible execution for his conviction on charges of treason. Prior to the pronouncement of his sentence, Mandela made this statement:

> During my lifetime I have dedicated myself to this struggle of the African people. I have fought against white domination, and I have fought against black domination. I have cherished the ideal of a democratic and free society in which all persons live together in harmony and with equal opportunities. It is an ideal which I hope to live for and to achieve. But if needs be, it is an ideal for which I am prepared to die.[2]

Mandela proved the power of his conviction through the sacrifice of his freedom. Decades later, he was released from prison and apartheid came to an end. In 1994, he was elected the first black head of state in South Africa.

However, Mandela served only a single term in that office. Having launched an effort at national reconciliation, he believed that a good foundation had been set for the future. Although he was eligible for another five-year term, Mandela chose to walk away from the power he had worked so long to achieve because he believed it to be in the best interest of the country.[3] That act cemented his legacy as a leader who was willing to put the needs of others ahead of his own privilege and power. That kind of sacrifice is rare and always revered. We find it astounding when someone voluntarily surrenders their rights, privileges, or power on behalf of others.

You may never have the occasion to sacrifice power in such a grand way, but you will certainly face occasions when you have the choice to hold on to your rights or to surrender them to meet the needs of others. When you choose to forgive another person, you sacrifice your right for personal justice or compensation—and when you do that as an act of mercy or compassion, you gain rather than lose respect. When you strike a compromise with an employee or coworker that allows their agenda to advance, you may surrender a bit of the control that was due to you. Yet when others see you have put the needs of the group ahead of your own career or reputation, your influence will grow. Even simple acts such as allowing a person to enter ahead of you or to take a parking spot that could have been yours enhance your leadership.

Notice two aspects of this surrender of privilege or power: it is done voluntarily and for the sake of others. This is not submitting to the victimization perpetrated by others in order to advance themselves. That kind of injustice is not to be tolerated. We are speaking here of the willing surrender of your rights in order to meet the genuine needs of another. When you put others first, they will notice. And when they have a genuine need, your gift will not be seen as a sign of weakness, but of strength. Your influence will grow as a result.

### Transferring Your Wealth

A second area in which we may sacrifice ourselves for the benefit of others is in the use of our wealth. Few of us feel as if we are wealthy, but we are. If you are reading this book, chances are good that you have enough disposable income to buy the book and enough spare time to read it. In a world in which an estimated three billion people live in poverty,[4] requiring all their time and energy be devoted to gaining enough food to survive, those two facts indicate you have wealth. And it's possible you have even more resources than that. One definition of wealth is excess, so if you have more food, money, clothing, and resources than you need to survive, by that definition you are wealthy. Since we all value wealth—which is usually reckoned in terms of money—very highly, those who are willing to give money away, especially when it changes their own financial status, are rare indeed.

Warren Buffett, one of the wealthiest people on earth, made headlines when he announced that he would give away nearly all his fortune. The highly successful investor has a vision for giving back to society, and he elected to do so by granting the bulk of his money to philanthropic causes—notably the Bill & Melinda Gates Foundation, which is active in improving health care and reducing poverty worldwide. The total value of Buffett's planned gifts, to be given over a period of years, was calculated at some $37 billion, an astoundingly generous amount by any standard, and possibly the largest sum ever given away. The gift—if given all at once—would have reduced the value of Buffett's fortune (in Berkshire Hathaway stock) to *only* $6.8 billion.[5]

Buffett's gift sets a marvelous example for others to follow, and we must note that he also pledged to donate the remainder of his wealth by the time of his death.[6] We should all use our resources to impact the world in such positive ways.

While Buffett's example powerfully illustrates generosity, he is giving out of his abundance. As someone has aptly put it, the true measure of your sacrifice is not how much you give, but how much you have left after you give. Generosity is impressive; sacrifice is extraordinary.

Jesus, the greatest teacher of all time, illustrated this point while watching people make donations to a religious institution. Observing many wealthy people giving large gifts, he also noticed a poor woman who put in two copper coins—essentially two cents. And he said, "This poor widow has put in more than all the others. All these people gave their gifts out of their wealth; but she out of her poverty put in all she had to live on."[7]

As a boy, I saw countless examples of this very same sacrificial giving. Poor as our family was, my father always insisted we boys take a few cents with us to church to put in the offering plate. Dad knew that some of the money went to help families who were even harder hit than we were. And when things were at their worst for the Toler household, we received a gift of groceries from folks at the church. Some of them had barely enough to eat themselves, yet they were willing to share with others.

When you give sacrificially to benefit others, whether it is to a food program, an educational initiative, or a fight for justice, you demonstrate that your own status means less to you than the welfare of others. When you donate to a scholarship fund while still paying off your own student loans, you demonstrate your commitment to doing good in the world. When you place a few food items in the collection box outside the supermarket despite the fact you're living paycheck to paycheck, you make a tangible sacrifice to benefit others. When you give to support a missionary, you forego buying certain things for yourself. When others see your dedication to helping others by sharing what you have, you gain respect in their eyes and the influence that goes along with it.

### Risking Your Safety

A third area in which we may sacrifice for others is in risking our safety for their care or survival. Though there have been many brave souls who have literally given up their lives to save another person—like Father Maximilian Kolbe, who volunteered to take the place of a condemned man at Auschwitz[8]—most of us will never be called upon to knowingly make such a sacrifice. However, there are many occasions on which we may place our wealth, reputation, or health at risk on behalf of others. Our willingness to disregard our own safety is a powerful statement of our concern for others, and that concern brings great respect.

On November 9, 2007, a group of soldiers was en route from the village of Aranas, Afghanistan, to their remote combat outpost. They had hoped to spend the day meeting with a group of village elders, but the soldiers suspected trouble when the elders delayed the meeting for several hours and an unusually large group of villagers turned out for the meeting. Some of the villagers trailed the soldiers toward their outpost, then launched an attack. Sgt. Kyle White began to engage the attackers but was rendered unconscious by a rocket-propelled grenade. As he awoke, an enemy round exploded near his head, sending shrapnel into his face.

Shaking off his wounds, Sgt. White noticed a fellow soldier who had been shot in the arm. Without hesitation, Sgt. White moved to help the soldier, exposing himself to enemy fire in the process. He then went to help an injured marine, offering aid until the man died from his wounds. After, Sgt. White returned to help the other soldier—again under heavy enemy fire—who had been shot a second time. Sgt. White applied a tourniquet that stopped the bleeding.

Realizing that both his radio and his comrade's radio were broken, Sgt. White braved enemy fire yet again to retrieve a radio from the deceased marine. With it, he provided information that allowed friendly forces to make air strikes that subdued the enemy attack and called for medical evacuation of his fellow soldiers, marines, and Afghan Army soldiers.

For displaying extraordinary heroism and selflessness by risking his own life for others, Sgt. Kyle J. White was awarded the Medal of Honor, his country's highest award for bravery. Sgt. White later recalled thinking, "It's just a matter of time before I'm dead. If that's going to happen, I might as well help someone while I can."[9, 10, 11] That attitude exemplifies not only the heroism of a Medal of Honor recipient but also the attitude of all who risk their comfort and security for the benefit of others.

Opportunities to display heroic, life-endangering selflessness are rare in wartime and rarer in civilian life. Yet we all have occasion to leave the safety and comfort of our own lives behind in order to benefit others. When you take up the call for justice on behalf of the oppressed, you risk your reputation and possibly sacrifice the comfortable life you've been used to. When you decide to promote change in your home or workplace, you leave the comfort zone of conformity. When you do that not merely for your own interests, but also to better the lives of others, you make a sacrifice that's worth noting. When you risk your health, wealth, comfort, or reputation in order to advance the well-being of those around you, you merit their respect.

As Sgt. White said, "When you're deployed, those people become your family. What you really care about is: I want to get this guy to the left and to the right home."[12] When the welfare of the people on your left and right becomes as important to you as your own well-being, you will have earned the right to be an influencer in their lives.

## EVERYDAY HERO

Civil rights leaders, billionaires, Medal of Honor recipients. Having read this chapter, you might conclude that only extraordinary sacrifices of courage, generosity, or heroism are worthy of respect. Not so. Every day, ordinary folks like you and me make the unexceptional sacrifices that make a home, classroom, office, or neighborhood better than they were before.

When a dad like mine goes to work every day, risking his own health for the security of his children, he leaves a powerful legacy. When a student gives up his time to tutor another student, helping them succeed, she makes a sacrifice worth remembering. When a teacher or employer, mom or mentor, classmate or coworker sacrifices time, contributes money, risks their reputation, or moves out of their comfort zone not to make themselves a star, but to provide for the needs of others, we all are richer for it.

Every day, you have opportunities large and small to sacrifice yourself on behalf of others. There is no question about whether or not your sacrifice will be worthwhile, or whether or not it will be rewarded with increased esteem, respect, and attention. It certainly will be. The only question is this: Will you live your life for Christ and others, or only for yourself? Your answer to that question will, in large measure, determine the level of your influence.

### · · · · · · · · · · · · · · · THE KEY THREE · · · · · · · · · · · · · ·

1. Name the person you most respect, then state what you have seen them sacrifice for others.

2. Review the three areas in which we often make sacrifices for others, and name the one that you find most challenging. Discuss this finding with a friend or mentor.

3. Name the most pressing need you see within your family, church, school, neighborhood, or workplace. Now ask God what you should sacrifice in order to meet that need.

# YOU CAN!

Let's go back to the beginning. At the start of this book, I asked you to state your vision for the world, the positive change you hope to make in your home, community, workplace, or even your nation. This vision is the reason you want to be an influencer in the first place. Take a moment to review that positive change. Call it to mind. Literally envision it. What will the world look like when you succeed in influencing others to change? It's an inspiring picture, isn't it?

Yet it is not without challenges. By now you've realized that achieving this vision will not be easy. Perhaps it seems too big for you to tackle. You may be wondering, "What have I gotten myself into?" If so, you're not alone. Everyone who envisions a better world faces that moment of apprehension, and that's the way it should be. If your vision seems within easy reach, it's too small to be worthy of your commitment and sacrifice. Every worthwhile dream seems a bit terrifying at the start. But take courage. You *can* do this. You can influence the world. The leap from where you are now to your vision for the future may seem great, but you can bridge the gap.

Remember that influencing others is a long game. This is a marathon, not a sprint. It will take months or even years to draw others toward your positive vision. And remember that your influence begins within yourself. If you hope to influence others, you must first gain control of yourself—your thoughts, attitudes, and actions. If you don't know where to begin, start there. You must become the change you hope to see in the world.

Next you will influence others through your vision, thoughts, words, habits, presence, encouragement, and generosity—and through the compelling power of your commitment and sacrifice. If you are diligent, your influence will not stop there. Through those with whom you come into contact, your vision will ripple outward, affecting more and more people over time. Ultimately, you will change the world.

Impossible? No. This result is entirely possible if you are able to harness the incredible power of your influence. Remember, you are influencing others all the time, whether you are aware of it or not. And that influence is never neutral. You constantly affect others in either negative or positive ways. When you are able to seize that power and harness it to further your vision, nothing can stop you from achieving your goal.

I believe in you! I am convinced you have what it takes to gain mastery of yourself, influence others, and impact the world. Only one question remains for you to answer: When will you begin?

# NOTES

## INTRODUCTION: THE POWER TO CHANGE THE FUTURE

1. Ken Blanchard and Phil Hodges, *Servant Leader: Transforming your Heart, Head, Hands and Habits* (Nashville: Thomas Nelson, 2003), 10.

2. Loren Eiseley, "The Star Thrower" as found in *The Unexpected Universe* (New York: Harcourt, 1969).

3. Michael Karson, "Punishment Doesn't Work," *Psychology Today*, January 14, 2014, https://www.psychologytoday.com/blog/feeling-our-way/201401/punishment-doesnt-work.

4. Martin Luther King Jr., "I Have a Dream," *American Rhetoric: Top 100 Speeches*, accessed February 7, 2017, http://www.americanrhetoric.com/speeches/mlkihaveadream.htm.

## CHAPTER 1: THE NATURE OF INFLUENCE

1. Ralph Waldo Emerson, *The Conduct of Life* (Boston: Houghton Mifflin, 1860), 258.

2. Zig Ziglar, "Little Things Make a Big Difference: The Choice Is Yours," *AdvantEdge Newsletter*, 2013, http://www.nightingale.com/newsletters/zig-ziglar-little-things-make-a-big-difference-the-choice-is-yours-577/.

3. Howard Zinn, *You Can't Be Neutral on a Moving Train*, a documentary released in 2004.

4. Ezekiel 22:29-30.

## CHAPTER 2: THREE DIMENSIONS OF INFLUENCE

1. John C. Maxwell, *The 5 Levels of Leadership: Proven Steps to Maximize Your Potential* (New York: Center Street, 2011), 44.

2. The Associated Press, "The Latest: Melenchon Is in 7 Places at Once, With Hologram," *The New York Times*, April 18, 2017, https://www.nytimes.com/aponline/2017/04/18/world/europe/ap-eu-france-election-the-latest.html (article no longer available).

3. The Associated Press, "French Candidate Uses Hologram to Travel Campaign Trail," *U.S. News & World Report*, February 5, 2017, https://www.usnews.com/news/world/articles/2017-02-05/french-candidate-uses-hologram-to-travel-campaign-trail.

4. See Colossians 3:9-10.

5. 1 Timothy 3:5.

6. Eliott C. McLaughlin, "Man Dragged off United Flight Has Concussion, Will File Suit, Lawyer Says," *CNN*, April 14, 2017, http://www.cnn.com/2017/04/13/travel/united-passenger-pulled-off-flight-lawsuit-family-attorney-speak/.

7. Brad Tuttle, "Warren Buffett's Boring, Brilliant Wisdom," *Time*, March 1, 2010, http://business.time.com/2010/03/01/warren-buffetts-boring-brilliant-wisdom/.

8. Jon Ronson, "How One Stupid Tweet Blew Up Justine Sacco's Life," *The New York Times*, February 12, 2015, https://www.nytimes.com/2015/02/15/magazine/how-one-stupid-tweet-ruined-justine-saccos-life.html.

9. "About Anne Frank" at Anne Frank Center for Mutual Respect, http://annefrank.com/about-anne-frank/.

10. Anne Frank, *The Diary of a Young Girl,* trans. B. M. Mooyaart-Doubleday (New York: Bantam, 1993), 197.

11. Anne Frank, *Anne Frank's Tales from the Secret Annex,* trans. Ralph Manheim and Michel Mok (Garden City: Doubleday, 1984), 131.

12. Frank, *Anne Frank's Tales from the Secret Annex.*

## CHAPTER 3: THE POWER OF YOUR VISION

1. Walt Disney, as quoted in Pat Williams with Jim Denney, *How to Be Like Walt: Capturing the Disney Magic Every Day of Your Life* (Deerfield Beach: Health Communications, 2004), 69.

2. Harry Readhead, "This Train Driver Got on the Wrong Service and Then Set Off in the Wrong Direction," *Metro,* April 9, 2015, http://metro.co.uk/2015/04/09/this-train-driver-got-on-the-wrong-service-and-then-set-off-in-the-wrong-direction-5141303/.

3. "How Does GPS Work?" *NASA Space Place,* May 6, 2015, https://spaceplace.nasa.gov/gps/en/.

4. Martin Luther King, Jr., "I Have a Dream…," *National Archives,* 1963, https://www.archives.gov/files/press/exhibits/dream-speech.pdf.

5. John F. Kennedy, "Excerpt from an Address Before a Joint Session of Congress, 25 May 1961," *John F. Kennedy Presidential Library and Museum,* May 25, 1961, https://www.jfklibrary.org/Asset-Viewer/xzw1gaeeTES6khED14P1Iw.aspx.

6. "Alzheimer's Association FY15–FY18 Strategic Plan," *Alzheimer's Association,* accessed May 23, 2017, http://www.alz.org/about_us_strategic_plan.asp.

7. "Our Purpose and Beliefs," *Oxfam International,* accessed May 23, 2017, https://www.oxfam.org/en/our-purpose-and-beliefs.

8. John C. Maxwell, "People Do What People See," *Bloomberg,* November 19, 2007, https://www.bloomberg.com/news/articles/2007-11-19/people-do-what-people-seebusinessweek-business-news-stock-market-and-financial-advice.

9. Andy Stanley, "Creating a Culture of Continual Improvement, Part 1," *The Andy Stanley Leadership Podcast,* podcast audio, March 3, 2017, https://itunes.apple.com/us/podcast/andy-stanley-leadership-podcast/id290055666?mt=2.

## CHAPTER 4: THE POWER OF YOUR THOUGHTS

1. Bob Selden, "The Train Story—a Journey, an Experience, and a Feeling!" *A Gift of Inspiration,* accessed May 23, 2017, http://www.agiftofinspiration.com.au/stories/attitude/.

2. Barbara L. Fredrickson, "The Broaden-and-Build Theory of Positive Emotions," *The Royal Society,* August 17, 2004, 1367, https://www.ncbi.nlm.nih.gov/pmc/.

3. Fredrickson, 1367.

4. Fredrickson, 1375.

5. Luke 6:45.

6. Gottfried Wilhelm Leibniz, *Theodicy: Essays on the Goodness of God, the Freedom of Man and the Origin of Evil,* trans. E. M. Huggard (New York: Cosimo, 2009), 128.

7. Justin Kruger and David Dunning, "Unskilled and Unaware of It: How Difficulties in Recognizing One's Own Incompetence Lead to Inflated Self-Assessments," *Journal of Personality and Social Psychology* 77 (December 1999): 1121–1134.

8. Luke 6:38.

9. Robert H. Schuller, *Move Ahead with Possibility Thinking* (New York: Jove, 1978), 15.

10. George Bernard Shaw, as quoted in Robert F. Kennedy, "Remarks at the University of Kansas, March 18, 1968," *John F. Kennedy Presidential Library and Museum*, March 18, 1968, https://www.jfklibrary.org/Research/Research-Aids/Ready-Reference/RFK-Speeches/Remarks-of-Robert-F-Kennedy-at-the-University-of-Kansas-March-18-1968.aspx.

11. Kate Harkness, as cited in Robert Biswas-Diener and Todd B. Kashdan, "What Happy People Do Differently," *Psychology Today*, July 2, 2013, https://www.psychologytoday.com/articles/201307/what-happy-people-do-differently.

## CHAPTER 5: THE POWER OF YOUR WORDS

1. Ingrid Bengis, *Combat in the Erogenous Zone* (New York: Alfred A. Knopf, 1972), 46.

2. "The Power of Words," YouTube video, 1:47, *Purple Feather*, February 23, 2010, http://purplefeather.co.uk/our-story.

3. See Matthew 7:3–5.

4. Proverbs 24:26.

5. Ann Landers, "Surrounded by Love, He Was Ready for a Miracle," *Chicago Tribune*, March 2, 1993, http://articles.chicagotribune.com/1993-03-02/features/9303186542_1_dear-ann-landers-diets-don-t-work-long-distance-truck-driver.

## CHAPTER 6: THE POWER OF YOUR EXAMPLE

1. Henry David Thoreau, *Letters to a Spiritual Seeker*, ed. Bradley P. Dean (New York: W. W. Norton, 2004), 38.

2. As cited in Michelle Trudeau and Jane Greenhalgh, "Yawning May Promote Social Bonding Even Between between Dogs and Humans," Morning Edition, National Public Radio, May 15, 2017, http://www.npr.org/sections/health-shots/2017/05/15/527106576/yawning-may-promote-social-bonding-even-between-dogs-and-humans.

3. Brad Tuttle, "Warren Buffett's Boring, Brilliant Wisdom," *Time*, March 1, 2010, http://business.time.com/2010/03/01/warren-buffetts-boring-brilliant-wisdom/.

## CHAPTER 7: THE POWER OF YOUR PRESENCE

1. Joe Gibbs, as quoted in "Joe Gibbs: Leaving a Legacy," *CBN*, http://www1.cbn.com/700club/joe-gibbs-leaving-legacy.http://www.npr.org/templates/story/story.php?storyId=5064534.

2. Debbie Hall, "The Power of Presence," NPR, December 26, 2005, https://www.npr.org/templates/story/story.php?storyId=5064534.

3. Jo Anne Lyon, *The Ultimate Blessing: My Journey to Discover God's Presence* (Indianapolis: Wesleyan, 2009), 27.

4. Woody Allen, as quoted in Susan Braudy, "He's Woody Allen's Not-So-Silent Partner," *The New York Times Archives*, August 21, 1977, http://www.nytimes.com/1977/08/21/archives/hes-woody-allens-notsosilent-partner.html.

5. Matthew 7:12.

6. Barry Corey, "Loving Others through the Power of Presence," *Tyndale*, accessed June 8, 2017, https://www.tyndale.com/stories/the-power-of-presence.

## CHAPTER 8: THE POWER OF YOUR ENCOURAGEMENT

1. Abigail Van Buren, "Exercise in Self-Esteem Is Lesson for a Lifetime," Dear Abby, *UExpress*, January 10, 1999, http://www.uexpress.com/dearabby/1999/1/10/exercise-in-self-esteem-is-lesson.

2. Garson O'Toole, "Be Kind; Everyone You Meet Is Fighting a Hard Battle," *Quote Investigator*, June 29, 2010, https://quoteinvestigator.com/2010/06/29/be-kind/.

3. Dale Carnegie, *How to Win Friends and Influence People*, rev. ed. (1936; repr., New York: Gallery, 1936), 227.

4. Ann Landers, "Simple Words Can Comfort," *Sun Sentinel*, December 30, 1993, http://articles.sun-sentinel.com/1993-12-30/lifestyle/9312290209_1_dear-ann-landers-new-jersey-woman-daughter.

## CHAPTER 9: THE POWER OF YOUR GENEROSITY

1. These statements all appear in the same source, but not worded exactly this way as a single quotation. Nonetheless, they represent the essence of John Wesley's thinking on generosity. John Wesley, "The Use of Money," *The Works of John Wesley*, 3rd ed. (Kansas City: Beacon Hill, 1979), 126, 131, 133.

2. "Tom Bloch," *Big Think*, http://bigthink.com/experts/tombloch.

3. "A CEO Who Left His Family's Company to Follow His Heart," Donor Stories, *Greater Kansas City Community Foundation*, https://www.growyourgiving.org/donor-stories.

4. See at http://bigthink.com/experts/tombloch.

5. Luke 6:38.

6. See Luke 6:38.

7. "Quotes," Chi Chi Rodriguez, *Biography*, November 16, 2016, https://www.biography.com/people/chi-chi-rodriguez-189145.

8. See at https://www.biography.com/people/chi-chi-rodriguez-189145.

9. Chi Chi Rodriguez, as quoted in Bob Verdi, "Be Like Chi Chi: Be a Good Giver," *Chicago Tribune*, November 26, 1991, http://articles.chicagotribune.com/1991-11-26/sports/9104170126_1_chi-chi-rodriguez-new-york-yankees-front-agents.

10. See at http://articles.chicagotribune.com/1991-11-26/sports/9104170126_1_chi-chi-rodriguez-new-york-yankees-front-agents.

## CHAPTER 10: THE POWER OF YOUR COMMITMENT

1. Ernest Shackleton, as quoted in Roland Huntford, *Shackleton* (New York: Carroll & Graf, 1985), 261.

2. "Athletics at the 1968 Ciudad de México Summer Games: Men's Marathon," *Sports Reference*, http://www.sports-reference.com/olympics/summer/1968/ATH/mens-marathon.html; "The Incredible Story of Tanzania's John-Stephen Akhwari - Mexico 1968 Olympics," YouTube video, :41, posted by "Olympic," May 1, 2013, https://www.youtube.com/watch?v=eNt_jynuAtI. See video description.

3. Seth Godin, *The Dip: A Little Book That Teaches You When to Quit (and When to Stick)* (New York: Portfolio, 2007), 4.

4. Søren Kierkegaard, "Gilleleie, August 1, 1835," *Søren Kierkegaard's Journals and Papers*, trans. and ed. Howard V. Hong and Edna H. Hong, vol. 5 (Bloomington: Indiana University, 1978), 34.

5. Muhammad Ali, Twitter post, April 30, 2009, 7:36 a.m., https://twitter.com/MuhammadAli/status/1659370445.

6. Ecclesiastes 4:12.

7. Lance Armstrong with Sally Jenkins, *It's Not About the Bike: My Journey Back to Life* (New York: Berkley, 2001), 269.

## CHAPTER 11: THE POWER OF YOUR SACRIFICE

1. Robert F. Kennedy, "Day of Affirmation Address, University of Capetown, Capetown, South Africa, June 6, 1966," *John F. Kennedy Presidential Library and Museum*, June 6, 1966, https://www.jfklibrary.org/Research/Research-Aids/Ready-Reference/RFK-Speeches/Day-of-Affirmation-Address-as-delivered.aspx.

2. Nelson Mandela, as quoted in "I Am Prepared to Die": Document Recalls Famous Speech from the Dock," *Nelson Mandela Foundation*, April 20, 2011, https://www.nelsonmandela.org/news/entry/i-am-prepared-to-die.

3. "SA President Nelson Mandela to Step Down," *South African History Online*, March 16, 2011, http://www.sahistory.org.za/dated-event/sa-president-nelson-mandela-step-down.

4. Anup Shah, "Poverty Facts and Stats," *Global Issues*, http://www.globalissues.org/article/26/poverty-facts-and-stats. In this article, poverty is defined as living on less than $2.50 a day.

5. Carol J. Loomis, "Warren Buffett Gives Away His Fortune," *Fortune Magazine: Archives*, June 25, 2006, http://archive.fortune.com/2006/06/25/magazines/fortune/charity1.fortune/index.htm.

6 Loomis, "Warren Buffet Gives Away His Fortune."

7. Luke 21:1-4.

8 "Maximilian Kolbe," Jewish Virtual Library, http://www.jewishvirtuallibrary.org/maximilian-kolbe.

9. David Hudson, "President Obama Awards the Medal of Honor to Sgt. Kyle J. White," *The White House: President Barack Obama*, May 13, 2014, https://obamawhitehouse.archives.gov/blog/2014/05/13/president-obama-awards-medal-honor-sgt-kyle-j-white.

10. "Sergeant Kyle J. White Medal of Honor Operation Enduring Freedom," at https://www.army.mil/medalofhonor/white/battle/index.html#full_narrative.

11. See at http://www.presidency.ucsb.edu/ws/index.php?pid=105185.

12. Kyle J. White, as quoted in David Hudson, "President Obama Awards the Medal of Honor to Sgt. Kyle J. White," *The White House: President Barack Obama*, May 13, 2014, https://obamawhitehouse.archives.gov/blog/2014/05/13/president-obama-awards-medal-honor-sgt-kyle-j-white.

## THE POWER OF YOUR ATTITUDE

As much as you try, sometimes you just can't change your circumstances—and never the actions of others. But you do have the power to choose how your attitude affects your outlook on your day and those you influence in your life.

Join Stan Toler as he shares the *what, why,* and *how* behind the transformation you desire. With this book, you'll...

- release the thoughts and habits that keep you from experiencing joy on a daily basis
- learn the seven choices you can make to get out of a rut and into greater success
- implement a plan to improve your outlook in three vital areas and conquer negativity

Having lost his father in an industrial accident as a boy, Toler knows about coping with unexpected tragedies and harsh realities. He will gently guide you through the internal processes that can positively change any life—including yours.

## THE POWER OF YOUR BRAIN

Do you find yourself stuck in negative thought patterns? Is your thinking disrupting your day and thwarting your goals?

When you choose to take each thought captive to the obedience of Christ, you drive out the world's way of thinking that breeds depression, discontent, and despair—and make room for more joy, faith, and purpose. Let Stan teach you an easy four-step process for restoring order to your brain:

- *Detoxification*—remove clutter from your mind
- *Realignment*—establish your thoughts on God's truth
- *Reinforcement*—bring others along on the journey
- *Perseverance*—maintain your positive momentum

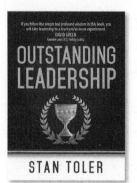

## OUTSTANDING LEADERSHIP

What makes a leader stand out? What are the keys to truly making a difference? And how can you become the influencer you were created to be? With more than 40 years of leadership experience, Stan Toler knows what it takes to empower people to reach organizational and personal goals. He cuts through the mystery and confusion and provides clear guidelines to help you accomplish vital leadership tasks, including...

- defining your vision, developing your plan, and communicating clearly to help people buy in to your shared goal
- overcoming common leadership challenges to create a culture of success
- building strong relationships and effective teams that make working hard worthwhile

You'll find all the tools, tips, and practical guidance you need to help individuals and groups reach their highest potential and fulfill their God-given purpose.

## MINUTE MOTIVATORS FOR LEADERS

You are a leader—people look to you to be an example, offer direction, and provide inspiration. But with so much to do, how can you keep fresh, focused, and excited about your opportunity to make a difference in people's lives? Stan Toler provides inspirational quotes, one-page gems of wisdom, and memorable taglines to fuel your passion and clarify your vision. You'll find plenty of helpful reminders that...

- Leaders are in the people business. As a leader, your primary function is not to buy, sell, or ply a trade. It is to understand and work with people.
- Bureaucrats run institutions. Leaders lead people. You can make the difference.
- Leadership is a team sport. Do more than direct individuals—build a team.

This treasure of tried-and-true principles will be your on-the-go source for the motivation and encouragement you need to be the effective leader you were created to be.

## MINUTE MOTIVATORS FOR WOMEN
### STAN TOLER AND LINDA TOLER

Whether you pick up this book first thing in the morning or when you're winding down at bedtime, you'll be inspired and encouraged over and over again!

Author Stan Toler and his wife, Linda, share thought-provoking quotes and beautiful words of hope within these pages. Each chapter will draw your attention to a single attribute every godly woman wants to cultivate in her life, such as patience, wisdom, persistence, courage, and gratitude.

Bite-size portions of inspiration make this the perfect devotional for, well, anytime—especially those days when you feel like you can never get ahead. Recharge in the middle of a hectic schedule or end your day with a much-needed reminder that God has every aspect of your life under control.

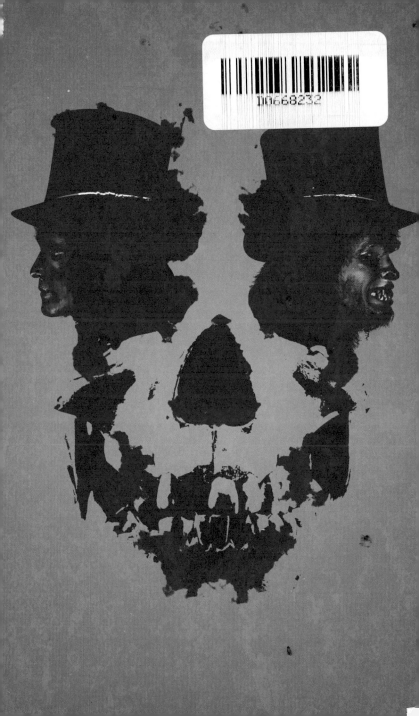

# Strange Case of
# Dr. Jekyll and Mr. Hyde
# & Other Stories

# Strange Case of Dr. Jekyll and Mr. Hyde & Other Stories

*ROBERT LOUIS STEVENSON*

**Word Cloud Classics**

San Diego

© 2014 Canterbury Classics

Canterbury Classics
An imprint of Printers Row Publishing Group
10350 Barnes Canyon Road, Suite 100, San Diego, CA 92121
www.thunderbaybooks.com

Printers Row Publishing Group is a division of Readerlink Distribution Services, LLC. The Canterbury Classics and Word Cloud Classics names and logos are trademarks of Readerlink Distribution Services, LLC.

All correspondence concerning the content of this book should be addressed to Canterbury Classics, Editorial Department, at the above address.

Publisher: Peter Norton
Publishing Team: Lori Asbury, Ana Parker, Laura Vignale
Editorial Team: JoAnn Padgett, Melinda Allman, Dan Mansfield
Production Team: Blake Mitchum, Rusty von Dyl

Library of Congress Cataloging-in-Publication Data

Stevenson, Robert Louis, 1850-1894.
  [Works. Selections]
  The Strange Case of Dr. Jekyll and Mr. Hyde and Other Stories / Robert Louis Stevenson.
      pages cm. -- (Word Cloud Classics)
  Summary: "A book so iconic that its title is synonymous with split personalities, The Strange Case of Dr. Jekyll and Mr. Hyde by Scottish author Robert Louis Stevenson was first released in 1886. The story of a virtuous Dr. Jekyll who mistakenly creates an alter ego of unadulterated evil serves as an examination of the duality of human nature and the battle between good and evil. Full of mystery and fright, this story has remained popular for more than a century and has been adapted countless times - over 132 in film alone. An instant success and popular with students of morality, this thrilling tale is now available as part of the Word Cloud Classics series, making it a chic and affordable addition to any library"-- Provided by publisher.
  ISBN 978-1-62686-255-5 (paperback) -- ISBN 1-62686-255-9
  I. Title.

PR5482 2014
823'.8--dc23

                    2014006984

Printed in China

20 19 18 17 16   3 4 5 6 7

# CONTENTS

# Strange Case of Dr. Jekyll and Mr. Hyde

# Story of the Door

Mr. Utterson the lawyer was a man of a rugged countenance, that was never lighted by a smile; cold, scanty and embarrassed in discourse; backward in sentiment; lean, long, dusty, dreary, and yet somehow lovable. At friendly meetings, and when the wine was to his taste, something eminently human beaconed from his eye; something indeed which never found its way into his talk, but which spoke not only in these silent symbols of the after-dinner face, but more often and loudly in the acts of his life. He was austere with himself; drank gin when he was alone, to mortify a taste for vintages; and though he enjoyed the theatre, had not crossed the doors of one for twenty years. But he had an approved tolerance for others; sometimes wondering, almost with envy, at the high pressure of spirits involved in their misdeeds; and in any extremity inclined to help rather than to reprove. "I incline to Cain's heresy," he used to say quaintly: "I let my brother go to the devil in his own way." In this character, it was frequently his fortune to be the last reputable acquaintance and the last good influence in the lives of down-going men. And to such as these, so long as they came about his chambers, he never marked a shade of change in his demeanour.

No doubt the feat was easy to Mr. Utterson; for he was undemonstrative at the best, and even his friendship seemed to be founded in a similar catholicity of good-nature. It is the mark of a modest man to accept his friendly circle ready-made from the hands of opportunity; and that was the lawyer's way. His friends were those of his own blood or those whom he had known the longest; his affections, like ivy, were the growth of time, they implied no aptness in the object. Hence, no doubt, the bond that united him to Mr. Richard Enfield, his distant kinsman, the well-known man about town. It was a nut to crack for many, what these two could see in each other, or what subject they could find in common. It was reported by those who encountered them in their Sunday walks, that they said nothing, looked singularly dull, and would hail with obvious relief the appearance of a friend. For all that, the two men put the greatest store by these excursions, counted them the chief jewel of each week, and not only set aside occasions of pleasure, but even resisted the calls of business, that they might enjoy them uninterrupted.

It chanced on one of these rambles that their way led them down a by-street in a busy quarter of London. The street was small and what is called quiet, but it drove a thriving trade on the weekdays. The inhabitants were all doing well, it seemed, and all emulously hoping to do better still, and laying out the surplus of their gains in coquetry; so that the shop fronts stood along that thoroughfare with an air of invitation, like rows of smiling saleswomen. Even on Sunday, when it veiled its more florid charms and lay comparatively empty of passage, the street shone out in contrast to its dingy neighbourhood, like a fire in a forest; and with its freshly painted shutters, well-polished brasses, and general cleanliness and gaiety of note, instantly caught and pleased the eye of the passenger.

Two doors from one corner, on the left hand going east, the line was broken by the entry of a court; and just at that point, a certain sinister block of building thrust forward its gable on the street. It was two stories high; showed no window, nothing but a door on the lower storey and a blind forehead of discoloured wall on the upper; and bore in every feature, the marks of prolonged and sordid negligence. The door, which was equipped with neither bell nor knocker, was blistered and distained. Tramps slouched into the recess and struck matches on the panels; children kept shop upon the steps; the schoolboy had tried his knife on the mouldings; and for close on a generation, no one had appeared to drive away these random visitors or to repair their ravages.

Mr. Enfield and the lawyer were on the other side of the by-street; but when they came abreast of the entry, the former lifted up his cane and pointed.

"Did you ever remark that door?" he asked; and when his companion had replied in the affirmative, "It is connected in my mind," added he, "with a very odd story."

"Indeed?" said Mr. Utterson, with a slight change of voice, "and what was that?"

"Well, it was this way," returned Mr. Enfield: "I was coming home from some place at the end of the world, about three o'clock of a black winter morning, and my way lay through a part of town where there was literally nothing to be seen but lamps. Street after street, and all the folks asleep—street after street, all lighted up as if for a procession and all as empty as a church—till at last I got into that state of mind when a man listens and listens and begins to long for the sight of a policeman. All at once, I saw two figures: one a little man who was stumping along eastward at a good walk, and the other a girl of maybe eight or ten who was running as hard as she was able down a cross street. Well, sir, the two ran into one another naturally enough at the corner; and then came the horrible part of the thing; for the man trampled calmly over the child's body and left her screaming on the ground. It sounds nothing to hear, but it was hellish to see. It wasn't like a man; it was like some damned Juggernaut. I gave a view-halloo, took to my heels, collared my gentleman, and brought him back to where there was already quite a group about the screaming child. He was perfectly cool and made no resistance, but gave me one look, so ugly that it brought out the sweat on me like running. The people who had turned out were the girl's own family; and pretty soon, the doctor, for whom she had been sent, put in his appearance. Well, the child was not much the worse, more frightened, according to the Sawbones; and there you might have supposed would be an end to it. But there was one curious circumstance. I had taken a loathing to my gentleman at first sight. So had the child's family, which was only natural. But the doctor's case was what struck me. He was the usual cut-and-dry apothecary, of no particular age and colour, with a strong Edinburgh accent, and about as emotional as a bagpipe. Well, sir, he was like the rest of us; every time he looked at my prisoner, I saw that Sawbones turn sick and white with the desire to kill him. I knew what was in his mind, just as he knew what was in mine; and killing being out of the question, we did the next best. We told the man we could and would make such a scandal out of this, as should make his name stink from one end of London to the other. If he had any friends or any credit, we undertook that he should lose them. And all the time, as we were pitching it in red hot, we were keeping the women off him as best we could, for they were as wild as harpies. I never saw a circle of such hateful faces; and there was the man in the middle, with a kind of black, sneering coolness—frightened too, I could see that—but carrying it off, sir, really like Satan. 'If you choose to make capital out of this accident,' said he, 'I am naturally helpless. No gentleman but wishes to avoid a scene,' says he. 'Name your figure.' Well, we screwed him up to a hundred pounds for the child's family; he would have clearly liked to stick out; but there was something about the lot of us that meant mischief, and at last he struck. The next thing was to get the money; and where do you think he carried us but to that place with the door?—whipped out a key, went in, and presently came back with the matter of ten pounds in gold and a cheque for the balance on Coutts's, drawn payable to bearer and signed with a name that I can't mention, though it's one of the points of my story, but it was a name at least very well known and often printed. The figure was stiff; but the signature was good for more than that, if it was only genuine. I took the liberty of pointing out to my gentleman that the whole business looked apocryphal, and that a man does not, in real life, walk into a cellar door at four in the morning and come out of it with another man's cheque for close upon a hundred pounds. But he was quite easy and sneering. 'Set your mind at rest,' says he, 'I will stay with you till the banks open and cash the cheque myself.' So we all set off, the doctor, and the child's father, and our friend and myself, and passed the rest of the night in my chambers; and next day, when we had breakfasted, went in a body to the bank. I gave in the check myself, and said I had every reason to believe it was a forgery. Not a bit of it. The cheque was genuine."

"Tut-tut," said Mr. Utterson.

"I see you feel as I do," said Mr. Enfield. "Yes, it's a bad story. For my man was a fellow that nobody could have to do with, a really damnable man; and the person that drew the cheque is the very pink of the proprieties, celebrated too, and (what makes it worse) one of your fellows who do what they call good. Blackmail, I suppose; an honest man paying through the nose for some of the capers of his youth. Black-Mail House is what I call that place with the door, in consequence. Though even that, you know, is far from explaining all," he added, and with the words fell into a vein of musing.

From this he was recalled by Mr. Utterson asking rather suddenly: "And you don't know if the drawer of the cheque lives there?"

"A likely place, isn't it?" returned Mr. Enfield. "But I happen to have noticed his address; he lives in some square or other."

"And you never asked about the—place with the door?" said Mr. Utterson.

"No, sir: I had a delicacy," was the reply. "I feel very strongly about putting questions; it partakes too much of the style of the day of judgment. You start a question, and it's like starting a stone. You sit quietly on the top of a hill; and away the stone goes, starting others; and presently some bland old bird (the last you would have thought of) is knocked on the head in his own back garden and the family have to change their name. No, sir, I make it a rule of mine: the more it looks like Queer Street, the less I ask."

"A very good rule, too," said the lawyer.

"But I have studied the place for myself," continued Mr. Enfield. "It seems scarcely a house. There is no other door, and nobody goes in or out of that one but, once in a great while, the gentleman of my adventure. There are three windows looking on the court on the first floor; none below; the windows are always shut but they're clean. And then there is a chimney which is generally smoking; so somebody must live there. And yet it's not so sure; for the buildings are so packed together about that court, that it's hard to say where one ends and another begins." The pair walked on again for a while in silence; and then, "Enfield," said Mr. Utterson, "that's a good rule of yours."

"Yes, I think it is," returned Enfield.

"But for all that," continued the lawyer, "there's one point I want to ask: I want to ask the name of that man who walked over the child."

"Well," said Mr. Enfield, "I can't see what harm it would do. It was a man of the name of Hyde."

"Hm," said Mr. Utterson. "What sort of a man is he to see?"

"He is not easy to describe. There is something wrong with his appearance; something displeasing, something downright detestable. I never saw a man I so disliked, and yet I scarce know why. He must be deformed somewhere; he gives a strong feeling of deformity, although I couldn't specify the point. He's an extraordinary-looking man, and yet I really can name nothing out of the way. No, sir; I can make no hand of it; I can't describe him. And it's not want of memory; for I declare I can see him this moment."

Mr. Utterson again walked some way in silence and obviously under a weight of consideration.

"You are sure he used a key?" he inquired at last.

"My dear sir . . ." began Enfield, surprised out of himself.

"Yes, I know," said Utterson; "I know it must seem strange. The fact is, if I do not ask you the name of the other party, it is because I know it already. You see, Richard, your tale has gone home. If you have been inexact in any point, you had better correct it."

"I think you might have warned me," returned the other, with a touch of sullenness. "But I have been pedantically exact, as you call it. The fellow had a key; and what's more, he has it still. I saw him use it, not a week ago."

Mr. Utterson sighed deeply but said never a word; and the young man presently resumed. "Here is another lesson to say nothing," said he. "I am ashamed of my long tongue. Let us make a bargain never to refer to this again."

"With all my heart," said the lawyer. "I shake hands on that, Richard."

## Search for Mr. Hyde

That evening Mr. Utterson came home to his bachelor house in sombre spirits and sat down to dinner without relish. It was his custom of a Sunday, when this meal was over, to sit close by the fire, a volume of some dry divinity on his reading-desk, until the clock of the neighbouring church rang out the hour of twelve, when he would go soberly and gratefully to bed. On this night, however, as soon as the cloth was taken away, he took up a candle and went into his business-room. There he opened his safe, took from the most private part of it a document endorsed on the envelope as Dr. Jekyll's Will, and sat down with a clouded brow to study its contents. The will was holograph, for Mr. Utterson, though he took charge of it now that it was made, had refused to lend the least assistance in the making of it; it provided not only that, in case of the decease of Henry Jekyll, M.D., D.C.L., LL.D., F.R.S., etc., all his possessions were to pass into the hands of his "friend and benefactor Edward Hyde," but that in case of Dr. Jekyll's "disappearance or unexplained absence for any period exceeding three calendar months," the said Edward Hyde should step into the said Henry Jekyll's shoes without further delay and free from any burthen or obligation, beyond the payment of a few small sums to the members of the doctor's household. This document had long been the lawyer's eyesore. It offended him both as a lawyer and as a lover of the sane and customary sides of life, to whom the fanciful was the immodest. And hitherto it was his ignorance of Mr. Hyde that had swelled his indignation; now, by a sudden turn, it was his knowledge. It was already bad enough when the name was but a name of which he could learn no more. It was worse when it began to be clothed upon with detestable attributes; and out of the shifting, insubstantial mists that had so long baffled his eye, there leaped up the sudden, definite presentment of a fiend.

"I thought it was madness," he said, as he replaced the obnoxious paper in the safe, "and now I begin to fear it is disgrace."

With that he blew out his candle, put on a great-coat, and set forth in the direction of Cavendish Square, that citadel of medicine, where his friend, the great Dr. Lanyon, had his house and received his crowding patients. "If any one knows, it will be Lanyon," he had thought.

The solemn butler knew and welcomed him; he was subjected to no stage of delay, but ushered direct from the door to the dining-room where Dr. Lanyon sat alone over his wine. This was a hearty, healthy, dapper, red-faced gentleman, with a shock of hair prematurely white, and a boisterous and decided manner. At sight of Mr. Utterson, he sprang up from his chair and welcomed him with both hands. The geniality, as was the way of the man, was somewhat theatrical to the eye; but it reposed on genuine feeling. For these two were old friends, old mates both at school and college, both thorough respecters of themselves and of each other, and, what does not always follow, men who thoroughly enjoyed each other's company.

After a little rambling talk, the lawyer led up to the subject which so disagreeably preoccupied his mind.

"I suppose, Lanyon," said he "you and I must be the two oldest friends that Henry Jekyll has?"

"I wish the friends were younger," chuckled Dr. Lanyon. "But I suppose we are. And what of that? I see little of him now."

"Indeed?" said Utterson. "I thought you had a bond of common interest."

"We had," was the reply. "But it is more than ten years since Henry Jekyll became too fanciful for me. He began to go wrong, wrong in mind; and though of course I continue to take an interest in him for old sake's sake, as they say, I see and I have seen devilish little of the man. Such unscientific balderdash," added the doctor, flushing suddenly purple, "would have estranged Damon and Pythias."

This little spirit of temper was somewhat of a relief to Mr. Utterson. "They have only differed on some point of science," he thought; and being a man of no scientific passions (except in the matter of conveyancing), he even added: "It is nothing worse than that!" He gave his friend a few seconds to recover his composure, and then approached the question he had come to put. "Did you ever come across a protégé of his—one Hyde?" he asked.

"Hyde?" repeated Lanyon. "No. Never heard of him. Since my time."

That was the amount of information that the lawyer carried back with him to the great, dark bed on which he tossed to and fro, until the small hours of the morning began to grow large. It was a night of little ease to his toiling mind, toiling in mere darkness and besieged by questions.

Six o'clock struck on the bells of the church that was so conveniently near to Mr. Utterson's dwelling, and still he was digging at the problem. Hitherto it had touched him on the intellectual side alone; but now his imagination also was engaged, or rather enslaved; and as he lay and tossed in the gross darkness of the night and the curtained room, Mr. Enfield's tale went by before his mind in a scroll of lighted pictures. He would be aware of the great field of lamps of a nocturnal city; then of the figure of a man walking swiftly; then of a child running from the doctor's; and then these met, and that human Juggernaut trod the child down and passed on regardless of her screams. Or else he would see a room in a rich house, where his friend lay asleep, dreaming and smiling at his dreams; and then the door of that room would be opened, the curtains of the bed plucked apart, the sleeper recalled, and lo! there would stand by his side a figure to whom power was given, and even at that dead hour, he must rise and do its bidding. The figure in these two phases haunted the lawyer all night; and if at any time he dozed over, it was but to see it glide more stealthily through sleeping houses, or move the more swiftly and still the more swiftly, even to dizziness, through wider labyrinths of lamplighted city, and at every street-corner crush a child and leave her screaming. And still the figure had no face by which he might know it; even in his dreams, it had no face, or one that baffled him and melted before his eyes; and thus it was that there sprang up and grew apace in the lawyer's mind a singularly strong, almost an inordinate, curiosity to behold the features of the real Mr. Hyde. If he could but once set eyes on him, he thought the mystery would lighten and perhaps roll altogether away, as was the habit of mysterious things when well examined. He might see a reason for his friend's strange preference or bondage (call it which you please) and even for the startling clause of the will. At least it would be a face worth seeing: the face of a man who was without bowels of mercy: a face which had but to show itself to raise up, in the mind of the unimpressionable Enfield, a spirit of enduring hatred.

From that time forward, Mr. Utterson began to haunt the door in the by-street of shops. In the morning before office hours, at noon when business was plenty, and time scarce, at night under the face of the fogged city moon, by all lights and at all hours of solitude or concourse, the lawyer was to be found on his chosen post.

"If he be Mr. Hyde," he had thought, "I shall be Mr. Seek."

And at last his patience was rewarded. It was a fine dry night; frost in the air; the streets as clean as a ballroom floor; the lamps, unshaken by any wind, drawing a regular pattern of light and shadow. By ten o'clock, when the shops were closed, the by-street was very solitary and, in spite of the low growl of London from all round, very silent. Small sounds carried far; domestic sounds out of the houses were clearly audible on either side of the roadway; and the rumour of the approach of any passenger preceded him by a long time. Mr. Utterson had been some minutes at his post, when he was aware of an odd, light footstep drawing near. In the course of his nightly patrols, he had long grown accustomed to the quaint effect with which the footfalls of a single person, while he is still a great way off, suddenly spring out distinct from the vast hum and clatter of the city. Yet his attention had never before been so sharply and decisively arrested; and it was with a strong, superstitious prevision of success that he withdrew into the entry of the court.

The steps drew swiftly nearer, and swelled out suddenly louder as they turned the end of the street. The lawyer, looking forth from the entry, could soon see what manner of man he had to deal with. He was small and very plainly dressed, and the look of him, even at that distance, went somehow strongly against the watcher's inclination. But he made straight for the door, crossing the roadway to save time; and as he came, he drew a key from his pocket like one approaching home.

Mr. Utterson stepped out and touched him on the shoulder as he passed. "Mr. Hyde, I think?"

Mr. Hyde shrank back with a hissing intake of the breath. But his fear was only momentary; and though he did not look the lawyer in the face, he answered coolly enough: "That is my name. What do you want?"

"I see you are going in," returned the lawyer. "I am an old friend of Dr. Jekyll's—Mr. Utterson of Gaunt Street—you must have heard my name; and meeting you so conveniently, I thought you might admit me."

"You will not find Dr. Jekyll; he is from home," replied Mr. Hyde, blowing in the key. And then suddenly, but still without looking up, "How did you know me?" he asked.

"On your side," said Mr. Utterson, "will you do me a favour?"

"With pleasure," replied the other. "What shall it be?"

"Will you let me see your face?" asked the lawyer.

Mr. Hyde appeared to hesitate, and then, as if upon some sudden reflection, fronted about with an air of defiance; and the pair stared at each other pretty fixedly for a few seconds. "Now I shall know you again," said Mr. Utterson. "It may be useful."

"Yes," returned Mr. Hyde, "it is as well we have met; and apropos, you should have my address." And he gave a number of a street in Soho.

"Good God!" thought Mr. Utterson, "can he, too, have been thinking of the will?" But he kept his feelings to himself and only grunted in acknowledgment of the address.

"And now," said the other, "how did you know me?"

"By description," was the reply.

"Whose description?"

"We have common friends," said Mr. Utterson.

"Common friends?" echoed Mr. Hyde, a little hoarsely. "Who are they?"

"Jekyll, for instance," said the lawyer.

"He never told you," cried Mr. Hyde, with a flush of anger. "I did not think you would have lied."

"Come," said Mr. Utterson, "that is not fitting language."

The other snarled aloud into a savage laugh; and the next moment, with extraordinary quickness, he had unlocked the door and disappeared into the house.

The lawyer stood awhile when Mr. Hyde had left him, the picture of disquietude. Then he began slowly to mount the street, pausing every step or two and putting his hand to his brow like a man in mental perplexity. The problem he was thus debating as he walked, was one of a class that is rarely solved. Mr. Hyde was pale and dwarfish, he gave an impression of deformity without any nameable malformation, he had a displeasing smile, he had borne himself to the lawyer with a sort of murderous mixture of timidity and boldness, and he spoke with a husky, whispering and somewhat broken voice; all these were points against him, but not all of these together could explain the hitherto unknown disgust, loathing, and fear with which Mr. Utterson regarded him. "There must be something else," said the perplexed gentleman. "There is something more, if I could find a name for it. God bless me, the man seems hardly human! Something troglodytic, shall we say? or can it be the old story of Dr. Fell? or is it the mere radiance of a foul soul that thus transpires through, and transfigures, its clay continent? The last, I think; for, O my poor old Harry Jekyll, if ever I read Satan's signature upon a face, it is on that of your new friend."

Round the corner from the by-street, there was a square of ancient, handsome houses, now for the most part decayed from their high estate and let in flats and chambers to all sorts and conditions of men: map-engravers, architects, shady lawyers, and the agents of obscure enterprises. One house, however, second from the corner, was still occupied entire; and at the door of this, which wore a great air of wealth and comfort, though it was now plunged in darkness except for the fan-light, Mr. Utterson stopped and knocked. A well-dressed, elderly servant opened the door.

"Is Dr. Jekyll at home, Poole?" asked the lawyer.

"I will see, Mr. Utterson," said Poole, admitting the visitor, as he spoke, into a large, low-roofed, comfortable hall, paved with flags, warmed (after the fashion of a country house) by a bright, open fire, and furnished with costly cabinets of oak. "Will you wait here by the fire, sir? or shall I give you a light in the dining room?"

"Here, thank you," said the lawyer, and he drew near and leaned on the tall fender. This hall, in which he was now left alone, was a pet fancy of his friend the doctor's; and Utterson himself was wont to speak of it as the pleasantest room in London. But to-night there was a shudder in his blood; the face of Hyde sat heavy on his memory; he felt (what was rare with him) a nausea and distaste of life; and in the gloom of his spirits, he seemed to read a menace in the flickering of the firelight on the polished cabinets and the uneasy starting of the shadow on the roof. He was ashamed of his relief, when Poole presently returned to announce that Dr. Jekyll was gone out.

"I saw Mr. Hyde go in by the old dissecting-room door, Poole," he said. "Is that right, when Dr. Jekyll is from home?"

"Quite right, Mr. Utterson, sir," replied the servant. "Mr. Hyde has a key."

"Your master seems to repose a great deal of trust in that young man, Poole," resumed the other musingly.

"Yes, sir, he does indeed," said Poole. "We have all orders to obey him."

"I do not think I ever met Mr. Hyde?" asked Utterson.

"O, dear no, sir. He never dines here," replied the butler. "Indeed we see very little of him on this side of the house; he mostly comes and goes by the laboratory."

"Well, good-night, Poole."

"Good-night, Mr. Utterson." And the lawyer set out homeward with a very heavy heart. "Poor Harry Jekyll," he thought, "my mind misgives me he is in deep waters! He was wild when he was young; a long while ago to be sure; but in the law of God, there is no statute of limitations. Ay, it must be that; the ghost of some old sin, the cancer of some concealed disgrace: punishment coming, *pede claudo*, years after memory has forgotten and self-love condoned the fault." And the lawyer, scared by the thought, brooded a while on his own past, groping in all the corners of memory, lest by chance some Jack-in-the-Box of an old iniquity should leap to light there. His past was fairly blameless; few men could read the rolls of their life with less apprehension; yet he was humbled to the dust by the many ill things he had done, and raised up again into a sober and fearful gratitude by the many that he had come so near to doing, yet avoided. And then by a return on his former subject, he conceived a spark of hope. "This Master Hyde, if he were studied," thought he, "must have secrets of his own; black secrets, by the look of him; secrets compared to which poor Jekyll's worst would be like sunshine. Things cannot continue as they are. It turns me cold to think of this creature stealing like a thief to Harry's bedside; poor Harry, what a wakening! And the danger of it; for if this Hyde suspects the existence of the will, he may grow impatient to inherit. Ay, I must put my shoulder to the wheel if Jekyll will but let me," he added, "if Jekyll will only let me." For once more he saw before his mind's eye, as clear as a transparency, the strange clauses of the will.

# Dr. Jekyll Was Quite at Ease

A fortnight later, by excellent good fortune, the doctor gave one of his pleasant dinners to some five or six old cronies, all intelligent, reputable men and all judges of good wine; and Mr. Utterson so contrived that he remained behind after the others had departed. This was no new arrangement, but a thing that had befallen many scores of times. Where Utterson was liked, he was liked well. Hosts loved to detain the dry lawyer, when the light-hearted and the loose-tongued had already their foot on the threshold; they liked to sit a while in his unobtrusive company, practising for solitude, sobering their minds in the man's rich silence after the expense and strain of gaiety. To this rule, Dr. Jekyll was no exception; and as he now sat on the opposite side of the fire—a large, well-made, smooth-faced man of fifty, with something of a slyish cast perhaps, but every mark of capacity and kindness—you could see by his looks that he cherished for Mr. Utterson a sincere and warm affection.

"I have been wanting to speak to you, Jekyll," began the latter. "You know that will of yours?"

A close observer might have gathered that the topic was distasteful; but the doctor carried it off gaily. "My poor Utterson," said he, "you are unfortunate in such a client. I never saw a man so distressed as you were by my will; unless it were that hide-bound pedant, Lanyon, at what he called my scientific heresies. Oh, I know he's a good fellow—you needn't frown—an excellent fellow, and I always mean to see more of him; but a hide-bound pedant for all that; an ignorant, blatant pedant. I was never more disappointed in any man than Lanyon."

"You know I never approved of it," pursued Utterson, ruthlessly disregarding the fresh topic.

"My will? Yes, certainly, I know that," said the doctor, a trifle sharply. "You have told me so."

"Well, I tell you so again," continued the lawyer. "I have been learning something of young Hyde."

The large handsome face of Dr. Jekyll grew pale to the very lips, and there came a blackness about his eyes. "I do not care to hear more," said he. "This is a matter I thought we had agreed to drop."

"What I heard was abominable," said Utterson.

"It can make no change. You do not understand my position," returned the doctor, with a certain incoherency of manner. "I am painfully situated, Utterson; my position is a very strange—a very strange one. It is one of those affairs that cannot be mended by talking."

"Jekyll," said Utterson, "you know me: I am a man to be trusted. Make a clean breast of this in confidence; and I make no doubt I can get you out of it."

"My good Utterson," said the doctor, "this is very good of you, this is downright good of you, and I cannot find words to thank you in. I believe you fully; I would trust you before any man alive, ay, before myself, if I could make the choice; but indeed it isn't what you fancy; it is not so bad as that; and just to put your good heart at rest, I will tell you one thing: the moment I choose, I can be rid of Mr. Hyde. I give you my hand upon that; and I thank you again and again; and I will just add one little word, Utterson, that I'm sure you'll take in good part: this is a private matter, and I beg of you to let it sleep."

Utterson reflected a little, looking in the fire.

"I have no doubt you are perfectly right," he said at last, getting to his feet.

"Well, but since we have touched upon this business, and for the last time I hope," continued the doctor, "there is one point I should like you to understand. I have really a very great interest in poor Hyde. I know you have seen him; he told me so; and I fear he was rude. But I do sincerely take a great, a very great interest in that young man; and if I am taken away, Utterson, I wish you to promise me that you will bear with him and get his rights for him. I think you would, if you knew all; and it would be a weight off my mind if you would promise."

"I can't pretend that I shall ever like him," said the lawyer.

"I don't ask that," pleaded Jekyll, laying his hand upon the other's arm; "I only ask for justice; I only ask you to help him for my sake, when I am no longer here."

Utterson heaved an irrepressible sigh. "Well," said he, "I promise."

## The Carew Murder Case

Nearly a year later, in the month of October, 18——, London was startled by a crime of singular ferocity and rendered all the more notable by the high position of the victim. The details were few and startling. A maid servant living alone in a house not far from the river, had gone upstairs to bed about eleven. Although a fog rolled over the city in the small hours, the early part of the night was cloudless, and the lane, which the maid's window overlooked, was brilliantly lit by the full moon. It seems she was romantically given, for she sat down upon her box, which stood immediately under the window, and fell into a dream of musing. Never (she used to say, with streaming tears, when she narrated that experience), never had she felt more at peace with all men or thought more kindly of the world. And as she so sat she became aware of an aged and beautiful gentleman with white hair, drawing near along the lane; and advancing to meet him, another and very small gentleman, to whom at first she paid less attention. When they had come within speech (which was just under the maid's eyes) the older man bowed and accosted the other with a very pretty manner of politeness. It did not seem as if the subject of his address were of great importance; indeed, from his pointing, it sometimes appeared as if he were only inquiring his way; but the moon shone on his face as he spoke, and the girl was pleased to watch it, it seemed to breathe such an innocent and old-world kindness of disposition, yet with something high too, as of a well-founded self-content. Presently her eye wandered to the other, and she was surprised to recognise in him a certain Mr. Hyde, who had once visited her master and for whom she had conceived a dislike. He had in his hand a heavy cane, with which he was trifling; but he answered never a word, and seemed to listen with an ill-contained impatience. And then all of a sudden he broke out in a great flame of anger, stamping with his foot, brandishing the cane, and carrying on (as the maid described it) like a madman. The old gentleman took a step back, with the air of one very much surprised and a trifle hurt; and at that Mr. Hyde broke out of all bounds and clubbed him to the earth. And next moment, with ape-like fury, he was trampling his victim under foot and hailing down a storm of blows, under which the bones were audibly shattered and the body jumped upon the roadway. At the horror of these sights and sounds, the maid fainted.

It was two o'clock when she came to herself and called for the police. The murderer was gone long ago; but there lay his victim in the middle of the lane, incredibly mangled. The stick with which the deed had been done, although it was of some rare and very tough and heavy wood, had broken in the middle under the stress of this insensate cruelty; and one splintered half had rolled in the neighbouring gutter—the other, without doubt, had been carried away by the murderer. A purse and a gold watch were found upon the victim: but no cards or papers, except a sealed and stamped envelope, which he had been probably carrying to the post, and which bore the name and address of Mr. Utterson.

This was brought to the lawyer the next morning, before he was out of bed; and he had no sooner seen it, and been told the circumstances, than he shot out a solemn lip. "I shall say nothing till I have seen the body," said he; "this may be very serious. Have the kindness to wait while I dress." And with the same grave countenance he hurried through his breakfast and drove to the police station, whither the body had been carried. As soon as he came into the cell, he nodded.

"Yes," said he, "I recognise him. I am sorry to say that this is Sir Danvers Carew."

"Good God, sir," exclaimed the officer, "is it possible?" And the next moment his eye lighted up with professional ambition. "This will make a deal of noise," he said. "And perhaps you can help us to the man." And he briefly narrated what the maid had seen, and showed the broken stick.

Mr. Utterson had already quailed at the name of Hyde; but when the stick was laid before him, he could doubt no longer; broken and battered as it was, he recognised it for one that he had himself presented many years before to Henry Jekyll.

"Is this Mr. Hyde a person of small stature?" he inquired.

"Particularly small and particularly wicked-looking, is what the maid calls him," said the officer.

Mr. Utterson reflected; and then, raising his head, "If you will come with me in my cab," he said, "I think I can take you to his house."

It was by this time about nine in the morning, and the first fog of the season. A great chocolate-coloured pall lowered over heaven, but the wind was continually charging and routing these embattled vapours; so that as the cab crawled from street to street, Mr. Utterson beheld a marvellous number of degrees and hues of twilight; for here it would be dark like the back-end of evening; and there would be a glow of a rich, lurid brown, like the light of some strange conflagration; and here, for a moment, the fog would be quite broken up, and a haggard shaft of daylight would glance in between the swirling wreaths. The dismal quarter of Soho seen under these changing glimpses, with its muddy ways, and slatternly passengers, and its lamps, which had never been extinguished or had been kindled afresh to combat this mournful reinvasion of darkness, seemed, in the lawyer's eyes, like a district of some city in a nightmare. The thoughts of his mind, besides, were of the gloomiest dye; and when he glanced at the companion of his drive, he was conscious of some touch of that terror of the law and the law's officers, which may at times assail the most honest.

As the cab drew up before the address indicated, the fog lifted a little and showed him a dingy street, a gin palace, a low French eating-house, a shop for the retail of penny numbers and twopenny salads, many ragged children huddled in the doorways, and many women of different nationalities passing out, key in hand, to have a morning glass; and the next moment the fog settled down again upon that part, as brown as umber, and cut him off from his blackguardly surroundings. This was the home of Henry Jekyll's favourite; of a man who was heir to a quarter of a million sterling.

An ivory-faced and silvery-haired old woman opened the door. She had an evil face, smoothed by hypocrisy; but her manners were excellent. Yes, she said, this was Mr. Hyde's, but he was not at home; he had been in that night very late, but had gone away again in less than an hour; there was nothing strange in that; his habits were very irregular, and he was often absent;

for instance, it was nearly two months since she had seen him till yesterday.

"Very well, then, we wish to see his rooms," said the lawyer; and when the woman began to declare it was impossible, "I had better tell you who this person is," he added. "This is Inspector Newcomen of Scotland Yard."

A flash of odious joy appeared upon the woman's face. "Ah!" said she, "he is in trouble! What has he done?"

Mr. Utterson and the inspector exchanged glances. "He don't seem a very popular character," observed the latter. "And now, my good woman, just let me and this gentleman have a look about us."

In the whole extent of the house, which but for the old woman remained otherwise empty, Mr. Hyde had only used a couple of rooms; but these were furnished with luxury and good taste. A closet was filled with wine; the plate was of silver, the napery elegant; a good picture hung upon the walls, a gift (as Utterson supposed) from Henry Jekyll, who was much of a connoisseur; and the carpets were of many plies and agreeable in colour. At this moment, however, the rooms bore every mark of having been recently and hurriedly ransacked; clothes lay about the floor, with their pockets inside out; lockfast drawers stood open; and on the hearth there lay a pile of grey ashes, as though many papers had been burned. From these embers the inspector disinterred the butt end of a green cheque-book, which had resisted the action of the fire; the other half of the stick was found behind the door; and as this clinched his suspicions, the officer declared himself delighted. A visit to the bank, where several thousand pounds were found to be lying to the murderer's credit, completed his gratification.

"You may depend upon it, sir," he told Mr. Utterson: "I have him in my hand. He must have lost his head, or he never would have left the stick or, above all, burned the cheque-book. Why, money's life to the man. We have nothing to do but wait for him at the bank, and get out the handbills."

This last, however, was not so easy of accomplishment; for Mr. Hyde had numbered few familiars—even the master of the servant-maid had only seen him twice; his family could nowhere be traced; he had never been photographed; and the few who could describe him differed widely, as common observers will. Only on one point, were they agreed; and that was the haunting sense of unexpressed deformity with which the fugitive impressed his beholders.

## Incident of the Letter

It was late in the afternoon, when Mr. Utterson found his way to Dr. Jekyll's door, where he was at once admitted by Poole, and carried down by the kitchen offices and across a yard which had once been a garden, to the building which was indifferently known as the laboratory or the dissecting-rooms. The doctor had bought the house from the heirs of a celebrated surgeon; and his own tastes being rather chemical than anatomical, had changed the destination of the block at the bottom of the garden. It was the first time that the lawyer had been received in that part of his friend's quarters; and he eyed the dingy, windowless structure with curiosity, and gazed round with a distasteful sense of strangeness as he crossed the theatre, once crowded with eager students and now lying gaunt and silent, the tables laden with chemical apparatus, the floor strewn with crates and littered with packing straw, and the light falling dimly through the foggy cupola. At the further end, a flight of stairs mounted to a door covered with red baize; and through this, Mr. Utterson was at last received into the doctor's cabinet. It was a large room, fitted round with glass presses, furnished, among other things, with a cheval-glass and a business table, and looking out upon the court by three dusty windows barred with iron. A fire burned in the grate; a lamp was set lighted on the chimney shelf, for even in the houses the fog began to lie thickly; and there, close up to the warmth, sat Dr. Jekyll, looking deadly sick. He did not rise to meet his visitor, but held out a cold hand and bade him welcome in a changed voice.

"And now," said Mr. Utterson, as soon as Poole had left them, "you have heard the news?"

The doctor shuddered. "They were crying it in the square," he said. "I heard them in my dining-room."

"One word," said the lawyer. "Carew was my client, but so are you, and I want to know what I am doing. You have not been mad enough to hide this fellow?"

"Utterson, I swear to God," cried the doctor, "I swear to God I will never set eyes on him again. I bind my honour to you that I am done with him in this world. It is all at an end. And indeed he does not want my help; you do not know him as I do; he is safe, he is quite safe; mark my words, he will never more be heard of."

The lawyer listened gloomily; he did not like his friend's feverish manner. "You seem pretty sure of him," said he; "and for your sake, I hope you may be right. If it came to a trial, your name might appear."

"I am quite sure of him," replied Jekyll; "I have grounds for certainty that I cannot share with anyone. But there is one thing on which you may advise me. I have—I have received a letter; and I am at a loss whether I should show it to the police. I should like to leave it in your hands, Utterson; you would judge wisely, I am sure; I have so great a trust in you."

"You fear, I suppose, that it might lead to his detection?" asked the lawyer.

"No," said the other. "I cannot say that I care what becomes of Hyde; I am quite done with him. I was thinking of my own character, which this hateful business has rather exposed."

Utterson ruminated a while; he was surprised at his friend's selfishness, and yet relieved by it. "Well," said he, at last, "let me see the letter."

The letter was written in an odd, upright hand and signed "Edward Hyde": and it signified, briefly enough, that the writer's benefactor, Dr. Jekyll, whom he had long so unworthily repaid for a thousand generosities, need labour under no alarm for his safety, as he had means of escape on which he placed a sure dependence. The lawyer liked this letter well enough; it put a better colour on the intimacy than he had looked for; and he blamed himself for some of his past suspicions.

"Have you the envelope?" he asked.

"I burned it," replied Jekyll, "before I thought what I was about. But it bore no postmark. The note was handed in."

"Shall I keep this and sleep upon it?" asked Utterson.

"I wish you to judge for me entirely," was the reply. "I have lost confidence in myself."

"Well, I shall consider," returned the lawyer. "And now one word more: it was Hyde who dictated the terms in your will about that disappearance?"

The doctor seemed seized with a qualm of faintness: he shut his mouth tight and nodded.

"I knew it," said Utterson. "He meant to murder you. You have had a fine escape."

"I have had what is far more to the purpose," returned the doctor solemnly: "I have had a lesson—O God, Utterson, what a lesson I have had!" And he covered his face for a moment with his hands.

On his way out, the lawyer stopped and had a word or two with Poole. "By the by," said he, "there was a letter handed in to-day: what was the messenger like?" But Poole was positive nothing had come except by post; "and only circulars by that," he added.

This news sent off the visitor with his fears renewed. Plainly the letter had come by the laboratory door; possibly, indeed, it had been written in the cabinet; and if that were so, it must be differently judged, and handled with the more caution. The newsboys, as he went, were crying themselves hoarse along the footways: "Special edition. Shocking murder of an MP." That was the funeral oration of one friend and client; and he could not help a certain apprehension lest the good name of another should be sucked down in the eddy of the scandal. It was, at least, a ticklish decision that he had to make; and self-reliant as he was by habit, he began to cherish a longing for advice. It was not to be had directly; but perhaps, he thought, it might be fished for.

Presently after, he sat on one side of his own hearth, with Mr. Guest, his head clerk, upon the other, and midway between, at a nicely calculated distance from the fire, a bottle of a particular old wine that had long dwelt unsunned in the foundations of his house. The fog still slept on the wing above the drowned city, where the lamps glimmered like carbuncles; and through the muffle and smother of these fallen clouds, the procession of the town's life was still rolling in through the great arteries with a sound as of a mighty wind. But the room was gay with firelight. In the bottle the acids were long ago resolved; the imperial dye had softened with time, as the colour grows richer in stained windows; and the glow of hot autumn afternoons on hillside vineyards was ready to be set free and to disperse the fogs of

London. Insensibly the lawyer melted. There was no man from whom he kept fewer secrets than Mr. Guest; and he was not always sure that he kept as many as he meant. Guest had often been on business to the doctor's; he knew Poole; he could scarce have failed to hear of Mr. Hyde's familiarity about the house; he might draw conclusions: was it not as well, then, that he should see a letter which put that mystery to rights? and above all since Guest, being a great student and critic of handwriting, would consider the step natural and obliging? The clerk, besides, was a man of counsel; he would scarce read so strange a document without dropping a remark; and by that remark Mr. Utterson might shape his future course.

"This is a sad business about Sir Danvers," he said.

"Yes, sir, indeed. It has elicited a great deal of public feeling," returned Guest. "The man, of course, was mad."

"I should like to hear your views on that," replied Utterson. "I have a document here in his handwriting; it is between ourselves, for I scarce know what to do about it; it is an ugly business at the best. But there it is; quite in your way a murderer's autograph."

Guest's eyes brightened, and he sat down at once and studied it with passion. "No, sir," he said: "not mad; but it is an odd hand."

"And by all accounts a very odd writer," added the lawyer.

Just then the servant entered with a note.

"Is that from Dr. Jekyll, sir?" inquired the clerk. "I thought I knew the writing. Anything private, Mr. Utterson?"

"Only an invitation to dinner. Why? Do you want to see it?"

"One moment. I thank you, sir"; and the clerk laid the two sheets of paper alongside and sedulously compared their contents. "Thank you, sir," he said at last, returning both; "it's a very interesting autograph."

There was a pause, during which Mr. Utterson struggled with himself. "Why did you compare them, Guest?" he inquired suddenly.

"Well, sir," returned the clerk, "there's a rather singular resemblance; the two hands are in many points identical: only differently sloped."

"Rather quaint," said Utterson.

"It is, as you say, rather quaint," returned Guest.

"I wouldn't speak of this note, you know," said the master.

"No, sir," said the clerk. "I understand."

But no sooner was Mr. Utterson alone that night than he locked the note into his safe, where it reposed from that time forward. "What!" he thought. "Henry Jekyll forge for a murderer!" And his blood ran cold in his veins.

# Remarkable Incident of Dr. Lanyon

Time ran on; thousands of pounds were offered in reward, for the death of Sir Danvers was resented as a public injury; but Mr. Hyde had disappeared out of the ken of the police as though he had never existed. Much of his past was unearthed, indeed, and all disreputable: tales came out of the man's cruelty, at once so callous and violent; of his vile life, of his strange associates, of the hatred that seemed to have surrounded his career; but of his present whereabouts, not a whisper. From the time he had left the house in Soho on the morning of the murder, he was simply blotted out; and gradually, as time drew on, Mr. Utterson began to recover from the hotness of his alarm, and to grow more at quiet with himself. The death of Sir Danvers was, to his way of thinking, more than paid for by the disappearance of Mr. Hyde. Now that that evil influence had been withdrawn, a new life began for Dr. Jekyll. He came out of his seclusion, renewed relations with his friends, became once more their familiar guest and entertainer; and whilst he had always been known for charities, he was now no less distinguished for religion. He was busy, he was much in the open air, he did good; his face seemed to open and brighten, as if with an inward consciousness of service; and for more than two months, the doctor was at peace.

On the 8th of January Utterson had dined at the doctor's with a small party; Lanyon had been there; and the face of the host had looked from one to the other as in the old days when the trio were inseparable friends. On the 12th, and again on the 14th, the door was shut against the lawyer. "The doctor was confined to the house," Poole said, "and saw no one." On the 15th, he tried again, and was again refused; and having now been used for the last two months to see his friend almost daily, he found this return of solitude to weigh upon his spirits. The fifth night he had in Guest to dine with him; and the sixth he betook himself to Dr. Lanyon's.

There at least he was not denied admittance; but when he came in, he was shocked at the change which had taken place in the doctor's appearance. He had his death-warrant written legibly upon his face. The rosy man had grown pale; his flesh had fallen away; he was visibly balder and older; and yet it was not so much, these tokens of a swift physical decay that arrested the lawyer's notice, as a look in the eye and quality of manner that seemed to testify to some deep-seated terror of the mind. It was unlikely that the doctor should fear death; and yet that was what Utterson was tempted to suspect. "Yes," he thought; "he is a doctor, he must know his own state and that his days are counted; and the knowledge is more than he can bear." And yet when Utterson remarked on his ill-looks, it was with an air of greatness that Lanyon declared himself a doomed man.

"I have had a shock," he said, "and I shall never recover. It is a question of weeks. Well, life has been pleasant; I liked it; yes, sir, I used to like it. I sometimes think if we knew all, we should be more glad to get away."

"Jekyll is ill, too," observed Utterson. "Have you seen him?"

But Lanyon's face changed, and he held up a trembling hand. "I wish to see or hear no more of Dr. Jekyll," he said in a loud, unsteady voice. "I am quite done with that person; and I beg that you will spare me any allusion to one whom I regard as dead."

"Tut-tut," said Mr. Utterson; and then after a considerable pause, "Can't I do anything?" he inquired. "We are three very old friends, Lanyon; we shall not live to make others."

"Nothing can be done," returned Lanyon; "ask himself."

"He will not see me," said the lawyer.

"I am not surprised at that," was the reply. "Some day, Utterson, after I am dead, you may perhaps come to learn the right and wrong of this. I cannot tell you. And in the meantime, if you can sit and talk with me of other things, for God's sake, stay and do so; but if you cannot keep clear of this accursed topic, then, in God's name, go, for I cannot bear it."

As soon as he got home, Utterson sat down and wrote to Jekyll, complaining of his exclusion from the house, and asking the cause of this unhappy break with Lanyon; and the next day brought him a long answer, often very pathetically worded, and sometimes darkly mysterious in drift. The quarrel with Lanyon was incurable. "I do not blame our old friend," Jekyll wrote, "but

I share his view that we must never meet. I mean from henceforth to lead a life of extreme seclusion; you must not be surprised, nor must you doubt my friendship, if my door is often shut even to you. You must suffer me to go my own dark way. I have brought on myself a punishment and a danger that I cannot name. If I am the chief of sinners, I am the chief of sufferers also. I could not think that this earth contained a place for sufferings and terrors so unmanning; and you can do but one thing, Utterson, to lighten this destiny, and that is to respect my silence." Utterson was amazed; the dark influence of Hyde had been withdrawn, the doctor had returned to his old tasks and amities; a week ago, the prospect had smiled with every promise of a cheerful and an honoured age; and now in a moment, friendship, and peace of mind, and the whole tenor of his life were wrecked. So great and unprepared a change pointed to madness; but in view of Lanyon's manner and words, there must lie for it some deeper ground.

A week afterwards Dr. Lanyon took to his bed, and in something less than a fortnight he was dead. The night after the funeral, at which he had been sadly affected, Utterson locked the door of his business room, and sitting there by the light of a melancholy candle, drew out and set before him an envelope addressed by the hand and sealed with the seal of his dead friend. "*Private:* for the hands of G. J. Utterson *alone* and in case of his predecease to be destroyed unread," so it was emphatically superscribed; and the lawyer dreaded to behold the contents. "I have buried one friend to-day," he thought: "what if this should cost me another?" And then he condemned the fear as a disloyalty, and broke the seal. Within there was another enclosure, likewise sealed, and marked upon the cover as "not to be opened till the death or disappearance of Dr. Henry Jekyll." Utterson could not trust his eyes. Yes, it was disappearance; here again, as in the mad will which he had long ago restored to its author, here again were the idea of a disappearance and the name of Henry Jekyll bracketed. But in the will, that idea had sprung from the sinister suggestion of the man Hyde; it was set there with a purpose all too plain and horrible. Written by the hand of Lanyon, what should it mean? A great curiosity came on the trustee, to disregard the prohibition and dive at once to the bottom of these mysteries; but professional honour and faith to his dead friend were stringent obligations; and the packet slept in the inmost corner of his private safe.

It is one thing to mortify curiosity, another to conquer it; and it may be doubted if, from that day forth, Utterson desired the society of his surviving friend with the same eagerness. He thought of him kindly; but his thoughts were disquieted and fearful. He went to call indeed; but he was perhaps relieved to be denied admittance; perhaps, in his heart, he preferred to speak with Poole upon the doorstep and surrounded by the air and sounds of the open city, rather than to be admitted into that house of voluntary bondage, and to sit and speak with its inscrutable recluse. Poole had, indeed, no very pleasant news to communicate. The doctor, it appeared, now more than ever confined himself to the cabinet over the laboratory, where he would sometimes even sleep; he was out of spirits, he had grown very silent, he did not read; it seemed as if he had something on his mind. Utterson became so used to the unvarying character of these reports, that he fell off little by little in the frequency of his visits.

## *Incident at the Window*

It chanced on Sunday, when Mr. Utterson was on his usual walk with Mr. Enfield, that their way lay once again through the by-street; and that when they came in front of the door, both stopped to gaze on it.

"Well," said Enfield, "that story's at an end at least. We shall never see more of Mr. Hyde."

"I hope not," said Utterson. "Did I ever tell you that I once saw him, and shared your feeling of repulsion?"

"It was impossible to do the one without the other," returned Enfield. "And by the way, what an ass you must have thought me, not to know that this was a back way to Dr. Jekyll's! It was partly your own fault that I found it out, even when I did."

"So you found it out, did you?" said Utterson. "But if that be so, we may step into the court and take a look at the windows. To tell you the truth, I am uneasy about poor Jekyll; and even outside, I feel as if the presence of a friend might do him good."

The court was very cool and a little damp, and full of premature twilight, although the sky, high up overhead, was still bright with sunset. The middle one of the three windows was half-way open; and sitting close beside it, taking the air with an infinite sadness of mien, like some disconsolate prisoner, Utterson saw Dr. Jekyll.

"What! Jekyll!" he cried. "I trust you are better."

"I am very low, Utterson," replied the doctor, drearily, "very low. It will not last long, thank God."

"You stay too much indoors," said the lawyer. "You should be out, whipping up the circulation like Mr. Enfield and me. (This is my cousin—Mr. Enfield—Dr. Jekyll.) Come, now; get your hat and take a quick turn with us."

"You are very good," sighed the other. "I should like to very much; but no, no, no, it is quite impossible; I dare not. But indeed, Utterson, I am very glad to see you; this is really a great pleasure; I would ask you and Mr. Enfield up, but the place is really not fit."

"Why then," said the lawyer, good-naturedly, "the best thing we can do is to stay down here and speak with you from where we are."

"That is just what I was about to venture to propose," returned the doctor with a smile. But the words were hardly uttered, before the smile was struck out of his face and succeeded by an expression of such abject terror and despair, as froze the very blood of the two gentlemen below. They saw it but for a glimpse, for the window was instantly thrust down; but that glimpse had been sufficient, and they turned and left the court without a word. In silence, too, they traversed the by-street; and it was not until they had come into a neighbouring thoroughfare, where even upon a Sunday there were still some stirrings of life, that Mr. Utterson at last turned and looked at his companion. They were both pale; and there was an answering horror in their eyes.

"God forgive us, God forgive us," said Mr. Utterson.

But Mr. Enfield only nodded his head very seriously and walked on once more in silence.

# The Last Night

M r. Utterson was sitting by his fireside one evening after dinner, when he was surprised to receive a visit from Poole.

"Bless me, Poole, what brings you here?" he cried; and then taking a second look at him, "What ails you?" he added; "is the doctor ill?"

"Mr. Utterson," said the man, "there is something wrong."

"Take a seat, and here is a glass of wine for you," said the lawyer. "Now, take your time, and tell me plainly what you want."

"You know the doctor's ways, sir," replied Poole, "and how he shuts himself up. Well, he's shut up again in the cabinet; and I don't like it, sir—I wish I may die if I like it. Mr. Utterson, sir, I'm afraid."

"Now, my good man," said the lawyer, "be explicit. What are you afraid of?"

"I've been afraid for about a week," returned Poole, doggedly disregarding the question, "and I can bear it no more."

The man's appearance amply bore out his words; his manner was altered for the worse; and except for the moment when he had first announced his terror, he had not once looked the lawyer in the face. Even now, he sat with the glass of wine untasted on his knee, and his eyes directed to a corner of the floor. "I can bear it no more," he repeated.

"Come," said the lawyer, "I see you have some good reason, Poole; I see there is something seriously amiss. Try to tell me what it is."

"I think there's been foul play," said Poole, hoarsely.

"Foul play!" cried the lawyer, a good deal frightened and rather inclined to be irritated in consequence. "What foul play? What does the man mean?"

"I daren't say, sir," was the answer; "but will you come along with me and see for yourself?"

Mr. Utterson's only answer was to rise and get his hat and great-coat; but he observed with wonder the greatness of the relief that appeared upon the butler's face, and perhaps with no less, that the wine was still untasted when he set it down to follow.

It was a wild, cold, seasonable night of March, with a pale moon, lying on her back as though the wind had tilted her, and a flying wrack of the most diaphanous and lawny texture. The wind made talking difficult, and flecked the blood into the face. It seemed to have swept the streets unusually bare of passengers, besides; for Mr. Utterson thought he had never seen that part of London so deserted. He could have wished it otherwise; never in his life had he been conscious of so sharp a wish to see and touch his fellow-creatures; for struggle as he might, there was borne in upon his mind a crushing anticipation of calamity. The square, when they got there, was all full of wind and dust, and the thin trees in the garden were lashing themselves along the railing. Poole, who had kept all the way a pace or two ahead, now pulled up in the middle of the pavement, and in spite of the biting weather, took off his hat and mopped his brow with a red pocket-handkerchief. But for all the hurry of his cowing, these were not the dews of exertion that he wiped away, but the moisture of some strangling anguish; for his face was white and his voice, when he spoke, harsh and broken.

"Well, sir," he said, "here we are, and God grant there be nothing wrong."

"Amen, Poole," said the lawyer.

Thereupon the servant knocked in a very guarded manner; the door was opened on the chain; and a voice asked from within, "Is that you, Poole?"

"It's all right," said Poole. "Open the door." The hall, when they entered it, was brightly lighted up; the fire was built high; and about the hearth the whole of the servants, men and women, stood huddled together like a flock of sheep. At the sight of Mr. Utterson, the housemaid broke into hysterical whimpering; and the cook, crying out, "Bless God! it's Mr. Utterson," ran forward as if to take him in her arms.

"What, what? Are you all here?" said the lawyer peevishly. "Very irregular, very unseemly; your master would be far from pleased."

"They're all afraid," said Poole.

Blank silence followed, no one protesting; only the maid lifted up her voice and now wept loudly.

"Hold your tongue!" Poole said to her, with a ferocity of accent that testified to his own jangled nerves; and indeed, when the girl had so suddenly raised the note of her lamentation, they had all started and turned toward the inner door with faces of dreadful expectation. "And now," continued the butler, addressing the knife-boy, "reach me a candle, and we'll get this through hands at once." And then he begged Mr. Utterson to follow him, and led the way to the back garden.

"Now, sir," said he, "you come as gently as you can. I want you to hear, and I don't want you to be heard. And see here, sir, if by any chance he was to ask you in, don't go."

Mr. Utterson's nerves, at this unlooked-for termination, gave a jerk that nearly threw him from his balance; but he re-collected his courage and followed the butler into the laboratory building and through the surgical theatre, with its lumber of crates and bottles, to the foot of the stair. Here Poole motioned him to stand on one side and listen; while he himself, setting down the candle and making a great and obvious call on his resolution, mounted the steps and knocked with a somewhat uncertain hand on the red baize of the cabinet door.

"Mr. Utterson, sir, asking to see you," he called; and even as he did so, once more violently signed to the lawyer to give ear.

A voice answered from within: "Tell him I cannot see any one," it said complainingly.

"Thank you, sir," said Poole, with a note of something like triumph in his voice; and taking up his candle, he led Mr. Utterson back across the yard and into the great kitchen, where the fire was out and the beetles were leaping on the floor.

"Sir," he said, looking Mr. Utterson in the eyes, "was that my master's voice?"

"It seems much changed," replied the lawyer, very pale, but giving look for look.

"Changed? Well, yes, I think so," said the butler. "Have I been twenty years in this man's house, to be deceived about his voice? No, sir; master's made away with; he was made, away with eight days ago, when we heard him cry out upon the name of God; and who's in there instead of him, and why it stays there, is a thing that cries to Heaven, Mr. Utterson!"

"This is a very strange tale, Poole; this is rather a wild tale, my man," said Mr. Utterson, biting his finger. "Suppose it were as you suppose, supposing Dr. Jekyll to have been—well, murdered, what could induce the murderer to stay? That won't hold water; it doesn't commend itself to reason."

"Well, Mr. Utterson, you are a hard man to satisfy, but I'll do it yet," said Poole. "All this last week (you must know) him, or it, or whatever it is that lives in that cabinet, has been crying night and day for some sort of medicine and cannot get it to his mind. It was sometimes his way—the master's, that is—to write his orders on a sheet of paper and throw it on the stair. We've had nothing else this week back; nothing but papers, and a closed door, and the very meals left there to be smuggled in when nobody was looking. Well, sir, every day, ay, and twice and thrice in the same day, there have been orders and complaints, and I have been sent flying to all the wholesale chemists in town. Every time I brought the stuff back, there would be another paper telling me to return it, because it was not pure, and another order to a different firm. This drug is wanted bitter bad, sir, whatever for."

"Have you any of these papers?" asked Mr. Utterson.

Poole felt in his pocket and handed out a crumpled note, which the lawyer, bending nearer to the candle, carefully examined. Its contents ran thus: "Dr. Jekyll presents his compliments to Messrs. Maw. He assures them that their last sample is impure and quite useless for his present purpose. In the year 18—, Dr. J. purchased a somewhat large quantity from Messrs. M. He now begs them to search with the most sedulous care, and should any of the same quality be left, to forward it to him at once. Expense is no consideration. The importance of this to Dr. J. can hardly be exaggerated." So far the letter had run composedly enough, but here with a sudden splutter of the pen, the writer's emotion had broken loose. "For God's sake," he had added, "find me some of the old."

"This is a strange note," said Mr. Utterson; and then sharply, "How do you come to have it open?"

"The man at Maw's was main angry, sir, and he threw it back to me like so much dirt," returned Poole.

"This is unquestionably the doctor's hand, do you know?" resumed the lawyer.

"I thought it looked like it," said the servant rather sulkily; and then, with another voice, "But what matters hand-of-write?" he said. "I've seen him!"

"Seen him?" repeated Mr. Utterson. "Well?"

"That's it!" said Poole. "It was this way. I came suddenly into the theatre from the garden. It seems he had slipped out to look for this drug or whatever it is; for the cabinet door was open, and there he was at the far end of the room digging among the crates. He looked up when I came in, gave a kind of cry, and whipped upstairs into the cabinet. It was but for one minute that I saw him, but the hair stood upon my head like quills. Sir, if that was my master, why had he a mask upon his face? If it was my master, why did he cry out like a rat, and run from me? I have served him long enough. And then . . ." The man paused and passed his hand over his face.

"These are all very strange circumstances," said Mr. Utterson, "but I think I begin to see daylight. Your master, Poole, is plainly seized with one of those maladies that both torture and deform the sufferer; hence, for aught I know, the alteration of his voice; hence the mask and the avoidance of his friends; hence his eagerness to find this drug, by means of which the poor soul retains some hope of ultimate recovery—God grant that he be not deceived! There is my explanation; it is sad enough, Poole, ay, and appalling to consider; but it is plain and natural, hangs well together, and delivers us from all exorbitant alarms."

"Sir," said the butler, turning to a sort of mottled pallor, "that thing was not my master, and there's the truth. My master"—here he looked round him and began to whisper—"is a tall, fine build of a man, and this was more of a dwarf." Utterson attempted to protest. "Oh, sir," cried Poole, "do you think I do not know my master after twenty years? Do you think I do not know where his head comes to in the cabinet door, where I saw him every morning of my life? No, sir, that thing in the mask was never Dr. Jekyll—God knows what it was, but it was never Dr. Jekyll; and it is the belief of my heart that there was murder done."

"Poole," replied the lawyer, "if you say that, it will become my duty to make certain. Much as I desire to spare your master's feelings, much as I am puzzled by this note which seems to prove him to be still alive, I shall consider it my duty to break in that door."

"Ah Mr. Utterson, that's talking!" cried the butler.

"And now comes the second question," resumed Utterson: "Who is going to do it?"

"Why, you and me," was the undaunted reply.

"That's very well said," returned the lawyer; "and whatever comes of it, I shall make it my business to see you are no loser."

"There is an axe in the theatre," continued Poole; "and you might take the kitchen poker for yourself."

The lawyer took that rude but weighty instrument into his hand, and balanced it. "Do you know, Poole," he said, looking up, "that you and I are about to place ourselves in a position of some peril?"

"You may say so, sir, indeed," returned the butler.

"It is well, then, that we should be frank," said the other. "We both think more than we have said; let us make a clean breast. This masked figure that you saw, did you recognise it?"

"Well, sir, it went so quick, and the creature was so doubled up, that I could hardly swear to that," was the answer. "But if you mean, was it Mr. Hyde?—why, yes, I think it was! You see, it was much of the same bigness; and it had the same quick, light way with it; and then who else could have got in by the laboratory door? You have not forgot, sir, that at the time of the murder he had still the key with him? But that's not all. I don't know, Mr. Utterson, if ever you met this Mr. Hyde?"

"Yes," said the lawyer, "I once spoke with him."

"Then you must know as well as the rest of us that there was something queer about that gentleman—something that gave a man a turn—I don't know rightly how to say it, sir, beyond this: that you felt it in your marrow kind of cold and thin."

"I own I felt something of what you describe," said Mr. Utterson.

"Quite so, sir," returned Poole. "Well, when that masked thing like a monkey jumped from among the chemicals and whipped into the cabinet, it went down my spine like ice. Oh, I know it's not evidence, Mr. Utterson. I'm book-learned enough for that; but a man has his feelings, and I give you my Bible-word it was Mr. Hyde!"

"Ay, ay," said the lawyer. "My fears incline to the same point. Evil, I fear, founded—evil was sure to come—of that connection. Ay, truly, I believe you; I believe poor Harry is killed; and I believe his murderer (for what purpose, God alone can tell) is still lurking in his victim's room. Well, let our name be vengeance. Call Bradshaw."

The footman came at the summons, very white and nervous.

"Pull yourself together, Bradshaw," said the lawyer. "This suspense, I know, is telling upon all of you; but it is now our intention to make an end of it. Poole, here, and I are going to force our way into the cabinet. If all is well, my shoulders are broad enough to bear the blame. Meanwhile, lest anything should really be amiss, or any malefactor seek to escape by the back, you and the boy must go round the corner with a pair of good sticks and take your post at the laboratory door. We give you ten minutes to get to your stations."

As Bradshaw left, the lawyer looked at his watch. "And now, Poole, let us get to ours," he said; and taking the poker under his arm, led the way into the yard. The scud had banked over the moon, and it was now quite dark. The wind, which only broke in puffs and draughts into that deep well of building, tossed the light of the candle to and fro about their steps, until they came into the shelter of the theatre, where they sat down silently to wait. London hummed solemnly all around; but nearer at hand, the stillness was only broken by the sounds of a footfall moving to and fro along the cabinet floor.

"So it will walk all day, sir," whispered Poole; "ay, and the better part of the night. Only when a new sample comes from the chemist, there's a bit of a break. Ah, it's an ill conscience that's such an enemy to rest! Ah, sir, there's blood foully shed in every step of it! But hark again, a little closer—put your heart in your ears, Mr. Utterson, and tell me, is that the doctor's foot?"

The steps fell lightly and oddly, with a certain swing, for all they went so slowly; it was different indeed from the heavy creaking tread of Henry Jekyll. Utterson sighed. "Is there never anything else?" he asked.

Poole nodded. "Once," he said. "Once I heard it weeping!"

"Weeping? how that?" said the lawyer, conscious of a sudden chill of horror.

"Weeping like a woman or a lost soul," said the butler. "I came away with that upon my heart, that I could have wept too."

But now the ten minutes drew to an end. Poole disinterred the axe from under a stack of packing straw; the candle was set upon the nearest table to light them to the attack; and they drew near with bated breath to where that patient foot was still going up and down, up and down, in the quiet of the night.

"Jekyll," cried Utterson, with a loud voice, "I demand to see you." He paused a moment, but there came no reply. "I give you fair warning, our suspicions are aroused, and I must and shall see you," he resumed; "if not by fair means, then by foul! if not of your consent, then by brute force!"

"Utterson," said the voice, "for God's sake, have mercy!"

"Ah, that's not Jekyll's voice—it's Hyde's!" cried Utterson. "Down with the door, Poole!"

Poole swung the axe over his shoulder; the blow shook the building, and the red baize door leaped against the lock and hinges. A dismal screech, as of mere animal terror, rang from the cabinet. Up went the axe again, and again the panels crashed and the frame bounded; four times the blow fell; but the wood was tough and the fittings were of excellent workmanship; and it was not until the fifth, that the lock burst in sunder and the wreck of the door fell inwards on the carpet.

The besiegers, appalled by their own riot and the stillness that had succeeded, stood back a little and peered in. There lay the cabinet before their eyes in the quiet lamplight, a good fire glowing and chattering on the hearth, the kettle singing its thin strain, a drawer or two open, papers neatly set forth on the business-table, and nearer the fire, the things laid out for tea: the quietest room, you would have said, and, but for the glazed presses full of chemicals, the most commonplace that night in London.

Right in the midst there lay the body of a man sorely contorted and still twitching. They drew near on tiptoe, turned it on its back and beheld the face of Edward Hyde. He was dressed in clothes far too large for him, clothes of the doctor's bigness; the cords of his face still moved with a semblance of life, but life was quite gone; and by the crushed phial in the hand and the strong smell of kernels that hung upon the air, Utterson knew that he was looking on the body of a self-destroyer.

"We have come too late," he said sternly, "whether to save or punish. Hyde is gone to his account; and it only remains for us to find the body of your master."

The far greater proportion of the building was occupied by the theatre, which filled almost the whole ground storey and was lighted from above, and by the cabinet, which formed an upper storey at one end and looked upon the court. A corridor joined the theatre to the door on the by-street; and with this the cabinet communicated separately by a second flight of stairs. There were besides a few dark closets and a spacious cellar. All these they now thoroughly examined. Each closet needed but a glance, for all were empty, and all, by the dust that fell from their doors, had stood long unopened. The cellar, indeed, was filled with crazy lumber, mostly dating from the times of the surgeon who was Jekyll's predecessor; but even as they opened the door they were advertised of the uselessness of further search, by the fall of a perfect mat of cobweb which had for years sealed up the entrance. Nowhere was there any trace of Henry Jekyll, dead or alive.

Poole stamped on the flags of the corridor. "He must be buried here," he said, hearkening to the sound.

"Or he may have fled," said Utterson, and he turned to examine the door in the by-street. It was locked; and lying near by on the flags, they found the key, already stained with rust.

"This does not look like use," observed the lawyer.

"Use!" echoed Poole. "Do you not see, sir, it is broken? much as if a man had stamped on it."

"Ay," continued Utterson, "and the fractures, too, are rusty." The two men looked at each other with a scare. "This is beyond me, Poole," said the lawyer. "Let us go back to the cabinet."

They mounted the stair in silence, and still with an occasional awe-struck glance at the dead body, proceeded more thoroughly to examine the contents of the cabinet. At one table, there were traces of chemical work, various measured heaps of some white salt being laid on glass saucers, as though for an experiment in which the unhappy man had been prevented.

"That is the same drug that I was always bringing him," said Poole; and even as he spoke, the kettle with a startling noise boiled over.

This brought them to the fireside, where the easy-chair was drawn cosily up, and the tea things stood ready to the sitter's elbow, the very sugar in the cup. There were several books on a shelf; one lay beside the tea things, open, and Utterson was amazed to find it a copy of a pious work, for which Jekyll had several times expressed a great esteem, annotated, in his own hand, with startling blasphemies.

Next, in the course of their review of the chamber, the searchers came to the cheval glass, into whose depths they looked with an involuntary horror. But it was so turned as to show them nothing but the rosy glow playing on the roof, the fire sparkling in a hundred repetitions along the glazed front of the presses, and their own pale and fearful countenances stooping to look in.

"This glass have seen some strange things, sir," whispered Poole.

"And surely none stranger than itself," echoed the lawyer in the same tones. "For what did Jekyll"—he caught himself up at the word with a start, and then conquering the weakness—"what could Jekyll want with it?" he said.

"You may say that!" said Poole. Next they turned to the business-table. On the desk among the neat array of papers, a large envelope was uppermost, and bore, in the doctor's hand, the name of Mr. Utterson. The lawyer unsealed it, and several enclosures fell to the floor. The first was a will, drawn in the same eccentric terms as the one which he had returned six months before, to serve as a testament in case of death and as a deed of gift in case of disappearance; but, in place of the name of Edward Hyde, the lawyer, with indescribable amazement, read the name of Gabriel John Utterson. He looked at Poole, and then back at the paper, and last of all at the dead malefactor stretched upon the carpet.

"My head goes round," he said. "He has been all these days

in possession; he had no cause to like me; he must have raged to see himself displaced; and he has not destroyed this document."

He caught up the next paper; it was a brief note in the doctor's hand and dated at the top.

"O Poole!" the lawyer cried, "he was alive and here this day. He cannot have been disposed of in so short a space, he must be still alive, he must have fled! And then, why fled? and how? and in that case, can we venture to declare this suicide? Oh, we must be careful. I foresee that we may yet involve your master in some dire catastrophe."

"Why don't you read it, sir?" asked Poole.

"Because I fear," replied the lawyer solemnly. "God grant I have no cause for it!" And with that he brought the paper to his eyes and read as follows:

MY DEAR UTTERSON—When this shall fall into your hands, I shall have disappeared, under what circumstances I have not the penetration to foresee, but my instinct and all the circumstances of my nameless situation tell me that the end is sure and must be early. Go then, and first read the narrative which Lanyon warned me he was to place in your hands; and if you care to hear more, turn to the confession of

Your unworthy and unhappy friend,
HENRY JEKYLL

"There was a third enclosure?" asked Utterson.

"Here, sir," said Poole, and gave into his hands a considerable packet sealed in several places.

The lawyer put it in his pocket. "I would say nothing of this paper. If your master has fled or is dead, we may at least save his credit. It is now ten; I must go home and read these documents in quiet; but I shall be back before midnight, when we shall send for the police."

They went out, locking the door of the theatre behind them; and Utterson, once more leaving the servants gathered about the fire in the hall, trudged back to his office to read the two narratives in which this mystery was now to be explained.

# Dr. Lanyon's Narrative

On the ninth of January, now four days ago, I received by the evening delivery a registered envelope, addressed in the hand of my colleague and old school-companion, Henry Jekyll. I was a good deal surprised by this; for we were by no means in the habit of correspondence; I had seen the man, dined with him, indeed, the night before; and I could imagine nothing in our intercourse that should justify formality of registration. The contents increased my wonder; for this is how the letter ran:

10th December, 18—

Dear Lanyon—You are one of my oldest friends; and although we may have differed at times on scientific questions, I cannot remember, at least on my side, any break in our affection. There was never a day when, if you had said to me, "Jekyll, my life, my honour, my reason, depend upon you," I would not have sacrificed my left hand to help you. Lanyon, my life, my honour my reason, are all at your mercy; if you fail me to-night I am lost. You might suppose, after this preface, that I am going to ask you for something dishonourable to grant. Judge for yourself.

I want you to postpone all other engagements for to-night—ay, even if you were summoned to the bedside of an emperor; to take a cab, unless your carriage should be actually at the door; and with this letter in your hand for consultation, to drive straight to my house. Poole, my butler, has his orders; you will find him waiting your arrival with a locksmith. The door of my cabinet is then to be forced: and you are to go in alone; to open the glazed press (letter E) on the left hand, breaking the lock if it be shut; and to draw out, with all its contents as they stand, the fourth drawer from the top or (which is the same thing) the third from the bottom. In my extreme distress of wind, I have a morbid fear of misdirecting you; but even if I am in error, you may know the right drawer by its contents: some powders, a phial and a paper book. This drawer I beg of you to carry back with you to Cavendish Square exactly as it stands.

That is the first part of the service: now for the second. You should be back, if you set out at once on the receipt of this, long before midnight; but I will leave you that amount of margin, not only in the fear of one of those obstacles that can neither be prevented nor foreseen, but because an hour when your servants are in bed is to be preferred for what will then remain to do. At midnight, then, I have to ask you to be alone in your consulting-room, to admit with your own hand into the house a man who will present himself in my name, and to place in his hands the drawer that you will have brought with you from my cabinet. Then you will have played your part and earned my gratitude completely. Five minutes afterwards, if you insist upon an explanation, you will have understood that these arrangements are of capital importance; and that by the neglect of one of them, fantastic as they must appear, you might have charged your conscience with my death or the shipwreck of my reason.

Confident as I am that you will not trifle with this appeal, my heart sinks and my hand trembles at the bare thought of such a possibility. Think of me at this hour, in a strange place, labouring under a blackness of distress that no fancy can exaggerate, and yet well aware that, if you will but punctually serve me, my troubles will roll away like a story that is told. Serve me, my dear Lanyon, and save

Your friend,
H. J.

P.S. I had already sealed this up when a fresh terror struck upon my soul. It is possible that the post office may fail me, and this letter not come into your hands until to-morrow morning. In that case, dear Lanyon, do my errand when it shall be most convenient for you in the course of the day; and once more expect my messenger at midnight. It may then already be too late; and if that night passes without event, you will know that you have seen the last of Henry Jekyll.

Upon the reading of this letter, I made sure my colleague was insane; but till that was proved beyond the possibility of doubt, I felt bound to do as he requested. The less I understood of this farrago, the less I was in a position to judge of its importance; and an appeal so worded could not be set aside without a grave responsibility. I rose accordingly from table, got into a hansom, and drove straight to Jekyll's house. The butler was awaiting my arrival; he had received by the same post as mine a registered letter of instruction, and had sent at once for a locksmith and a carpenter. The tradesmen came while we were yet speaking; and we moved in a body to old Dr. Denman's surgical theatre, from which (as you are doubtless aware) Jekyll's private cabinet is most conveniently entered. The door was very strong, the lock excellent; the carpenter avowed he would have great trouble and have to do much damage, if force were to be used; and the locksmith was near despair. But this last was a handy fellow, and after two hours' work, the door stood open. The press marked E was unlocked; and I took out the drawer, had it filled up with straw and tied in a sheet, and returned with it to Cavendish Square.

Here I proceeded to examine its contents. The powders were neatly enough made up, but not with the nicety of the dispensing chemist; so that it was plain they were of Jekyll's private manufacture; and when I opened one of the wrappers I found what seemed to me a simple crystalline salt of a white colour. The phial, to which I next turned my attention, might have been about half full of a blood-red liquor, which was highly pungent to the sense of smell and seemed to me to contain phosphorus and some volatile ether. At the other ingredients I could make no guess. The book was an ordinary version book and contained little but a series of dates. These covered a period of many years, but I observed that the entries ceased nearly a year ago and quite abruptly. Here and there a brief remark was appended to a date, usually no more than a single word: "double" occurring perhaps six times in a total of several hundred entries; and once very early in the list and followed by several marks of exclamation, "total failure!!!" All this, though it whetted my curiosity, told me little that was definite. Here were a phial of some tincture, a paper of some salt, and the record of a series of experiments that had led (like too many of Jekyll's investigations) to no end of practical usefulness. How could the presence of these articles in my house affect either the honour, the sanity, or the life of my flighty colleague? If his messenger could go to one place, why could he not go to another? And even granting some impediment, why was this gentleman to be received by me in secret? The more I reflected the more convinced I grew that I was dealing with a case of cerebral disease: and though I dismissed my servants to bed, I loaded an old revolver, that I might be found in some posture of self-defence.

Twelve o'clock had scarce rung out over London, ere the knocker sounded very gently on the door. I went myself at the summons, and found a small man crouching against the pillars of the portico.

"Are you come from Dr. Jekyll?" I asked.

He told me "yes" by a constrained gesture; and when I had bidden him enter, he did not obey me without a searching backward glance into the darkness of the square. There was a policeman not far off, advancing with his bull's-eye open; and at the sight, I thought my visitor started and made greater haste.

These particulars struck me, I confess, disagreeably; and as I followed him into the bright light of the consulting-room, I kept my hand ready on my weapon. Here, at last, I had a chance of clearly seeing him. I had never set eyes on him before, so much was certain. He was small, as I have said; I was struck besides with the shocking expression of his face, with his remarkable combination of great muscular activity and great apparent debility of constitution, and—last but not least—with the odd, subjective disturbance caused by his neighbourhood. This bore some resemblance to incipient rigour, and was accompanied by a marked sinking of the pulse. At the time, I set it down to some idiosyncratic, personal distaste, and merely wondered at the acuteness of the symptoms; but I have since had reason to believe the cause to lie much deeper in the nature of man, and to turn on some nobler hinge than the principle of hatred.

This person (who had thus, from the first moment of his entrance, struck in me what I can only describe as a disgustful curiosity) was dressed in a fashion that would have made an ordinary person laughable; his clothes, that is to say, although they were of rich and sober fabric, were enormously too large for him in every measurement—the trousers hanging on his legs and rolled up to keep them from the ground, the waist of the coat below his haunches, and the collar sprawling wide upon his shoulders. Strange to relate, this ludicrous accoutrement was far from moving me to laughter. Rather, as there was something abnormal and misbegotten in the very essence of the creature that now faced me—something seizing, surprising, and revolting—this fresh disparity seemed but to fit in with and to reinforce it; so that to my interest in the man's nature and character, there was added a curiosity as to his origin, his life, his fortune and status in the world.

These observations, though they have taken so great a space to be set down in, were yet the work of a few seconds. My visitor was, indeed, on fire with sombre excitement.

"Have you got it?" he cried. "Have you got it?" And so lively was his impatience that he even laid his hand upon my arm and sought to shake me.

I put him back, conscious at his touch of a certain icy pang along my blood. "Come, sir," said I. "You forget that I have not yet the pleasure of your acquaintance. Be seated, if you please." And I showed him an example, and sat down myself in my customary seat and with as fair an imitation of my ordinary manner to a patient, as the lateness of the hour, the nature of my preoccupations, and the horror I had of my visitor, would suffer me to muster.

"I beg your pardon, Dr. Lanyon," he replied civilly enough. "What you say is very well founded; and my impatience has shown its heels to my politeness. I come here at the instance of your colleague, Dr. Henry Jekyll, on a piece of business of some moment; and I understood . . ." He paused and put his hand to his throat, and I could see, in spite of his collected manner, that he was wrestling against the approaches of the hysteria—"I understood, a drawer . . ."

But here I took pity on my visitor's suspense, and some perhaps on my own growing curiosity.

"There it is, sir," said I, pointing to the drawer, where it lay on the floor behind a table and still covered with the sheet.

He sprang to it, and then paused, and laid his hand upon his heart: I could hear his teeth grate with the convulsive action of his jaws; and his face was so ghastly to see that I grew alarmed both for his life and reason.

"Compose yourself," said I.

He turned a dreadful smile to me, and as if with the decision of despair, plucked away the sheet. At sight of the contents, he uttered one loud sob of such immense relief that I sat petrified. And the next moment, in a voice that was already fairly well under control, "Have you a graduated glass?" he asked.

I rose from my place with something of an effort and gave him what he asked.

He thanked me with a smiling nod, measured out a few minims of the red tincture and added one of the powders. The mixture, which was at first of a reddish hue, began, in proportion as the crystals melted, to brighten in colour, to effervesce audibly, and to throw off small fumes of vapour. Suddenly and at the same moment, the ebullition ceased and the compound changed to a dark purple, which faded again more slowly to a watery green. My visitor, who had watched these metamorphoses with a keen eye, smiled, set down the glass upon the table, and then turned and looked upon me with an air of scrutiny.

"And now," said he, "to settle what remains. Will you be wise? will you be guided? will you suffer me to take this glass in my hand and to go forth from your house without further parley? or has the greed of curiosity too much command of you? Think before you answer, for it shall be done as you decide. As you decide, you shall be left as you were before, and neither richer nor wiser, unless the sense of service rendered to a man in mortal distress may be counted as a kind of riches of the soul. Or, if you shall so prefer to choose, a new province of knowledge and new avenues to fame and power shall be laid open to you, here, in this room, upon the instant; and your sight shall be blasted by a prodigy to stagger the unbelief of Satan."

"Sir," said I, affecting a coolness that I was far from truly possessing, "you speak enigmas, and you will perhaps not wonder that I hear you with no very strong impression of belief. But I have gone too far in the way of inexplicable services to pause before I see the end."

"It is well," replied my visitor. "Lanyon, you remember your vows: what follows is under the seal of our profession. And now, you who have so long been bound to the most narrow and material views, you who have denied the virtue of transcendental medicine, you who have derided your superiors—behold!"

He put the glass to his lips and drank at one gulp. A cry followed; he reeled, staggered, clutched at the table and held on, staring with injected eyes, gasping with open mouth; and as I looked there came, I thought, a change—he seemed to swell—his face became suddenly black and the features seemed to melt and alter—and the next moment, I had sprung to my feet and leaped back against the wall, my arm raised to shield me from that prodigy, my mind submerged in terror.

"O God!" I screamed, and "O God!" again and again; for there before my eyes—pale and shaken, and half-fainting, and groping before him with his hands, like a man restored from death—there stood Henry Jekyll!

What he told me in the next hour, I cannot bring my mind to set on paper. I saw what I saw, I heard what I heard, and my soul sickened at it; and yet now when that sight has faded from my eyes, I ask myself if I believe it, and I cannot answer. My life is shaken to its roots; sleep has left me; the deadliest terror sits by me at all hours of the day and night; I feel that my days are numbered, and that I must die; and yet I shall die incredulous. As for the moral turpitude that man unveiled to me, even with tears of penitence, I cannot, even in memory, dwell on it without a start of horror. I will say but one thing, Utterson, and that (if you can bring your mind to credit it) will be more than enough. The creature who crept into my house that night was, on Jekyll's own confession, known by the name of Hyde and hunted for in every corner of the land as the murderer of Carew.

HASTIE LANYON

# Henry Jekyll's Full Statement
## of the Case

I was born in the year 18— to a large fortune, endowed besides with excellent parts, inclined by nature to industry, fond of the respect of the wise and good among my fellow-men, and thus, as might have been supposed, with every guarantee of an honourable and distinguished future. And indeed the worst of my faults was a certain impatient gaiety of disposition, such as has made the happiness of many, but such as I found it hard to reconcile with my imperious desire to carry my head high, and wear a more than commonly grave countenance before the public. Hence it came about that I concealed my pleasures; and that when I reached years of reflection, and began to look round me and take stock of my progress and position in the world, I stood already committed to a profound duplicity of life. Many a man would have even blazoned such irregularities as I was guilty of; but from the high views that I had set before me, I regarded and hid them with an almost morbid sense of shame. It was thus rather the exacting nature of my aspirations than any particular degradation in my faults, that made me what I was and, with even a deeper trench than in the majority of men, severed in me those provinces of good and ill which divide and compound man's dual nature. In this case, I was driven to reflect deeply and inveterately on that hard law of life, which lies at the root of religion and is one of the most plentiful springs of distress. Though so profound a double-dealer, I was in no sense a hypocrite; both sides of me were in dead earnest; I was no more myself when I laid aside restraint and plunged in shame, than when I laboured, in the eye of day, at the furtherance of knowledge or the relief of sorrow and suffering. And it chanced that the direction of my scientific studies, which led wholly toward the mystic and the transcendental, reacted and shed a strong light on this consciousness of the perennial war among my members. With every day, and from both sides of my intelligence, the moral and the intellectual, I thus drew steadily nearer to that truth, by whose partial discovery I have been doomed to such a dreadful shipwreck: that man is not truly one, but truly two. I say two, because the state of my own knowledge does not pass beyond that point. Others will follow, others will outstrip me on the same lines; and I hazard the guess that man will be ultimately known for a mere polity of multifarious, incongruous, and independent denizens. I, for my part, from the nature of my life, advanced infallibly in one direction and in one direction only. It was on the moral side, and in my own person, that I learned to recognise the thorough and primitive duality of man; I saw that, of the two natures that contended in the field of my consciousness, even if I could rightly be said to be either, it was only because I was radically both; and from an early date, even before the course of my scientific discoveries had begun to suggest the most naked possibility of such a miracle, I had learned to dwell with pleasure, as a beloved daydream, on the thought of the separation of these elements. If each, I told myself, could but be housed in separate identities, life would be relieved of all that was unbearable; the unjust delivered from the aspirations might go his way, and remorse of his more upright twin; and the just could walk steadfastly and securely on his upward path, doing the good things in which he found his pleasure, and no longer exposed to disgrace and penitence by the hands of this extraneous evil. It was the curse of mankind that these incongruous fagots were thus bound together that in the agonised womb of consciousness, these polar twins should be continuously struggling. How, then, were they dissociated?

I was so far in my reflections when, as I have said, a sidelight began to shine upon the subject from the laboratory table. I began to perceive more deeply than it has ever yet been stated, the trembling immateriality, the mistlike transience of this seemingly so solid body in which we walk attired. Certain agents I found to have the power to shake and to pluck back that fleshly vestment, even as a wind might toss the curtains of a pavilion. For two good reasons, I will not enter deeply into this scientific branch of my confession. First, because I have been made to learn that the doom and burthen of our life is bound forever on man's shoulders, and when the attempt is made to cast it off, it but returns upon us with more unfamiliar and more awful pressure. Second, because, as my narrative will make, alas! too evident, my discoveries were incomplete. Enough, then, that I not only recognised my natural body for the mere aura and effulgence of certain of the powers that made up my spirit, but managed to compound a drug by which these powers should be dethroned from their supremacy, and a second form and countenance substituted, none the less natural to me because they were the expression, and bore the stamp, of lower elements in my soul.

I hesitated long before I put this theory to the test of practice. I knew well that I risked death; for any drug that so potently controlled and shook the very fortress of identity, might by the least scruple of an overdose or at the least inopportunity in the moment of exhibition, utterly blot out that immaterial tabernacle which I looked to it to change. But the temptation of a discovery so singular and profound, at last overcame the suggestions of alarm. I had long since prepared my tincture; I purchased at once, from a firm of wholesale chemists, a large quantity of a particular salt which I knew, from my experiments, to be the last ingredient required; and late one accursed night, I compounded the elements, watched them boil and smoke together in the glass, and when the ebullition had subsided, with a strong glow of courage, drank off the potion.

The most racking pangs succeeded: a grinding in the bones, deadly nausea, and a horror of the spirit that cannot be exceeded at the hour of birth or death. Then these agonies began swiftly to subside, and I came to myself as if out of a great sickness. There was something strange in my sensations, something indescribably new and, from its very novelty, incredibly sweet. I felt younger, lighter, happier in body; within I was conscious of a heady recklessness, a current of disordered sensual images running like a millrace in my fancy, a solution of the bonds of obligation, an unknown but not an innocent freedom of the soul. I knew myself, at the first breath of this new life, to be more wicked, tenfold more wicked, sold a slave to my original evil; and the thought, in that moment, braced and delighted me like wine. I stretched out my hands, exulting in the freshness of these sensations; and in the act, I was suddenly aware that I had lost in stature.

There was no mirror, at that date, in my room; that which stands beside me as I write, was brought there later on and for the very purpose of these transformations. The night, however, was far gone into the morning—the morning, black as it was, was nearly ripe for the conception of the day—the inmates of my house were locked in the most rigorous hours of slumber; and I determined, flushed as I was with hope and triumph, to venture in my new shape as far as to my bedroom. I crossed the yard, wherein the constellations looked down upon me, I could have thought, with wonder, the first creature of that sort that their unsleeping vigilance had yet disclosed to them; I stole through the corridors, a stranger in my own house; and coming to my room, I saw for the first time the appearance of Edward Hyde.

I must here speak by theory alone, saying not that which I know, but that which I suppose to be most probable. The evil side of my nature, to which I had now transferred the stamping efficacy, was less robust and less developed than the good which I had just deposed. Again, in the course of my life, which had been, after all, nine-tenths a life of effort, virtue, and control, it had been much less exercised and much less exhausted. And hence, as I think, it came about that Edward Hyde was so much smaller, slighter, and younger than Henry Jekyll. Even as good shone upon the countenance of the one, evil was written broadly and plainly on the face of the other. Evil besides (which I must still believe to be the lethal side of man) had left on that body an imprint of deformity and decay. And yet when I looked upon that ugly idol in the glass, I was conscious of no repugnance, rather of a leap of welcome. This, too, was myself. It seemed natural and human. In my eyes it bore a livelier image of the spirit, it seemed more express and single, than the imperfect and divided countenance I had been hitherto accustomed to call mine. And in so far I was doubtless right. I have observed that when I wore the semblance of Edward Hyde, none could come near to me at first without a visible misgiving of the flesh. This, as I take it, was because all human beings, as we meet them, are commingled out of good and evil: and Edward Hyde, alone in the ranks of mankind, was pure evil.

I lingered but a moment at the mirror: the second and

conclusive experiment had yet to be attempted; it yet remained to be seen if I had lost my identity beyond redemption and must flee before daylight from a house that was no longer mine; and hurrying back to my cabinet, I once more prepared and drank the cup, once more suffered the pangs of dissolution, and came to myself once more with the character, the stature, and the face of Henry Jekyll.

That night I had come to the fatal cross-roads. Had I approached my discovery in a more noble spirit, had I risked the experiment while under the empire of generous or pious aspirations, all must have been otherwise, and from these agonies of death and birth, I had come forth an angel instead of a fiend. The drug had no discriminating action; it was neither diabolical nor divine; it but shook the doors of the prison-house of my disposition; and like the captives of Philippi, that which stood within ran forth. At that time my virtue slumbered; my evil, kept awake by ambition, was alert and swift to seize the occasion; and the thing that was projected was Edward Hyde. Hence, although I had now two characters as well as two appearances, one was wholly evil, and the other was still the old Henry Jekyll, that incongruous compound of whose reformation and improvement I had already learned to despair. The movement was thus wholly toward the worse.

Even at that time, I had not yet conquered my aversion to the dryness of a life of study. I would still be merrily disposed at times; and as my pleasures were (to say the least) undignified, and I was not only well known and highly considered, but growing toward the elderly man, this incoherency of my life was daily growing more unwelcome. It was on this side that my new power tempted me until I fell in slavery. I had but to drink the cup, to doff at once the body of the noted professor, and to assume, like a thick cloak, that of Edward Hyde. I smiled at the notion; it seemed to me at the time to be humorous; and I made my preparations with the most studious care. I took and furnished that house in Soho, to which Hyde was tracked by the police; and engaged as housekeeper a creature whom I well knew to be silent and unscrupulous. On the other side, I announced to my servants that a Mr. Hyde (whom I described) was to have full liberty and power about my house in the square; and to parry mishaps, I even called and made myself a familiar object, in my second character. I next drew up that will to which you so much objected; so that if anything befell me in the person of Dr. Jekyll, I could enter on that of Edward Hyde without pecuniary loss. And thus fortified, as I supposed, on every side, I began to profit by the strange immunities of my position.

Men have before hired bravos to transact their crimes, while their own person and reputation sat under shelter. I was the first that ever did so for his pleasures. I was the first that could thus plod in the public eye with a load of genial respectability, and in a moment, like a schoolboy, strip off these lendings and spring headlong into the sea of liberty. But for me, in my impenetrable mantle, the safety was complete. Think of it—I did not even exist! Let me but escape into my laboratory door, give me but a second or two to mix and swallow the draught that I had always standing ready; and whatever he had done, Edward Hyde would pass away like the stain of breath upon a mirror; and there in his stead, quietly at home, trimming the midnight lamp in his study, a man who could afford to laugh at suspicion, would be Henry Jekyll.

The pleasures which I made haste to seek in my disguise were, as I have said, undignified; I would scarce use a harder term. But in the hands of Edward Hyde, they soon began to turn toward the monstrous. When I would come back from these excursions, I was often plunged into a kind of wonder at my vicarious depravity. This familiar that I called out of my own soul, and sent forth alone to do his good pleasure, was a being inherently malign and villainous; his every act and thought centred on self; drinking pleasure with bestial avidity from any degree of torture to another; relentless like a man of stone. Henry Jekyll stood at times aghast before the acts of Edward Hyde; but the situation was apart from ordinary laws, and insidiously relaxed the grasp of conscience. It was Hyde, after all, and Hyde alone, that was guilty. Jekyll was no worse; he woke again to his good qualities seemingly unimpaired; he would even make haste, where it was possible, to undo the evil done by Hyde. And thus his conscience slumbered.

Into the details of the infamy at which I thus connived (for even now I can scarce grant that I committed it) I have no design of entering; I mean but to point out the warnings and the successive steps with which my chastisement approached. I met with one accident which, as it brought on no consequence, I shall no more than mention. An act of cruelty to a child aroused against me the anger of a passer-by, whom I recognised the other day in the person of your kinsman; the doctor and the child's family joined him; there were moments when I feared for my life; and at last, in order to pacify their too just resentment, Edward Hyde had to bring them to the door, and pay them in a cheque drawn in the name of Henry Jekyll. But this danger was easily eliminated from the future, by opening an account at another bank in the name of Edward Hyde himself; and when, by sloping my own hand backward, I had supplied my double with a signature, I thought I sat beyond the reach of fate.

Some two months before the murder of Sir Danvers, I had been out for one of my adventures, had returned at a late hour, and woke the next day in bed with somewhat odd sensations. It was in vain I looked about me; in vain I saw the decent furniture and tall proportions of my room in the square; in vain that I recognised the pattern of the bed-curtains and the design of the mahogany frame; something still kept insisting that I was not where I was, that I had not wakened where I seemed to be, but in the little room in Soho where I was accustomed to sleep in the body of Edward Hyde. I smiled to myself, and, in my psychological way began lazily to inquire into the elements of this illusion, occasionally, even as I did so, dropping back into a comfortable morning doze. I was still so engaged when, in one of my more wakeful moments, my eyes fell upon my hand. Now the hand of Henry Jekyll (as you have often remarked) was professional in shape and size: it was large, firm, white, and comely. But the hand which I now saw, clearly enough, in the yellow light of a mid-London morning, lying half shut on the bedclothes, was lean, corded, knuckly, of a dusky pallor and thickly shaded with a swart growth of hair. It was the hand of Edward Hyde.

I must have stared upon it for near half a minute, sunk as I was in the mere stupidity of wonder, before terror woke up in my breast as sudden and startling as the crash of cymbals; and bounding from my bed, I rushed to the mirror. At the sight that met my eyes, my blood was changed into something exquisitely thin and icy. Yes, I had gone to bed Henry Jekyll, I had awakened Edward Hyde. How was this to be explained? I asked myself, and then, with another bound of terror—how was it to be remedied? It was well on in the morning; the servants were up; all my drugs were in the cabinet—a long journey down two pairs of stairs, through the back passage, across the open court and through the anatomical theatre, from where I was then standing horror-struck. It might indeed be possible to cover my face; but of what use was that, when I was unable to conceal the alteration in my stature? And then with an overpowering sweetness of relief, it came back upon my mind that the servants were already used to the coming and going of my second self. I had soon dressed, as well as I was able, in clothes of my own size: had soon passed through the house, where Bradshaw stared and drew back at seeing Mr. Hyde at such an hour and in such a strange array; and ten minutes later, Dr. Jekyll had returned to his own shape and was sitting down, with a darkened brow, to make a feint of breakfasting.

Small indeed was my appetite. This inexplicable incident, this reversal of my previous experience, seemed, like the Babylonian finger on the wall, to be spelling out the letters of my judgment; and I began to reflect more seriously than ever before on the issues and possibilities of my double existence. That part of me which I had the power of projecting, had lately been much exercised and nourished; it had seemed to me of late as though the body of Edward Hyde had grown in stature, as though (when I wore that form) I were conscious of a more generous tide of blood; and I began to spy a danger that, if this were much prolonged, the balance of my nature might be permanently overthrown, the power of voluntary change be forfeited, and the character of Edward Hyde become irrevocably mine. The power of the drug had not been always equally displayed. Once, very early in my career, it had totally failed me; since then I had been obliged on more than one occasion to double, and once, with infinite risk of death, to treble the amount; and these rare uncertainties had cast hitherto the sole shadow on my contentment. Now, however, and in the light of that morning's accident, I was led to remark that whereas, in the beginning, the difficulty had been to throw off the body of Jekyll, it had of late gradually but decidedly transferred itself to the other side. All things therefore seemed to point to this: that I was slowly losing hold of my original and better self, and becoming slowly incorporated with my second and worse.

Between these two, I now felt I had to choose. My two natures had memory in common, but all other faculties were most unequally shared between them. Jekyll (who was composite) now with the most sensitive apprehensions, now with a greedy gusto, projected and shared in the pleasures and adventures of Hyde; but Hyde was indifferent to Jekyll, or but remembered him as the mountain bandit remembers the cavern in which he conceals himself from pursuit. Jekyll had more than a father's interest; Hyde had more than a son's indifference. To cast in my lot with Jekyll, was to die to those appetites which I had long secretly indulged and had of late begun to pamper. To cast it in with Hyde, was to die to a thousand interests and aspirations, and to become, at a blow and forever, despised and friendless. The bargain might appear unequal; but there was still another consideration in the scales; for while Jekyll would suffer smartingly in the fires of abstinence, Hyde would be not even conscious of all that he had lost. Strange as my circumstances were, the terms of this debate are as old and commonplace as man; much the same inducements and alarms cast the die for any tempted and trembling sinner; and it fell out with me, as it falls with so vast a majority of my fellows, that I chose the better part and was found wanting in the strength to keep to it.

Yes, I preferred the elderly and discontented doctor, surrounded by friends and cherishing honest hopes; and bade a resolute farewell to the liberty, the comparative youth, the light step, leaping impulses and secret pleasures, that I had enjoyed in the disguise of Hyde. I made this choice perhaps with some unconscious reservation, for I neither gave up the house in Soho, nor destroyed the clothes of Edward Hyde, which still lay ready in my cabinet. For two months, however, I was true to my determination; for two months I led a life of such severity as I had never before attained to, and enjoyed the compensations of an approving conscience. But time began at last to obliterate the freshness of my alarm; the praises of conscience began to grow into a thing of course; I began to be tortured with throes and longings, as of Hyde struggling after freedom; and at last, in an hour of moral weakness, I once again compounded and swallowed the transforming draught.

I do not suppose that, when a drunkard reasons with himself upon his vice, he is once out of five hundred times affected by the dangers that he runs through his brutish, physical insensibility; neither had I, long as I had considered my position, made enough allowance for the complete moral insensibility and insensate readiness to evil, which were the leading characters of Edward Hyde. Yet it was by these that I was punished. My devil had been long caged, he came out roaring. I was conscious, even when I took the draught, of a more unbridled, a more furious propensity to ill. It must have been this, I suppose, that stirred in my soul that tempest of impatience with which I listened to the civilities of my unhappy victim; I declare, at least, before God, no man morally sane could have been guilty of that crime upon so pitiful a provocation; and that I struck in no more reasonable spirit than that in which a sick child may break a plaything. But I had voluntarily stripped myself of all those balancing instincts by which even the worst of us continues to walk with some degree of steadiness among temptations; and in my case, to be tempted, however slightly, was to fall.

Instantly the spirit of hell awoke in me and raged. With a transport of glee, I mauled the unresisting body, tasting delight from every blow; and it was not till weariness had begun to succeed, that I was suddenly, in the top fit of my delirium, struck through the heart by a cold thrill of terror. A mist dispersed; I saw my life to be forfeit; and fled from the scene of these excesses, at once glorying and trembling, my lust of evil gratified and stimulated, my love of life screwed to the topmost peg. I ran to the house in Soho, and (to make assurance doubly sure) destroyed my papers; thence I set out through the lamplit streets, in the same divided ecstasy of mind, gloating on my crime, light-headedly devising others in the future, and yet still hastening and still hearkening in my wake for the steps of the avenger. Hyde had a song upon his lips as he compounded the draught, and as he drank it, pledged the dead man. The pangs of transformation had not done tearing him, before Henry Jekyll, with streaming tears of gratitude and remorse, had fallen upon his knees and lifted his clasped hands to God. The veil of self-indulgence was rent from head to foot, I saw my life as a whole: I followed it up from the days of childhood, when I had walked with my father's hand, and through the self-denying toils of my professional life, to arrive again and again, with the same sense of unreality, at the damned horrors of the evening. I could have screamed aloud; I sought with tears and prayers to smother down the crowd of hideous images and sounds with which my memory swarmed against me; and still, between the petitions, the ugly face of my iniquity stared into my soul. As the acuteness of this remorse began to die away, it was succeeded by a sense of joy. The problem of my conduct was solved. Hyde was thenceforth impossible; whether I would or not, I was now confined to the better part of my existence; and oh, how I rejoiced to think it! with what willing humility, I embraced anew the restrictions of natural life! with what sincere renunciation, I locked the door by which I had so often gone and come, and ground the key under my heel!

The next day, came the news that the murder had been overlooked, that the guilt of Hyde was patent to the world, and that the victim was a man high in public estimation. It was not only a crime, it had been a tragic folly. I think I was glad to know it; I think I was glad to have my better impulses thus buttressed and guarded by the terrors of the scaffold. Jekyll was now my city of refuge; let but Hyde peep out an instant, and the hands of all men would be raised to take and slay him.

I resolved in my future conduct to redeem the past; and I can say with honesty that my resolve was fruitful of some good. You know yourself how earnestly in the last months of last year, I laboured to relieve suffering; you know that much was done for others, and that the days passed quietly, almost happily for myself. Nor can I truly say that I wearied of this beneficent and innocent life; I think instead that I daily enjoyed it more completely; but I was still cursed with my duality of purpose; and as the first edge of my penitence wore off, the lower side of me, so long indulged, so recently chained down, began to growl for licence. Not that I dreamed of resuscitating Hyde; the bare idea of that would startle me to frenzy: no, it was in my own person, that I was once more tempted to trifle with my conscience; and it was as an ordinary secret sinner, that I at last fell before the assaults of temptation.

There comes an end to all things; the most capacious measure is filled at last; and this brief condescension to evil finally destroyed the balance of my soul. And yet I was not alarmed; the fall seemed natural, like a return to the old days before I had made discovery. It was a fine, clear, January day, wet under foot where the frost had melted, but cloudless overhead; and the Regent's Park was full of winter chirrupings and sweet with spring odours. I sat in the sun on a bench; the animal within me licking the chops of memory; the spiritual side a little drowsed, promising subsequent penitence, but not yet moved to begin. After all, I reflected, I was like my neighbours; and then I smiled, comparing myself with other men, comparing my active good will with the lazy cruelty of their neglect. And at the very moment of that vainglorious thought, a qualm came over me, a horrid nausea and the most deadly shuddering. These passed away, and left me faint; and then as in its turn the faintness subsided, I began to be aware of a change in the temper of my thoughts, a greater boldness, a contempt of danger, a solution of the bonds of obligation. I looked down; my clothes hung formlessly on my shrunken limbs; the hand that lay on my knee was corded and hairy. I was once more Edward Hyde. A moment before I had been safe of all men's respect, wealthy, beloved—the cloth laying for me in the dining-room at home; and now I was the common quarry of mankind, hunted, houseless, a known murderer, thrall to the gallows.

My reason wavered, but it did not fail me utterly. I have more than once observed that, in my second character, my faculties seemed sharpened to a point and my spirits more tensely elastic; thus it came about that, where Jekyll perhaps might have succumbed, Hyde rose to the importance of the moment. My drugs were in one of the presses of my cabinet; how was I to reach them? That was the problem that (crushing my temples in my hands) I set myself to solve. The laboratory door I had closed. If I sought to enter by the house, my own servants would consign me to the gallows. I saw I must employ another hand, and thought of Lanyon. How was he to be reached? how persuaded? Supposing that I escaped capture in the streets, how was I to make my way into his presence? and how should I, an unknown and displeasing visitor, prevail on the famous physician to rifle the study of his colleague, Dr. Jekyll? Then I remembered that of my original character, one part remained to me: I could write my own hand; and once I had conceived that kindling spark, the way that I must follow became lighted up from end to end.

Thereupon, I arranged my clothes as best I could, and summoning a passing hansom, drove to an hotel in Portland Street, the name of which I chanced to remember. At my appearance (which was indeed comical enough, however tragic a fate these garments covered) the driver could not conceal his mirth. I gnashed my teeth upon him with a gust of devilish fury; and the smile withered from his face—happily for him—yet more happily for myself, for in another instant I had certainly dragged him from his perch. At the inn, as I entered, I looked about me with so black a countenance as made the attendants tremble; not a look did they exchange in my presence; but obsequiously took my orders, led me to a private room, and brought me wherewithal to write. Hyde in danger of his life was a creature new to me; shaken with inordinate anger, strung to the pitch of murder, lusting to inflict pain. Yet the creature was astute; mastered his fury with a great effort of the will; composed his two important letters, one to Lanyon and one to Poole; and that he might receive actual evidence of their being posted, sent them out with directions that they should be registered.

Thenceforward, he sat all day over the fire in the private room, gnawing his nails; there he dined, sitting alone with his fears, the waiter visibly quailing before his eye; and thence, when the night was fully come, he set forth in the corner of a closed cab, and was driven to and fro about the streets of the city. He, I say—I cannot say, I. That child of Hell had nothing human; nothing lived in him but fear and hatred. And when at last, thinking the driver had begun to grow suspicious, he discharged the cab and ventured on foot, attired in his misfitting clothes, an object marked out for observation, into the midst of the nocturnal passengers, these two base passions raged within him like a tempest. He walked fast, hunted by his fears, chattering to himself, skulking through the less-frequented thoroughfares, counting the minutes that still divided him from midnight. Once a woman spoke to him, offering, I think, a box of lights. He smote her in the face, and she fled.

When I came to myself at Lanyon's, the horror of my old friend perhaps affected me somewhat: I do not know; it was at least but a drop in the sea to the abhorrence with which I looked back upon these hours. A change had come over me. It was no longer the fear of the gallows, it was the horror of being Hyde that racked me. I received Lanyon's condemnation partly in a dream; it was partly in a dream that I came home to my own house and got into bed. I slept after the prostration of the day, with a stringent and profound slumber which not even the nightmares that wrung me could avail to break. I awoke in the morning shaken, weakened, but refreshed. I still hated and feared the thought of the brute that slept within me, and I had not of course forgotten the appalling dangers of the day before; but I was once more at home, in my own house and close to my drugs; and gratitude for my escape shone so strong in my soul that it almost rivalled the brightness of hope.

I was stepping leisurely across the court after breakfast, drinking the chill of the air with pleasure, when I was seized again with those indescribable sensations that heralded the change; and I had but the time to gain the shelter of my cabinet, before I was once again raging and freezing with the passions of Hyde. It took on this occasion a double dose to recall me to myself; and alas! Six hours after, as I sat looking sadly in the fire, the pangs returned, and the drug had to be readministered. In short, from that day forth it seemed only by a great effort as of gymnastics, and only under the immediate stimulation of the drug, that I was able to wear the countenance of Jekyll. At all hours of the day and night, I would be taken with the premonitory shudder; above all, if I slept, or even dozed for a moment in my chair, it was always as Hyde that I awakened. Under the strain of this continually-impending doom and by the sleeplessness to which I now condemned myself, ay, even beyond what I had thought possible to man, I became, in my own person, a creature eaten up and emptied by fever, languidly weak both in body and mind, and solely occupied by one thought: the horror of my other self. But when I slept, or when the virtue of the medicine wore off, I would leap almost without transition (for the pangs of transformation grew daily less marked) into the possession of a fancy brimming with images of terror, a soul boiling with causeless hatreds, and a body that seemed not strong enough to contain the raging energies of life. The powers of Hyde seemed to have grown with the sickliness of Jekyll. And certainly the hate that now divided them was equal on each side. With Jekyll, it was a thing of vital instinct. He had now seen the full deformity of that creature that shared with him some of the phenomena of consciousness, and was co-heir with him to death: and beyond these links of community, which in themselves made the most poignant part of his distress, he thought of Hyde, for all his energy of life, as of something not only hellish but inorganic. This was the shocking thing; that the slime of the pit seemed to utter cries and voices; that the amorphous dust gesticulated and sinned; that what was dead, and had no shape, should usurp the offices of life. And this again, that that insurgent horror was knit to him closer than a wife, closer than an eye; lay caged in his flesh, where he heard it mutter and felt it struggle to be born; and at every hour of weakness, and in the confidence of slumber, prevailed against him and deposed him out of life. The hatred of Hyde for Jekyll, was of a different order. His terror of the gallows drove him continually to commit temporary suicide, and return to his subordinate station of a part instead of a person; but he loathed the necessity, he loathed the despondency into which Jekyll was now fallen, and he resented the dislike with which he was himself regarded. Hence the apelike tricks that he would play me, scrawling in my own hand blasphemies on the pages of my books, burning the letters and destroying the portrait of my father; and indeed, had it not been for his fear of death, he would long ago have ruined himself in order to involve me in the ruin. But his love of life is wonderful; I go further: I, who sicken and freeze at the mere thought of him, when I recall the abjection and passion of this attachment, and when I know how he fears my power to cut him off by suicide, I find it in my heart to pity him.

It is useless, and the time awfully fails me, to prolong this description; no one has ever suffered such torments, let that suffice; and yet even to these, habit brought—no, not alleviation—but a certain callousness of soul, a certain acquiescence of despair; and my punishment might have gone on for years, but for the last calamity which has now fallen, and which has finally severed me from my own face and nature. My provision of the salt, which had never been renewed since the date of the first experiment, began to run low. I sent out for a fresh supply, and mixed the draught; the ebullition followed, and the first change of colour, not the second; I drank it and it was without efficiency. You will learn from Poole how I have had London ransacked; it was in vain; and I am now persuaded that my first supply was impure, and that it was that unknown impurity which lent efficacy to the draught.

About a week has passed, and I am now finishing this statement under the influence of the last of the old powders. This, then, is the last time, short of a miracle, that Henry Jekyll can think his own thoughts or see his own face (now how sadly altered!) in the glass. Nor must I delay too long to bring my writing to an end; for if my narrative has hitherto escaped destruction, it has been by a combination of great prudence and great good luck. Should the throes of change take me in the act of writing it, Hyde will tear it in pieces; but if some time shall have elapsed after I have laid it by, his wonderful selfishness and circumscription to the moment will probably save it once again from the action of his apelike spite. And indeed the doom that is closing on us both, has already changed and crushed him. Half-an-hour from now, when I shall again and for ever reindue that hated personality, I know how I shall sit shuddering and weeping in my chair, or continue, with the most strained and fear-struck ecstasy of listening, to pace up and down this room (my last earthly refuge) and give ear to every sound of menace. Will Hyde die upon the scaffold? or will he find courage to release himself at the last moment? God knows; I am careless; this is my true hour of death, and what is to follow concerns another than myself. Here then, as I lay down the pen and proceed to seal up my confession, I bring the life of that unhappy Henry Jekyll to an end.

# THE SUICIDE CLUB

## Story of the Young Man
## with the Cream Tarts

During his residence in London, the accomplished Prince Florizel of Bohemia gained the affection of all classes by the seduction of his manner and by a well-considered generosity. He was a remarkable man even by what was known of him; and that was but a small part of what he actually did. Although of a placid temper in ordinary circumstances, and accustomed to take the world with as much philosophy as any ploughman, the Prince of Bohemia was not without a taste for ways of life more adventurous and eccentric than that to which he was destined by his birth. Now and then, when he fell into a low humour, when there was no laughable play to witness in any of the London theatres, and when the season of the year was unsuitable to those field sports in which he excelled all competitors, he would summon his confidant and Master of the Horse, Colonel Geraldine, and bid him prepare himself against an evening ramble. The Master of the Horse was a young officer of a brave and even temerarious disposition. He greeted the news with delight, and hastened to make ready. Long practice and a varied acquaintance of life had given him a singular facility in disguise; he could adapt not only his face and bearing, but his voice and almost his thoughts, to those of any rank, character, or nation; and in this way he diverted attention from the Prince, and sometimes gained admission for the pair into strange societies. The civil authorities were never taken into the secret of these adventures; the imperturbable courage of the one and the ready invention and chivalrous devotion of the other had brought them through a score of dangerous passes; and they grew in confidence as time went on.

One evening in March they were driven by a sharp fall of sleet into an Oyster Bar in the immediate neighbourhood of Leicester Square. Colonel Geraldine was dressed and painted to represent a person connected with the Press in reduced circumstances; while the Prince had, as usual, travestied his appearance by the addition of false whiskers and a pair of large adhesive eyebrows.

These lent him a shaggy and weather-beaten air, which, for one of his urbanity, formed the most impenetrable disguise. Thus equipped, the commander and his satellite sipped their brandy and soda in security.

The bar was full of guests, male and female; but though more than one of these offered to fall into talk with our adventurers, none of them promised to grow interesting upon a nearer acquaintance. There was nothing present but the lees of London and the commonplace of disrespectability; and the Prince had already fallen to yawning, and was beginning to grow weary of the whole excursion, when the swing doors were pushed violently open, and a young man, followed by a couple of commissionaires, entered the bar. Each of the commissionaires carried a large dish of cream tarts under a cover, which they at once removed; and the young man made the round of the company, and pressed these confections upon every one's acceptance with an exaggerated courtesy. Sometimes his offer was laughingly accepted; sometimes it was firmly, or even harshly, rejected. In these latter cases the new-comer always ate the tart himself, with some more or less humorous commentary.

At last he accosted Prince Florizel.

"Sir," said he, with a profound obeisance, proffering the tart at the same time between his thumb and forefinger, "will you so far honour an entire stranger? I can answer for the quality of the pastry, having eaten two dozen and three of them myself since five o'clock."

"I am in the habit," replied the Prince, "of looking not so much to the nature of a gift as to the spirit in which it is offered."

"The spirit, sir," returned the young man, with another bow, "is one of mockery."

"Mockery?" repeated Florizel. "And whom do you propose to mock?"

"I am not here to expound my philosophy," replied the other, "but to distribute these cream tarts. If I mention that I heartily include myself in the ridicule of the transaction, I hope you will consider honour satisfied and condescend. If not, you will constrain me to eat my twenty-eighth, and I own to being weary of the exercise."

"You touch me," said the Prince, "and I have all the will in the world to rescue you from this dilemma, but upon one condition. If my friend and I eat your cakes—for which we have neither of us any natural inclination—we shall expect you to join us at supper by way of recompense."

The young man seemed to reflect.

"I have still several dozen upon hand," he said at last; "and that will make it necessary for me to visit several more bars before my great affair is concluded. This will take some time; and if you are hungry—"

The Prince interrupted him with a polite gesture.

"My friend and I will accompany you," he said; "for we have already a deep interest in your very agreeable mode of passing an evening. And now that the preliminaries of peace are settled, allow me to sign the treaty for both."

And the Prince swallowed the tart with the best grace imaginable.

"It is delicious," said he.

"I perceive you are a connoisseur," replied the young man.

Colonel Geraldine likewise did honour to the pastry; and every one in that bar having now either accepted or refused his delicacies, the young man with the cream tarts led the way to another and similar establishment. The two commissionaires, who seemed to have grown accustomed to their absurd employment, followed immediately after; and the Prince and the Colonel brought up the rear, arm in arm, and smiling to each other as they went. In this order the company visited two other taverns, where scenes were enacted of a like nature to that already described— some refusing, some accepting, the favours of this vagabond hospitality, and the young man himself eating each rejected tart.

On leaving the third saloon the young man counted his store. There were but nine remaining, three in one tray and six in the other.

"Gentlemen," said he, addressing himself to his two new followers, "I am unwilling to delay your supper. I am positively sure you must be hungry. I feel that I owe you a special consideration. And on this great day for me, when I am closing a career of folly by my most conspicuously silly action, I wish to behave handsomely to all who give me countenance. Gentlemen, you shall wait no longer. Although my constitution is shattered by previous excesses, at the risk of my life I liquidate the suspensory condition."

With these words he crushed the nine remaining tarts into his mouth, and swallowed them at a single movement each. Then, turning to the commissionaires, he gave them a couple of sovereigns.

"I have to thank you," said he, "for your extraordinary patience."

And he dismissed them with a bow apiece. For some seconds he stood looking at the purse from which he had just paid his assistants, then, with a laugh, he tossed it into the middle of the street, and signified his readiness for supper.

In a small French restaurant in Soho, which had enjoyed an exaggerated reputation for some little while, but had already begun to be forgotten, and in a private room up two pair of stairs, the three companions made a very elegant supper, and drank three or four bottles of champagne, talking the while upon indifferent subjects. The young man was fluent and gay, but he laughed louder than was natural in a person of polite breeding; his hands trembled violently, and his voice took sudden and surprising inflections, which seemed to be independent of his will. The dessert had been cleared away, and all three had lighted their cigars, when the Prince addressed him in these words:—

"You will, I am sure, pardon my curiosity. What I have seen of you has greatly pleased but even more puzzled me. And though I should be loth to seem indiscreet, I must tell you that my friend and I are persons very well worthy to be entrusted with a secret. We have many of our own, which we are continually revealing to improper ears. And if, as I suppose, your story is a silly one, you need have no delicacy with us, who are two of the silliest men in England. My name is Godall, Theophilus Godall; my friend is Major Alfred Hammersmith—or at least, such is the name by which he chooses to be known. We pass our lives entirely in the search for extravagant adventures; and there is no extravagance with which we are not capable of sympathy."

"I like you, Mr. Godall," returned the young man; "you

inspire me with a natural confidence; and I have not the slightest objection to your friend the Major, whom I take to be a nobleman in masquerade. At least, I am sure he is no soldier."

The Colonel smiled at this compliment to the perfection of his art; and the young man went on in a more animated manner.

"There is every reason why I should not tell you my story. Perhaps that is just the reason why I am going to do so. At least, you seem so well prepared to hear a tale of silliness that I cannot find it in my heart to disappoint you. My name, in spite of your example, I shall keep to myself. My age is not essential to the narrative. I am descended from my ancestors by ordinary generation, and from them I inherited the very eligible human tenement which I still occupy and a fortune of three hundred pounds a year. I suppose they also handed on to me a hare-brain humour, which it has been my chief delight to indulge. I received a good education. I can play the violin nearly well enough to earn money in the orchestra of a penny gaff, but not quite. The same remark applies to the flute and the French horn. I learned enough of whist to lose about a hundred a year at that scientific game. My acquaintance with French was sufficient to enable me to squander money in Paris with almost the same facility as in London. In short, I am a person full of manly accomplishments. I have had every sort of adventure, including a duel about nothing. Only two months ago I met a young lady exactly suited to my taste in mind and body; I found my heart melt; I saw that I had come upon my fate at last, and was in the way to fall in love. But when I came to reckon up what remained to me of my capital, I found it amounted to something less than four hundred pounds! I ask you fairly—can a man who respects himself fall in love on four hundred pounds? I concluded, certainly not; left the presence of my charmer, and slightly accelerating my usual rate of expenditure, came this morning to my last eighty pounds. This I divided into two equal parts; forty I reserved for a particular purpose; the remaining forty I was to dissipate before the night. I have passed a very entertaining day, and played many farces besides that of the cream tarts which procured me the advantage of your acquaintance; for I was determined, as I told you, to bring a foolish career to a still more foolish conclusion; and when you saw me throw my purse into the street, the forty pounds were at an end. Now you know me as well as I know myself: a fool, but consistent in his folly; and, as I will ask you to believe, neither a whimperer nor a coward."

From the whole tone of the young man's statement it was plain that he harboured very bitter and contemptuous thoughts about himself. His auditors were led to imagine that his love affair was nearer his heart than he admitted, and that he had a design on his own life. The farce of the cream tarts began to have very much the air of a tragedy in disguise.

"Why, is this not odd," broke out Geraldine, giving a look to Prince Florizel, "that we three fellows should have met by the merest accident in so large a wilderness as London, and should be so nearly in the same condition?"

"How?" cried the young man. "Are you, too, ruined? Is this supper a folly like my cream tarts? Has the devil brought three of his own together for a last carouse?"

"The devil, depend upon it, can sometimes do a very gentlemanly thing," returned Prince Florizel; "and I am so much touched by this coincidence, that, although we are not entirely in the same case, I am going to put an end to the disparity. Let your heroic treatment of the last cream tarts be my example."

So saying, the Prince drew out his purse and took from it a small bundle of bank-notes.

"You see, I was a week or so behind you, but I mean to catch you up and come neck and neck into the winning-post," he continued. "This," laying one of the notes upon the table, "will suffice for the bill. As for the rest—"

He tossed them into the fire, and they went up the chimney in a single blaze.

The young man tried to catch his arm, but as the table was between them his interference came too late.

"Unhappy man," he cried, "you should not have burned them all! You should have kept forty pounds."

"Forty pounds!" repeated the Prince. "Why, in heaven's name, forty pounds?"

"Why not eighty?" cried the Colonel; "for to my certain knowledge there must have been a hundred in the bundle."

"It was only forty pounds he needed," said the young man gloomily. "But without them there is no admission. The rule is strict. Forty pounds for each. Accursed life, where a man cannot even die without money!"

The Prince and the Colonel exchanged glances. "Explain yourself," said the latter. "I have still a pocket-book tolerably well lined, and I need not say how readily I should share my wealth with Godall. But I must know to what end: you must certainly tell us what you mean."

The young man seemed to awaken; he looked uneasily from one to the other, and his face flushed deeply.

"You are not fooling me?" he asked. "You are indeed ruined men like me?"

"Indeed, I am for my part," replied the Colonel.

"And for mine," said the Prince, "I have given you proof. Who but a ruined man would throw his notes into the fire? The action speaks for itself."

"A ruined man—yes," returned the other suspiciously, "or else a millionaire."

"Enough, sir," said the Prince; "I have said so, and I am not accustomed to have my word remain in doubt."

"Ruined?" said the young man. "Are you ruined, like me? Are you, after a life of indulgence, come to such a pass that you can only indulge yourself in one thing more? Are you"— he kept lowering his voice as he went on—"are you going to give yourselves that last indulgence? Are you going to avoid the consequences of your folly by the one infallible and easy path? Are you going to give the slip to the sheriff's officers of conscience by the one open door?"

Suddenly he broke off and attempted to laugh.

"Here is your health!" he cried, emptying his glass, "and good night to you, my merry ruined men."

Colonel Geraldine caught him by the arm as he was about to rise.

"You lack confidence in us," he said, "and you are wrong. To all your questions I make answer in the affirmative. But I am not so timid, and can speak the Queen's English plainly. We too, like yourself, have had enough of life, and are determined to die.

Sooner or later, alone or together, we meant to seek out death and beard him where he lies ready. Since we have met you, and your case is more pressing, let it be to-night—and at once—and, if you will, all three together. Such a penniless trio," he cried, "should go arm in arm into the halls of Pluto, and give each other some countenance among the shades!"

Geraldine had hit exactly on the manners and intonations that became the part he was playing. The Prince himself was disturbed, and looked over at his confidant with a shade of doubt. As for the young man, the flush came back darkly into his cheek, and his eyes threw out a spark of light.

"You are the men for me!" he cried, with an almost terrible gaiety. "Shake hands upon the bargain!" (his hand was cold and wet). "You little know in what a company you will begin the march! You little know in what a happy moment for yourselves you partook of my cream tarts! I am only a unit, but I am a unit in an army. I know Death's private door. I am one of his familiars, and can show you into eternity without ceremony and yet without scandal."

They called upon him eagerly to explain his meaning.

"Can you muster eighty pounds between you?" he demanded.

Geraldine ostentatiously consulted his pocket-book, and replied in the affirmative.

"Fortunate beings!" cried the young man. "Forty pounds is the entry money of the Suicide Club."

"The Suicide Club," said the Prince, "why, what the devil is that?"

"Listen," said the young man; "this is the age of conveniences, and I have to tell you of the last perfection of the sort. We have affairs in different places; and hence railways were invented. Railways separated us infallibly from our friends; and so telegraphs were made that we might communicate speedier at great distances. Even in hotels we have lifts to spare us a climb of some hundred steps. Now, we know that life is only a stage to play the fool upon as long as the part amuses us. There was one more convenience lacking to modern comfort; a decent, easy way to quit that stage; the back stairs to liberty; or, as I said this moment, Death's private door. This, my two fellow-rebels, is supplied by the Suicide Club. Do not suppose that you and I are alone, or even exceptional in the highly reasonable desire that we profess. A large number of our fellowmen, who have grown heartily sick of the performance in which they are expected to join daily and all their lives long, are only kept from flight by one or two considerations. Some have families who would be shocked, or even blamed, if the matter became public; others have a weakness at heart and recoil from the circumstances of death. That is, to some extent, my own experience. I cannot put a pistol to my head and draw the trigger; for something stronger than myself withholds the act; and although I loathe life, I have not strength enough in my body to take hold of death and be done with it. For such as I, and for all who desire to be out of the coil without posthumous scandal, the Suicide Club has been inaugurated. How this has been managed, what is its history, or what may be its ramifications in other lands, I am myself uninformed; and what I know of its constitution, I am not at liberty to communicate to you. To this extent, however, I am at your service. If you are truly tired of life, I will introduce you to-night to a meeting; and if not to-night, at least some time within the week, you will be easily relieved of your existences. It is now (consulting his watch) eleven; by half-past, at latest, we must leave this place; so that you have half-an-hour before you to consider my proposal. It is more serious than a cream tart," he added, with a smile; "and I suspect more palatable."

"More serious, certainly," returned Colonel Geraldine; "and as it is so much more so, will you allow me five minutes' speech in private with my friend, Mr. Godall?"

"It is only fair," answered the young man. "If you will permit, I will retire."

"You will be very obliging," said the Colonel.

As soon as the two were alone—"What," said Prince Florizel, "is the use of this confabulation, Geraldine? I see you are flurried, whereas my mind is very tranquilly made up. I will see the end of this."

"Your Highness," said the Colonel, turning pale; "let me ask you to consider the importance of your life, not only to your friends, but to the public interest. 'If not to-night,' said this madman; but supposing that to-night some irreparable disaster were to overtake your Highness's person, what, let me ask you, what would be my despair, and what the concern and disaster of a great nation?"

"I will see the end of this," repeated the Prince in his most deliberate tones; "and have the kindness, Colonel Geraldine, to remember and respect your word of honour as a gentleman. Under no circumstances, recollect, nor without my special authority, are you to betray the incognito under which I choose to go abroad. These were my commands, which I now reiterate. And now," he added, "let me ask you to call for the bill."

Colonel Geraldine bowed in submission; but he had a very white face as he summoned the young man of the cream tarts, and issued his directions to the waiter. The Prince preserved his undisturbed demeanour, and described a Palais Royal farce to the young suicide with great humour and gusto. He avoided the Colonel's appealing looks without ostentation, and selected another cheroot with more than usual care. Indeed, he was now the only man of the party who kept any command over his nerves.

The bill was discharged, the Prince giving the whole change of the note to the astonished waiter; and the three drove off in a four-wheeler. They were not long upon the way before the cab stopped at the entrance to a rather dark court. Here all descended.

After Geraldine had paid the fare, the young man turned, and addressed Prince Florizel as follows:—

"It is still time, Mr. Godall, to make good your escape into thraldom. And for you too, Major Hammersmith. Reflect well before you take another step; and if your hearts say no—here are the cross-roads."

"Lead on, sir," said the Prince. "I am not the man to go back from a thing once said."

"Your coolness does me good," replied their guide. "I have never seen any one so unmoved at this conjuncture; and yet you are not the first whom I have escorted to this door. More than one of my friends has preceded me, where I knew I must shortly follow. But this is of no interest to you. Wait me here for only a few moments; I shall return as soon as I have arranged the preliminaries of your introduction."

And with that the young man, waving his hand to his companions, turned into the court, entered a doorway and disappeared.

"Of all our follies," said Colonel Geraldine in a low voice, "this is the wildest and most dangerous."

"I perfectly believe so," returned the Prince.

"We have still," pursued the Colonel, "a moment to ourselves. Let me beseech your Highness to profit by the opportunity and retire. The consequences of this step are so dark, and may be so grave, that I feel myself justified in pushing a little farther than usual the liberty which your Highness is so condescending as to allow me in private."

"Am I to understand that Colonel Geraldine is afraid?" asked his Highness, taking his cheroot from his lips, and looking keenly into the other's face.

"My fear is certainly not personal," replied the other proudly; "of that your Highness may rest well assured."

"I had supposed as much," returned the Prince, with undisturbed good humour; "but I was unwilling to remind you of the difference in our stations. No more—no more," he added, seeing Geraldine about to apologise, "you stand excused."

And he smoked placidly, leaning against a railing, until the young man returned.

"Well," he asked, "has our reception been arranged?"

"Follow me," was the reply. "The President will see you in the cabinet. And let me warn you to be frank in your answers. I have stood your guarantee; but the club requires a searching inquiry before admission; for the indiscretion of a single member would lead to the dispersion of the whole society for ever."

The Prince and Geraldine put their heads together for a moment. "Bear me out in this," said the one; and "bear me out in that," said the other; and by boldly taking up the characters of men with whom both were acquainted, they had come to an agreement in a twinkling, and were ready to follow their guide into the President's cabinet.

There were no formidable obstacles to pass. The outer door stood open; the door of the cabinet was ajar; and there, in a small but very high apartment, the young man left them once more.

"He will be here immediately," he said, with a nod, as he disappeared.

Voices were audible in the cabinet through the folding doors which formed one end; and now and then the noise of a champagne cork, followed by a burst of laughter, intervened among the sounds of conversation. A single tall window looked out upon the river and the embankment; and by the disposition of the lights they judged themselves not far from Charing Cross station. The furniture was scanty, and the coverings worn to the thread; and there was nothing movable except a hand-bell in the centre of a round table, and the hats and coats of a considerable party hung round the wall on pegs.

"What sort of a den is this?" said Geraldine.

"That is what I have come to see," replied the Prince. "If they keep live devils on the premises, the thing may grow amusing."

Just then the folding door was opened no more than was necessary for the passage of a human body; and there entered at the same moment a louder buzz of talk, and the redoubtable President of the Suicide Club. The President was a man of fifty or upwards; large and rambling in his gait, with shaggy side whiskers, a bald top to his head, and a veiled grey eye, which now and then emitted a twinkle. His mouth, which embraced a large cigar, he kept continually screwing round and round and from side to side, as he looked sagaciously and coldly at the strangers. He was dressed in light tweeds, with his neck very open in a striped shirt collar; and carried a minute book under one arm.

"Good evening," said he, after he had closed the door behind him. "I am told you wish to speak with me."

"We have a desire, sir, to join the Suicide Club," replied the Colonel.

The President rolled his cigar about in his mouth. "What is that?" he said abruptly.

"Pardon me," returned the Colonel, "but I believe you are the person best qualified to give us information on that point."

"I?" cried the President. "A Suicide Club? Come, come! this is a frolic for All Fools' Day. I can make allowances for gentlemen who get merry in their liquor; but let there be an end to this."

"Call your Club what you will," said the Colonel, "you have some company behind these doors, and we insist on joining it."

"Sir," returned the President curtly, "you have made a mistake. This is a private house, and you must leave it instantly."

The Prince had remained quietly in his seat throughout this little colloquy; but now, when the Colonel looked over to him, as much as to say, "Take your answer and come away, for God's sake!" he drew his cheroot from his mouth, and spoke—

"I have come here," said he, "upon the invitation of a friend of yours. He has doubtless informed you of my intention in thus intruding on your party. Let me remind you that a person in my circumstances has exceedingly little to bind him, and is not at all likely to tolerate much rudeness. I am a very quiet man, as a usual thing; but, my dear sir, you are either going to oblige me in the little matter of which you are aware, or you shall very bitterly repent that you ever admitted me to your ante-chamber."

The President laughed aloud.

"That is the way to speak," said he. "You are a man who is a man. You know the way to my heart, and can do what you like with me. Will you," he continued, addressing Geraldine, "will you step aside for a few minutes? I shall finish first with your companion, and some of the club's formalities require to be fulfilled in private."

With these words he opened the door of a small closet, into which he shut the Colonel.

"I believe in you," he said to Florizel, as soon as they were alone; "but are you sure of your friend?"

"Not so sure as I am of myself, though he has more cogent reasons," answered Florizel, "but sure enough to bring him here without alarm. He has had enough to cure the most tenacious man of life. He was cashiered the other day for cheating at cards."

"A good reason, I daresay," replied the President; "at least, we have another in the same case, and I feel sure of him. Have you also been in the Service, may I ask?"

"I have," was the reply; "but I was too lazy, I left it early."

"What is your reason for being tired of life?" pursued the President.

"The same, as near as I can make out," answered the Prince; "unadulterated laziness."

The President started. "D——n it," said he, "you must have something better than that."

"I have no more money," added Florizel. "That is also a vexation, without doubt. It brings my sense of idleness to an acute point."

The President rolled his cigar round in his mouth for some seconds, directing his gaze straight into the eyes of this unusual neophyte; but the Prince supported his scrutiny with unabashed good temper.

"If I had not a deal of experience," said the President at last, "I should turn you off. But I know the world; and this much any way, that the most frivolous excuses for a suicide are often the toughest to stand by. And when I downright like a man, as I do you, sir, I would rather strain the regulation than deny him."

The Prince and the Colonel, one after the other, were subjected to a long and particular interrogatory: the Prince alone; but Geraldine in the presence of the Prince, so that the President might observe the countenance of the one while the other was being warmly cross-examined. The result was satisfactory; and the President, after having booked a few details of each case, produced a form of oath to be accepted. Nothing could be conceived more passive than the obedience promised, or more stringent than the terms by which the juror bound himself. The man who forfeited a pledge so awful could scarcely have a rag of honour or any of the consolations of religion left to him. Florizel signed the document, but not without a shudder; the Colonel followed his example with an air of great depression. Then the President received the entry money; and without more ado, introduced the two friends into the smoking-room of the Suicide Club.

The smoking-room of the Suicide Club was the same height as the cabinet into which it opened, but much larger, and papered from top to bottom with an imitation of oak wainscot. A large and cheerful fire and a number of gas-jets illuminated the company. The Prince and his follower made the number up to eighteen. Most of the party were smoking, and drinking champagne; a feverish hilarity reigned, with sudden and rather ghastly pauses.

"Is this a full meeting?" asked the Prince.

"Middling," said the President. "By the way," he added, "if you have any money, it is usual to offer some champagne. It keeps up a good spirit, and is one of my own little perquisites."

"Hammersmith," said Florizel, "I may leave the champagne to you."

And with that he turned away and began to go round among the guests. Accustomed to play the host in the highest circles, he charmed and dominated all whom he approached; there was something at once winning and authoritative in his address; and his extraordinary coolness gave him yet another distinction in this half maniacal society. As he went from one to another he kept both his eyes and ears open, and soon began to gain a general idea of the people among whom he found himself. As in all other places of resort, one type predominated: people in the prime of youth, with every show of intelligence and sensibility in their appearance, but with little promise of strength or the quality that makes success. Few were much above thirty, and not a few were still in their teens. They stood, leaning on tables and shifting on their feet; sometimes they smoked extraordinarily fast, and sometimes they let their cigars go out; some talked well, but the conversation of others was plainly the result of nervous tension, and was equally without wit or purport. As each new bottle of champagne was opened, there was a manifest improvement in gaiety. Only two were seated—one in a chair in the recess of the window, with his head hanging and his hands plunged deep into his trouser pockets, pale, visibly moist with perspiration, saying never a word, a very wreck of soul and body; the other sat on the divan close by the chimney, and attracted notice by a trenchant dissimilarity from all the rest. He was probably upwards of forty, but he looked fully ten years older; and Florizel thought he had never seen a man more naturally hideous, nor one more ravaged by disease and ruinous excitements. He was no more than skin and bone, was partly paralysed, and wore spectacles of such unusual power, that his eyes appeared through the glasses greatly magnified and distorted in shape. Except the Prince and the President, he was the only person in the room who preserved the composure of ordinary life.

There was little decency among the members of the club. Some boasted of the disgraceful actions, the consequences of which had reduced them to seek refuge in death; and the others listened without disapproval. There was a tacit understanding against moral judgments; and whoever passed the club doors enjoyed already some of the immunities of the tomb. They drank to each other's memories, and to those of notable suicides in the past. They compared and developed their different views of death—some declaring that it was no more than blackness and cessation; others full of a hope that that very night they should be scaling the stars and commencing with the mighty dead.

"To the eternal memory of Baron Trenck, the type of suicides!" cried one. "He went out of a small cell into a smaller, that he might come forth again to freedom."

"For my part," said a second, "I wish no more than a bandage for my eyes and cotton for my ears. Only they have no cotton thick enough in this world."

A third was for reading the mysteries of life in a future state; and a fourth professed that he would never have joined the club, if he had not been induced to believe in Mr. Darwin.

"I could not bear," said this remarkable suicide, "to be descended from an ape."

Altogether, the Prince was disappointed by the bearing and conversation of the members.

"It does not seem to me," he thought, "a matter for so much disturbance. If a man has made up his mind to kill himself, let him do it, in God's name, like a gentleman. This flutter and big talk is out of place."

In the meanwhile Colonel Geraldine was a prey to the blackest apprehensions; the club and its rules were still a mystery, and he looked round the room for some one who should be able to set his mind at rest. In this survey his eye lighted on the paralytic person with the strong spectacles; and seeing him so exceedingly tranquil, he besought the President, who was going in and out of the room under a pressure of business, to present him to the gentleman on the divan.

The functionary explained the needlessness of all such

formalities within the club, but nevertheless presented Mr. Hammersmith to Mr. Malthus.

Mr. Malthus looked at the Colonel curiously, and then requested him to take a seat upon his right.

"You are a new-comer," he said, "and wish information? You have come to the proper source. It is two years since I first visited this charming club."

The Colonel breathed again. If Mr. Malthus had frequented the place for two years there could be little danger for the Prince in a single evening. But Geraldine was none the less astonished, and began to suspect a mystification.

"What!" cried he, "two years! I thought—but indeed I see I have been made the subject of a pleasantry."

"By no means," replied Mr. Malthus mildly. "My case is peculiar. I am not, properly speaking, a suicide at all; but, as it were, an honorary member. I rarely visit the club twice in two months. My infirmity and the kindness of the President have procured me these little immunities, for which besides I pay at an advanced rate. Even as it is my luck has been extraordinary."

"I am afraid," said the Colonel, "that I must ask you to be more explicit. You must remember that I am still most imperfectly acquainted with the rules of the club."

"An ordinary member who comes here in search of death like yourself," replied the paralytic, "returns every evening until fortune favours him. He can even, if he is penniless, get board and lodging from the President: very fair, I believe, and clean, although, of course, not luxurious; that could hardly be, considering the exiguity (if I may so express myself) of the subscription. And then the President's company is a delicacy in itself."

"Indeed!" cried Geraldine, "he had not greatly prepossessed me."

"Ah!" said Mr. Malthus, "you do not know the man: the drollest fellow! What stories! What cynicism! He knows life to admiration and, between ourselves, is probably the most corrupt rogue in Christendom."

"And he also," asked the Colonel, "is a permanency—like yourself, if I may say so without offence?"

"Indeed, he is a permanency in a very different sense from me," replied Mr. Malthus. "I have been graciously spared, but I must go at last. Now he never plays. He shuffles and deals for the club, and makes the necessary arrangements. That man, my dear Mr. Hammersmith, is the very soul of ingenuity. For three years he has pursued in London his useful and, I think I may add, his artistic calling; and not so much as a whisper of suspicion has been once aroused. I believe him myself to be inspired. You doubtless remember the celebrated case, six months ago, of the gentleman who was accidentally poisoned in a chemist's shop? That was one of the least rich, one of the least racy, of his notions; but then, how simple! and how safe!"

"You astound me," said the Colonel. "Was that unfortunate gentleman one of the—" He was about to say "victims"; but bethinking himself in time, he substituted—"members of the club?"

In the same flash of thought, it occurred to him that Mr. Malthus himself had not at all spoken in the tone of one who is in love with death; and he added hurriedly:

"But I perceive I am still in the dark. You speak of shuffling and dealing; pray for what end? And since you seem rather unwilling to die than otherwise, I must own that I cannot conceive what brings you here at all."

"You say truly that you are in the dark," replied Mr. Malthus with more animation. "Why, my dear sir, this club is the temple of intoxication. If my enfeebled health could support the excitement more often, you may depend upon it I should be more often here. It requires all the sense of duty engendered by a long habit of ill-health and careful regimen, to keep me from excess in this, which is, I may say, my last dissipation. I have tried them all, sir," he went on, laying his hand on Geraldine's arm, "all without exception, and I declare to you, upon my honour, there is not one of them that has not been grossly and untruthfully overrated. People trifle with love. Now, I deny that love is a strong passion. Fear is the strong passion; it is with fear that you must trifle, if you wish to taste the intensest joys of living. Envy me—envy me, sir," he added with a chuckle, "I am a coward!"

Geraldine could scarcely repress a movement of repulsion

for this deplorable wretch; but he commanded himself with an effort, and continued his inquiries.

"How, sir," he asked, "is the excitement so artfully prolonged? and where is there any element of uncertainty?"

"I must tell you how the victim for every evening is selected," returned Mr. Malthus; "and not only the victim, but another member, who is to be the instrument in the club's hands, and death's high priest for that occasion."

"Good God!" said the Colonel, "do they then kill each other?"

"The trouble of suicide is removed in that way," returned Malthus with a nod.

"Merciful heavens!" ejaculated the Colonel, "and may you—may I—may the—my friend I mean—may any of us be pitched upon this evening as the slayer of another man's body and immortal spirit? Can such things be possible among men born of women? Oh! infamy of infamies!"

He was about to rise in his horror, when he caught the Prince's eye. It was fixed upon him from across the room with a frowning and angry stare. And in a moment Geraldine recovered his composure.

"After all," he added, "why not? And since you say the game is interesting, *vogue la galère*—I follow the club!"

Mr. Malthus had keenly enjoyed the Colonel's amazement and disgust. He had the vanity of wickedness; and it pleased him to see another man give way to a generous movement, while he felt himself, in his entire corruption, superior to such emotions.

"You now, after your first moment of surprise," said he, "are in a position to appreciate the delights of our society. You can see how it combines the excitement of a gaming-table, a duel, and a Roman amphitheatre. The Pagans did well enough; I cordially admire the refinement of their minds; but it has been reserved for a Christian country to attain this extreme, this quintessence, this absolute of poignancy. You will understand how vapid are all amusements to a man who has acquired a taste for this one. The game we play," he continued, "is one of extreme simplicity. A full pack—but I perceive you are about to see the thing in progress. Will you lend me the help of your arm? I am unfortunately paralysed."

Indeed, just as Mr. Malthus was beginning his description, another pair of folding-doors was thrown open, and the whole club began to pass, not without some hurry, into the adjoining room. It was similar in every respect to the one from which it was entered, but somewhat differently furnished. The centre was occupied by a long green table, at which the President sat shuffling a pack of cards with great particularity. Even with the stick and the Colonel's arm, Mr. Malthus walked with so much difficulty that every one was seated before this pair and the Prince, who had waited for them, entered the apartment; and, in consequence, the three took seats close together at the lower end of the board.

"It is a pack of fifty-two," whispered Mr. Malthus. "Watch for the ace of spades, which is the sign of death, and the ace of clubs, which designates the official of the night. Happy, happy young men!" he added. "You have good eyes, and can follow the game. Alas! I cannot tell an ace from a deuce across the table."

And he proceeded to equip himself with a second pair of spectacles.

"I must at least watch the faces," he explained.

The Colonel rapidly informed his friend of all that he had learned from the honorary member, and of the horrible alternative that lay before them. The Prince was conscious of a deadly chill and a contraction about his heart; he swallowed with difficulty, and looked from side to side like a man in a maze.

"One bold stroke," whispered the Colonel, "and we may still escape."

But the suggestion recalled the Prince's spirits.

"Silence!" said he. "Let me see that you can play like a gentleman for any stake, however serious."

And he looked about him, once more to all appearance at his ease, although his heart beat thickly, and he was conscious of an unpleasant heat in his bosom. The members were all very quiet and intent; every one was pale, but none so pale as Mr. Malthus. His eyes protruded; his head kept nodding involuntarily upon his spine; his hands found their way, one after the other, to his mouth, where they made clutches at his tremulous and ashen lips. It was plain that the honorary member enjoyed his membership on very startling terms.

"Attention, gentlemen!" said the President.

And he began slowly dealing the cards about the table in the reverse direction, pausing until each man had shown his card. Nearly every one hesitated; and sometimes you would see a player's fingers stumble more than once before he could turn over the momentous slip of pasteboard. As the Prince's turn drew nearer, he was conscious of a growing and almost suffocating excitement; but he had somewhat of the gambler's nature, and recognised almost with astonishment, that there was a degree of pleasure in his sensations. The nine of clubs fell to his lot; the three of spades was dealt to Geraldine; and the queen of hearts to Mr. Malthus, who was unable to suppress a sob of relief. The young man of the cream tarts almost immediately afterwards turned over the ace of clubs, and remained frozen with horror, the card still resting on his finger; he had not come there to kill, but to be killed; and the Prince in his generous sympathy with his position almost forgot the peril that still hung over himself and his friend.

The deal was coming round again, and still Death's card had not come out. The players held their respiration, and only breathed by gasps. The Prince received another club; Geraldine had a diamond; but when Mr. Malthus turned up his card a horrible noise, like that of something breaking, issued from his mouth; and he rose from his seat and sat down again, with no sign of his paralysis. It was the ace of spades. The honorary member had trifled once too often with his terrors.

Conversation broke out again almost at once. The players relaxed their rigid attitudes, and began to rise from the table and stroll back by twos and threes into the smoking-room. The President stretched his arms and yawned, like a man who has finished his day's work. But Mr. Malthus sat in his place, with his head in his hands, and his hands upon the table, drunk and motionless—a thing stricken down.

The Prince and Geraldine made their escape at once. In the cold night air their horror of what they had witnessed was redoubled.

"Alas!" cried the Prince, "to be bound by an oath in such a matter! to allow this wholesale trade in murder to be continued with profit and impunity! If I but dared to forfeit my pledge!"

"That is impossible for your Highness," replied the Colonel, "whose honour is the honour of Bohemia. But I dare, and may with propriety, forfeit mine."

"Geraldine," said the Prince, "if your honour suffers in any of the adventures into which you follow me, not only will I never pardon you, but—what I believe will much more sensibly affect you—I should never forgive myself."

"I receive your Highness's commands," replied the Colonel. "Shall we go from this accursed spot?"

"Yes," said the Prince. "Call a cab in Heaven's name, and let me try to forget in slumber the memory of this night's disgrace."

But it was notable that he carefully read the name of the court before he left it.

The next morning, as soon as the Prince was stirring, Colonel Geraldine brought him a daily newspaper, with the following paragraph marked:—

"*Melancholy Accident.*—This morning, about two o'clock, Mr. Bartholomew Malthus, of 16 Chepstow Place, Westbourne Grove, on his way home from a party at a friend's house, fell over the upper parapet in Trafalgar Square, fracturing his skull and breaking a leg and an arm. Death was instantaneous. Mr. Malthus, accompanied by a friend, was engaged in looking for a cab at the time of the unfortunate occurrence. As Mr. Malthus was paralytic, it is thought that his fall may have been occasioned by another seizure. The unhappy gentleman was well known in the most respectable circles, and his loss will be widely and deeply deplored."

"If ever a soul went straight to Hell," said Geraldine solemnly, "it was that paralytic man's."

The Prince buried his face in his hands, and remained silent.

"I am almost rejoiced," continued the Colonel, "to know that he is dead. But for our young man of the cream tarts I confess my heart bleeds."

"Geraldine," said the Prince, raising his face, "that unhappy lad was last night as innocent as you and I; and this morning the guilt of blood is on his soul. When I think of the President, my heart grows sick within me. I do not know how it shall be done, but I shall have that scoundrel at my mercy as there is a God in heaven. What an experience, what a lesson, was that game of cards!"

"One," said the Colonel, "never to be repeated."

The Prince remained so long without replying, that Geraldine grew alarmed.

"You cannot mean to return," he said. "You have suffered too much and seen too much horror already. The duties of your high position forbid the repetition of the hazard."

"There is much in what you say," replied Prince Florizel, "and I am not altogether pleased with my own determination. Alas! in the clothes of the greatest potentate, what is there but a man? I never felt my weakness more acutely than now, Geraldine, but it is stronger than I. Can I cease to interest myself in the fortunes of the unhappy young man who supped with us some hours ago? Can I leave the President to follow his nefarious career unwatched? Can I begin an adventure so entrancing, and not follow it to an end? No, Geraldine: you ask of the Prince more than the man is able to perform. To-night, once more, we take our places at the table of the Suicide Club."

Colonel Geraldine fell upon his knees.

"Will your Highness take my life?" he cried. "It is his—his freely; but do not, O do not! let him ask me to countenance so terrible a risk."

"Colonel Geraldine," replied the Prince, with some haughtiness of manner, "your life is absolutely your own. I only looked for obedience; and when that is unwillingly rendered, I shall look for that no longer. I add one word: your importunity in this affair has been sufficient."

The Master of the Horse regained his feet at once.

"Your Highness," he said, "may I be excused in my attendance this afternoon? I dare not, as an honourable man, venture a second time into that fatal house until I have perfectly ordered my affairs. Your Highness shall meet, I promise him, with no more opposition from the most devoted and grateful of his servants."

"My dear Geraldine," returned Prince Florizel, "I always regret when you oblige me to remember my rank. Dispose of your day as you think fit, but be here before eleven in the same disguise."

The club, on this second evening, was not so fully attended; and when Geraldine and the Prince arrived, there were not above half-a-dozen persons in the smoking-room. His Highness took the President aside and congratulated him warmly on the demise of Mr. Malthus.

"I like," he said, "to meet with capacity, and certainly find much of it in you. Your profession is of a very delicate nature, but I see you are well qualified to conduct it with success and secrecy."

The President was somewhat affected by these compliments from one of his Highness's superior bearing. He acknowledged them almost with humility.

"Poor Malthy!" he added, "I shall hardly know the club without him. The most of my patrons are boys, sir, and poetical boys, who are not much company for me. Not but what Malthy had some poetry, too; but it was of a kind that I could understand."

"I can readily imagine you should find yourself in sympathy with Mr. Malthus," returned the Prince. "He struck me as a man of a very original disposition."

The young man of the cream tarts was in the room, but painfully depressed and silent. His late companions sought in vain to lead him into conversation.

"How bitterly I wish," he cried, "that I had never brought you to this infamous abode! Begone, while you are clean-handed. If you could have heard the old man scream as he fell, and the noise of his bones upon the pavement! Wish me, if you have any kindness to so fallen a being—wish the ace of spades for me to-night!"

A few more members dropped in as the evening went on, but the club did not muster more than the devil's dozen when they took their places at the table. The Prince was again conscious of a certain joy in his alarms; but he was astonished to see Geraldine so much more self-possessed than on the night before.

"It is extraordinary," thought the Prince, "that a will, made or unmade, should so greatly influence a young man's spirit."

"Attention, gentlemen!" said the President, and he began to deal.

Three times the cards went all round the table, and neither of the marked cards had yet fallen from his hand. The excitement as he began the fourth distribution was overwhelming. There were just cards enough to go once more entirely round. The Prince, who sat second from the dealer's left, would receive, in the reverse mode of dealing practised at the club, the second last card. The third player turned up a black ace—it was the ace of clubs. The next received a diamond, the next a heart, and so on; but the ace of spades was still undelivered. At last, Geraldine, who sat upon the Prince's left, turned his card; it was an ace, but the ace of hearts.

When Prince Florizel saw his fate upon the table in front of him, his heart stood still. He was a brave man, but the sweat poured off his face. There were exactly fifty chances out of a hundred that he was doomed. He reversed the card; it was the ace of spades. A loud roaring filled his brain, and the table swam before his eyes. He heard the player on his right break into a fit of laughter that sounded between mirth and disappointment; he saw the company rapidly dispersing, but his mind was full of other thoughts. He recognised how foolish, how criminal, had been his conduct. In perfect health, in the prime of his years, the heir to a throne, he had gambled away his future and that of a brave and loyal country. "God," he cried, "God forgive me!" And with that, the confusion of his senses passed away, and he regained his self-possession in a moment.

To his surprise Geraldine had disappeared. There was no one in the card-room but his destined butcher consulting with the President, and the young man of the cream tarts, who slipped up to the Prince, and whispered in his ear:—

"I would give a million, if I had it, for your luck."

His Highness could not help reflecting, as the young man departed, that he would have sold his opportunity for a much more moderate sum.

The whispered conference now came to an end. The holder of the ace of clubs left the room with a look of intelligence, and the President, approaching the unfortunate Prince, proffered him his hand.

"I am pleased to have met you, sir," said he, "and pleased to have been in a position to do you this trifling service. At least, you cannot complain of delay. On the second evening—what a stroke of luck!"

The Prince endeavoured in vain to articulate something in response, but his mouth was dry and his tongue seemed paralysed.

"You feel a little sickish?" asked the President, with some show of solicitude. "Most gentlemen do. Will you take a little brandy?"

The Prince signified in the affirmative, and the other immediately filled some of the spirit into a tumbler.

"Poor old Malthy!" ejaculated the President, as the Prince drained the glass. "He drank near upon a pint, and little enough good it seemed to do him!"

"I am more amenable to treatment," said the Prince, a good deal revived. "I am my own man again at once, as you perceive. And so, let me ask you, what are my directions?"

"You will proceed along the Strand in the direction of the City, and on the left-hand pavement, until you meet the gentleman who has just left the room. He will continue your instructions, and him you will have the kindness to obey; the authority of the club is vested in his person for the night. And now," added the President, "I wish you a pleasant walk."

Florizel acknowledged the salutation rather awkwardly, and took his leave. He passed through the smoking-room, where the bulk of the players were still consuming champagne, some of which he had himself ordered and paid for; and he was surprised to find himself cursing them in his heart. He put on his hat and greatcoat in the cabinet, and selected his umbrella from a corner. The familiarity of these acts, and the thought that he was about them for the last time, betrayed him into a fit of laughter which sounded unpleasantly in his own ears. He conceived a reluctance to leave the cabinet, and turned instead to the window. The sight of the lamps and the darkness recalled him to himself.

"Come, come, I must be a man," he thought, "and tear myself away."

At the corner of Box Court three men fell upon Prince Florizel and he was unceremoniously thrust into a carriage, which at once drove rapidly away. There was already an occupant.

"Will your Highness pardon my zeal?" said a well-known voice.

The Prince threw himself upon the Colonel's neck in a passion of relief.

"How can I ever thank you?" he cried. "And how was this effected?"

Although he had been willing to march upon his doom, he was overjoyed to yield to friendly violence, and return once more to life and hope.

"You can thank me effectually enough," replied the Colonel, "by avoiding all such dangers in the future. And as for your second question, all has been managed by the simplest means. I arranged this afternoon with a celebrated detective. Secrecy has been promised and paid for. Your own servants have been principally engaged in the affair. The house in Box Court has been surrounded since nightfall, and this, which is one of your own carriages, has been awaiting you for nearly an hour."

"And the miserable creature who was to have slain me—what of him?" inquired the Prince.

"He was pinioned as he left the club," replied the Colonel, "and now awaits your sentence at the Palace, where he will soon be joined by his accomplices."

"Geraldine," said the Prince, "you have saved me against my explicit orders, and you have done well. I owe you not only my life, but a lesson; and I should be unworthy of my rank if I did not show myself grateful to my teacher. Let it be yours to choose the manner."

There was a pause, during which the carriage continued to speed through the streets, and the two men were each buried in his own reflections. The silence was broken by Colonel Geraldine.

"Your Highness," said he, "has by this time a considerable body of prisoners. There is at least one criminal among the number to whom justice should be dealt. Our oath forbids us all recourse to law; and discretion would forbid it equally if the oath were loosened. May I inquire your Highness's intention?"

"It is decided," answered Florizel; "the President must fall in duel. It only remains to choose his adversary."

"Your Highness has permitted me to name my own recompense," said the Colonel. "Will he permit me to ask the appointment of my brother? It is an honourable post, but I dare assure your Highness that the lad will acquit himself with credit."

"You ask me an ungracious favour," said the Prince, "but I must refuse you nothing."

The Colonel kissed his hand with the greatest affection; and at that moment the carriage rolled under the archway of the Prince's splendid residence.

An hour after, Florizel in his official robes, and covered with all the orders of Bohemia, received the members of the Suicide Club.

"Foolish and wicked men," said he, "as many of you as have been driven into this strait by the lack of fortune shall receive employment and remuneration from my officers. Those who suffer under a sense of guilt must have recourse to a higher and more generous Potentate than I. I feel pity for all of you, deeper than you can imagine; to-morrow you shall tell me your stories; and as you answer more frankly, I shall be the more able to remedy your misfortunes. As for you," he added, turning to the President, "I should only offend a person of your parts by any offer of assistance; but I have instead a piece of diversion to propose to you. Here," laying his hand on the shoulder of Colonel Geraldine's young brother, "is an officer of mine who desires to make a little tour upon the Continent; and I ask you, as a favour, to accompany him on this excursion. Do you," he went on, changing his tone, "do you shoot well with the pistol? Because you may have need of that accomplishment. When two men go travelling together, it is best to be prepared for all. Let me add that, if by any chance you should lose young Mr. Geraldine upon the way, I shall always have another member of my household to place at your disposal; and I am known, Mr. President, to have long eyesight, and as long an arm."

With these words, said with much sternness, the Prince concluded his address. Next morning the members of the club were suitably provided for by his munificence, and the President set forth upon his travels, under the supervision of Mr. Geraldine, and a pair of faithful and adroit lackeys, well trained in the Prince's household. Not content with this, discreet agents were put in possession of the house in Box Court, and all letters or visitors for the Suicide Club or its officials were to be examined by Prince Florizel in person.

Here (says my Arabian author) ends the "Story of the Young Man with the Cream Tarts," who is now a comfortable householder in Wigmore Street, Cavendish Square. The number, for obvious reasons, I suppress. Those who care to pursue the adventures of Prince Florizel and the President of the Suicide Club, may read the "Story of the Physician and the Saratoga Trunk."

# Story of the Physician and the Saratoga Trunk

Mr. Silas Q. Scuddamore was a young American of a simple and harmless disposition, which was the more to his credit as he came from New England—a quarter of the New World not precisely famous for those qualities. Although he was exceedingly rich, he kept a note of all his expenses in a little paper pocket-book; and he had chosen to study the attractions of Paris from the seventh storey of what is called a furnished hotel, in the Latin Quarter. There was a great deal of habit in his penuriousness; and his virtue, which was very remarkable among his associates, was principally founded upon diffidence and youth.

The next room to his was inhabited by a lady, very attractive in her air and very elegant in toilette, whom, on his first arrival, he had taken for a Countess. In course of time he had learned that she was known by the name of Madame Zephyrine, and that whatever station she occupied in life it was not that of a person of title. Madame Zephyrine, probably in the hope of enchanting the young American, used to flaunt by him on the stairs with a civil inclination, a word of course, and a knock-down look out of her black eyes, and disappear in a rustle of silk, and with the revelation of an admirable foot and ankle. But these advances, so far from encouraging Mr. Scuddamore, plunged him into the depths of depression and bashfulness. She had come to him several times for a light, or to apologise for the imaginary depredations of her poodle; but his mouth was closed in the presence of so superior a being, his French promptly left him, and he could only stare and stammer until she was gone. The slenderness of their intercourse did not prevent him from throwing out insinuations of a very glorious order when he was safely alone with a few males.

The room on the other side of the American's—for there were three rooms on a floor in the hotel—was tenanted by an old English physician of rather doubtful reputation. Dr. Noel, for that was his name, had been forced to leave London, where he enjoyed a large and increasing practice; and it was hinted that the police had been the instigators of this change of scene. At least he, who had made something of a figure in earlier life, now dwelt in the Latin Quarter in great simplicity and solitude, and devoted much of his time to study. Mr. Scuddamore had made his acquaintance, and the pair would now and then dine together frugally in a restaurant across the street.

Silas Q. Scuddamore had many little vices of the more respectable order, and was not restrained by delicacy from indulging them in many rather doubtful ways. Chief among his foibles stood curiosity. He was a born gossip; and life, and especially those parts of it in which he had no experience, interested him to the degree of passion. He was a pert, invincible questioner, pushing his inquiries with equal pertinacity and indiscretion; he had been observed, when he took a letter to the post, to weigh it in his hand, to turn it over and over, and to study the address with care; and when he found a flaw in the partition between his room and Madame Zephyrine's, instead of filling it up, he enlarged and improved the opening, and made use of it as a spy-hole on his neighbour's affairs.

One day, in the end of March, his curiosity growing as it was indulged, he enlarged the hole a little further, so that he might command another corner of the room. That evening, when he went as usual to inspect Madame Zephyrine's movements, he was astonished to find the aperture obscured in an odd manner on the other side, and still more abashed when the obstacle was suddenly withdrawn and a titter of laughter reached his ears. Some of the plaster had evidently betrayed the secret of his spy-hole, and his neighbour had been returning the compliment in kind. Mr. Scuddamore was moved to a very acute feeling of annoyance; he condemned Madame Zephyrine unmercifully; he even blamed himself; but when he found, next day, that she had taken no means to baulk him of his favourite pastime, he continued to profit by her carelessness, and gratify his idle curiosity.

That next day Madame Zephyrine received a long visit from a tall, loosely-built man of fifty or upwards, whom Silas had not hitherto seen. His tweed suit and coloured shirt, no less than his shaggy side-whiskers, identified him as a Britisher, and his dull grey eye affected Silas with a sense of cold. He kept screwing his mouth from side to side and round and round during the whole colloquy, which was carried on in whispers. More than once it seemed to the young New Englander as if their gestures indicated his own apartment; but the only thing definite he could gather by the most scrupulous attention was this remark made by the Englishman in a somewhat higher key, as if in answer to some reluctance or opposition.

"I have studied his taste to a nicety, and I tell you again and again you are the only woman of the sort that I can lay my hands on."

In answer to this, Madame Zephyrine sighed, and appeared by a gesture to resign herself, like one yielding to unqualified authority.

That afternoon the observatory was finally blinded, a wardrobe having been drawn in front of it upon the other side; and while Silas was still lamenting over this misfortune, which he attributed to the Britisher's malign suggestion, the concierge brought him up a letter in a female handwriting. It was conceived in French of no very rigorous orthography, bore no signature, and in the most encouraging terms invited the young American to be present in a certain part of the Bullier Ball at eleven o'clock that night. Curiosity and timidity fought a long battle in his heart; sometimes he was all virtue, sometimes all fire and daring; and the result of it was that, long before ten, Mr. Silas Q. Scuddamore presented himself in unimpeachable attire at the door of the Bullier Ball Rooms, and paid his entry money with a sense of reckless devilry that was not without its charm.

It was Carnival time, and the Ball was very full and noisy. The lights and the crowd at first rather abashed our young adventurer, and then, mounting to his brain with a sort of intoxication, put him in possession of more than his own share of manhood. He felt ready to face the devil, and strutted in the ballroom with the swagger of a cavalier. While he was thus parading, he became aware of Madame Zephyrine and her Britisher in conference behind a pillar. The cat-like spirit of eaves-dropping overcame him at once. He stole nearer and nearer on the couple from behind, until he was within earshot.

"That is the man," the Britisher was saying; "there—with the long blond hair—speaking to a girl in green."

Silas identified a very handsome young fellow of small stature, who was plainly the object of this designation.

"It is well," said Madame Zephyrine. "I shall do my utmost. But, remember, the best of us may fail in such a matter."

"Tut!" returned her companion; "I answer for the result. Have I not chosen you from thirty? Go; but be wary of the Prince. I cannot think what cursed accident has brought him here to-night. As if there were not a dozen balls in Paris better worth his notice than this riot of students and counter-jumpers! See him where he sits, more like a reigning Emperor at home than a Prince upon his holidays!"

Silas was again lucky. He observed a person of rather a full build, strikingly handsome, and of a very stately and courteous demeanour, seated at table with another handsome young man, several years his junior, who addressed him with conspicuous deference. The name of Prince struck gratefully on Silas's Republican hearing, and the aspect of the person to whom that name was applied exercised its usual charm upon his mind. He left Madame Zephyrine and her Englishman to take care of each other, and threading his way through the assembly, approached the table which the Prince and his confidant had honoured with their choice.

"I tell you, Geraldine," the former was saying, "the action is madness. Yourself (I am glad to remember it) chose your brother for this perilous service, and you are bound in duty to have a guard upon his conduct. He has consented to delay so many days in Paris; that was already an imprudence, considering the character of the man he has to deal with; but now, when he is within eight-and-forty hours of his departure, when he is within two or three days of the decisive trial, I ask you, is this a place for him to spend his time? He should be in a gallery at practice; he should be sleeping long hours and taking moderate exercise on foot; he should be on a rigorous diet, without white wines or brandy. Does the dog imagine we are all playing comedy? The thing is deadly earnest, Geraldine."

"I know the lad too well to interfere," replied Colonel Geraldine, "and well enough not to be alarmed. He is more cautious than you fancy, and of an indomitable spirit. If it had been a woman I should not say so much, but I trust the President to him and the two valets without an instant's apprehension."

"I am gratified to hear you say so," replied the Prince; "but my mind is not at rest. These servants are well-trained spies, and already has not this miscreant succeeded three times in eluding their observation and spending several hours on end in private, and most likely dangerous, affairs? An amateur might have lost him by accident, but if Rudolph and Jerome were thrown off the scent, it must have been done on purpose, and by a man who had a cogent reason and exceptional resources."

"I believe the question is now one between my brother and myself," replied Geraldine, with a shade of offence in his tone.

"I permit it to be so, Colonel Geraldine," returned Prince Florizel. "Perhaps, for that very reason, you should be all the more ready to accept my counsels. But enough. That girl in yellow dances well."

And the talk veered into the ordinary topics of a Paris ballroom in the Carnival.

Silas remembered where he was, and that the hour was already near at hand when he ought to be upon the scene of his assignation. The more he reflected the less he liked the prospect, and as at that moment an eddy in the crowd began to draw him in the direction of the door, he suffered it to carry him away without resistance. The eddy stranded him in a corner under the gallery, where his ear was immediately struck with the voice of Madame Zephyrine. She was speaking in French with the young man of the blond locks who had been pointed out by the strange Britisher not half-an-hour before.

"I have a character at stake," she said, "or I would put no other condition than my heart recommends. But you have only to say so much to the porter, and he will let you go by without a word."

"But why this talk of debt?" objected her companion.

"Heavens!" said she, "do you think I do not understand my own hotel?"

And she went by, clinging affectionately to her companion's arm.

This put Silas in mind of his billet.

"Ten minutes hence," thought he, "and I may be walking with

as beautiful a woman as that, and even better dressed—perhaps a real lady, possibly a woman or title."

And then he remembered the spelling, and was a little downcast.

"But it may have been written by her maid," he imagined.

The clock was only a few minutes from the hour, and this immediate proximity set his heart beating at a curious and rather disagreeable speed. He reflected with relief that he was in no way bound to put in an appearance. Virtue and cowardice were together, and he made once more for the door, but this time of his own accord, and battling against the stream of people which was now moving in a contrary direction. Perhaps this prolonged resistance wearied him, or perhaps he was in that frame of mind when merely to continue in the same determination for a certain number of minutes produces a reaction and a different purpose. Certainly, at least, he wheeled about for a third time, and did not stop until he had found a place of concealment within a few yards of the appointed place.

Here he went through an agony of spirit, in which he several times prayed to God for help, for Silas had been devoutly educated. He had now not the least inclination for the meeting; nothing kept him from flight but a silly fear lest he should be thought unmanly; but this was so powerful that it kept head against all other motives; and although it could not decide him to advance, prevented him from definitely running away. At last the clock indicated ten minutes past the hour. Young Scuddamore's spirit began to rise; he peered round the corner and saw no one at the place of meeting; doubtless his unknown correspondent had wearied and gone away. He became as bold as he had formerly been timid. It seemed to him that if he came at all to the appointment, however late, he was clear from the charge of cowardice. Nay, now he began to suspect a hoax, and actually complimented himself on his shrewdness in having suspected and outmanoeuvred his mystifiers. So very idle a thing is a boy's mind!

Armed with these reflections, he advanced boldly from his corner; but he had not taken above a couple of steps before a hand was laid upon his arm. He turned and beheld a lady cast in a very large mould and with somewhat stately features, but bearing no mark of severity in her looks.

"I see that you are a very self-confident lady-killer," said she; "for you make yourself expected. But I was determined to meet you. When a woman has once so far forgotten herself as to make the first advance, she has long ago left behind her all considerations of petty pride."

Silas was overwhelmed by the size and attractions of his correspondent and the suddenness with which she had fallen upon him. But she soon set him at his ease. She was very towardly and lenient in her behaviour; she led him on to make pleasantries, and then applauded him to the echo; and in a very short time, between blandishments and a liberal exhibition of warm brandy, she had not only induced him to fancy himself in love, but to declare his passion with the greatest vehemence.

"Alas!" she said; "I do not know whether I ought not to deplore this moment, great as is the pleasure you give me by your words. Hitherto I was alone to suffer; now, poor boy, there will be two. I am not my own mistress. I dare not ask you to visit me at my own house, for I am watched by jealous eyes. Let me see," she added; "I am older than you, although so much weaker; and while I trust in your courage and determination, I must employ my own knowledge of the world for our mutual benefit. Where do you live?"

He told her that he lodged in a furnished hotel, and named the street and number.

She seemed to reflect for some minutes, with an effort of mind.

"I see," she said at last. "You will be faithful and obedient, will you not?"

Silas assured her eagerly of his fidelity.

"To-morrow night, then," she continued, with an encouraging smile, "you must remain at home all the evening; and if any friends should visit you, dismiss them at once on any pretext that most readily presents itself. Your door is probably shut by ten?" she asked.

"By eleven," answered Silas.

"At a quarter past eleven," pursued the lady, "leave the house. Merely cry for the door to be opened, and be sure you fall into no talk with the porter, as that might ruin everything. Go straight to the corner where the Luxembourg Gardens join the Boulevard; there you will find me waiting you. I trust you to follow my advice from point to point: and remember, if you fail me in only one particular, you will bring the sharpest trouble on a woman whose only fault is to have seen and loved you."

"I cannot see the use of all these instructions," said Silas.

"I believe you are already beginning to treat me as a master," she cried, tapping him with her fan upon the arm. "Patience, patience! that should come in time. A woman loves to be obeyed at first, although afterwards she finds her pleasure in obeying. Do as I ask you, for Heaven's sake, or I will answer for nothing. Indeed, now I think of it," she added, with the manner of one who has just seen further into a difficulty, "I find a better plan of keeping importunate visitors away. Tell the porter to admit no one for you, except a person who may come that night to claim a debt; and speak with some feeling, as though you feared the interview, so that he may take your words in earnest."

"I think you may trust me to protect myself against intruders," he said, not without a little pique.

"That is how I should prefer the thing arranged," she answered coldly. "I know you men; you think nothing of a woman's reputation."

Silas blushed and somewhat hung his head; for the scheme he had in view had involved a little vain-glorying before his acquaintances.

"Above all," she added, "do not speak to the porter as you come out."

"And why?" said he. "Of all your instructions, that seems to me the least important."

"You at first doubted the wisdom of some of the others, which you now see to be very necessary," she replied. "Believe me, this also has its uses; in time you will see them; and what am I to think of your affection, if you refuse me such trifles at our first interview?"

Silas confounded himself in explanations and apologies; in the middle of these she looked up at the clock and clapped her hands together with a suppressed scream.

"Heavens!" she cried, "is it so late? I have not an instant to lose. Alas, we poor women, what slaves we are! What have I not risked for you already?"

And after repeating her directions, which she artfully combined with caresses and the most abandoned looks, she bade him farewell and disappeared among the crowd.

The whole of the next day Silas was filled with a sense of great importance; he was now sure she was a countess; and when evening came he minutely obeyed her orders and was at the corner of the Luxembourg Gardens by the hour appointed. No one was there. He waited nearly half-an-hour, looking in the face of every one who passed or loitered near the spot; he even visited the neighbouring corners of the Boulevard and made a complete circuit of the garden railings; but there was no beautiful countess to throw herself into his arms. At last, and most reluctantly, he began to retrace his steps towards his hotel. On the way he remembered the words he had heard pass between Madame Zephyrine and the blond young man, and they gave him an indefinite uneasiness.

"It appears," he reflected, "that every one has to tell lies to our porter."

He rang the bell, the door opened before him, and the porter in his bed-clothes came to offer him a light.

"Has he gone?" inquired the porter.

"He? Whom do you mean?" asked Silas, somewhat sharply, for he was irritated by his disappointment.

"I did not notice him go out," continued the porter, "but I trust you paid him. We do not care, in this house, to have lodgers who cannot meet their liabilities."

"What the devil do you mean?" demanded Silas rudely. "I cannot understand a word of this farrago."

"The short blond young man who came for his debt," returned the other. "Him it is I mean. Who else should it be, when I had your orders to admit no one else?"

"Why, good God, of course he never came," retorted Silas.

"I believe what I believe," returned the porter, putting his tongue into his cheek with a most roguish air.

"You are an insolent scoundrel," cried Silas, and, feeling that he had made a ridiculous exhibition of asperity, and at the same time bewildered by a dozen alarms, he turned and began to run upstairs.

"Do you not want a light then?" cried the porter.

But Silas only hurried the faster, and did not pause until he had reached the seventh landing and stood in front of his own door. There he waited a moment to recover his breath, assailed by the worst forebodings and almost dreading to enter the room.

When at last he did so he was relieved to find it dark, and to all appearance, untenanted. He drew a long breath. Here he was, home again in safety, and this should be his last folly as certainly as it had been his first. The matches stood on a little table by the bed, and he began to grope his way in that direction. As he moved, his apprehensions grew upon him once more, and he was pleased, when his foot encountered an obstacle, to find it nothing more alarming than a chair. At last he touched curtains. From the position of the window, which was faintly visible, he knew he must be at the foot of the bed, and had only to feel his way along it in order to reach the table in question.

He lowered his hand, but what it touched was not simply a counterpane—it was a counterpane with something underneath it like the outline of a human leg. Silas withdrew his arm and stood a moment petrified.

"What, what," he thought, "can this betoken?"

He listened intently, but there was no sound of breathing. Once more, with a great effort, he reached out the end of his finger to the spot he had already touched; but this time he leaped back half a yard, and stood shivering and fixed with terror. There was something in his bed. What it was he knew not, but there was something there.

It was some seconds before he could move. Then, guided by an instinct, he fell straight upon the matches, and keeping his back towards the bed lighted a candle. As soon as the flame had kindled, he turned slowly round and looked for what he feared to see. Sure enough, there was the worst of his imaginations realised. The coverlid was drawn carefully up over the pillow, but it moulded the outline of a human body lying motionless; and when he dashed forward and flung aside the sheets, he beheld the blond young man whom he had seen in the Bullier Ball the night before, his eyes open and without speculation, his face swollen and blackened, and a thin stream of blood trickling from his nostrils.

Silas uttered a long, tremulous wail, dropped the candle, and fell on his knees beside the bed.

Silas was awakened from the stupor into which his terrible discovery had plunged him by a prolonged but discreet tapping at the door. It took him some seconds to remember his position; and when he hastened to prevent anyone from entering it was already too late. Dr. Noel, in a tall night-cap, carrying a lamp which lighted up his long white countenance, sidling in his gait, and peering and cocking his head like some sort of bird, pushed the door slowly open, and advanced into the middle of the room.

"I thought I heard a cry," began the Doctor, "and fearing you might be unwell I did not hesitate to offer this intrusion."

Silas, with a flushed face and a fearful beating heart, kept between the Doctor and the bed; but he found no voice to answer.

"You are in the dark," pursued the Doctor; "and yet you have not even begun to prepare for rest. You will not easily persuade me against my own eyesight; and your face declares most eloquently that you require either a friend or a physician—which is it to be? Let me feel your pulse, for that is often a just reporter of the heart."

He advanced to Silas, who still retreated before him backwards, and sought to take him by the wrist; but the strain on the young American's nerves had become too great for endurance. He avoided the Doctor with a febrile movement, and, throwing himself upon the floor, burst into a flood of weeping.

As soon as Dr. Noel perceived the dead man in the bed his face darkened; and hurrying back to the door which he had left ajar, he hastily closed and double-locked it.

"Up!" he cried, addressing Silas in strident tones; "this is no time for weeping. What have you done? How came this body in your room? Speak freely to one who may be helpful. Do you imagine I would ruin you? Do you think this piece of dead flesh on your pillow can alter in any degree the sympathy with which you have inspired me? Credulous youth, the horror with which blind and unjust law regards an action never attaches to the doer in the eyes of those who love him; and if I saw the friend of my heart return to me out of seas of blood he would be in no way changed in my affection. Raise yourself," he said; "good and ill are a chimera; there is nought in life except destiny, and however you may be circumstanced there is one at your side who will help you to the last."

Thus encouraged, Silas gathered himself together, and in a broken voice, and helped out by the Doctor's interrogations, contrived at last to put him in possession of the facts. But the conversation between the Prince and Geraldine he altogether omitted, as he had understood little of its purport, and had no idea that it was in any way related to his own misadventure.

"Alas!" cried Dr. Noel, "I am much abused, or you have fallen innocently into the most dangerous hands in Europe. Poor boy, what a pit has been dug for your simplicity! into what a deadly peril have your unwary feet been conducted! This man," he said, "this Englishman, whom you twice saw, and whom I suspect to be the soul of the contrivance, can you describe him? Was he young or old? tall or short?"

But Silas, who, for all his curiosity, had not a seeing eye in his head, was able to supply nothing but meagre generalities, which it was impossible to recognise.

"I would have it a piece of education in all schools!" cried the Doctor angrily. "Where is the use of eyesight and articulate speech if a man cannot observe and recollect the features of his enemy? I, who know all the gangs of Europe, might have identified him, and gained new weapons for your defence. Cultivate this art in future, my poor boy; you may find it of momentous service."

"The future!" repeated Silas. "What future is there left for me except the gallows?"

"Youth is but a cowardly season," returned the Doctor; "and a man's own troubles look blacker than they are. I am old, and yet I never despair."

"Can I tell such a story to the police?" demanded Silas.

"Assuredly not," replied the Doctor. "From what I see already of the machination in which you have been involved, your case is desperate upon that side; and for the narrow eye of the authorities you are infallibly the guilty person. And remember that we only know a portion of the plot; and the same infamous contrivers have doubtless arranged many other circumstances which would be elicited by a police inquiry, and help to fix the guilt more certainly upon your innocence."

"I am then lost, indeed!" cried Silas.

"I have not said so," answered Dr. Noel "for I am a cautious man."

"But look at this!" objected Silas, pointing to the body. "Here is this object in my bed; not to be explained, not to be disposed of, not to be regarded without horror."

"Horror?" replied the Doctor. "No. When this sort of clock has run down, it is no more to me than an ingenious piece of mechanism, to be investigated with the bistoury. When blood is once cold and stagnant, it is no longer human blood; when flesh is once dead, it is no longer that flesh which we desire in our lovers and respect in our friends. The grace, the attraction, the terror, have all gone from it with the animating spirit. Accustom yourself to look upon it with composure; for if my scheme is practicable you will have to live some days in constant proximity to that which now so greatly horrifies you."

"Your scheme?" cried Silas. "What is that? Tell me speedily, Doctor; for I have scarcely courage enough to continue to exist."

Without replying, Doctor Noel turned towards the bed, and proceeded to examine the corpse.

"Quite dead," he murmured. "Yes, as I had supposed, the pockets empty. Yes, and the name cut off the shirt. Their work has been done thoroughly and well. Fortunately, he is of small stature."

Silas followed these words with an extreme anxiety. At last the Doctor, his autopsy completed, took a chair and addressed the young American with a smile.

"Since I came into your room," said he, "although my ears and my tongue have been so busy, I have not suffered my eyes to remain idle. I noted a little while ago that you have there, in the corner, one of those monstrous constructions which your fellow-countrymen carry with them into all quarters of the globe—in a word, a Saratoga trunk. Until this moment I have never been able to conceive the utility of these erections; but then I began to have a glimmer. Whether it was for convenience in the slave trade, or to obviate the results of too ready an employment of the bowie-knife, I cannot bring myself to decide. But one thing I see plainly—the object of such a box is to contain a human body.

"Surely," cried Silas, "surely this is not a time for jesting."

"Although I may express myself with some degree of pleasantry," replied the Doctor, "the purport of my words is entirely serious. And the first thing we have to do, my young friend, is to empty your coffer of all that it contains."

Silas, obeying the authority of Doctor Noel, put himself at his disposition. The Saratoga trunk was soon gutted of its contents, which made a considerable litter on the floor; and then—Silas taking the heels and the Doctor supporting the shoulders—the body of the murdered man was carried from the bed, and, after some difficulty, doubled up and inserted whole into the empty box. With an effort on the part of both, the lid was forced down upon this unusual baggage, and the trunk was locked and corded by the Doctor's own hand, while Silas disposed of what had been taken out between the closet and a chest of drawers.

"Now," said the Doctor, "the first step has been taken on the way to your deliverance. To-morrow, or rather to-day, it must be your task to allay the suspicions of your porter, paying him all that you owe; while you may trust me to make the arrangements necessary to a safe conclusion. Meantime, follow me to my room, where I shall give you a safe and powerful opiate; for, whatever you do, you must have rest."

The next day was the longest in Silas's memory; it seemed as if it would never be done. He denied himself to his friends, and sat in a corner with his eyes fixed upon the Saratoga trunk in dismal contemplation. His own former indiscretions were now returned upon him in kind; for the observatory had been once more opened, and he was conscious of an almost continual study from Madame Zephyrine's apartment. So distressing did this become, that he was at last obliged to block up the spy-hole from his own side; and when he was thus secured from observation he spent a considerable portion of his time in contrite tears and prayer.

Late in the evening Dr. Noel entered the room carrying in his hand a pair of sealed envelopes without address, one somewhat bulky, and the other so slim as to seem without enclosure.

"Silas," he said, seating himself at the table, "the time has now come for me to explain my plan for your salvation. To-morrow morning, at an early hour, Prince Florizel of Bohemia returns to London, after having diverted himself for a few days with the Parisian Carnival. It was my fortune, a good while ago, to do Colonel Geraldine, his Master of the Horse, one of those services, so common in my profession, which are never forgotten upon either side. I have no need to explain to you the nature of the obligation under which he was laid; suffice it to say that I knew him ready to serve me in any practicable manner. Now, it was necessary for you to gain London with your trunk unopened. To this the Custom House seemed to oppose a fatal difficulty; but I bethought me that the baggage of so considerable a person as the Prince, is, as a matter of courtesy, passed without examination by the officers of Custom. I applied to Colonel Geraldine, and succeeded in obtaining a favourable answer. To-morrow, if you go before six to the hotel where the Prince lodges, your baggage will be passed over as a part of his, and you yourself will make the journey as a member of his suite."

"It seems to me, as you speak, that I have already seen both the Prince and Colonel Geraldine; I even overheard some of their conversation the other evening at the Bullier Ball."

"It is probable enough; for the Prince loves to mix with all societies," replied the Doctor. "Once arrived in London," he pursued, "your task is nearly ended. In this more bulky envelope I have given you a letter which I dare not address; but in the other you will find the designation of the house to which you must carry it along with your box, which will there be taken from you and not trouble you any more."

"Alas!" said Silas, "I have every wish to believe you; but how is it possible? You open up to me a bright prospect, but, I ask you, is my mind capable of receiving so unlikely a solution? Be more generous, and let me further understand your meaning."

The Doctor seemed painfully impressed.

"Boy," he answered, "you do not know how hard a thing you ask of me. But be it so. I am now inured to humiliation; and it would be strange if I refused you this, after having granted you so much. Know, then, that although I now make so quiet an appearance—frugal, solitary, addicted to study—when I was younger, my name was once a rallying-cry among the most astute and dangerous spirits of London; and while I was outwardly an object for respect and consideration, my true power resided in the most secret, terrible, and criminal relations. It is to one of the persons who then obeyed me that I now address myself to deliver you from your burden. They were men of many different nations and dexterities, all bound together by a formidable oath, and working to the same purposes; the trade of the association was in murder; and I who speak to you, innocent as I appear, was the chieftain of this redoubtable crew."

"What?" cried Silas. "A murderer? And one with whom murder was a trade? Can I take your hand? Ought I so much as to accept your services? Dark and criminal old man, would you make an accomplice of my youth and my distress?"

The Doctor bitterly laughed.

"You are difficult to please, Mr. Scuddamore," said he; "but I now offer you your choice of company between the murdered man and the murderer. If your conscience is too nice to accept my aid, say so, and I will immediately leave you. Thenceforward you can deal with your trunk and its belongings as best suits your upright conscience."

"I own myself wrong," replied Silas. "I should have remembered how generously you offered to shield me, even before I had convinced you of my innocence, and I continue to listen to your counsels with gratitude."

"That is well," returned the Doctor; "and I perceive you are beginning to learn some of the lessons of experience."

"At the same time," resumed the New-Englander, "as you confess yourself accustomed to this tragical business, and the people to whom you recommend me are your own former associates and friends, could you not yourself undertake the transport of the box, and rid me at once of its detested presence?"

"Upon my word," replied the Doctor, "I admire you cordially. If you do not think I have already meddled sufficiently in your concerns, believe me, from my heart I think the contrary. Take or leave my services as I offer them; and trouble me with no more words of gratitude, for I value your consideration even more lightly than I do your intellect. A time will come, if you should be spared to see a number of years in health of mind, when you will think differently of all this, and blush for your to-night's behaviour."

So saying, the Doctor arose from his chair, repeated his directions briefly and clearly, and departed from the room without permitting Silas any time to answer.

The next morning Silas presented himself at the hotel, where he was politely received by Colonel Geraldine, and relieved, from that moment, of all immediate alarm about his trunk and its grisly contents. The journey passed over without much incident, although the young man was horrified to overhear the sailors and railway porters complaining among themselves about the unusual weight of the Prince's baggage. Silas travelled in a carriage with the valets, for Prince Florizel chose to be alone with his Master of the Horse. On board the steamer, however, Silas attracted his Highness's attention by the melancholy of his air and attitude as he stood gazing at the pile of baggage; for he was still full of disquietude about the future.

"There is a young man," observed the Prince, "who must have some cause for sorrow."

"That," replied Geraldine, "is the American for whom I obtained permission to travel with your suite."

"You remind me that I have been remiss in courtesy," said Prince Florizel, and advancing to Silas, he addressed him with the most exquisite condescension in these words:—"I was charmed, young sir, to be able to gratify the desire you made known to me through Colonel Geraldine. Remember, if you please, that I shall be glad at any future time to lay you under a more serious obligation."

And he then put some questions as to the political condition of America, which Silas answered with sense and propriety.

"You are still a young man," said the Prince; "but I observe you to be very serious for your years. Perhaps you allow your attention to be too much occupied with grave studies. But, perhaps, on the other hand, I am myself indiscreet and touch upon a painful subject."

"I have certainly cause to be the most miserable of men," said

Silas; "never has a more innocent person been more dismally abused."

"I will not ask you for your confidence," returned Prince Florizel. "But do not forget that Colonel Geraldine's recommendation is an unfailing passport; and that I am not only willing, but possibly more able than many others, to do you a service."

Silas was delighted with the amiability of this great personage; but his mind soon returned upon its gloomy preoccupations; for not even the favour of a Prince to a Republican can discharge a brooding spirit of its cares.

The train arrived at Charing Cross, where the officers of the Revenue respected the baggage of Prince Florizel in the usual manner. The most elegant equipages were in waiting; and Silas was driven, along with the rest, to the Prince's residence. There Colonel Geraldine sought him out, and expressed himself pleased to have been of any service to a friend of the physician's, for whom he professed a great consideration.

"I hope," he added, "that you will find none of your porcelain injured. Special orders were given along the line to deal tenderly with the Prince's effects."

And then, directing the servants to place one of the carriages at the young gentleman's disposal, and at once to charge the Saratoga trunk upon the dickey, the Colonel shook hands and excused himself on account of his occupations in the princely household.

Silas now broke the seal of the envelope containing the address, and directed the stately footman to drive him to Box Court, opening off the Strand. It seemed as if the place were not at all unknown to the man, for he looked startled and begged a repetition of the order. It was with a heart full of alarms, that Silas mounted into the luxurious vehicle, and was driven to his destination. The entrance to Box Court was too narrow for the passage of a coach; it was a mere footway between railings, with a post at either end. On one of these posts was seated a man, who at once jumped down and exchanged a friendly sign with the driver, while the footman opened the door and inquired of Silas whether he should take down the Saratoga trunk, and to what number it should be carried.

"If you please," said Silas. "To number three."

The footman and the man who had been sitting on the post, even with the aid of Silas himself, had hard work to carry in the trunk; and before it was deposited at the door of the house in question, the young American was horrified to find a score of loiterers looking on. But he knocked with as good a countenance as he could muster up, and presented the other envelope to him who opened.

"He is not at home," said he, "but if you will leave your letter and return to-morrow early, I shall be able to inform you whether and when he can receive your visit. Would you like to leave your box?" he added.

"Dearly," cried Silas; and the next moment he repented his precipitation, and declared, with equal emphasis, that he would rather carry the box along with him to the hotel.

The crowd jeered at his indecision and followed him to the carriage with insulting remarks; and Silas, covered with shame and terror, implored the servants to conduct him to some quiet and comfortable house of entertainment in the immediate neighbourhood.

The Prince's equipage deposited Silas at the Craven Hotel in Craven Street, and immediately drove away, leaving him alone with the servants of the inn. The only vacant room, it appeared, was a little den up four pairs of stairs, and looking towards the back. To this hermitage, with infinite trouble and complaint, a pair of stout porters carried the Saratoga trunk. It is needless to mention that Silas kept closely at their heels throughout the ascent, and had his heart in his mouth at every corner. A single false step, he reflected, and the box might go over the banisters and land its fatal contents, plainly discovered, on the pavement of the hall.

Arrived in the room, he sat down on the edge of his bed to recover from the agony that he had just endured; but he had hardly taken his position when he was recalled to a sense of his peril by the action of the boots, who had knelt beside the trunk, and was proceeding officiously to undo its elaborate fastenings.

"Let it be!" cried Silas. "I shall want nothing from it while I stay here."

"You might have let it lie in the hall, then," growled the man; "a thing as big and heavy as a church. What you have inside I cannot fancy. If it is all money, you are a richer man than me."

"Money?" repeated Silas, in a sudden perturbation. "What do you mean by money? I have no money, and you are speaking like a fool."

"All right, captain," retorted the boots with a wink. "There's nobody will touch your lordship's money. I'm as safe as the bank," he added; "but as the box is heavy, I shouldn't mind drinking something to your lordship's health."

Silas pressed two Napoleons upon his acceptance, apologising, at the same time, for being obliged to trouble him with foreign money, and pleading his recent arrival for excuse. And the man, grumbling with even greater fervour, and looking contemptuously from the money in his hand to the Saratoga trunk and back again from the one to the other, at last consented to withdraw.

For nearly two days the dead body had been packed into Silas's box; and as soon as he was alone the unfortunate New-Englander nosed all the cracks and openings with the most passionate attention. But the weather was cool, and the trunk still managed to contain his shocking secret.

He took a chair beside it, and buried his face in his hands, and his mind in the most profound reflection. If he were not speedily relieved, no question but he must be speedily discovered. Alone in a strange city, without friends or accomplices, if the Doctor's introduction failed him, he was indubitably a lost New-Englander. He reflected pathetically over his ambitious designs for the future; he should not now become the hero and spokesman of his native place of Bangor, Maine; he should not, as he had fondly anticipated, move on from office to office, from honour to honour; he might as well divest himself at once of all hope of being acclaimed President of the United States, and leaving behind him a statue, in the worst possible style of art, to adorn the Capitol at Washington. Here he was, chained to a dead Englishman doubled up inside a Saratoga trunk; whom he must get rid of, or perish from the rolls of national glory!

I should be afraid to chronicle the language employed by this young man to the Doctor, to the murdered man, to Madame

Zephyrine, to the boots of the hotel, to the Prince's servants, and, in a word, to all who had been ever so remotely connected with his horrible misfortune.

He slunk down to dinner about seven at night; but the yellow coffee-room appalled him, the eyes of the other diners seemed to rest on his with suspicion, and his mind remained upstairs with the Saratoga trunk. When the waiter came to offer him cheese, his nerves were already so much on edge that he leaped half-way out of his chair and upset the remainder of a pint of ale upon the table-cloth.

The fellow offered to show him to the smoking-room when he had done; and although he would have much preferred to return at once to his perilous treasure, he had not the courage to refuse, and was shown downstairs to the black, gas-lit cellar, which formed, and possibly still forms, the divan of the Craven Hotel.

Two very sad betting men were playing billiards, attended by a moist, consumptive marker; and for the moment Silas imagined that these were the only occupants of the apartment. But at the next glance his eye fell upon a person smoking in the farthest corner, with lowered eyes and a most respectable and modest aspect. He knew at once that he had seen the face before; and, in spite of the entire change of clothes, recognised the man whom he had found seated on a post at the entrance to Box Court, and who had helped him to carry the trunk to and from the carriage. The New-Englander simply turned and ran, nor did he pause until he had locked and bolted himself into his bedroom.

There, all night long, a prey to the most terrible imaginations, he watched beside the fatal boxful of dead flesh. The suggestion of the boots that his trunk was full of gold inspired him with all manner of new terrors, if he so much as dared to close an eye; and the presence in the smoking-room, and under an obvious disguise, of the loiterer from Box Court convinced him that he was once more the centre of obscure machinations.

Midnight had sounded some time, when, impelled by uneasy suspicions, Silas opened his bedroom door and peered into the passage. It was dimly illuminated by a single jet of gas; and some distance off he perceived a man sleeping on the floor in the costume of an hotel under-servant. Silas drew near the man on tiptoe. He lay partly on his back, partly on his side, and his right forearm concealed his face from recognition. Suddenly, while the American was still bending over him, the sleeper removed his arm and opened his eyes, and Silas found himself once more face to face with the loiterer of Box Court.

"Good-night, sir," said the man, pleasantly.

But Silas was too profoundly moved to find an answer, and regained his room in silence.

Towards morning, worn out by apprehension, he fell asleep on his chair, with his head forward on the trunk. In spite of so constrained an attitude and such a grisly pillow, his slumber was sound and prolonged, and he was only awakened at a late hour and by a sharp tapping at the door.

He hurried to open, and found the boots without.

"You are the gentleman who called yesterday at Box Court?" he asked.

Silas, with a quaver, admitted that he had done so.

"Then this note is for you," added the servant, proffering a sealed envelope.

Silas tore it open, and found inside the words: "Twelve o'clock."

He was punctual to the hour; the trunk was carried before him by several stout servants; and he was himself ushered into a room, where a man sat warming himself before the fire with his back towards the door. The sound of so many persons entering and leaving, and the scraping of the trunk as it was deposited upon the bare boards, were alike unable to attract the notice of the occupant; and Silas stood waiting, in an agony of fear, until he should deign to recognise his presence.

Perhaps five minutes had elapsed before the man turned leisurely about, and disclosed the features of Prince Florizel of Bohemia.

"So, sir," he said, with great severity, "this is the manner in which you abuse my politeness. You join yourselves to persons of condition, I perceive, for no other purpose than to escape the consequences of your crimes; and I can readily understand your embarrassment when I addressed myself to you yesterday."

"Indeed," cried Silas, "I am innocent of everything except misfortune."

And in a hurried voice, and with the greatest ingenuousness, he recounted to the Prince the whole history of his calamity.

"I see I have been mistaken," said his Highness, when he had heard him to an end. "You are no other than a victim, and since I am not to punish you may be sure I shall do my utmost to help. And now," he continued, "to business. Open your box at once, and let me see what it contains."

Silas changed colour.

"I almost fear to look upon it," he exclaimed.

"Nay," replied the Prince, "have you not looked at it already? This is a form of sentimentality to be resisted. The sight of a sick man, whom we can still help, should appeal more directly to the feelings than that of a dead man who is equally beyond help or harm, love or hatred. Nerve yourself, Mr. Scuddamore," and then, seeing that Silas still hesitated, "I do not desire to give another name to my request," he added.

The young American awoke as if out of a dream, and with a shiver of repugnance addressed himself to loose the straps and open the lock of the Saratoga trunk. The Prince stood by, watching with a composed countenance and his hands behind his back. The body was quite stiff, and it cost Silas a great effort, both moral and physical, to dislodge it from its position, and discover the face.

Prince Florizel started back with an exclamation of painful surprise.

"Alas!" he cried, "you little know, Mr. Scuddamore, what a cruel gift you have brought me. This is a young man of my own suite, the brother of my trusted friend; and it was upon matters of my own service that he has thus perished at the hands of violent and treacherous men. Poor Geraldine," he went on, as if to himself, "in what words am I to tell you of your brother's fate? How can I excuse myself in your eyes, or in the eyes of God, for the presumptuous schemes that led him to this bloody and unnatural death? Ah, Florizel! Florizel! when will you learn the discretion that suits mortal life, and be no longer dazzled with the image of power at your disposal? Power!" he cried; "who is more powerless? I look upon this young man whom I have sacrificed, Mr. Scuddamore, and feel how small a thing it is to be a Prince."

Silas was moved at the sight of his emotion. He tried to murmur some consolatory words, and burst into tears.

The Prince, touched by his obvious intention, came up to him and took him by the hand.

"Command yourself," said he. "We have both much to learn, and we shall both be better men for to-day's meeting."

Silas thanked him in silence with an affectionate look.

"Write me the address of Doctor Noel on this piece of paper," continued the Prince, leading him towards the table; "and let me recommend you, when you are again in Paris, to avoid the society of that dangerous man. He has acted in this matter on a generous inspiration; that I must believe; had he been privy to young Geraldine's death he would never have despatched the body to the care of the actual criminal."

"The actual criminal!" repeated Silas in astonishment.

"Even so," returned the Prince. "This letter, which the disposition of Almighty Providence has so strangely delivered into my hands, was addressed to no less a person than the criminal himself, the infamous President of the Suicide Club. Seek to pry no further in these perilous affairs, but content yourself with your own miraculous escape, and leave this house at once. I have pressing affairs, and must arrange at once about this poor clay, which was so lately a gallant and handsome youth."

Silas took a grateful and submissive leave of Prince Florizel, but he lingered in Box Court until he saw him depart in a splendid carriage on a visit to Colonel Henderson of the police. Republican as he was, the young American took off his hat with almost a sentiment of devotion to the retreating carriage. And the same night he started by rail on his return to Paris.

Here (observes my Arabian author) is the end of the "Story of the Physician and the Saratoga Trunk." Omitting some reflections on the power of Providence, highly pertinent in the original, but little suited to our occidental taste, I shall only add that Mr. Scuddamore has already begun to mount the ladder of political fame, and by last advices was the Sheriff of his native town.

# *The Adventure of the Hansom Cab*

Lieutenant Brackenbury Rich had greatly distinguished himself in one of the lesser Indian hill wars. He it was who took the chieftain prisoner with his own hand; his gallantry was universally applauded; and when he came home, prostrated by an ugly sabre cut and a protracted jungle fever, society was prepared to welcome the Lieutenant as a celebrity of minor lustre. But his was a character remarkable for unaffected modesty; adventure was dear to his heart, but he cared little for adulation; and he waited at foreign watering-places and in Algiers until the fame of his exploits had run through its nine days' vitality and begun to be forgotten. He arrived in London at last, in the early season, with as little observation as he could desire; and as he was an orphan and had none but distant relatives who lived in the provinces, it was almost as a foreigner that he installed himself in the capital of the country for which he had shed his blood.

On the day following his arrival he dined alone at a military club. He shook hands with a few old comrades, and received their warm congratulations; but as one and all had some engagement for the evening, he found himself left entirely to his own resources. He was in dress, for he had entertained the notion of visiting a theatre. But the great city was new to him; he had gone from a provincial school to a military college, and thence direct to the Eastern Empire; and he promised himself a variety of delights in this world for exploration. Swinging his cane, he took his way westward. It was a mild evening, already dark, and now and then threatening rain. The succession of faces in the lamplight stirred the Lieutenant's imagination; and it seemed to him as if he could walk for ever in that stimulating city atmosphere and surrounded by the mystery of four million private lives. He glanced at the houses, and marvelled what was passing behind those warmly-lighted windows; he looked into face after face, and saw them each intent upon some unknown interest, criminal or kindly.

"They talk of war," he thought, "but this is the great battlefield of mankind."

And then he began to wonder that he should walk so long in this complicated scene, and not chance upon so much as the shadow of an adventure for himself.

"All in good time," he reflected. "I am still a stranger, and perhaps wear a strange air. But I must be drawn into the eddy before long."

The night was already well advanced when a plump of cold rain fell suddenly out of the darkness. Brackenbury paused under some trees, and as he did so he caught sight of a hansom cabman making him a sign that he was disengaged. The circumstance fell in so happily to the occasion that he at once raised his cane in answer, and had soon ensconced himself in the London gondola.

"Where to, sir?" asked the driver.

"Where you please," said Brackenbury.

And immediately, at a pace of surprising swiftness, the hansom drove off through the rain into a maze of villas. One villa was so like another, each with its front garden, and there was so little to distinguish the deserted lamp-lit streets and crescents through which the flying hansom took its way, that Brackenbury soon lost all idea of direction.

He would have been tempted to believe that the cabman was amusing himself by driving him round and round and in and out about a small quarter, but there was something business-like in the speed which convinced him of the contrary. The man had an object in view, he was hastening towards a definite end; and Brackenbury was at once astonished at the fellow's skill in picking a way through such a labyrinth, and a little concerned to imagine what was the occasion of his hurry. He had heard tales of strangers falling ill in London. Did the driver belong to some bloody and treacherous association? and was he himself being whirled to a murderous death?

The thought had scarcely presented itself, when the cab swung sharply round a corner and pulled up before the garden gate of a villa in a long and wide road. The house was brilliantly lighted up. Another hansom had just driven away, and Brackenbury could see a gentleman being admitted at the front door and received by several liveried servants. He was surprised that the cabman should have stopped so immediately in front of a house where a reception was being held; but he did not doubt it was the result of accident, and sat placidly smoking where he was, until he heard the trap thrown open over his head.

"Here we are, sir," said the driver.

"Here!" repeated Brackenbury. "Where?"

"You told me to take you where I pleased, sir," returned the man with a chuckle, "and here we are."

It struck Brackenbury that the voice was wonderfully smooth and courteous for a man in so inferior a position; he remembered the speed at which he had been driven; and now it occurred to him that the hansom was more luxuriously appointed than the common run of public conveyances.

"I must ask you to explain," said he. "Do you mean to turn me out into the rain? My good man, I suspect the choice is mine."

"The choice is certainly yours," replied the driver; "but when I tell you all, I believe I know how a gentleman of your figure will decide. There is a gentlemen's party in this house. I do not know whether the master be a stranger to London and without acquaintances of his own; or whether he is a man of odd notions. But certainly I was hired to kidnap single gentlemen in evening dress, as many as I pleased, but military officers by preference. You have simply to go in and say that Mr. Morris invited you."

"Are you Mr. Morris?" inquired the Lieutenant.

"Oh, no," replied the cabman. "Mr. Morris is the person of the house."

"It is not a common way of collecting guests," said Brackenbury: "but an eccentric man might very well indulge the whim without any intention to offend. And suppose that I refuse Mr. Morris's invitation," he went on, "what then?"

"My orders are to drive you back where I took you from," replied the man, "and set out to look for others up to midnight. Those who have no fancy for such an adventure, Mr. Morris said, were not the guests for him."

These words decided the Lieutenant on the spot.

"After all," he reflected, as he descended from the hansom, "I have not had long to wait for my adventure."

He had hardly found footing on the side-walk, and was still feeling in his pocket for the fare, when the cab swung about and drove off by the way it came at the former break-neck velocity. Brackenbury shouted after the man, who paid no heed, and continued to drive away; but the sound of his voice was overheard in the house, the door was again thrown open, emitting a flood of light upon the garden, and a servant ran down to meet him holding an umbrella.

"The cabman has been paid," observed the servant in a very civil tone; and he proceeded to escort Brackenbury along the path and up the steps. In the hall several other attendants relieved him of his hat, cane, and paletot, gave him a ticket with a number in return, and politely hurried him up a stair adorned with tropical flowers, to the door of an apartment on the first storey. Here a grave butler inquired his name, and announcing "Lieutenant Brackenbury Rich," ushered him into the drawing-room of the house.

A young man, slender and singularly handsome, came forward and greeted him with an air at once courtly and affectionate. Hundreds of candles, of the finest wax, lit up a room that was perfumed, like the staircase, with a profusion of rare and beautiful flowering shrubs. A side-table was loaded with tempting viands. Several servants went to and fro with fruits and goblets of champagne. The company was perhaps sixteen in number, all men, few beyond the prime of life, and with hardly an exception, of a dashing and capable exterior. They were divided into two groups, one about a roulette board, and the other surrounding a table at which one of their number held a bank of baccarat.

"I see," thought Brackenbury, "I am in a private gambling saloon, and the cabman was a tout."

His eye had embraced the details, and his mind formed the conclusion, while his host was still holding him by the hand; and to him his looks returned from this rapid survey. At a second view Mr. Morris surprised him still more than on the first. The easy elegance of his manners, the distinction, amiability, and courage that appeared upon his features, fitted very ill with the Lieutenant's preconceptions on the subject of the proprietor of a hell; and the tone of his conversation seemed to mark him out for a man of position and merit. Brackenbury found he had an instinctive liking for his entertainer; and though he chid himself for the weakness, he was unable to resist a sort of friendly attraction for Mr. Morris's person and character.

"I have heard of you, Lieutenant Rich," said Mr. Morris, lowering his tone; "and believe me I am gratified to make your acquaintance. Your looks accord with the reputation that has preceded you from India. And if you will forget for a while the irregularity of your presentation in my house, I shall feel it not only an honour, but a genuine pleasure besides. A man who makes a mouthful of barbarian cavaliers," he added with a laugh, "should not be appalled by a breach of etiquette, however serious."

And he led him towards the sideboard and pressed him to partake of some refreshment.

"Upon my word," the Lieutenant reflected, "this is one of the pleasantest fellows and, I do not doubt, one of the most agreeable societies in London."

He partook of some champagne, which he found excellent; and observing that many of the company were already smoking, he lit one of his own Manillas, and strolled up to the roulette board, where he sometimes made a stake and sometimes looked on smilingly on the fortune of others. It was while he was thus idling that he became aware of a sharp scrutiny to which the whole of the guests were subjected. Mr. Morris went here and there, ostensibly busied on hospitable concerns; but he had ever a shrewd glance at disposal; not a man of the party escaped his sudden, searching looks; he took stock of the bearing of heavy losers, he valued the amount of the stakes, he paused behind couples who were deep in conversation; and, in a word, there was hardly a characteristic of any one present but he seemed to catch and make a note of it. Brackenbury began to wonder if this were indeed a gambling hell: it had so much the air of a private inquisition. He followed Mr. Morris in all his movements; and although the man had a ready smile, he seemed to perceive, as it were under a mask, a haggard, careworn, and preoccupied spirit. The fellows around him laughed and made their game; but Brackenbury had lost interest in the guests.

"This Morris," thought he, "is no idler in the room. Some deep purpose inspires him; let it be mine to fathom it."

Now and then Mr. Morris would call one of his visitors aside; and after a brief colloquy in an ante-room, he would return alone, and the visitors in question reappeared no more. After a certain number of repetitions, this performance excited Brackenbury's curiosity to a high degree. He determined to be at the bottom of this minor mystery at once; and strolling into the ante-room, found a deep window recess concealed by curtains of the fashionable green. Here he hurriedly ensconced himself; nor had he to wait long before the sound of steps and voices drew near him from the principal apartment. Peering through the division, he saw Mr. Morris escorting a fat and ruddy personage, with somewhat the look of a commercial traveller, whom Brackenbury had already remarked for his coarse laugh and under-bred behaviour at the table. The pair halted immediately before the window, so that Brackenbury lost not a word of the following discourse:—

"I beg you a thousand pardons!" began Mr. Morris, with the most conciliatory manner; "and, if I appear rude, I am sure you will readily forgive me. In a place so great as London accidents must continually happen; and the best that we can hope is to remedy them with as small delay as possible. I will not deny that I fear you have made a mistake and honoured my poor house by inadvertence; for, to speak openly, I cannot at all remember your appearance. Let me put the question without unnecessary circumlocution—between gentlemen of honour a word will suffice—Under whose roof do you suppose yourself to be?"

"That of Mr. Morris," replied the other, with a prodigious display of confusion, which had been visibly growing upon him throughout the last few words.

"Mr. John or Mr. James Morris?" inquired the host.

"I really cannot tell you," returned the unfortunate guest. "I am not personally acquainted with the gentleman, any more than I am with yourself."

"I see," said Mr. Morris. "There is another person of the same name farther down the street; and I have no doubt the policeman will be able to supply you with his number. Believe me, I felicitate myself on the misunderstanding which has procured me the pleasure of your company for so long; and let me express a hope that we may meet again upon a more regular footing.

Meantime, I would not for the world detain you longer from your friends. John," he added, raising his voice, "will you see that this gentleman finds his great-coat?"

And with the most agreeable air Mr. Morris escorted his visitor as far as the ante-room door, where he left him under conduct of the butler. As he passed the window, on his return to the drawing-room, Brackenbury could hear him utter a profound sigh, as though his mind was loaded with a great anxiety, and his nerves already fatigued with the task on which he was engaged.

For perhaps an hour the hansoms kept arriving with such frequency, that Mr. Morris had to receive a new guest for every old one that he sent away, and the company preserved its number undiminished. But towards the end of that time the arrivals grew few and far between, and at length ceased entirely, while the process of elimination was continued with unimpaired activity. The drawing-room began to look empty: the baccarat was discontinued for lack of a banker; more than one person said good-night of his own accord, and was suffered to depart without expostulation; and in the meanwhile Mr. Morris redoubled in agreeable attentions to those who stayed behind. He went from group to group and from person to person with looks of the readiest sympathy and the most pertinent and pleasing talk; he was not so much like a host as like a hostess, and there was a feminine coquetry and condescension in his manner which charmed the hearts of all.

As the guests grew thinner, Lieutenant Rich strolled for a moment out of the drawing-room into the hall in quest of fresher air. But he had no sooner passed the threshold of the ante-chamber than he was brought to a dead halt by a discovery of the most surprising nature. The flowering shrubs had disappeared from the staircase; three large furniture waggons stood before the garden gate; the servants were busy dismantling the house upon all sides; and some of them had already donned their great-coats and were preparing to depart. It was like the end of a country ball, where everything has been supplied by contract. Brackenbury had indeed some matter for reflection. First, the guests, who were no real guests after all, had been dismissed;

and now the servants, who could hardly be genuine servants, were actively dispersing.

"Was the whole establishment a sham?" he asked himself. "The mushroom of a single night which should disappear before morning?"

Watching a favourable opportunity, Brackenbury dashed upstairs to the highest regions of the house. It was as he had expected. He ran from room to room, and saw not a stick of furniture nor so much as a picture on the walls. Although the house had been painted and papered, it was not only uninhabited at present, but plainly had never been inhabited at all. The young officer remembered with astonishment its specious, settled, and hospitable air on his arrival.

It was only at a prodigious cost that the imposture could have been carried out upon so great a scale.

Who, then, was Mr. Morris? What was his intention in thus playing the householder for a single night in the remote west of London? And why did he collect his visitors at hazard from the streets?

Brackenbury remembered that he had already delayed too long, and hastened to join the company. Many had left during his absence; and counting the Lieutenant and his host, there were not more than five persons in the drawing-room—recently so thronged. Mr. Morris greeted him, as he re-entered the apartment, with a smile, and immediately rose to his feet.

"It is now time, gentlemen," said he, "to explain my purpose in decoying you from your amusements. I trust you did not find the evening hang very dully on your hands; but my object, I will confess it, was not to entertain your leisure, but to help myself in an unfortunate necessity. You are all gentlemen," he continued, "your appearance does you that much justice, and I ask for no better security. Hence, I speak it without concealment, I ask you to render me a dangerous and delicate service; dangerous because you may run the hazard of your lives, and delicate because I must ask an absolute discretion upon all that you shall see or hear. From an utter stranger the request is almost comically extravagant; I am well aware of this; and I would add at once, if there be any one present who has heard enough, if there be one among the party who recoils from a dangerous confidence and a piece of Quixotic devotion to he knows not whom—here is my hand ready, and I shall wish him good-night and God-speed with all the sincerity in the world."

A very tall, black man, with a heavy stoop, immediately responded to this appeal.

"I commend your frankness, sir," said he; "and, for my part, I go. I make no reflections; but I cannot deny that you fill me with suspicious thoughts. I go myself, as I say; and perhaps you will think I have no right to add words to my example."

"On the contrary," replied Mr. Morris, "I am obliged to you for all you say. It would be impossible to exaggerate the gravity of my proposal."

"Well, gentlemen, what do you say?" said the tall man, addressing the others. "We have had our evening's frolic; shall we all go homeward peaceably in a body? You will think well of my suggestion in the morning, when you see the sun again in innocence and safety."

The speaker pronounced the last words with an intonation which added to their force; and his face wore a singular expression, full of gravity and significance. Another of the company rose hastily, and, with some appearance of alarm, prepared to take his leave. There were only two who held their ground, Brackenbury and an old red-nosed cavalry Major; but these two preserved a nonchalant demeanour, and, beyond a look of intelligence which they rapidly exchanged, appeared entirely foreign to the discussion that had just been terminated.

Mr. Morris conducted the deserters as far as the door, which he closed upon their heels; then he turned round, disclosing a countenance of mingled relief and animation, and addressed the two officers as follows.

"I have chosen my men like Joshua in the Bible," said Mr. Morris, "and I now believe I have the pick of London. Your appearance pleased my hansom cabmen; then it delighted me; I have watched your behaviour in a strange company, and under the most unusual circumstances: I have studied how you played and how you bore your losses; lastly, I have put you to the test of a staggering announcement, and you received it like an invitation to dinner. It is not for nothing," he cried, "that I have been for years the companion and the pupil of the bravest and wisest potentate in Europe."

"At the affair of Bunderchang," observed the Major, "I asked for twelve volunteers, and every trooper in the ranks replied to my appeal. But a gaming party is not the same thing as a regiment under fire. You may be pleased, I suppose, to have found two, and two who will not fail you at a push. As for the pair who ran away, I count them among the most pitiful hounds I ever met with. Lieutenant Rich," he added, addressing Brackenbury, "I have heard much of you of late; and I cannot doubt but you have also heard of me. I am Major O'Rooke."

And the veteran tendered his hand, which was red and tremulous, to the young Lieutenant.

"Who has not?" answered Brackenbury.

"When this little matter is settled," said Mr. Morris, "you will think I have sufficiently rewarded you; for I could offer neither a more valuable service than to make him acquainted with the other."

"And now," said Major O'Rooke, "is it a duel?"

"A duel after a fashion," replied Mr. Morris, "a duel with unknown and dangerous enemies, and, as I gravely fear, a duel to the death. I must ask you," he continued, "to call me Morris no longer; call me, if you please, Hammersmith; my real name, as well as that of another person to whom I hope to present you before long, you will gratify me by not asking and not seeking to discover for yourselves. Three days ago the person of whom I speak disappeared suddenly from home; and, until this morning, I received no hint of his situation. You will fancy my alarm when I tell you that he is engaged upon a work of private justice. Bound by an unhappy oath, too lightly sworn, he finds it necessary, without the help of law, to rid the earth of an insidious and bloody villain. Already two of our friends, and one of them my own born brother, have perished in the enterprise. He himself, or I am much deceived, is taken in the same fatal toils. But at least he still lives and still hopes, as this billet sufficiently proves."

And the speaker, no other than Colonel Geraldine, proffered a letter, thus conceived:—

"MAJOR HAMMERSMITH,—On Wednesday, at 3 A.M., you will be admitted by the small door to the gardens of Rochester House, Regent's Park, by a man who is entirely in my interest. I must request you not to fail me by a second. Pray bring my case of swords, and, if you can find them, one or two gentlemen of conduct and discretion to whom my person is unknown. My name must not be used in this affair.

T. GODALL."

"From his wisdom alone, if he had no other title," pursued Colonel Geraldine, when the others had each satisfied his curiosity, "my friend is a man whose directions should implicitly be followed. I need not tell you, therefore, that I have not so much as visited the neighbourhood of Rochester House; and that I am still as wholly in the dark as either of yourselves as to the nature of my friend's dilemma. I betook myself, as soon as I had received this order, to a furnishing contractor, and, in a few hours, the house in which we now are had assumed its late air of festival. My scheme was at least original; and I am far from regretting an action which has procured me the services of Major O'Rooke and Lieutenant Brackenbury Rich. But the servants in the street will have a strange awakening. The house which this evening was full of lights and visitors they will find uninhabited and for sale to-morrow morning. Thus even the most serious concerns," added the Colonel, "have a merry side."

"And let us add a merry ending," said Brackenbury.

The Colonel consulted his watch.

"It is now hard on two," he said. "We have an hour before us, and a swift cab is at the door. Tell me if I may count upon your help."

"During a long life," replied Major O'Rooke, "I never took back my hand from anything, nor so much as hedged a bet."

Brackenbury signified his readiness in the most becoming terms; and after they had drunk a glass or two of wine, the Colonel gave each of them a loaded revolver, and the three mounted into the cab and drove off for the address in question.

Rochester House was a magnificent residence on the banks of the canal. The large extent of the garden isolated it in an unusual degree from the annoyances of neighbourhood. It seemed the *parc aux cerfs* of some great nobleman or millionaire. As far as could be seen from the street, there was not a glimmer of light in any of the numerous windows of the mansion; and the place had a look of neglect, as though the master had been long from home.

The cab was discharged, and the three gentlemen were not long in discovering the small door, which was a sort of postern in a lane between two garden walls. It still wanted ten or fifteen minutes of the appointed time; the rain fell heavily, and the adventurers sheltered themselves below some pendant ivy, and spoke in low tones of the approaching trial.

Suddenly Geraldine raised his finger to command silence, and all three bent their hearing to the utmost. Through the continuous noise of the rain, the steps and voices of two men became audible from the other side of the wall; and, as they drew nearer, Brackenbury, whose sense of hearing was remarkably acute, could even distinguish some fragments of their talk.

"Is the grave dug?" asked one.

"It is," replied the other; "behind the laurel hedge. When the job is done, we can cover it with a pile of stakes."

The first speaker laughed, and the sound of his merriment was shocking to the listeners on the other side.

"In an hour from now," he said.

And by the sound of the steps it was obvious that the pair had separated, and were proceeding in contrary directions.

Almost immediately after the postern door was cautiously opened, a white face was protruded into the lane, and a hand was seen beckoning to the watchers. In dead silence the three passed the door, which was immediately locked behind them, and followed their guide through several garden alleys to the kitchen entrance of the house. A single candle burned in the great paved kitchen, which was destitute of the customary furniture; and as the party proceeded to ascend from thence by a flight of winding stairs, a prodigious noise of rats testified still more plainly to the dilapidation of the house.

Their conductor preceded them, carrying the candle. He was a lean man, much bent, but still agile; and he turned from time to time and admonished silence and caution by his gestures. Colonel Geraldine followed on his heels, the case of swords under one arm, and a pistol ready in the other. Brackenbury's heart beat thickly. He perceived that they were still in time; but he judged from the alacrity of the old man that the hour of action must be near at hand; and the circumstances of this adventure were so obscure and menacing, the place seemed so well chosen for the darkest acts, that an older man than Brackenbury might have been pardoned a measure of emotion as he closed the procession up the winding stair.

At the top the guide threw open a door and ushered the three officers before him into a small apartment, lighted by a smoky lamp and the glow of a modest fire. At the chimney corner sat a man in the early prime of life, and of a stout but courtly and commanding appearance. His attitude and expression were those of the most unmoved composure; he was smoking a cheroot with much enjoyment and deliberation, and on a table by his elbow stood a long glass of some effervescing beverage which diffused an agreeable odour through the room.

"Welcome," said he, extending his hand to Colonel Geraldine. "I knew I might count on your exactitude."

"On my devotion," replied the Colonel, with a bow.

"Present me to your friends," continued the first; and, when that ceremony had been performed, "I wish, gentlemen," he added, with the most exquisite affability, "that I could offer you a more cheerful programme; it is ungracious to inaugurate an acquaintance upon serious affairs; but the compulsion of events is stronger than the obligations of good-fellowship. I hope and believe you will be able to forgive me this unpleasant evening; and for men of your stamp it will be enough to know that you are conferring a considerable favour."

"Your Highness," said the Major, "must pardon my bluntness. I am unable to hide what I know. For some time back I have suspected Major Hammersmith, but Mr. Godall is unmistakable. To seek two men in London unacquainted with Prince Florizel of Bohemia was to ask too much at Fortune's hands."

"Prince Florizel!" cried Brackenbury in amazement.

And he gazed with the deepest interest on the features of the celebrated personage before him.

"I shall not lament the loss of my incognito," remarked the

Prince, "for it enables me to thank you with the more authority. You would have done as much for Mr. Godall, I feel sure, as for the Prince of Bohemia; but the latter can perhaps do more for you. The gain is mine," he added, with a courteous gesture.

And the next moment he was conversing with the two officers about the Indian army and the native troops, a subject on which, as on all others, he had a remarkable fund of information and the soundest views.

There was something so striking in this man's attitude at a moment of deadly peril that Brackenbury was overcome with respectful admiration; nor was he less sensible to the charm of his conversation or the surprising amenity of his address. Every gesture, every intonation, was not only noble in itself, but seemed to ennoble the fortunate mortal for whom it was intended; and Brackenbury confessed to himself with enthusiasm that this was a sovereign for whom a brave man might thankfully lay down his life.

Many minutes had thus passed, when the person who had introduced them into the house, and who had sat ever since in a corner, and with his watch in his hand, arose and whispered a word into the Prince's ear.

"It is well, Dr. Noel," replied Florizel, aloud; and then addressing the others, "You will excuse me, gentlemen," he added, "if I have to leave you in the dark. The moment now approaches."

Dr. Noel extinguished the lamp. A faint, grey light, premonitory of the dawn, illuminated the window, but was not sufficient to illuminate the room; and when the Prince rose to his feet, it was impossible to distinguish his features or to make a guess at the nature of the emotion which obviously affected him as he spoke. He moved towards the door, and placed himself at one side of it in an attitude of the wariest attention.

"You will have the kindness," he said, "to maintain the strictest silence, and to conceal yourselves in the densest of the shadow."

The three officers and the physician hastened to obey, and for nearly ten minutes the only sound in Rochester House was occasioned by the excursions of the rats behind the woodwork. At the end of that period, a loud creak of a hinge broke in with surprising distinctness on the silence; and shortly after, the watchers could distinguish a slow and cautious tread approaching up the kitchen stair. At every second step the intruder seemed to pause and lend an ear, and during these intervals, which seemed of an incalculable duration, a profound disquiet possessed the spirit of the listeners. Dr. Noel, accustomed as he was to dangerous emotions, suffered an almost pitiful physical prostration; his breath whistled in his lungs, his teeth grated one upon another, and his joints cracked aloud as he nervously shifted his position.

At last a hand was laid upon the door, and the bolt shot back with a slight report. There followed another pause, during which Brackenbury could see the Prince draw himself together noiselessly as if for some unusual exertion. Then the door opened, letting in a little more of the light of the morning; and the figure of a man appeared upon the threshold and stood motionless. He was tall, and carried a knife in his hand. Even in the twilight they could see his upper teeth bare and glistening, for his mouth was open like that of a hound about to leap. The man had evidently been over the head in water but a minute or two before; and even while he stood there the drops kept falling from his wet clothes and pattered on the floor.

The next moment he crossed the threshold. There was a leap, a stifled cry, an instantaneous struggle; and before Colonel Geraldine could spring to his aid, the Prince held the man disarmed and helpless, by the shoulders.

"Dr. Noel," he said, "you will be so good as to re-light the lamp."

And relinquishing the charge of his prisoner to Geraldine and Brackenbury, he crossed the room and set his back against the chimney-piece. As soon as the lamp had kindled, the party beheld an unaccustomed sternness on the Prince's features. It was no longer Florizel, the careless gentleman; it was the Prince of Bohemia, justly incensed and full of deadly purpose, who now raised his head and addressed the captive President of the Suicide Club.

"President," he said, "you have laid your last snare, and your own feet are taken in it. The day is beginning; it is your last morning. You have just swum the Regent's Canal; it is your last bathe in this world. Your old accomplice, Dr. Noel, so far from betraying me, has delivered you into my hands for judgment. And the grave you had dug for me this afternoon shall serve, in God's almighty providence, to hide your own just doom from the curiosity of mankind. Kneel and pray, sir, if you have a mind that way; for your time is short, and God is weary of your iniquities."

The President made no answer either by word or sign; but continued to hang his head and gaze sullenly on the floor, as though he were conscious of the Prince's prolonged and unsparing regard.

"Gentlemen," continued Florizel, resuming the ordinary tone of his conversation, "this is a fellow who has long eluded me, but whom, thanks to Dr. Noel, I now have tightly by the heels. To tell the story of his misdeeds would occupy more time than we can now afford; but if the canal had contained nothing but the blood of his victims, I believe the wretch would have been no drier than you see him. Even in an affair of this sort I desire to preserve the forms of honour. But I make you the judges, gentlemen— this is more an execution than a duel and to give the rogue his choice of weapons would be to push too far a point of etiquette. I cannot afford to lose my life in such a business," he continued, unlocking the case of swords; "and as a pistol-bullet travels so often on the wings of chance, and skill and courage may fall by the most trembling marksman, I have decided, and I feel sure you will approve my determination, to put this question to the touch of swords."

When Brackenbury and Major O'Rooke, to whom these remarks were particularly addressed, had each intimated his approval, "Quick, sir," added Prince Florizel to the President, "choose a blade and do not keep me waiting; I have an impatience to be done with you for ever."

For the first time since he was captured and disarmed the President raised his head, and it was plain that he began instantly to pluck up courage.

"Is it to be stand up?" he asked eagerly, "and between you and me?"

"I mean so far to honour you," replied the Prince.

"Oh, come!" cried the President. "With a fair field, who knows how things may happen? I must add that I consider it handsome behaviour on your Highness's part; and if the worst comes to the worst I shall die by one of the most gallant gentlemen in Europe."

And the President, liberated by those who had detained him, stepped up to the table and began, with minute attention, to select a sword. He was highly elated, and seemed to feel no doubt that he should issue victorious from the contest. The spectators grew alarmed in the face of so entire a confidence, and adjured Prince Florizel to reconsider his intention.

"It is but a farce," he answered; "and I think I can promise you, gentlemen, that it will not be long a-playing."

"Your Highness will be careful not to over-reach," said Colonel Geraldine.

"Geraldine," returned the Prince, "did you ever know me fail in a debt of honour? I owe you this man's death, and you shall have it."

The President at last satisfied himself with one of the rapiers, and signified his readiness by a gesture that was not devoid of a rude nobility. The nearness of peril, and the sense of courage, even to this obnoxious villain, lent an air of manhood and a certain grace.

The Prince helped himself at random to a sword.

"Colonel Geraldine and Doctor Noel," he said, "will have the goodness to await me in this room. I wish no personal friend of mine to be involved in this transaction. Major O'Rooke, you are a man of some years and a settled reputation—let me recommend the President to your good graces. Lieutenant Rich will be so good as lend me his attentions: a young man cannot have too much experience in such affairs."

"Your Highness," replied Brackenbury, "it is an honour I shall prize extremely."

"It is well," returned Prince Florizel; "I shall hope to stand your friend in more important circumstances."

And so saying he led the way out of the apartment and down the kitchen stairs.

The two men who were thus left alone threw open the window and leaned out, straining every sense to catch an indication of the tragical events that were about to follow. The rain was now over; day had almost come, and the birds were piping in the shrubbery and on the forest trees of the garden. The Prince and his companions were visible for a moment as they followed an alley between two flowering thickets; but at the first corner a clump of foliage intervened, and they were again concealed from view. This was all that the Colonel and the Physician had an opportunity to see, and the garden was so vast, and the place of combat evidently so remote from the house, that not even the noise of sword-play reached their ears.

"He has taken him towards the grave," said Dr. Noel, with a shudder.

"God," cried the Colonel, "God defend the right!"

And they awaited the event in silence, the Doctor shaking with fear, the Colonel in an agony of sweat. Many minutes must have elapsed, the day was sensibly broader, and the birds were singing more heartily in the garden before a sound of returning footsteps recalled their glances towards the door. It was the Prince and the two Indian officers who entered. God had defended the right.

"I am ashamed of my emotion," said Prince Florizel; "I feel it is a weakness unworthy of my station, but the continued existence of that hound of hell had begun to prey upon me like a disease, and his death has more refreshed me than a night of slumber. Look, Geraldine," he continued, throwing his sword upon the floor, "there is the blood of the man who killed your brother. It should be a welcome sight. And yet," he added, "see how strangely we men are made! my revenge is not yet five minutes old, and already I am beginning to ask myself if even revenge be attainable on this precarious stage of life. The ill he did, who can undo it? The career in which he amassed a huge fortune (for the house itself in which we stand belonged to him)—that career is now a part of the destiny of mankind for ever; and I might weary myself making thrusts in carte until the crack of judgment, and Geraldine's brother would be none the less dead, and a thousand other innocent persons would be none the less dishonoured and debauched! The existence of a man is so small a thing to take, so mighty a thing to employ! Alas!" he cried, "is there anything in life so disenchanting as attainment?"

"God's justice has been done," replied the Doctor. "So much

I behold. The lesson, your Highness, has been a cruel one for me; and I await my own turn with deadly apprehension."

"What was I saying?" cried the Prince. "I have punished, and here is the man beside us who can help me to undo. Ah, Dr. Noel! you and I have before us many a day of hard and honourable toil; and perhaps, before we have none, you may have more than redeemed your early errors."

"And in the meantime," said the Doctor, "let me go and bury my oldest friend."

(And this, observes the erudite Arabian, is the fortunate conclusion of the tale. The Prince, it is superfluous to mention, forgot none of those who served him in this great exploit; and to this day his authority and influence help them forward in their public career, while his condescending friendship adds a charm to their private life. To collect, continues my author, all the strange events in which this Prince has played the part of Providence were to fill the habitable globe with books. But the stories which relate to the fortunes of the Rajah's Diamond are of too entertaining a description, says he, to be omitted. Following prudently in the footsteps of this Oriental, we shall now begin the series to which he refers with the "Story of the Bandbox.")

# THE RAJAH'S DIAMOND

# Story of the Bandbox

U p to the age of sixteen, at a private school and afterwards at one of those great institutions for which England is justly famous, Mr. Harry Hartley had received the ordinary education of a gentleman. At that period, he manifested a remarkable distaste for study; and his only surviving parent being both weak and ignorant, he was permitted thenceforward to spend his time in the attainment of petty and purely elegant accomplishments. Two years later, he was left an orphan and almost a beggar. For all active and industrious pursuits, Harry was unfitted alike by nature and training. He could sing romantic ditties, and accompany himself with discretion on the piano; he was a graceful although a timid cavalier; he had a pronounced taste for chess; and nature had sent him into the world with one of the most engaging exteriors that can well be fancied. Blond and pink, with dove's eyes and a gentle smile, he had an air of agreeable tenderness and melancholy, and the most submissive and caressing manners. But when all is said, he was not the man to lead armaments of war, or direct the councils of a State.

A fortunate chance and some influence obtained for Harry, at the time of his bereavement, the position of private secretary to Major-General Sir Thomas Vandeleur, C.B. Sir Thomas was a man of sixty, loud-spoken, boisterous, and domineering. For some reason, some service the nature of which had been often whispered and repeatedly denied, the Rajah of Kashgar had presented this officer with the sixth known diamond of the world. The gift transformed General Vandeleur from a poor into a wealthy man, from an obscure and unpopular soldier into one of the lions of London society; the possessor of the Rajah's Diamond was welcome in the most exclusive circles; and he had found a lady, young, beautiful, and well-born, who was willing to call the diamond hers even at the price of marriage with Sir Thomas Vandeleur. It was commonly said at the time that, as like draws to like, one jewel had attracted another; certainly Lady Vandeleur was not only a gem of the finest water in her own person, but she showed herself to the world in a very costly setting; and she was considered by many respectable authorities, as one among the three or four best dressed women in England.

Harry's duty as secretary was not particularly onerous; but he had a dislike for all prolonged work; it gave him pain to ink his fingers; and the charms of Lady Vandeleur and her toilettes drew him often from the library to the boudoir. He had the prettiest ways among women, could talk fashions with enjoyment, and was never more happy than when criticising a shade of ribbon, or running on an errand to the milliner's. In short, Sir Thomas's correspondence fell into pitiful arrears, and my Lady had another lady's maid.

At last the General, who was one of the least patient of military commanders, arose from his place in a violent access of passion, and indicated to his secretary that he had no further need for his services, with one of those explanatory gestures which are most rarely employed between gentlemen. The door being unfortunately open, Mr. Hartley fell downstairs head foremost.

He arose somewhat hurt and very deeply aggrieved. The life in the General's house precisely suited him; he moved, on a more or less doubtful footing, in very genteel company, he did little, he ate of the best, and he had a lukewarm satisfaction in the presence of Lady Vandeleur, which, in his own heart, he dubbed by a more emphatic name.

Immediately after he had been outraged by the military foot, he hurried to the boudoir and recounted his sorrows.

"You know very well, my dear Harry," replied Lady Vandeleur, for she called him by name like a child or a domestic servant, "that you never by any chance do what the General tells you. No more do I, you may say. But that is different. A woman can earn her pardon for a good year of disobedience by a single adroit submission; and, besides, no one is married to his private secretary. I shall be sorry to lose you; but since you cannot stay longer in a house where you have been insulted, I shall wish you good-bye, and I promise you to make the General smart for his behaviour."

Harry's countenance fell; tears came into his eyes, and he gazed on Lady Vandeleur with a tender reproach.

"My Lady," said he, "what is an insult? I should think little indeed of any one who could not forgive them by the score. But to leave one's friends; to tear up the bonds of affection——"

He was unable to continue, for his emotion choked him, and he began to weep.

Lady Vandeleur looked at him with a curious expression. "This little fool," she thought, "imagines himself to be in love with me. Why should he not become my servant instead of the General's? He is good-natured, obliging, and understands dress; and besides it will keep him out of mischief. He is positively too pretty to be unattached." That night she talked over the General, who was already somewhat ashamed of his vivacity; and Harry was transferred to the feminine department, where his life was little short of heavenly. He was always dressed with uncommon nicety, wore delicate flowers in his button-hole, and could entertain a visitor with tact and pleasantry. He took a pride in servility to a beautiful woman; received Lady Vandeleur's commands as so many marks of favour; and was pleased to exhibit himself before other men, who derided and despised him, in his character of male lady's-maid and man milliner. Nor could he think enough of his existence from a moral point of view. Wickedness seemed to him an essentially male attribute, and to pass one's days with a delicate woman, and principally occupied about trimmings, was to inhabit an enchanted isle among the storms of life.

One fine morning he came into the drawing-room and began to arrange some music on the top of the piano. Lady Vandeleur, at the other end of the apartment, was speaking somewhat eagerly with her brother, Charlie Pendragon, an elderly young man, much broken with dissipation, and very lame of one foot. The private secretary, to whose entrance they paid no regard, could not avoid overhearing a part of their conversation.

"To-day or never," said the lady. "Once and for all, it shall be done to-day."

"To-day, if it must be," replied the brother, with a sigh. "But it is a false step, a ruinous step, Clara; and we shall live to repent it dismally."

Lady Vandeleur looked her brother steadily and somewhat strangely in the face.

"You forget," she said; "the man must die at last."

"Upon my word, Clara," said Pendragon, "I believe you are the most heartless rascal in England."

"You men," she returned, "are so coarsely built, that you can never appreciate a shade of meaning. You are yourselves rapacious, violent, immodest, careless of distinction; and yet the least thought for the future shocks you in a woman. I have no patience with such stuff. You would despise in a common banker the imbecility that you expect to find in us."

"You are very likely right," replied her brother; "you were always cleverer than I. And, anyway, you know my motto: The family before all."

"Yes, Charlie," she returned, taking his hand in hers, "I know your motto better than you know it yourself. 'And Clara before the family!' Is not that the second part of it? Indeed, you are the best of brothers, and I love you dearly."

Mr. Pendragon got up, looking a little confused by these family endearments.

"I had better not be seen," said he. "I understand my part to a miracle, and I'll keep an eye on the Tame Cat."

"Do," she replied. "He is an abject creature, and might ruin all."

She kissed the tips of her fingers to him daintily; and the brother withdrew by the boudoir and the back stair.

"Harry," said Lady Vandeleur, turning towards the secretary as soon as they were alone, "I have a commission for you this morning. But you shall take a cab; I cannot have my secretary freckled."

She spoke the last words with emphasis and a look of half-motherly pride that caused great contentment to poor Harry; and he professed himself charmed to find an opportunity of serving her.

"It is another of our great secrets," she went on archly, "and no one must know of it but my secretary and me. Sir Thomas would make the saddest disturbance; and if you only knew how weary I am of these scenes! Oh, Harry, Harry, can you explain to me what makes you men so violent and unjust? But, indeed, I know you cannot; you are the only man in the world who knows nothing of these shameful passions; you are so good, Harry, and so kind; you, at least, can be a woman's friend; and, do you know? I think you make the others more ugly by comparison."

"It is you," said Harry gallantly, "who are so kind to me. You treat me like—"

"Like a mother," interposed Lady Vandeleur; "I try to be a mother to you. Or, at least," she corrected herself with a smile, "almost a mother. I am afraid I am too young to be your mother really. Let us say a friend—a dear friend."

She paused long enough to let her words take effect in Harry's sentimental quarters, but not long enough to allow him a reply.

"But all this is beside our purpose," she resumed. "You will find a bandbox in the left-hand side of the oak wardrobe; it is underneath the pink slip that I wore on Wednesday with my Mechlin. You will take it immediately to this address," and she gave him a paper, "but do not, on any account, let it out of your hands until you have received a receipt written by myself. Do you understand? Answer, if you please—answer! This is extremely important, and I must ask you to pay some attention."

Harry pacified her by repeating her instructions perfectly; and she was just going to tell him more when General Vandeleur flung into the apartment, scarlet with anger, and holding a long and elaborate milliner's bill in his hand.

"Will you look at this, madam?" cried he. "Will you have the goodness to look at this document? I know well enough you married me for my money, and I hope I can make as great allowances as any other man in the service; but, as sure as God made me, I mean to put a period to this disreputable prodigality."

"Mr. Hartley," said Lady Vandeleur, "I think you understand what you have to do. May I ask you to see to it at once?"

"Stop," said the General, addressing Harry, "one word before you go." And then, turning again to Lady Vandeleur, "What is this precious fellow's errand?" he demanded. "I trust him no further than I do yourself, let me tell you. If he had as much as the rudiments of honesty, he would scorn to stay in this house; and what he does for his wages is a mystery to all the world. What is his errand, madam? and why are you hurrying him away?"

"I supposed you had something to say to me in private," replied the lady.

"You spoke about an errand," insisted the General. "Do not attempt to deceive me in my present state of temper. You certainly spoke about an errand."

"If you insist on making your servants privy to our humiliating dissensions," replied Lady Vandeleur, "perhaps I had better ask Mr. Hartley to sit down. No?" she continued; "then you may go, Mr. Hartley. I trust you may remember all that you have heard in this room; it may be useful to you."

Harry at once made his escape from the drawing-room; and as he ran upstairs he could hear the General's voice upraised in declamation, and the thin tones of Lady Vandeleur planting icy repartees at every opening. How cordially he admired the wife! How skilfully she could evade an awkward question! with what secure effrontery she repeated her instructions under the very guns of the enemy! and on the other hand, how he detested the husband!

There had been nothing unfamiliar in the morning's events, for he was continually in the habit of serving Lady Vandeleur on secret missions, principally connected with millinery. There was a skeleton in the house, as he well knew. The bottomless extravagance and the unknown liabilities of the wife had long since swallowed her own fortune, and threatened day by day to engulph that of the husband. Once or twice in every year exposure and ruin seemed imminent, and Harry kept trotting round to all sorts of furnishers' shops, telling small fibs, and paying small advances on the gross amount, until another term was tided over, and the lady and her faithful secretary breathed again. For Harry, in a double capacity, was heart and soul upon that side of the war: not only did he adore Lady Vandeleur and fear and dislike her husband, but he naturally sympathised with the love of finery, and his own single extravagance was at the tailor's.

He found the bandbox where it had been described, arranged his toilette with care, and left the house. The sun shone brightly; the distance he had to travel was considerable, and he remembered with dismay that the General's sudden irruption had prevented Lady Vandeleur from giving him money for a cab. On this sultry day there was every chance that his complexion would suffer severely; and to walk through so much of London with a bandbox on his arm was a humiliation almost insupportable to a youth of his character. He paused, and took counsel with himself. The Vandeleurs lived in Eaton Place; his destination was near Notting Hill; plainly, he might cross the Park by keeping well in the open and avoiding populous alleys; and he thanked his stars when he reflected that it was still comparatively early in the day.

Anxious to be rid of his incubus, he walked somewhat faster than his ordinary, and he was already some way through Kensington Gardens when, in a solitary spot among trees, he found himself confronted by the General.

"I beg your pardon, Sir Thomas," observed Harry, politely falling on one side; for the other stood directly in his path.

"Where are you going, sir?" asked the General.

"I am taking a little walk among the trees," replied the lad.

The General struck the bandbox with his cane.

"With that thing?" he cried; "you lie, sir, and you know you lie!"

"Indeed, Sir Thomas," returned Harry, "I am not accustomed to be questioned in so high a key."

"You do not understand your position," said the General. "You are my servant, and a servant of whom I have conceived the most serious suspicions. How do I know but that your box is full of teaspoons?"

"It contains a silk hat belonging to a friend," said Harry.

"Very well," replied General Vandeleur. "Then I want to see your friend's silk hat. I have," he added grimly, "a singular curiosity for hats; and I believe you know me to be somewhat positive."

"I beg your pardon, Sir Thomas, I am exceedingly grieved," Harry apologised; "but indeed this is a private affair."

The General caught him roughly by the shoulder with one hand, while he raised his cane in the most menacing manner with the other. Harry gave himself up for lost; but at the same moment Heaven vouchsafed him an unexpected defender in the person of Charlie Pendragon, who now strode forward from behind the trees.

"Come, come, General, hold your hand," said he, "this is neither courteous nor manly."

"Aha!" cried the General, wheeling round upon his new antagonist, "Mr. Pendragon! And do you suppose, Mr. Pendragon, that because I have had the misfortune to marry your sister, I shall suffer myself to be dogged and thwarted by a discredited and bankrupt libertine like you? My acquaintance with Lady Vandeleur, sir, has taken away all my appetite for the other members of her family."

"And do you fancy, General Vandeleur," retorted Charlie, "that because my sister has had the misfortune to marry you, she there and then forfeited her rights and privileges as a lady? I own, sir, that by that action she did as much as anybody could to derogate from her position; but to me she is still a Pendragon. I make it my business to protect her from ungentlemanly outrage, and if you were ten times her husband I would not permit her liberty to be restrained, nor her private messengers to be violently arrested."

"How is that, Mr. Hartley?" interrogated the General. "Mr. Pendragon is of my opinion, it appears. He too suspects that Lady Vandeleur has something to do with your friend's silk hat."

Charlie saw that he had committed an unpardonable blunder, which he hastened to repair.

"How, sir?" he cried; "I suspect, do you say? I suspect nothing. Only where I find strength abused and a man brutalising his inferiors, I take the liberty to interfere."

As he said these words he made a sign to Harry, which the latter was too dull or too much troubled to understand.

"In what way am I to construe your attitude, sir?" demanded Vandeleur.

"Why, sir, as you please," returned Pendragon.

The General once more raised his cane, and made a cut for Charlie's head; but the latter, lame foot and all, evaded the blow with his umbrella, ran in, and immediately closed with his formidable adversary.

"Run, Harry, run!" he cried; "run, you dolt! Harry stood petrified for a moment, watching the two men sway together in this fierce embrace; then he turned and took to his heels. When he cast a glance over his shoulder he saw the General prostrate under Charlie's knee, but still making desperate efforts to reverse the situation; and the Gardens seemed to have filled with people, who were running from all directions towards the scene of fight. This spectacle lent the secretary wings; and he did not relax his pace until he had gained the Bayswater road, and plunged at random into an unfrequented by-street.

To see two gentlemen of his acquaintance thus brutally mauling each other was deeply shocking to Harry. He desired to forget the sight; he desired, above all, to put as great a distance as possible between himself and General Vandeleur; and in his eagerness for this he forgot everything about his destination, and hurried before him headlong and trembling. When he remembered that Lady Vandeleur was the wife of one and the sister of the other of these gladiators, his heart was touched with sympathy for a woman so distressingly misplaced in life. Even his own situation in the General's household looked hardly so pleasing as usual in the light of these violent transactions.

He had walked some little distance, busied with these meditations, before a slight collision with another passenger reminded him of the bandbox on his arm.

"Heavens!" cried he, "where was my head? and whither have I wandered?"

Thereupon he consulted the envelope which Lady Vandeleur had given him. The address was there, but without a name. Harry was simply directed to ask for "the gentleman who expected a parcel from Lady Vandeleur," and if he were not at home to await his return. The gentleman, added the note, should present a receipt in the handwriting of the lady herself. All this seemed mightily mysterious, and Harry was above all astonished at the omission of the name and the formality of the receipt. He had thought little of this last when he heard it dropped in conversation; but reading it in cold blood, and taking it in connection with the other strange particulars, he became convinced that he was engaged in perilous affairs. For half a moment he had a doubt of Lady Vandeleur herself; for he found these obscure proceedings somewhat unworthy of so high a lady, and became more critical when her secrets were preserved against himself. But her empire over his spirit was too complete, he dismissed his suspicions, and blamed himself roundly for having so much as entertained them.

In one thing, however, his duty and interest, his generosity and his terrors, coincided—to get rid of the bandbox with the greatest possible despatch.

He accosted the first policeman and courteously inquired his way. It turned out that he was already not far from his destination, and a walk of a few minutes brought him to a small house in a lane, freshly painted, and kept with the most scrupulous attention. The knocker and bell-pull were highly polished; flowering pot-herbs garnished the sills of the different windows; and curtains of some rich material concealed the interior from the eyes of curious passengers. The place had an air of repose and secrecy; and Harry was so far caught with this spirit that he knocked with more than usual discretion, and was more than usually careful to remove all impurity from his boots.

A servant-maid of some personal attractions immediately opened the door, and seemed to regard the secretary with no unkind eyes.

"This is the parcel from Lady Vandeleur," said Harry.

"I know," replied the maid, with a nod. "But the gentleman is from home. Will you leave it with me?"

"I cannot," answered Harry. "I am directed not to part with it but upon a certain condition, and I must ask you, I am afraid, to let me wait."

"Well," said she, "I suppose I may let you wait. I am lonely enough, I can tell you, and you do not look as though you would eat a girl. But be sure and do not ask the gentleman's name, for that I am not to tell you."

"Do you say so?" cried Harry. "Why, how strange! But indeed for some time back I walk among surprises. One question I think I may surely ask without indiscretion: Is he the master of this house?"

"He is a lodger, and not eight days old at that," returned the maid. "And now a question for a question: Do you know Lady Vandeleur?"

"I am her private secretary," replied Harry with a glow of modest pride.

"She is pretty, is she not?" pursued the servant.

"Oh, beautiful!" cried Harry; "wonderfully lovely, and not less good and kind!"

"You look kind enough yourself," she retorted; "and I wager you are worth a dozen Lady Vandeleurs."

Harry was properly scandalised.

"I!" he cried. "I am only a secretary!"

"Do you mean that for me?" said the girl. "Because I am only a housemaid, if you please." And then, relenting at the sight of Harry's obvious confusion, "I know you mean nothing of the sort," she added; "and I like your looks; but I think nothing of your Lady Vandeleur. Oh, these mistresses!" she cried. "To send out a real gentleman like you—with a bandbox—in broad day!"

During this talk they had remained in their original positions—she on the doorstep, he on the side-walk, bareheaded for the sake of coolness, and with the bandbox on his arm. But upon this last speech Harry, who was unable to support such point-blank compliments to his appearance, nor the encouraging look with which they were accompanied, began to change his attitude, and glance from left to right in perturbation. In so doing he turned his face towards the lower end of the lane, and there, to his indescribable dismay, his eyes encountered those of General Vandeleur. The General, in a prodigious fluster of heat, hurry, and indignation, had been scouring the streets in chase of his brother-in-law; but so soon as he caught a glimpse of the delinquent secretary, his purpose changed, his anger flowed into a new channel, and he turned on his heel and came tearing up the lane with truculent gestures and vociferations.

Harry made but one bolt of it into the house, driving the maid before him; and the door was slammed in his pursuer's countenance.

"Is there a bar? Will it lock?" asked Harry, while a salvo on the knocker made the house echo from wall to wall.

"Why, what is wrong with you?" asked the maid. "Is it this old gentleman?"

"If he gets hold of me," whispered Harry, "I am as good as dead. He has been pursuing me all day, carries a sword-stick, and is an Indian military officer."

"These are fine manners," cried the maid. "And what, if you please, may be his name?"

"It is the General, my master," answered Harry. "He is after this bandbox."

"Did not I tell you?" cried the maid in triumph. "I told you I thought worse than nothing of your Lady Vandeleur; and if you had an eye in your head you might see what she is for yourself. An ungrateful minx, I will be bound for that!"

The General renewed his attack upon the knocker, and his passion growing with delay, began to kick and beat upon the panels of the door.

"It is lucky," observed the girl, "that I am alone in the house; your General may hammer until he is weary, and there is none to open for him. Follow me!"

So saying she led Harry into the kitchen, where she made him sit down, and stood by him herself in an affectionate attitude, with a hand upon his shoulder. The din at the door, so far from abating, continued to increase in volume, and at each blow the unhappy secretary was shaken to the heart.

"What is your name?" asked the girl.

"Harry Hartley," he replied.

"Mine," she went on, "is Prudence. Do you like it?"

"Very much," said Harry. "But hear for a moment how the General beats upon the door. He will certainly break it in, and then, in heaven's name, what have I to look for but death?"

"You put yourself very much about with no occasion," answered Prudence. "Let your General knock, he will do no more than blister his hands. Do you think I would keep you here if I were not sure to save you? Oh, no, I am a good friend to those that please me! and we have a back door upon another lane. But," she added, checking him, for he had got upon his feet immediately on this welcome news, "but I will not show where it is unless you kiss me. Will you, Harry?"

"That I will," he cried, remembering his gallantry, "not for your back door, but because you are good and pretty."

And he administered two or three cordial salutes, which were returned to him in kind.

Then Prudence led him to the back gate, and put her hand upon the key.

"Will you come and see me?" she asked.

"I will indeed," said Harry. "Do not I owe you my life?"

"And now," she added, opening the door, "run as hard as you can, for I shall let in the General."

Harry scarcely required this advice; fear had him by the forelock; and he addressed himself diligently to flight. A few steps, and he believed he would escape from his trials, and return to Lady Vandeleur in honour and safety. But these few steps had not been taken before he heard a man's voice hailing him by name with many execrations, and, looking over his shoulder, he beheld Charlie Pendragon waving him with both arms to return. The shock of this new incident was so sudden and profound, and Harry was already worked into so high a state of nervous tension, that he could think of nothing better than to accelerate his pace, and continue running. He should certainly have remembered the scene in Kensington Gardens; he should certainly have concluded that, where the General was his enemy, Charlie Pendragon could be no other than a friend. But such was the fever and perturbation of his mind that he was struck by none of these considerations, and only continued to run the faster up the lane.

Charlie, by the sound of his voice and the vile terms that he hurled after the secretary, was obviously beside himself with rage. He, too, ran his very best; but, try as he might, the physical advantages were not upon his side, and his outcries and the fall of his lame foot on the macadam began to fall farther and farther into the wake.

Harry's hopes began once more to arise. The lane was both steep and narrow, but it was exceedingly solitary, bordered on either hand by garden walls, overhung with foliage; and, for as far as the fugitive could see in front of him, there was neither a creature moving nor an open door. Providence, weary of persecution, was now offering him an open field for his escape.

Alas! as he came abreast of a garden door under a tuft of chestnuts, it was suddenly drawn back, and he could see inside, upon a garden path, the figure of a butcher's boy with his tray upon his arm. He had hardly recognised the fact before he was some steps beyond upon the other side. But the fellow had had time to observe him; he was evidently much surprised to see a gentleman go by at so unusual a pace; and he came out into the lane and began to call after Harry with shouts of ironical encouragement.

His appearance gave a new idea to Charlie Pendragon, who, although he was now sadly out of breath, once more upraised his voice.

"Stop, thief!" he cried.

And immediately the butcher's boy had taken up the cry and joined in the pursuit.

This was a bitter moment for the hunted secretary. It is true that his terror enabled him once more to improve his pace, and gain with every step on his pursuers; but he was well aware that he was near the end of his resources, and should he meet any one coming the other way, his predicament in the narrow lane would be desperate indeed.

"I must find a place of concealment," he thought, "and that within the next few seconds, or all is over with me in this world."

Scarcely had the thought crossed his mind than the lane took a sudden turning; and he found himself hidden from his enemies. There are circumstances in which even the least energetic of mankind learn to behave with vigour and decision; and the most cautious forget their prudence and embrace foolhardy resolutions. This was one of those occasions for Harry Hartley; and those who knew him best would have been the most astonished at the lad's audacity. He stopped dead, flung the bandbox over a garden wall, and leaping upward with incredible agility and seizing the copestone with his hands, he tumbled headlong after it into the garden.

He came to himself a moment afterwards, seated in a border of small rosebushes. His hands and knees were cut and bleeding, for the wall had been protected against such an escalade by a liberal provision of old bottles; and he was conscious of a general dislocation and a painful swimming in the head. Facing him across the garden, which was in admirable order, and set with flowers of the most delicious perfume, he beheld the back of a house. It was of considerable extent, and plainly habitable; but, in odd contrast to the grounds, it was crazy, ill-kept, and of a mean appearance. On all other sides the circuit of the garden wall appeared unbroken.

He took in these features of the scene with mechanical glances, but his mind was still unable to piece together or draw a rational conclusion from what he saw. And when he heard footsteps advancing on the gravel, although he turned his eyes in that direction, it was with no thought either for defence or flight.

The new-comer was a large, coarse, and very sordid personage, in gardening clothes, and with a watering-pot in his left hand. One less confused would have been affected with some alarm at the sight of this man's huge proportions and black and lowering eyes. But Harry was too gravely shaken by his fall to be so much as terrified; and if he was unable to divert his glances from the gardener, he remained absolutely passive, and suffered him to draw near, to take him by the shoulder, and to plant him roughly on his feet, without a motion of resistance.

For a moment the two stared into each other's eyes, Harry fascinated, the man filled with wrath and a cruel, sneering humour.

"Who are you?" he demanded at last. "Who are you to come flying over my wall and break my *Gloire de Dijons!* What is your name?" he added, shaking him; "and what may be your business here?"

Harry could not as much as proffer a word in explanation.

But just at that moment Pendragon and the butcher's boy went clumping past, and the sound of their feet and their hoarse cries echoed loudly in the narrow lane. The gardener had received his answer; and he looked down into Harry's face with an obnoxious smile.

"A thief!" he said. "Upon my word, and a very good thing you must make of it; for I see you dressed like a gentleman from top to toe. Are you not ashamed to go about the world in such a trim, with honest folk, I dare say, glad to buy your cast-off finery second hand? Speak up, you dog," the man went on; "you can understand English, I suppose; and I mean to have a bit of talk with you before I march you to the station."

"Indeed, sir," said Harry, "this is all a dreadful misconception; and if you will go with me to Sir Thomas Vandeleur's in Eaton Place, I can promise that all will be made plain. The most upright person, as I now perceive, can be led into suspicious positions."

"My little man," replied the gardener, "I will go with you no farther than the station-house in the next street. The inspector, no doubt, will be glad to take a stroll with you as far as Eaton Place, and have a bit of afternoon tea with your great acquaintances. Or would you prefer to go direct to the Home Secretary? Sir Thomas Vandeleur, indeed! Perhaps you think I don't know a gentleman when I see one, from a common run-the-hedge like you? Clothes or no clothes, I can read you like a book. Here is a shirt that maybe cost as much as my Sunday hat; and that coat, I take it, has never seen the inside of Rag-fair, and then your boots—"

The man, whose eyes had fallen upon the ground, stopped short in his insulting commentary, and remained for a moment looking intently upon something at his feet. When he spoke his voice was strangely altered.

"What, in God's name," said he, "is all this?"

Harry, following the direction of the man's eyes, beheld a spectacle that struck him dumb with terror and amazement. In his fall he had descended vertically upon the bandbox and burst it open from end to end; thence a great treasure of diamonds had poured forth, and now lay abroad, part trodden in the soil, part scattered on the surface in regal and glittering profusion. There was a magnificent coronet which he had often admired on Lady Vandeleur; there were rings and brooches, ear-drops and bracelets, and even unset brilliants rolling here and there among the rosebushes like drops of morning dew. A princely fortune lay between the two men upon the ground—a fortune in the most inviting, solid, and durable form, capable of being carried in an apron, beautiful in itself, and scattering the sunlight in a million rainbow flashes.

"Good God!" said Harry, "I am lost!"

His mind raced backwards into the past with the incalculable velocity of thought, and he began to comprehend his day's adventures, to conceive them as a whole, and to recognise the sad imbroglio in which his own character and fortunes had become involved. He looked round him as if for help, but he was alone in the garden, with his scattered diamonds and his redoubtable interlocutor; and when he gave ear, there was no sound but the rustle of the leaves and the hurried pulsation of his heart. It was little wonder if the young man felt himself deserted by his spirits, and with a broken voice repeated his last ejaculation—"I am lost!"

The gardener peered in all directions with an air of guilt; but there was no face at any of the windows, and he seemed to breathe again.

"Pick up a heart," he said, "you fool! The worst of it is done. Why could you not say at first there was enough for two? Two?" he repeated, "aye, and for two hundred! But come away from here, where we may be observed; and, for the love of wisdom, straighten out your hat and brush your clothes. You could not travel two steps the figure of fun you look just now."

While Harry mechanically adopted these suggestions, the gardener, getting upon his knees, hastily drew together the scattered jewels and returned them to the bandbox. The touch of these costly crystals sent a shiver of emotion through the man's stalwart frame; his face was transfigured, and his eyes shone with concupiscence; indeed it seemed as if he luxuriously prolonged his occupation, and dallied with every diamond that he handled. At last, however, it was done; and, concealing the bandbox in his smock, the gardener beckoned to Harry and preceded him in the direction of the house.

Near the door they were met by a young man evidently in holy orders, dark and strikingly handsome, with a look of mingled weakness and resolution, and very neatly attired after the manner of his caste. The gardener was plainly annoyed by this encounter; but he put as good a face upon it as he could, and accosted the clergyman with an obsequious and smiling air.

"Here is a fine afternoon, Mr. Rolles," said he: "a fine afternoon, as sure as God made it! And here is a young friend of mine who had a fancy to look at my roses. I took the liberty to bring him in, for I thought none of the lodgers would object."

"Speaking for myself," replied the Reverend Mr. Rolles, "I do not; nor do I fancy any of the rest of us would be more difficult upon so small a matter. The garden is your own, Mr. Raeburn; we must none of us forget that; and because you give us liberty to walk there we should be indeed ungracious if we so far presumed upon your politeness as to interfere with the convenience of your friends. But, on second thoughts," he added, "I believe that this gentleman and I have met before. Mr. Hartley, I think. I regret to observe that you have had a fall."

And he offered his hand.

A sort of maiden dignity and a desire to delay as long as possible the necessity for explanation moved Harry to refuse this chance of help, and to deny his own identity. He chose the tender mercies of the gardener, who was at least unknown to him, rather than the curiosity and perhaps the doubts of an acquaintance.

"I fear there is some mistake," said he. "My name is Thomlinson and I am a friend of Mr. Raeburn's."

"Indeed?" said Mr. Rolles. "The likeness is amazing."

Mr. Raeburn, who had been upon thorns throughout this colloquy, now felt it high time to bring it to a period.

"I wish you a pleasant saunter, sir," said he.

And with that he dragged Harry after him into the house, and then into a chamber on the garden. His first care was to draw down the blind, for Mr. Rolles still remained where they had left him, in an attitude of perplexity and thought. Then he emptied the broken bandbox on the table, and stood before the treasure, thus fully displayed, with an expression of rapturous greed, and rubbing his hands upon his thighs. For Harry, the sight of the man's face under the influence of this base emotion, added another pang to those he was already suffering. It seemed incredible that, from his life of pure and delicate trifling, he should be plunged in a breath among sordid and criminal relations. He could reproach his conscience with no sinful act; and yet he was now suffering the punishment of sin in its most acute and cruel forms—the dread of punishment, the suspicions of the good, and the companionship and contamination of vile and brutal natures. He felt he could lay his life down with gladness to escape from the room and the society of Mr. Raeburn.

"And now," said the latter, after he had separated the jewels into two nearly equal parts, and drawn one of them nearer to himself; "and now," said he, "everything in this world has to be paid for, and some things sweetly. You must know, Mr. Hartley, if such be your name, that I am a man of a very easy temper, and good nature has been my stumbling-block from first to last. I could pocket the whole of these pretty pebbles, if I chose, and I should like to see you dare to say a word; but I think I must have taken a liking to you; for I declare I have not the heart to shave you so close. So, do you see, in pure kind feeling, I propose that we divide; and these," indicating the two heaps, "are the proportions that seem to me just and friendly. Do you see any objection, Mr. Hartley, may I ask? I am not the man to stick upon a brooch."

"But, sir," cried Harry, "what you propose to me is impossible. The jewels are not mine, and I cannot share what is another's, no matter with whom, nor in what proportions."

"They are not yours, are they not?" returned Raeburn. "And you could not share them with anybody, couldn't you? Well now, that is what I call a pity; for here am I obliged to take you to the station. The police—think of that," he continued; "think of the disgrace for your respectable parents; think," he went on, taking Harry by the wrist; "think of the Colonies and the Day of Judgment."

"I cannot help it," wailed Harry. "It is not my fault. You will not come with me to Eaton Place?"

"No," replied the man, "I will not, that is certain. And I mean to divide these playthings with you here."

And so saying he applied a sudden and severe torsion to the lad's wrist.

Harry could not suppress a scream, and the perspiration burst forth upon his face. Perhaps pain and terror quickened his intelligence, but certainly at that moment the whole business flashed across him in another light; and he saw that there was nothing for it but to accede to the ruffian's proposal, and trust to find the house and force him to disgorge, under more favourable circumstances, and when he himself was clear from all suspicion.

"I agree," he said.

"There is a lamb," sneered the gardener. "I thought you would recognise your interests at last. This bandbox," he continued, "I shall burn with my rubbish; it is a thing that curious folk might recognise; and as for you, scrape up your gaieties and put them in your pocket."

Harry proceeded to obey, Raeburn watching him, and every now and again his greed rekindled by some bright scintillation, abstracting another jewel from the secretary's share, and adding it to his own.

When this was finished, both proceeded to the front door, which Raeburn cautiously opened to observe the street. This was apparently clear of passengers; for he suddenly seized Harry by the nape of the neck, and holding his face downward so that he could see nothing but the roadway and the doorsteps of the houses, pushed him violently before him down one street and up another for the space of perhaps a minute and a half. Harry had counted three corners before the bully relaxed his grasp, and crying, "Now be off with you!" sent the lad flying head foremost with a well-directed and athletic kick.

When Harry gathered himself up, half-stunned and bleeding freely at the nose, Mr. Raeburn had entirely disappeared. For the first time, anger and pain so completely overcame the lad's spirits that he burst into a fit of tears and remained sobbing in the middle of the road.

After he had thus somewhat assuaged his emotion, he began to look about him and read the names of the streets at whose intersection he had been deserted by the gardener. He was still in an unfrequented portion of West London, among villas and large gardens; but he could see some persons at a window who had evidently witnessed his misfortune; and almost immediately after a servant came running from the house and offered him a glass of water. At the same time, a dirty rogue, who had been slouching somewhere in the neighbourhood, drew near him from the other side.

"Poor fellow," said the maid, "how vilely you have been handled, to be sure! Why, your knees are all cut, and your clothes ruined! Do you know the wretch who used you so?"

"That I do!" cried Harry, who was somewhat refreshed by the water; "and shall run him home in spite of his precautions. He shall pay dearly for this day's work, I promise you."

"You had better come into the house and have yourself washed and brushed," continued the maid. "My mistress will make you welcome, never fear. And see, I will pick up your hat. Why, love of mercy!" she screamed, "if you have not dropped diamonds all over the street!"

Such was the case; a good half of what remained to him after the depredations of Mr. Raeburn, had been shaken out of his pockets by the summersault and once more lay glittering on the ground. He blessed his fortune that the maid had been so quick of eye; "there is nothing so bad but it might be worse," thought he; and the recovery of these few seemed to him almost as great an affair as the loss of all the rest. But, alas! as he stooped to pick up his treasures, the loiterer made a rapid onslaught, overset both Harry and the maid with a movement of his arms, swept up a double handful of the diamonds, and made off along the street with an amazing swiftness.

Harry, as soon as he could get upon his feet, gave chase to the miscreant with many cries, but the latter was too fleet of foot, and probably too well acquainted with the locality; for turn where the pursuer would he could find no traces of the fugitive.

In the deepest despondency, Harry revisited the scene of his mishap, where the maid, who was still waiting, very honestly returned him his hat and the remainder of the fallen diamonds. Harry thanked her from his heart, and being now in no humour for economy, made his way to the nearest cab-stand and set off for Eaton Place by coach.

The house, on his arrival, seemed in some confusion, as if a catastrophe had happened in the family; and the servants clustered together in the hall, and were unable, or perhaps not altogether anxious, to suppress their merriment at the tatterdemalion figure of the secretary. He passed them with as good an air of dignity as he could assume, and made directly for the boudoir. When he opened the door an astonishing and even menacing spectacle presented itself to his eyes; for he beheld the General and his wife and, of all people, Charlie Pendragon, closeted together and speaking with earnestness and gravity on some important subject. Harry saw at once that there was little left for him to explain— plenary confession had plainly been made to the General of the intended fraud upon his pocket, and the unfortunate miscarriage of the scheme; and they had all made common cause against a common danger.

"Thank Heaven!" cried Lady Vandeleur, "here he is! The bandbox, Harry—the bandbox!"

But Harry stood before them silent and downcast.

"Speak!" she cried. "Speak! Where is the bandbox?"

And the men, with threatening gestures, repeated the demand.

Harry drew a handful of jewels from his pocket. He was very white.

"This is all that remains," said he. "I declare before Heaven it was through no fault of mine; and if you will have patience, although some are lost, I am afraid, for ever, others, I am sure, may be still recovered."

"Alas!" cried Lady Vandeleur, "all our diamonds are gone, and I owe ninety thousand pounds for dress!"

"Madam," said the General, "you might have paved the gutter with your own trash; you might have made debts to fifty times the sum you mention; you might have robbed me of my mother's coronet and ring; and Nature might have still so far prevailed that I could have forgiven you at last. But, madam, you have taken the Rajah's Diamond—the Eye of Light, as the Orientals poetically termed it—the Pride of Kashgar! You have taken from me the Rajah's Diamond," he cried, raising his hands, "and all, madam, all is at an end between us!"

"Believe me, General Vandeleur," she replied, "that is one of the most agreeable speeches that ever I heard from your lips; and since we are to be ruined, I could almost welcome the change, if it delivers me from you. You have told me often enough that I married you for your money; let me tell you now that I always bitterly repented the bargain; and if you were still marriageable, and had a diamond bigger than your head, I should counsel even my maid against a union so uninviting and disastrous. As for you, Mr. Hartley," she continued, turning on the secretary, "you have sufficiently exhibited your valuable qualities in this house; we are now persuaded that you equally lack manhood, sense, and self-respect; and I can see only one course open for you—to withdraw instanter, and, if possible, return no more. For your wages you may rank as a creditor in my late husband's bankruptcy."

Harry had scarcely comprehended this insulting address before the General was down upon him with another.

"And in the meantime," said that personage, "follow me before the nearest Inspector of Police. You may impose upon a simple-minded soldier, sir, but the eye of the law will read your disreputable secret. If I must spend my old age in poverty through your underhand intriguing with my wife, I mean at least that you shall not remain unpunished for your pains; and God, sir, will deny me a very considerable satisfaction if you do not pick oakum from now until your dying day."

With that, the General dragged Harry from the apartment, and hurried him downstairs and along the street to the police-station of the district.

Here (says my Arabian author) ended this deplorable business of the bandbox. But to the unfortunate Secretary the whole affair was the beginning of a new and manlier life. The police were easily persuaded of his innocence; and, after he had given what help he could in the subsequent investigations, he was even complemented by one of the chiefs of the detective department on the probity and simplicity of his behaviour. Several persons interested themselves in one so unfortunate; and soon after he inherited a sum of money from a maiden aunt in Worcestershire. With this he married Prudence, and set sail for Bendigo, or according to another account, for Trincomalee, exceedingly content, and with the best of prospects.

## Story of the Young Man in Holy Orders

The Reverend Mr. Simon Rolles had distinguished himself in the Moral Sciences, and was more than usually proficient in the study of Divinity. His essay "On the Christian Doctrine of the Social Obligations" obtained for him, at the moment of its production, a certain celebrity in the University of Oxford; and it was understood in clerical and learned circles that young Mr. Rolles had in contemplation a considerable work—a folio, it was said—on the authority of the Fathers of the Church. These attainments, these ambitious designs, however, were far from helping him to any preferment; and he was still in quest of his first curacy when a chance ramble in that part of London, the peaceful and rich aspect of the garden, a desire for solitude and study, and the cheapness of the lodging, led him to take up his abode with Mr. Raeburn, the nurseryman of Stockdove Lane.

It was his habit every afternoon, after he had worked seven or eight hours on St. Ambrose or St. Chrysostom, to walk for a while in meditation among the roses. And this was usually one of the most productive moments of his day. But even a sincere appetite for thought, and the excitement of grave problems awaiting solution, are not always sufficient to preserve the mind of the philosopher against the petty shocks and contacts of the world. And when Mr. Rolles found General Vandeleur's secretary, ragged and bleeding, in the company of his landlord; when he saw both change colour and seek to avoid his questions; and, above all, when the former denied his own identity with the most unmoved assurance, he speedily forgot the Saints and Fathers in the vulgar interest of curiosity.

"I cannot be mistaken," thought he. "That is Mr. Hartley beyond a doubt. How comes he in such a pickle? why does he deny his name? and what can be his business with that black-looking ruffian, my landlord?"

As he was thus reflecting, another peculiar circumstance attracted his attention. The face of Mr. Raeburn appeared at a low window next the door; and, as chance directed, his eyes met those of Mr. Rolles. The nurseryman seemed disconcerted, and even alarmed; and immediately after the blind of the apartment was pulled sharply down.

"This may all be very well," reflected Mr. Rolles; "it may be all excellently well; but I confess freely that I do not think so. Suspicious, underhand, untruthful, fearful of observation—I believe upon my soul," he thought, "the pair are plotting some disgraceful action."

The detective that there is in all of us awoke and became clamant in the bosom of Mr. Rolles; and with a brisk, eager step, that bore no resemblance to his usual gait, he proceeded to make the circuit of the garden. When he came to the scene of Harry's escalade, his eye was at once arrested by a broken rosebush and marks of trampling on the mould. He looked up, and saw scratches on the brick, and a rag of trouser floating from a broken bottle. This, then, was the mode of entrance chosen by Mr. Raeburn's particular friend! It was thus that General Vandeleur's secretary came to admire a flower-garden! The young clergyman whistled softly to himself as he stooped to examine the ground. He could make out where Harry had landed from his perilous leap; he recognised the flat foot of Mr. Raeburn where it had sunk deeply in the soil as he pulled up the Secretary by the collar; nay, on a closer inspection, he seemed to distinguish the marks of groping fingers, as though something had been spilt abroad and eagerly collected.

"Upon my word," he thought, "the thing grows vastly interesting."

And just then he caught sight of something almost entirely buried in the earth. In an instant he had disinterred a dainty morocco case, ornamented and clasped in gilt. It had been trodden heavily underfoot, and thus escaped the hurried search of Mr. Raeburn. Mr. Rolles opened the case, and drew a long breath of almost horrified astonishment; for there lay before him, in a cradle of green velvet, a diamond of prodigious magnitude and of the finest water. It was of the bigness of a duck's egg; beautifully shaped, and without a flaw; and as the sun shone upon it, it gave forth a lustre like that of electricity, and seemed to burn in his hand with a thousand internal fires.

He knew little of precious stones; but the Rajah's Diamond was a wonder that explained itself; a village child, if he found it, would run screaming for the nearest cottage; and a savage would prostrate himself in adoration before so imposing a fetish. The beauty of the stone flattered the young clergyman's eyes; the thought of its incalculable value overpowered his intellect. He knew that what he held in his hand was worth more than many years' purchase of an archiepiscopal see; that it would build cathedrals more stately than Ely or Cologne; that he who possessed it was set free for ever from the primal curse, and might follow his own inclinations without concern or hurry, without let or hindrance. And as he suddenly turned it, the rays leaped forth again with renewed brilliancy, and seemed to pierce his very heart.

Decisive actions are often taken in a moment and without any conscious deliverance from the rational parts of man. So it was now with Mr. Rolles. He glanced hurriedly round; beheld, like Mr. Raeburn before him, nothing but the sunlit flower-garden, the tall tree-tops, and the house with blinded windows; and in a trice he had shut the case, thrust it into his pocket, and was hastening to his study with the speed of guilt.

The Reverend Simon Rolles had stolen the Rajah's Diamond.

Early in the afternoon the police arrived with Harry Hartley. The nurseryman, who was beside himself with terror, readily discovered his hoard; and the jewels were identified and inventoried in the presence of the Secretary. As for Mr. Rolles, he showed himself in a most obliging temper, communicated what he knew with freedom, and professed regret that he could do no more to help the officers in their duty.

"Still," he added, "I suppose your business is nearly at an end."

"By no means," replied the man from Scotland Yard; and he narrated the second robbery of which Harry had been the immediate victim, and gave the young clergyman a description of the more important jewels that were still not found, dilating particularly on the Rajah's Diamond.

"It must be worth a fortune," observed Mr. Rolles.

"Ten fortunes—twenty fortunes," cried the officer.

"The more it is worth," remarked Simon shrewdly, "the more

difficult it must be to sell. Such a thing has a physiognomy not to be disguised, and I should fancy a man might as easily negotiate St. Paul's Cathedral."

"Oh, truly!" said the officer; "but if the thief be a man of any intelligence, he will cut it into three or four, and there will be still enough to make him rich."

"Thank you," said the clergyman. "You cannot imagine how much your conversation interests me."

Whereupon the functionary admitted that they knew many strange things in his profession, and immediately after took his leave.

Mr. Rolles regained his apartment. It seemed smaller and barer than usual; the materials for his great work had never presented so little interest; and he looked upon his library with the eye of scorn. He took down, volume by volume, several Fathers of the Church, and glanced them through; but they contained nothing to his purpose.

"These old gentlemen," thought he, "are no doubt very valuable writers, but they seem to me conspicuously ignorant of life. Here am I, with learning enough to be a Bishop, and I positively do not know how to dispose of a stolen diamond. I glean a hint from a common policeman, and, with all my folios, I cannot so much as put it into execution. This inspires me with very low ideas of University training."

Herewith he kicked over his book-shelf and, putting on his hat, hastened from the house to the club of which he was a member. In such a place of mundane resort he hoped to find some man of good counsel and a shrewd experience in life. In the reading-room he saw many of the country clergy and an Archdeacon; there were three journalists and a writer upon the Higher Metaphysic, playing pool; and at dinner only the raff of ordinary club frequenters showed their commonplace and obliterated countenances. None of these, thought Mr. Rolles, would know more on dangerous topics than he knew himself; none of them were fit to give him guidance in his present strait. At length in the smoking-room, up many weary stairs, he hit upon a gentleman of somewhat portly build and dressed with conspicuous plainness. He was smoking a cigar and reading the

*Fortnightly Review*; his face was singularly free from all sign of preoccupation or fatigue; and there was something in his air which seemed to invite confidence and to expect submission. The more the young clergyman scrutinised his features, the more he was convinced that he had fallen on one capable of giving pertinent advice.

"Sir," said he, "you will excuse my abruptness; but I judge you from your appearance to be pre-eminently a man of the world."

"I have indeed considerable claims to that distinction," replied the stranger, laying aside his magazine with a look of mingled amusement and surprise.

"I, sir," continued the Curate, "am a recluse, a student, a creature of ink-bottles and patristic folios. A recent event has brought my folly vividly before my eyes, and I desire to instruct myself in life. By life," he added, "I do not mean Thackeray's novels; but the crimes and secret possibilities of our society, and the principles of wise conduct among exceptional events. I am a patient reader; can the thing be learnt in books?"

"You put me in a difficulty," said the stranger. "I confess I have no great notion of the use of books, except to amuse a railway journey; although, I believe, there are some very exact treatises on astronomy, the use of the globes, agriculture, and the art of making paper flowers. Upon the less apparent provinces of life I fear you will find nothing truthful. Yet stay," he added, "have you read Gaboriau?"

Mr. Rolles admitted he had never even heard the name.

"You may gather some notions from Gaboriau," resumed the stranger. "He is at least suggestive; and as he is an author much studied by Prince Bismarck, you will, at the worst, lose your time in good society."

"Sir," said the Curate, "I am infinitely obliged by your politeness."

"You have already more than repaid me," returned the other.

"How?" inquired Simon.

"By the novelty of your request," replied the gentleman; and with a polite gesture, as though to ask permission, he resumed the study of the *Fortnightly Review*.

On his way home Mr. Rolles purchased a work on precious

stones and several of Gaboriau's novels. These last he eagerly skimmed until an advanced hour in the morning; but although they introduced him to many new ideas, he could nowhere discover what to do with a stolen diamond. He was annoyed, moreover, to find the information scattered amongst romantic story-telling, instead of soberly set forth after the manner of a manual; and he concluded that, even if the writer had thought much upon these subjects, he was totally lacking in educational method. For the character and attainments of Lecoq, however, he was unable to contain his admiration.

"He was truly a great creature," ruminated Mr. Rolles. "He knew the world as I know Paley's Evidences. There was nothing that he could not carry to a termination with his own hand, and against the largest odds. Heavens!" he broke out suddenly, "is not this the lesson? Must I not learn to cut diamonds for myself?"

It seemed to him as if he had sailed at once out of his perplexities; he remembered that he knew a jeweller, one B. Macculloch, in Edinburgh, who would be glad to put him in the way of the necessary training; a few months, perhaps a few years, of sordid toil, and he would be sufficiently expert to divide and sufficiently cunning to dispose with advantage of the Rajah's Diamond. That done, he might return to pursue his researches at leisure, a wealthy and luxurious student, envied and respected by all. Golden visions attended him through his slumber, and he awoke refreshed and light-hearted with the morning sun.

Mr. Raeburn's house was on that day to be closed by the police, and this afforded a pretext for his departure. He cheerfully prepared his baggage, transported it to King's Cross, where he left it in the cloak-room, and returned to the club to while away the afternoon and dine.

"If you dine here to-day, Rolles," observed an acquaintance, "you may see two of the most remarkable men in England— Prince Florizel of Bohemia, and old Jack Vandeleur."

"I have heard of the Prince," replied Mr. Rolles; "and General Vandeleur I have even met in society."

"General Vandeleur is an ass!" returned the other. "This is his brother John, the biggest adventurer, the best judge of precious stones, and one of the most acute diplomatists in Europe. Have you never heard of his duel with the Duc de Val d'Orge? of his exploits and atrocities when he was Dictator of Paraguay? of his dexterity in recovering Sir Samuel Levi's jewellery? nor of his services in the Indian Mutiny—services by which the Government profited, but which the Government dared not recognise? You make me wonder what we mean by fame, or even by infamy; for Jack Vandeleur has prodigious claims to both. Run downstairs," he continued, "take a table near them, and keep your ears open. You will hear some strange talk, or I am much misled."

"But how shall I know them?" inquired the clergyman.

"Know them!" cried his friend; "why, the Prince is the finest gentleman in Europe, the only living creature who looks like a king; and as for Jack Vandeleur, if you can imagine Ulysses at seventy years of age, and with a sabre-cut across his face, you have the man before you! Know them, indeed! Why, you could pick either of them out of a Derby day!"

Rolles eagerly hurried to the dining-room. It was as his friend had asserted; it was impossible to mistake the pair in question. Old John Vandeleur was of a remarkable force of body, and obviously broken to the most difficult exercises. He had neither the carriage of a swordsman, nor of a sailor, nor yet of one much inured to the saddle; but something made up of all these, and the result and expression of many different habits and dexterities. His features were bold and aquiline; his expression arrogant and predatory; his whole appearance that of a swift, violent, unscrupulous man of action; and his copious white hair and the deep sabre-cut that traversed his nose and temple added a note of savagery to a head already remarkable and menacing in itself.

In his companion, the Prince of Bohemia, Mr. Rolles was astonished to recognise the gentleman who had recommended him the study of Gaboriau. Doubtless Prince Florizel, who rarely visited the club, of which, as of most others, he was an honorary member, had been waiting for John Vandeleur when Simon accosted him on the previous evening.

The other diners had modestly retired into the angles of the room, and left the distinguished pair in a certain isolation, but the young clergyman was unrestrained by any sentiment of awe, and, marching boldly up, took his place at the nearest table.

The conversation was, indeed, new to the student's ears. The ex-Dictator of Paraguay stated many extraordinary experiences in different quarters of the world; and the Prince supplied a commentary which, to a man of thought, was even more interesting than the events themselves. Two forms of experience were thus brought together and laid before the young clergyman; and he did not know which to admire the most—the desperate actor or the skilled expert in life; the man who spoke boldly of his own deeds and perils, or the man who seemed, like a god, to know all things and to have suffered nothing. The manner of each aptly fitted with his part in the discourse. The Dictator indulged in brutalities alike of speech and gesture; his hand opened and shut and fell roughly on the table; and his voice was loud and heavy. The Prince, on the other hand, seemed the very type of urbane docility and quiet; the least movement, the least inflection, had with him a weightier significance than all the shouts and pantomime of his companion; and if ever, as must frequently have been the case, he described some experience personal to himself, it was so aptly dissimulated as to pass unnoticed with the rest.

At length the talk wandered on to the late robberies and the Rajah's Diamond.

"That diamond would be better in the sea," observed Prince Florizel.

"As a Vandeleur," replied the Dictator, "your Highness may imagine my dissent."

"I speak on grounds of public policy," pursued the Prince. "Jewels so valuable should be reserved for the collection of a Prince or the treasury of a great nation. To hand them about among the common sort of men is to set a price on Virtue's head; and if the Rajah of Kashgar—a Prince, I understand, of great enlightenment—desired vengeance upon the men of Europe, he could hardly have gone more efficaciously about his purpose than by sending us this apple of discord. There is no honesty too robust for such a trial. I myself, who have many duties and many privileges of my own—I myself, Mr. Vandeleur, could scarce handle the intoxicating crystal and be safe. As for you, who are a diamond hunter by taste and profession, I do not believe there is a crime in the calendar you would not perpetrate—I do not believe you have a friend in the world whom you would not eagerly betray—I do not know if you have a family, but if you have I declare you would sacrifice your children—and all this for what? Not to be richer, nor to have more comforts or more respect, but simply to call this diamond yours for a year or two until you die, and now and again to open a safe and look at it as one looks at a picture."

"It is true," replied Vandeleur. "I have hunted most things, from men and women down to mosquitos; I have dived for coral; I have followed both whales and tigers; and a diamond is the tallest quarry of the lot. It has beauty and worth; it alone can properly reward the ardours of the chase. At this moment, as your Highness may fancy, I am upon the trail; I have a sure knack, a wide experience; I know every stone of price in my brother's collection as a shepherd knows his sheep; and I wish I may die if I do not recover them every one!"

"Sir Thomas Vandeleur will have great cause to thank you," said the Prince.

"I am not so sure," returned the Dictator, with a laugh. "One of the Vandeleurs will. Thomas or John—Peter or Paul—we are all apostles."

"I did not catch your observation," said the Prince with some disgust.

And at the same moment the waiter informed Mr. Vandeleur that his cab was at the door.

Mr. Rolles glanced at the clock, and saw that he also must be moving; and the coincidence struck him sharply and unpleasantly, for he desired to see no more of the diamond hunter.

Much study having somewhat shaken the young man's nerves, he was in the habit of travelling in the most luxurious manner; and for the present journey he had taken a sofa in the sleeping carriage.

"You will be very comfortable," said the guard; "there is no one in your compartment, and only one old gentleman in the other end."

It was close upon the hour, and the tickets were being examined, when Mr. Rolles beheld this other fellow-passenger ushered by several porters into his place; certainly, there was not another man in the world whom he would not have preferred—for it was old John Vandeleur, the ex-Dictator.

The sleeping carriages on the Great Northern line were divided into three compartments—one at each end for travellers, and one in the centre fitted with the conveniences of a lavatory. A door running in grooves separated each of the others from the lavatory; but as there were neither bolts nor locks, the whole suite was practically common ground.

When Mr. Rolles had studied his position, he perceived himself without defence. If the Dictator chose to pay him a visit in the course of the night, he could do no less than receive it; he had no means of fortification, and lay open to attack as if he had been lying in the fields. This situation caused him some agony of mind. He recalled with alarm the boastful statements of his fellow-traveller across the dining-table, and the professions of immorality which he had heard him offering to the disgusted Prince. Some persons, he remembered to have read, are endowed with a singular quickness of perception for the neighbourhood of precious metals; through walls and even at considerable distances they are said to divine the presence of gold. Might it not be the same with diamonds? he wondered; and if so, who was more likely to enjoy this transcendental sense than the person who gloried in the appellation of the Diamond Hunter? From such a man he recognised that he had everything to fear, and longed eagerly for the arrival of the day.

In the meantime he neglected no precaution, concealed his diamond in the most internal pocket of a system of great-coats, and devoutly recommended himself to the care of Providence.

The train pursued its usual even and rapid course; and nearly half the journey had been accomplished before slumber began to triumph over uneasiness in the breast of Mr. Rolles. For some time he resisted its influence; but it grew upon him more and more, and a little before York he was fain to stretch himself upon one of the couches and suffer his eyes to close; and almost at the same instant consciousness deserted the young clergyman. His last thought was of his terrifying neighbour.

When he awoke it was still pitch dark, except for the flicker of the veiled lamp; and the continual roaring and oscillation testified to the unrelaxed velocity of the train. He sat upright in a panic, for he had been tormented by the most uneasy dreams; it was some seconds before he recovered his self-command; and even after he had resumed a recumbent attitude sleep continued to flee him, and he lay awake with his brain in a state of violent agitation, and his eyes fixed upon the lavatory door. He pulled his clerical felt hat over his brow still farther to shield him from the light; and he adopted the usual expedients, such as counting a thousand or banishing thought, by which experienced invalids are accustomed to woo the approach of sleep. In the case of Mr. Rolles they proved one and all vain; he was harassed by a dozen different anxieties—the old man in the other end of the carriage haunted him in the most alarming shapes; and in whatever attitude he chose to lie the diamond in his pocket occasioned him a sensible physical distress. It burned, it was too large, it bruised his ribs; and there were infinitesimal fractions of a second in which he had half a mind to throw it from the window.

While he was thus lying, a strange incident took place.

The sliding-door into the lavatory stirred a little, and then a little more, and was finally drawn back for the space of about twenty inches. The lamp in the lavatory was unshaded, and in the lighted aperture thus disclosed, Mr. Rolles could see the head of Mr. Vandeleur in an attitude of deep attention. He was conscious that the gaze of the Dictator rested intently on his own face; and the instinct of self-preservation moved him to hold his breath, to refrain from the least movement, and keeping his eyes lowered, to watch his visitor from underneath the lashes. After about a moment, the head was withdrawn and the door of the lavatory replaced.

The Dictator had not come to attack, but to observe; his action was not that of a man threatening another, but that of a man who was himself threatened; if Mr. Rolles was afraid of him, it appeared that he, in his turn, was not quite easy on the score of Mr. Rolles. He had come, it would seem, to make sure that his only fellow-traveller was asleep; and, when satisfied on that point, he had at once withdrawn.

The clergyman leaped to his feet. The extreme of terror

had given place to a reaction of foolhardy daring. He reflected that the rattle of the flying train concealed all other sounds, and determined, come what might, to return the visit he had just received. Divesting himself of his cloak, which might have interfered with the freedom of his action, he entered the lavatory and paused to listen. As he had expected, there was nothing to be heard above the roar of the train's progress; and laying his hand on the door at the farther side, he proceeded cautiously to draw it back for about six inches. Then he stopped, and could not contain an ejaculation of surprise.

John Vandeleur wore a fur travelling cap with lappets to protect his ears; and this may have combined with the sound of the express to keep him in ignorance of what was going forward. It is certain, at least, that he did not raise his head, but continued without interruption to pursue his strange employment. Between his feet stood an open hat-box; in one hand he held the sleeve of his sealskin great-coat; in the other a formidable knife, with which he had just slit up the lining of the sleeve. Mr. Rolles had read of persons carrying money in a belt; and as he had no acquaintance with any but cricket-belts, he had never been able rightly to conceive how this was managed. But here was a stranger thing before his eyes; for John Vandeleur, it appeared, carried diamonds in the lining of his sleeve; and even as the young clergyman gazed, he could see one glittering brilliant drop after another into the hat-box.

He stood riveted to the spot, following this unusual business with his eyes. The diamonds were, for the most part, small, and not easily distinguishable either in shape or fire. Suddenly the Dictator appeared to find a difficulty; he employed both hands and stooped over his task; but it was not until after considerable manoeuvring that he extricated a large tiara of diamonds from the lining, and held it up for some seconds' examination before he placed it with the others in the hat-box. The tiara was a ray of light to Mr. Rolles; he immediately recognised it for a part of the treasure stolen from Harry Hartley by the loiterer. There was no room for mistake; it was exactly as the detective had described it; there were the ruby stars, with a great emerald in the centre; there were the interlacing crescents; and there were the pear-shaped pendants, each a single stone, which gave a special value to Lady Vandeleur's tiara.

Mr. Rolles was hugely relieved. The Dictator was as deeply in the affair as he was; neither could tell tales upon the other. In the first glow of happiness, the clergyman suffered a deep sigh to escape him; and as his bosom had become choked and his throat dry during his previous suspense, the sigh was followed by a cough.

Mr. Vandeleur looked up; his face contracted with the blackest and most deadly passion; his eyes opened widely, and his under jaw dropped in an astonishment that was upon the brink of fury. By an instinctive movement he had covered the hat-box with the coat. For half a minute the two men stared upon each other in silence. It was not a long interval, but it sufficed for Mr. Rolles; he was one of those who think swiftly on dangerous occasions; he decided on a course of action of a singularly daring nature; and although he felt he was setting his life upon the hazard, he was the first to break silence.

"I beg your pardon," said he.

The Dictator shivered slightly, and when he spoke his voice was hoarse.

"What do you want here?" he asked.

"I take a particular interest in diamonds," replied Mr. Rolles, with an air of perfect self-possession. "Two connoisseurs should be acquainted. I have here a trifle of my own which may perhaps serve for an introduction."

And so saying, he quietly took the case from his pocket, showed the Rajah's Diamond to the Dictator for an instant, and replaced it in security.

"It was once your brother's," he added.

John Vandeleur continued to regard him with a look of almost painful amazement; but he neither spoke nor moved.

"I was pleased to observe," resumed the young man, "that we have gems from the same collection."

The Dictator's surprise overpowered him.

"I beg your pardon," he said; "I begin to perceive that I am growing old! I am positively not prepared for little incidents like this. But set my mind at rest upon one point: do my eyes deceive me, or are you indeed a parson?"

"I am in holy orders," answered Mr. Rolles.

"Well," cried the other, "as long as I live I will never hear another word against the cloth!"

"You flatter me," said Mr. Rolles.

"Pardon me," replied Vandeleur; "pardon me, young man. You are no coward, but it still remains to be seen whether you are not the worst of fools. Perhaps," he continued, leaning back upon his seat, "perhaps you would oblige me with a few particulars. I must suppose you had some object in the stupefying impudence of your proceedings, and I confess I have a curiosity to know it."

"It is very simple," replied the clergyman; "it proceeds from my great inexperience of life."

"I shall be glad to be persuaded," answered Vandeleur.

Whereupon Mr. Rolles told him the whole story of his connection with the Rajah's Diamond, from the time he found it in Raeburn's garden to the time when he left London in the Flying Scotchman. He added a brief sketch of his feelings and thoughts during the journey, and concluded in these words:—

"When I recognised the tiara I knew we were in the same attitude towards Society, and this inspired me with a hope, which I trust you will say was not ill-founded, that you might become in some sense my partner in the difficulties and, of course, the profits of my situation. To one of your special knowledge and obviously great experience the negotiation of the diamond would give but little trouble, while to me it was a matter of impossibility. On the other part, I judged that I might lose nearly as much by cutting the diamond, and that not improbably with an unskilful hand, as might enable me to pay you with proper generosity for your assistance. The subject was a delicate one to broach; and perhaps I fell short in delicacy. But I must ask you to remember that for me the situation was a new one, and I was entirely unacquainted with the etiquette in use. I believe without vanity that I could have married or baptized you in a very acceptable manner; but every man has his own aptitudes, and this sort of bargain was not among the list of my accomplishments."

"I do not wish to flatter you," replied Vandeleur; "but upon my word, you have an unusual disposition for a life of crime. You have more accomplishments than you imagine; and though

I have encountered a number of rogues in different quarters of the world, I never met with one so unblushing as yourself. Cheer up, Mr. Rolles, you are in the right profession at last! As for helping you, you may command me as you will. I have only a day's business in Edinburgh on a little matter for my brother; and once that is concluded, I return to Paris, where I usually reside. If you please, you may accompany me thither. And before the end of a month I believe I shall have brought your little business to a satisfactory conclusion."

(At this point, contrary to all the canons of his art, our Arabian author breaks off the "Story of the Young Man in Holy Orders." I regret and condemn such practices; but I must follow my original, and refer the reader for the conclusion of Mr. Rolles' adventures to the next number of the cycle, the "Story of the House with the Green Blinds.")

## Story of the House with
## the Green Blinds

Francis Scrymgeour, a clerk in the Bank of Scotland at Edinburgh, had attained the age of twenty-five in a sphere of quiet, creditable, and domestic life. His mother died while he was young; but his father, a man of sense and probity, had given him an excellent education at school, and brought him up at home to orderly and frugal habits. Francis, who was of a docile and affectionate disposition, profited by these advantages with zeal, and devoted himself heart and soul to his employment. A walk upon Saturday afternoon, an occasional dinner with members of his family, and a yearly tour of a fortnight in the Highlands or even on the continent of Europe, were his principal distractions, and, he grew rapidly in favour with his superiors, and enjoyed already a salary of nearly two hundred pounds a year, with the prospect of an ultimate advance to almost double that amount. Few young men were more contented, few more willing and laborious than Francis Scrymgeour. Sometimes at night, when he had read the daily paper, he would play upon the flute to amuse his father, for whose qualities he entertained a great respect.

One day he received a note from a well-known firm of Writers to the Signet, requesting the favour of an immediate interview with him. The letter was marked "Private and Confidential," and had been addressed to him at the bank, instead of at home—two unusual circumstances which made him obey the summons with the more alacrity. The senior member of the firm, a man of much austerity of manner, made him gravely welcome, requested him to take a seat, and proceeded to explain the matter in hand in the picked expressions of a veteran man of business. A person, who must remain nameless, but of whom the lawyer had every reason to think well—a man, in short, of some station in the country—desired to make Francis an annual allowance of five hundred pounds. The capital was to be placed under the control of the lawyer's firm and two trustees who must also remain anonymous. There were conditions annexed to this liberality, but he was of opinion that his new client would find nothing either excessive or dishonourable in the terms; and he repeated these two words with emphasis, as though he desired to commit himself to nothing more.

Francis asked their nature.

"The conditions," said the Writer to the Signet, "are, as I have twice remarked, neither dishonourable nor excessive. At the same time I cannot conceal from you that they are most unusual. Indeed, the whole case is very much out of our way; and I should certainly have refused it had it not been for the reputation of the gentleman who entrusted it to my care, and, let me add, Mr. Scrymgeour, the interest I have been led to take in yourself by many complimentary and, I have no doubt, well-deserved reports."

Francis entreated him to be more specific.

"You cannot picture my uneasiness as to these conditions," he said.

"They are two," replied the lawyer, "only two; and the sum, as you will remember, is five hundred a year—and unburdened, I forgot to add, unburdened."

And the lawyer raised his eyebrows at him with solemn gusto.

"The first," he resumed, "is of remarkable simplicity. You must be in Paris by the afternoon of Sunday, the 15th; there you will find, at the box-office of the Comédie Française, a ticket for admission taken in your name and waiting you. You are requested to sit out the whole performance in the seat provided, and that is all."

"I should certainly have preferred a week-day," replied Francis. "But, after all, once in a way——"

"And in Paris, my dear sir," added the lawyer soothingly. "I believe I am something of a precisian myself, but upon such a consideration, and in Paris, I should not hesitate an instant."

And the pair laughed pleasantly together.

"The other is of more importance," continued the Writer to the Signet. "It regards your marriage. My client, taking a deep interest in your welfare, desires to advise you absolutely in the choice of a wife. Absolutely, you understand," he repeated.

"Let us be more explicit, if you please," returned Francis. "Am I to marry any one, maid or widow, black or white, whom this invisible person chooses to propose?"

"I was to assure you that suitability of age and position should be a principle with your benefactor," replied the lawyer. "As to race, I confess the difficulty had not occurred to me, and I failed to inquire; but if you like I will make a note of it at once, and advise you on the earliest opportunity."

"Sir," said Francis, "it remains to be seen whether this whole affair is not a most unworthy fraud. The circumstances are inexplicable—I had almost said incredible; and until I see a little more daylight, and some plausible motive, I confess I should be very sorry to put a hand to the transaction. I appeal to you in this difficulty for information. I must learn what is at the bottom of it all. If you do not know, cannot guess, or are not at liberty to tell me, I shall take my hat and go back to my bank as I came."

"I do not know," answered the lawyer, "but I have an excellent guess. Your father, and no one else, is at the root of this apparently unnatural business."

"My father!" cried Francis, in extreme disdain. "Worthy man, I know every thought of his mind, every penny of his fortune!"

"You misinterpret my words," said the lawyer. "I do not refer to Mr. Scrymgeour, senior; for he is not your father. When he and his wife came to Edinburgh, you were already nearly one year old, and you had not yet been three months in their care. The secret has been well kept; but such is the fact. Your father is unknown, and I say again that I believe him to be the original of the offers I am charged at present to transmit to you."

It would be impossible to exaggerate the astonishment of Francis Scrymgeour at this unexpected information. He pled this confusion to the lawyer.

"Sir," said he, "after a piece of news so startling, you must grant me some hours for thought. You shall know this evening what conclusion I have reached."

The lawyer commended his prudence; and Francis, excusing himself upon some pretext at the bank, took a long walk into the country, and fully considered the different steps and aspects of the case. A pleasant sense of his own importance rendered him the more deliberate: but the issue was from the first not doubtful. His whole carnal man leaned irresistibly towards the five hundred a year, and the strange conditions with which it was burdened; he discovered in his heart an invincible repugnance to the name of Scrymgeour, which he had never hitherto disliked; he began to despise the narrow and unromantic interests of his former life; and when once his mind was fairly made up, he walked with a new feeling of strength and freedom, and nourished himself with the gayest anticipations.

He said but a word to the lawyer, and immediately received a cheque for two quarters' arrears; for the allowance was ante-dated from the first of January. With this in his pocket, he walked home. The flat in Scotland Street looked mean in his eyes; his nostrils, for the first time, rebelled against the odour of broth; and he observed little defects of manner in his adoptive father which filled him with surprise and almost with disgust. The next day, he determined, should see him on his way to Paris.

In that city, where he arrived long before the appointed date, he put up at a modest hotel frequented by English and Italians, and devoted himself to improvement in the French tongue; for this purpose he had a master twice a week, entered into conversation with loiterers in the Champs Elysées, and nightly frequented the theatre. He had his whole toilette fashionably renewed; and was shaved and had his hair dressed every morning by a barber in a neighbouring street. This gave him something of a foreign air, and seemed to wipe off the reproach of his past years.

At length, on the Saturday afternoon, he betook himself to the box-office of the theatre in the Rue Richelieu. No sooner had he mentioned his name than the clerk produced the order in an envelope of which the address was scarcely dry.

"It has been taken this moment," said the clerk.

"Indeed!" said Francis. "May I ask what the gentleman was like?"

"Your friend is easy to describe," replied the official. "He is old and strong and beautiful, with white hair and a sabre-cut across his face. You cannot fail to recognise so marked a person."

"No, indeed," returned Francis; "and I thank you for your politeness."

"He cannot yet be far distant," added the clerk. "If you make haste you might still overtake him."

Francis did not wait to be twice told; he ran precipitately

from the theatre into the middle of the street and looked in all directions. More than one white-haired man was within sight; but though he overtook each of them in succession, all wanted the sabre-cut. For nearly half-an-hour he tried one street after another in the neighbourhood, until at length, recognising the folly of continued search, he started on a walk to compose his agitated feelings; for this proximity of an encounter with him to whom he could not doubt he owed the day had profoundly moved the young man.

It chanced that his way lay up the Rue Drouot and thence up the Rue des Martyrs; and chance, in this case, served him better than all the forethought in the world. For on the outer boulevard he saw two men in earnest colloquy upon a seat. One was dark, young, and handsome, secularly dressed, but with an indelible clerical stamp; the other answered in every particular to the description given him by the clerk. Francis felt his heart beat high in his bosom; he knew he was now about to hear the voice of his father; and making a wide circuit, he noiselessly took his place behind the couple in question, who were too much interested in their talk to observe much else. As Francis had expected, the conversation was conducted in the English language.

"Your suspicions begin to annoy me, Rolles," said the older man. "I tell you I am doing my utmost; a man cannot lay his hand on millions in a moment. Have I not taken you up, a mere stranger, out of pure good-will? Are you not living largely on my bounty?"

"On your advances, Mr. Vandeleur," corrected the other.

"Advances, if you choose; and interest instead of goodwill, if you prefer it," returned Vandeleur angrily. "I am not here to pick expressions. Business is business; and your business, let me remind you, is too muddy for such airs. Trust me, or leave me alone and find some one else; but let us have an end, for God's sake, of your jeremiads."

"I am beginning to learn the world," replied the other, "and I see that you have every reason to play me false, and not one to deal honestly. I am not here to pick expressions either; you wish the diamond for yourself; you know you do—you dare not deny it. Have you not already forged my name, and searched my lodging in my absence? I understand the cause of your delays; you are lying in wait; you are the diamond hunter, forsooth; and sooner or later, by fair means or foul, you'll lay your hands upon it. I tell you, it must stop; push me much further and I promise you a surprise."

"It does not become you to use threats," returned Vandeleur. "Two can play at that. My brother is here in Paris; the police are on the alert; and if you persist in wearying me with your caterwauling, I will arrange a little astonishment for you, Mr. Rolles. But mine shall be once and for all. Do you understand, or would you prefer me to tell it you in Hebrew? There is an end to all things, and you have come to the end of my patience. Tuesday, at seven; not a day, not an hour sooner, not the least part of a second, if it were to save your life. And if you do not choose to wait, you may go to the bottomless pit for me, and welcome."

And so saying, the Dictator arose from the bench, and marched off in the direction of Montmartre, shaking his head and swinging his cane with a most furious air; while his companion remained where he was, in an attitude of great dejection.

Francis was at the pitch of surprise and horror; his sentiments had been shocked to the last degree; the hopeful tenderness with which he had taken his place upon the bench was transformed into repulsion and despair; old Mr. Scrymgeour, he reflected, was a far more kindly and creditable parent than this dangerous and violent intriguer; but he retained his presence of mind, and suffered not a moment to elapse before he was on the trail of the Dictator.

That gentleman's fury carried him forward at a brisk pace, and he was so completely occupied in his angry thoughts that he never so much as cast a look behind him till he reached his own door.

His house stood high up in the Rue Lepic, commanding a view of all Paris and enjoying the pure air of the heights. It was two storeys high, with green blinds and shutters; and all the windows looking on the street were hermetically closed. Tops of trees showed over the high garden wall, and the wall was protected by *chevaux-de-frise*. The Dictator paused a moment while he searched his pocket for a key; and then, opening a gate, disappeared within the enclosure.

Francis looked about him; the neighbourhood was very lonely, the house isolated in its garden. It seemed as if his observation must here come to an abrupt end. A second glance, however, showed him a tall house next door presenting a gable to the garden, and in this gable a single window. He passed to the front and saw a ticket offering unfurnished lodgings by the month; and, on inquiry, the room which commanded the Dictator's garden proved to be one of those to let. Francis did not hesitate a moment; he took the room, paid an advance upon the rent, and returned to his hotel to seek his baggage.

The old man with the sabre-cut might or might not be his father; he might or he might not be upon the true scent; but he was certainly on the edge of an exciting mystery, and he promised himself that he would not relax his observation until he had got to the bottom of the secret.

From the window of his new apartment Francis Scrymgeour commanded a complete view into the garden of the house with the green blinds. Immediately below him a very comely chestnut with wide boughs sheltered a pair of rustic tables where people might dine in the height of summer. On all sides save one a dense vegetation concealed the soil; but there, between the tables and the house, he saw a patch of gravel walk leading from the verandah to the garden-gate. Studying the place from between the boards of the Venetian shutters, which he durst not open for fear of attracting attention, Francis observed but little to indicate the manners of the inhabitants, and that little argued no more than a close reserve and a taste for solitude. The garden was conventual, the house had the air of a prison. The green blinds were all drawn down upon the outside; the door into the verandah was closed; the garden, as far as he could see it, was left entirely to itself in the evening sunshine. A modest curl of smoke from a single chimney alone testified to the presence of living people.

In order that he might not be entirely idle, and to give a certain colour to his way of life, Francis had purchased Euclid's Geometry in French, which he set himself to copy and translate on the top of his portmanteau and seated on the floor against the wall; for he was equally without chair or table. From time to time he would rise and cast a glance into the enclosure of the house with the green blinds; but the windows remained obstinately closed and the garden empty.

Only late in the evening did anything occur to reward his continued attention. Between nine and ten the sharp tinkle of a bell aroused him from a fit of dozing; and he sprang to his observatory in time to hear an important noise of locks being opened and bars removed, and to see Mr. Vandeleur, carrying a lantern and clothed in a flowing robe of black velvet with a skull-cap to match, issue from under the verandah and proceed leisurely towards the garden gate. The sound of bolts and bars was then repeated; and a moment after Francis perceived the Dictator escorting into the house, in the mobile light of the lantern, an individual of the lowest and most despicable appearance.

Half-an-hour afterwards the visitor was reconducted to the street; and Mr. Vandeleur, setting his light upon one of the rustic tables, finished a cigar with great deliberation under the foliage of the chestnut. Francis, peering through a clear space among the leaves, was able to follow his gestures as he threw away the ash or enjoyed a copious inhalation; and beheld a cloud upon the old man's brow and a forcible action of the lips, which testified to some deep and probably painful train of thought. The cigar was already almost at an end, when the voice of a young girl was heard suddenly crying the hour from the interior of the house.

"In a moment," replied John Vandeleur.

And, with that, he threw away the stump and, taking up the lantern, sailed away under the verandah for the night. As soon as the door was closed, absolute darkness fell upon the house; Francis might try his eyesight as much as he pleased, he could not detect so much as a single chink of light below a blind; and he concluded, with great good sense, that the bed-chambers were all upon the other side.

Early the next morning (for he was early awake after an uncomfortable night upon the floor), he saw cause to adopt a different explanation. The blinds rose, one after another, by means of a spring in the interior, and disclosed steel shutters such as we see on the front of shops; these in their turn were rolled up by a similar contrivance; and for the space of about an hour, the chambers were left open to the morning air. At the end of that time Mr. Vandeleur, with his own hand, once more closed the shutters and replaced the blinds from within.

While Francis was still marvelling at these precautions, the door opened and a young girl came forth to look about her in the garden. It was not two minutes before she re-entered the house, but even in that short time he saw enough to convince him that she possessed the most unusual attractions. His curiosity was not only highly excited by this incident, but his spirits were improved to a still more notable degree. The alarming manners and more than equivocal life of his father ceased from that moment to prey upon his mind; from that moment he embraced his new family with ardour; and whether the young lady should prove his sister or his wife, he felt convinced she was an angel in disguise. So much was this the case that he was seized with a sudden horror when he reflected how little he really knew, and how possible it was that he had followed the wrong person when he followed Mr. Vandeleur.

The porter, whom he consulted, could afford him little information; but, such as it was, it had a mysterious and questionable sound. The person next door was an English gentleman of extraordinary wealth, and proportionately eccentric in his tastes and habits. He possessed great collections, which he kept in the house beside him; and it was to protect these that he had fitted the place with steel shutters, elaborate fastenings, and *chevaux-de-frise* along the garden wall. He lived much alone, in spite of some strange visitors with whom, it seemed, he had business to transact; and there was no one else in the house, except Mademoiselle and an old woman servant.

"Is Mademoiselle his daughter?" inquired Francis.

"Certainly," replied the porter. "Mademoiselle is the daughter of the house; and strange it is to see how she is made to work. For all his riches, it is she who goes to market; and every day in the week you may see her going by with a basket on her arm."

"And the collections?" asked the other.

"Sir," said the man, "they are immensely valuable. More I cannot tell you. Since M. de Vandeleur's arrival no one in the quarter has so much as passed the door."

"Suppose not," returned Francis, "you must surely have some

notion what these famous galleries contain. Is it pictures, silks, statues, jewels, or what?"

"My faith, sir," said the fellow with a shrug, "it might be carrots, and still I could not tell you. How should I know? The house is kept like a garrison, as you perceive."

And then as Francis was returning disappointed to his room, the porter called him back.

"I have just remembered, sir," said he. "M. de Vandeleur has been in all parts of the world, and I once heard the old woman declare that he had brought many diamonds back with him. If that be the truth, there must be a fine show behind those shutters."

By an early hour on Sunday Francis was in his place at the theatre. The seat which had been taken for him was only two or three numbers from the left-hand side, and directly opposite one of the lower boxes. As the seat had been specially chosen there was doubtless something to be learned from its position; and he judged by an instinct that the box upon his right was, in some way or other, to be connected with the drama in which he ignorantly played a part. Indeed, it was so situated that its occupants could safely observe him from beginning to end of the piece, if they were so minded; while, profiting by the depth, they could screen themselves sufficiently well from any counter-examination on his side. He promised himself not to leave it for a moment out of sight; and whilst he scanned the rest of the theatre, or made a show of attending to the business of the stage, he always kept a corner of an eye upon the empty box.

The second act had been some time in progress, and was even drawing towards a close, when the door opened and two persons entered and ensconced themselves in the darkest of the shade. Francis could hardly control his emotion. It was Mr. Vandeleur and his daughter. The blood came and went in his arteries and veins with stunning activity; his ears sang; his head turned. He dared not look lest he should awake suspicion; his play-bill, which he kept reading from end to end and over and over again, turned from white to red before his eyes; and when he cast a glance upon the stage, it seemed incalculably far away, and he found the voices and gestures of the actors to the last degree impertinent and absurd.

From time to time he risked a momentary look in the direction which principally interested him; and once at least he felt certain that his eyes encountered those of the young girl. A shock passed over his body, and he saw all the colours of the rainbow. What would he not have given to overhear what passed between the Vandeleurs? What would he not have given for the courage to take up his opera-glass and steadily inspect their attitude and expression? There, for aught he knew, his whole life was being decided—and he not able to interfere, not able even to follow the debate, but condemned to sit and suffer where he was, in impotent anxiety.

At last the act came to an end. The curtain fell, and the people around him began to leave their places, for the interval. It was only natural that he should follow their example; and if he did so, it was not only natural but necessary that he should pass immediately in front of the box in question. Summoning all his courage, but keeping his eyes lowered, Francis drew near the spot. His progress was slow, for the old gentleman before him moved with incredible deliberation, wheezing as he went. What was he to do? Should he address the Vandeleurs by name as he went by? Should he take the flower from his button-hole and throw it into the box? Should he raise his face and direct one long and affectionate look upon the lady who was either his sister or his betrothed? As he found himself thus struggling among so many alternatives, he had a vision of his old equable existence in the bank, and was assailed by a thought of regret for the past.

By this time he had arrived directly opposite the box; and although he was still undetermined what to do or whether to do anything, he turned his head and lifted his eyes. No sooner had he done so than he uttered a cry of disappointment and remained rooted to the spot. The box was empty. During his slow advance Mr. Vandeleur and his daughter had quietly slipped away.

A polite person in his rear reminded him that he was stopping the path; and he moved on again with mechanical footsteps, and suffered the crowd to carry him unresisting out of the theatre. Once in the street, the pressure ceasing, he came to a halt, and the cool night air speedily restored him to the possession of his faculties. He was surprised to find that his head ached violently, and that he remembered not one word of the two acts which he had witnessed. As the excitement wore away, it was succeeded by an overweening appetite for sleep, and he hailed a cab and drove to his lodging in a state of extreme exhaustion and some disgust of life.

Next morning he lay in wait for Miss Vandeleur on her road to market, and by eight o'clock beheld her stepping down a lane. She was simply, and even poorly, attired; but in the carriage of her head and body there was something flexible and noble that would have lent distinction to the meanest toilette. Even her basket, so aptly did she carry it, became her like an ornament. It seemed to Francis, as he slipped into a doorway, that the sunshine followed and the shadows fled before her as she walked; and he was conscious, for the first time, of a bird singing in a cage above the lane.

He suffered her to pass the doorway, and then, coming forth once more, addressed her by name from behind. "Miss Vandeleur," said he.

She turned and, when she saw who he was, became deadly pale.

"Pardon me," he continued; "Heaven knows I had no will to startle you; and, indeed, there should be nothing startling in the presence of one who wishes you so well as I do. And, believe me, I am acting rather from necessity than choice. We have many things in common, and I am sadly in the dark. There is much that I should be doing, and my hands are tied. I do not know even what to feel, nor who are my friends and enemies."

She found her voice with an effort.

"I do not know who you are," she said.

"Ah, yes! Miss Vandeleur, you do," returned Francis "better than I do myself. Indeed, it is on that, above all, that I seek light. Tell me what you know," he pleaded. "Tell me who I am, who you are, and how our destinies are intermixed. Give me a little help with my life, Miss Vandeleur—only a word or two to guide me, only the name of my father, if you will—and I shall be grateful and content."

"I will not attempt to deceive you," she replied. "I know who you are, but I am not at liberty to say."

"Tell me, at least, that you have forgiven my presumption, and I shall wait with all the patience I have," he said. "If I am not to know, I must do without. It is cruel, but I can bear more upon a push. Only do not add to my troubles the thought that I have made an enemy of you."

"You did only what was natural," she said, "and I have nothing to forgive you. Farewell."

"Is it to be *farewell*?" he asked.

"Nay, that I do not know myself," she answered. "Farewell for the present, if you like."

And with these words she was gone.

Francis returned to his lodging in a state of considerable commotion of mind. He made the most trifling progress with his Euclid for that forenoon, and was more often at the window than at his improvised writing-table. But beyond seeing the return of Miss Vandeleur, and the meeting between her and her father, who was smoking a Trichinopoli cigar in the verandah, there was nothing notable in the neighbourhood of the house with the green blinds before the time of the mid-day meal. The young man hastily allayed his appetite in a neighbouring restaurant, and returned with the speed of unallayed curiosity to the house in the Rue Lepic. A mounted servant was leading a saddle-horse to and fro before the garden wall; and the porter of Francis's lodging was smoking a pipe against the door-post, absorbed in contemplation of the livery and the steeds.

"Look!" he cried to the young man, "what fine cattle! what an elegant costume! They belong to the brother of M. de Vandeleur, who is now within upon a visit. He is a great man, a general, in your country; and you doubtless know him well by reputation."

"I confess," returned Francis, "that I have never heard of General Vandeleur before. We have many officers of that grade, and my pursuits have been exclusively civil."

"It is he," replied the porter, "who lost the great diamond of the Indies. Of that at least you must have read often in the papers."

As soon as Francis could disengage himself from the porter he ran upstairs and hurried to the window. Immediately below the clear space in the chestnut leaves, the two gentlemen were seated in conversation over a cigar. The General, a red, military-looking man, offered some traces of a family resemblance to his brother; he had something of the same features, something, although very little, of the same free and powerful carriage; but he was older, smaller, and more common in air; his likeness was that of a caricature, and he seemed altogether a poor and debile being by the side of the Dictator.

They spoke in tones so low, leaning over the table with every appearance of interest, that Francis could catch no more than a word or two on an occasion. For as little as he heard, he was convinced that the conversation turned upon himself and his own career; several times the name of Scrymgeour reached his ear, for it was easy to distinguish, and still more frequently he fancied he could distinguish the name Francis.

At length the General, as if in a hot anger, broke forth into several violent exclamations.

"Francis Vandeleur!" he cried, accentuating the last word. "Francis Vandeleur, I tell you."

The Dictator made a movement of his whole body, half affirmative, half contemptuous, but his answer was inaudible to the young man.

Was he the Francis Vandeleur in question? he wondered. Were they discussing the name under which he was to be married? Or was the whole affair a dream and a delusion of his own conceit and self-absorption?

After another interval of inaudible talk, dissension seemed again to arise between the couple underneath the chestnut, and again the General raised his voice angrily so as to be audible to Francis.

"My wife?" he cried. "I have done with my wife for good. I will not hear her name. I am sick of her very name."

And he swore aloud and beat the table with his fist.

The Dictator appeared, by his gestures, to pacify him after a paternal fashion; and a little after he conducted him to the garden-gate. The pair shook hands affectionately enough; but so soon as the door had closed behind his visitor, John Vandeleur fell into a fit of laughter which sounded unkindly and even devilish in the ears of Francis Scrymgeour.

So another day had passed, and little more learnt. But the young man remembered that the morrow was Tuesday, and promised himself some curious discoveries; all might be well, or all might be ill; he was sure, at least, to glean some curious information, and, perhaps, by good luck, get at the heart of the mystery which surrounded his father and his family.

As the hour of the dinner drew near many preparations were made in the garden of the house with the green blinds. That table which was partly visible to Francis through the chestnut leaves was destined to serve as a sideboard, and carried relays of plates and the materials for salad: the other, which was almost entirely concealed, had been set apart for the diners, and Francis could catch glimpses of white cloth and silver plate.

Mr. Rolles arrived, punctual to the minute; he looked like a man upon his guard, and spoke low and sparingly. The Dictator, on the other hand, appeared to enjoy an unusual flow of spirits; his laugh, which was youthful and pleasant to hear, sounded frequently from the garden; by the modulation and the changes of his voice it was obvious that he told many droll stories and imitated the accents of a variety of different nations; and before he and the young clergyman had finished their vermouth all feeling of distrust was at an end, and they were talking together like a pair of school companions.

At length Miss Vandeleur made her appearance, carrying the soup-tureen. Mr. Rolles ran to offer her assistance which she laughingly refused; and there was an interchange of pleasantries among the trio which seemed to have reference to this primitive manner of waiting by one of the company.

"One is more at one's ease," Mr. Vandeleur was heard to declare.

Next moment they were all three in their places, and Francis could see as little as he could hear of what passed. But the dinner seemed to go merrily; there was a perpetual babble of voices and sound of knives and forks below the chestnut; and Francis, who had no more than a roll to gnaw, was affected with envy by the comfort and deliberation of the meal. The party lingered over one dish after another, and then over a delicate dessert, with a bottle of old wine carefully uncorked by the hand of the Dictator himself. As it began to grow dark a lamp was set upon the table and a couple of candles on the sideboard; for the night was perfectly pure, starry, and windless. Light overflowed besides from the door and window in the verandah, so that the garden was fairly illuminated and the leaves twinkled in the darkness.

For perhaps the tenth time Miss Vandeleur entered the house; and on this occasion she returned with the coffee-tray, which she placed upon the sideboard. At the same moment her father rose from his seat.

"The coffee is my province," Francis heard him say.

And next moment he saw his supposed father standing by the sideboard in the light of the candles.

Talking over his shoulder all the while, Mr. Vandeleur poured out two cups of the brown stimulant, and then, by a rapid act of prestidigitation, emptied the contents of a tiny phial into the smaller of the two. The thing was so swiftly done that even Francis, who looked straight into his face, had hardly time to perceive the movement before it was completed. And next instant, and still laughing, Mr. Vandeleur had turned again towards the table with a cup in either hand.

"Ere we have done with this," said he, "we may expect our famous Hebrew."

It would be impossible to depict the confusion and distress of Francis Scrymgeour. He saw foul play going forward before his eyes, and he felt bound to interfere, but knew not how. It might be a mere pleasantry, and then how should he look if he were to offer an unnecessary warning? Or again, if it were serious, the criminal might be his own father, and then how should he not lament if he were to bring ruin on the author of his days? For the first time he became conscious of his own position as a spy. To wait inactive at such a juncture and with such a conflict of sentiments in his bosom was to suffer the most acute torture; he clung to the bars of the shutters, his heart beat fast and with irregularity, and he felt a strong sweat break forth upon his body.

Several minutes passed.

He seemed to perceive the conversation die away and grow less and less in vivacity and volume; but still no sign of any alarming or even notable event.

Suddenly the ring of a glass breaking was followed by a faint and dull sound, as of a person who should have fallen forward with his head upon the table. At the same moment a piercing scream rose from the garden.

"What have you done?" cried Miss Vandeleur. "He is dead!"

The Dictator replied in a violent whisper, so strong and sibilant that every word was audible to the watcher at the window.

"Silence!" said Mr. Vandeleur; "the man is as well as I am. Take him by the heels whilst I carry him by the shoulders."

Francis heard Miss Vandeleur break forth into a passion of tears.

"Do you hear what I say?" resumed the Dictator, in the same tones. "Or do you wish to quarrel with me? I give you your choice, Miss Vandeleur."

There was another pause, and the Dictator spoke again.

"Take that man by the heels," he said. "I must have him brought into the house. If I were a little younger, I could help myself against the world. But now that years and dangers are upon me and my hands are weakened, I must turn to you for aid."

"It is a crime," replied the girl.

"I am your father," said Mr. Vandeleur.

This appeal seemed to produce its effect. A scuffling noise followed upon the gravel, a chair was overset, and then Francis saw the father and daughter stagger across the walk and disappear under the verandah, bearing the inanimate body of Mr. Rolles embraced about the knees and shoulders. The young clergyman was limp and pallid, and his head rolled upon his shoulders at every step.

Was he alive or dead? Francis, in spite of the Dictator's declaration, inclined to the latter view. A great crime had been committed; a great calamity had fallen upon the inhabitants of the house with the green blinds. To his surprise, Francis found all horror for the deed swallowed up in sorrow for a girl and an old man whom he judged to be in the height of peril. A tide of generous feeling swept into his heart; he, too, would help his father against man and mankind, against fate and justice; and casting open the shutters he closed his eyes and threw himself with out-stretched arms into the foliage of the chestnut.

Branch after branch slipped from his grasp or broke under his weight; then he caught a stalwart bough under his armpit, and hung suspended for a second; and then he let himself drop and fell heavily against the table. A cry of alarm from the house warned him that his entrance had not been effected unobserved. He recovered himself with a stagger, and in three bounds crossed the intervening space and stood before the door in the verandah.

In a small apartment, carpeted with matting and surrounded by glazed cabinets full of rare and costly curios, Mr. Vandeleur was stooping over the body of Mr. Rolles. He raised himself as Francis entered, and there was an instantaneous passage of hands. It was the business of a second; as fast as an eye can wink the thing was done; the young man had not the time to be sure, but it seemed to him as if the Dictator had taken something from the curate's breast, looked at it for the least fraction of time as it lay in his hand, and then suddenly and swiftly passed it to his daughter.

All this was over while Francis had still one foot upon the threshold, and the other raised in air. The next instant he was on his knees to Mr. Vandeleur.

"Father!" he cried. "Let me too help you. I will do what you wish and ask no questions; I will obey you with my life; treat me as a son, and you will find I have a son's devotion."

A deplorable explosion of oaths was the Dictator's first reply.

"Son and father?" he cried. "Father and son? What d—d unnatural comedy is all this? How do you come in my garden? What do you want? And who, in God's name, are you?"

Francis, with a stunned and shamefaced aspect, got upon his feet again, and stood in silence.

Then a light seemed to break upon Mr. Vandeleur, and he laughed aloud.

"I see," cried he. "It is the Scrymgeour. Very well, Mr. Scrymgeour. Let me tell you in a few words how you stand. You have entered my private residence by force, or perhaps by fraud, but certainly with no encouragement from me; and you come at a moment of some annoyance, a guest having fainted at my table, to besiege me with your protestations. You are no son of mine. You are my brother's bastard by a fishwife, if you want to know.

I regard you with an indifference closely bordering on aversion; and from what I now see of your conduct, I judge your mind to be exactly suitable to your exterior. I recommend you these mortifying reflections for your leisure; and, in the meantime, let me beseech you to rid us of your presence. If I were not occupied," added the Dictator, with a terrifying oath, "I should give you the unholiest drubbing ere you went!"

Francis listened in profound humiliation. He would have fled had it been possible; but as he had no means of leaving the residence into which he had so unfortunately penetrated, he could do no more than stand foolishly where he was.

It was Miss Vandeleur who broke the silence.

"Father," she said, "you speak in anger. Mr. Scrymgeour may have been mistaken, but he meant well and kindly."

"Thank you for speaking," returned the Dictator. "You remind me of some other observations which I hold it a point of honour to make to Mr. Scrymgeour. My brother," he continued, addressing the young man, "has been foolish enough to give you an allowance; he was foolish enough and presumptuous enough to propose a match between you and this young lady. You were exhibited to her two nights ago; and I rejoice to tell you that she rejected the idea with disgust. Let me add that I have considerable influence with your father; and it shall not be my fault if you are not beggared of your allowance and sent back to your scrivening ere the week be out."

The tones of the old man's voice were, if possible, more wounding than his language; Francis felt himself exposed to the most cruel, blighting, and unbearable contempt; his head turned, and he covered his face with his hands, uttering at the same time a tearless sob of agony. But Miss Vandeleur once again interfered in his behalf.

"Mr. Scrymgeour," she said, speaking in clear and even tones, "you must not be concerned at my father's harsh expressions. I felt no disgust for you; on the contrary, I asked an opportunity to make your better acquaintance. As for what has passed to-night, believe me it has filled my mind with both pity and esteem."

Just then Mr. Rolles made a convulsive movement with his arm, which convinced Francis that he was only drugged, and was beginning to throw off the influence of the opiate. Mr. Vandeleur stooped over him and examined his face for an instant.

"Come, come!" cried he, raising his head. "Let there be an end of this. And since you are so pleased with his conduct, Miss Vandeleur, take a candle and show the bastard out."

The young lady hastened to obey.

"Thank you," said Francis, as soon as he was alone with her in the garden. "I thank you from my soul. This has been the bitterest evening of my life, but it will have always one pleasant recollection."

"I spoke as I felt," she replied, "and in justice to you. It made my heart sorry that you should be so unkindly used."

By this time they had reached the garden gate; and Miss Vandeleur, having set the candle on the ground, was already unfastening the bolts.

"One word more," said Francis. "This is not for the last time—I shall see you again, shall I not?"

"Alas!" she answered. "You have heard my father. What can I do but obey?"

"Tell me at least that it is not with your consent," returned Francis; "tell me that you have no wish to see the last of me."

"Indeed," replied she, "I have none. You seem to me both brave and honest."

"Then," said Francis, "give me a keepsake."

She paused for a moment, with her hand upon the key; for the various bars and bolts were all undone, and there was nothing left but to open the lock.

"If I agree," she said, "will you promise to do as I tell you from point to point?"

"Can you ask?" replied Francis. "I would do so willingly on your bare word."

She turned the key and threw open the door.

"Be it so," said she. "You do not know what you ask, but be it so. Whatever you hear," she continued, "whatever happens, do not return to this house; hurry fast until you reach the lighted and populous quarters of the city; even there be upon your guard. You are in a greater danger than you fancy. Promise me you will not so much as look at my keepsake until you are in a place of safety."

"I promise," replied Francis.

She put something loosely wrapped in a handkerchief into the young man's hand; and at the same time, with more strength than he could have anticipated, she pushed him into the street.

"Now, run!" she cried.

He heard the door close behind him, and the noise of the bolts being replaced.

"My faith," said he, "since I have promised!"

And he took to his heels down the lane that leads into the Rue Ravignan.

He was not fifty paces from the house with the green blinds when the most diabolical outcry suddenly arose out of the stillness of the night. Mechanically he stood still; another passenger followed his example; in the neighbouring floors he saw people crowding to the windows; a conflagration could not have produced more disturbance in this empty quarter. And yet it seemed to be all the work of a single man, roaring between grief and rage, like a lioness robbed of her whelps; and Francis was surprised and alarmed to hear his own name shouted with English imprecations to the wind.

His first movement was to return to the house; his second, as he remembered Miss Vandeleur's advice, to continue his flight with greater expedition than before; and he was in the act of turning to put his thought in action, when the Dictator, bareheaded, bawling aloud, his white hair blowing about his head, shot past him like a ball out of the cannon's mouth, and went careering down the street.

"That was a close shave," thought Francis to himself. "What he wants with me, and why he should be so disturbed, I cannot think; but he is plainly not good company for the moment, and I cannot do better than follow Miss Vandeleur's advice."

So saying, he turned to retrace his steps, thinking to double and descend by the Rue Lepic itself while his pursuer should continue to follow after him on the other line of street. The plan was ill-devised: as a matter of fact, he should have taken his seat in the nearest café, and waited there until the first heat of the pursuit was over. But besides that Francis had no experience and little natural aptitude for the small war of private life, he was so unconscious of any evil on his part, that he saw nothing to fear beyond a disagreeable interview. And to disagreeable interviews he felt he had already served his apprenticeship that evening; nor could he suppose that Miss Vandeleur had left anything unsaid. Indeed, the young man was sore both in body and mind—the one was all bruised, the other was full of smarting arrows; and he owned to himself that Mr. Vandeleur was master of a very deadly tongue.

The thought of his bruises reminded him that he had not only come without a hat, but that his clothes had considerably suffered in his descent through the chestnut. At the first magazine he purchased a cheap wideawake, and had the disorder of his toilet summarily repaired. The keepsake, still rolled in the handkerchief, he thrust in the meanwhile into his trousers pocket.

Not many steps beyond the shop he was conscious of a sudden shock, a hand upon his throat, an infuriated face close to his own, and an open mouth bawling curses in his ear. The Dictator, having found no trace of his quarry, was returning by the other way. Francis was a stalwart young fellow; but he was no match for his adversary whether in strength or skill; and after a few ineffectual struggles he resigned himself entirely to his captor.

"What do you want with me?" said he.

"We will talk of that at home," returned the Dictator grimly.

And he continued to march the young man up hill in the direction of the house with the green blinds.

But Francis, although he no longer struggled, was only waiting an opportunity to make a bold push for freedom. With a sudden jerk he left the collar of his coat in the hands of Mr. Vandeleur, and once more made off at his best speed in the direction of the Boulevards.

The tables were now turned. If the Dictator was the stronger, Francis, in the top of his youth, was the more fleet of foot, and he had soon effected his escape among the crowds. Relieved for a moment, but with a growing sentiment of alarm and wonder in his mind, be walked briskly until he debauched upon the Place de l'Opéra, lit up like day with electric lamps.

"This, at least," thought he, "should satisfy Miss Vandeleur."

And turning to his right along the Boulevards, he entered the Café Americain and ordered some beer. It was both late and early for the majority of the frequenters of the establishment. Only two or three persons, all men, were dotted here and there at separate tables in the hall; and Francis was too much occupied by his own thoughts to observe their presence.

He drew the handkerchief from his pocket. The object wrapped in it proved to be a morocco case, clasped and ornamented in gilt, which opened by means of a spring, and disclosed to the horrified young man a diamond of monstrous bigness and extraordinary brilliancy. The circumstance was so inexplicable, the value of the stone was plainly so enormous, that Francis sat staring into the open casket without movement, without conscious thought, like a man stricken suddenly with idiocy.

A hand was laid upon his shoulder, lightly but firmly, and a quiet voice, which yet had in it the ring of command, uttered these words in his ear—

"Close the casket, and compose your face."

Looking up, he beheld a man, still young, of an urbane and tranquil presence, and dressed with rich simplicity. This personage had risen from a neighbouring table, and, bringing his glass with him, had taken a seat beside Francis.

"Close the casket," repeated the stranger, "and put it quietly back into your pocket, where I feel persuaded it should never have been. Try, if you please, to throw off your bewildered air, and act as though I were one of your acquaintances whom you had met by chance. So! Touch glasses with me. That is better. I fear, sir, you must be an amateur."

And the stranger pronounced these last words with a smile of peculiar meaning, leaned back in his seat and enjoyed a deep inhalation of tobacco.

"For God's sake," said Francis, "tell me who you are and what this means? Why I should obey your most unusual suggestions I am sure I know not; but the truth is, I have fallen this evening into so many perplexing adventures, and all I meet conduct themselves so strangely, that I think I must either have gone mad or wandered into another planet. Your face inspires me with confidence; you seem wise, good, and experienced; tell me, for heaven's sake, why you accost me in so odd a fashion?"

"All in due time," replied the stranger. "But I have the first hand, and you must begin by telling me how the Rajah's Diamond is in your possession."

"The Rajah's Diamond!" echoed Francis.

"I would not speak so loud, if I were you," returned the other. "But most certainly you have the Rajah's Diamond in your pocket. I have seen and handled it a score of times in Sir Thomas Vandeleur's collection."

"Sir Thomas Vandeleur! The General! My father!" cried Francis.

"Your father?" repeated the stranger. "I was not aware the General had any family."

"I am illegitimate, sir," replied Francis, with a flush.

The other bowed with gravity. It was a respectful bow, as of a man silently apologising to his equal; and Francis felt relieved and comforted, he scarce knew why. The society of this person did him good; he seemed to touch firm ground; a strong feeling of respect grew up in his bosom, and mechanically he removed his wideawake as though in the presence of a superior.

"I perceive," said the stranger, "that your adventures have not all been peaceful. Your collar is torn, your face is scratched, you have a cut upon your temple; you will, perhaps, pardon my curiosity when I ask you to explain how you came by these injuries, and how you happen to have stolen property to an enormous value in your pocket."

"I must differ from you!" returned Francis hotly. "I possess no stolen property. And if you refer to the diamond, it was given to me not an hour ago by Miss Vandeleur in the Rue Lepic."

"By Miss Vandeleur of the Rue Lepic!" repeated the other. "You interest me more than you suppose. Pray continue."

"Heavens!" cried Francis.

His memory had made a sudden bound. He had seen Mr. Vandeleur take an article from the breast of his drugged visitor, and that article, he was now persuaded, was a morocco case.

"You have a light?" inquired the stranger.

"Listen," replied Francis. "I know not who you are, but I believe you to be worthy of confidence and helpful; I find myself in strange waters; I must have counsel and support, and since you invite me I shall tell you all."

And he briefly recounted his experiences since the day when he was summoned from the bank by his lawyer.

"Yours is indeed a remarkable history," said the stranger, after the young man had made an end of his narrative; "and your position is full of difficulty and peril. Many would counsel you to seek out your father, and give the diamond to him; but I have other views. Waiter!" he cried.

The waiter drew near.

"Will you ask the manager to speak with me a moment?" said he; and Francis observed once more, both in his tone and manner, the evidence of a habit of command.

The waiter withdrew, and returned in a moment with the manager, who bowed with obsequious respect.

"What," said he, "can I do to serve you?"

"Have the goodness," replied the stranger, indicating Francis, "to tell this gentleman my name."

"You have the honour, sir," said the functionary, addressing young Scrymgeour, "to occupy the same table with His Highness Prince Florizel of Bohemia."

Francis rose with precipitation, and made a grateful reverence to the Prince, who bade him resume his seat.

"I thank you," said Florizel, once more addressing the functionary; "I am sorry to have deranged you for so small a matter."

And he dismissed him with a movement of his hand.

"And now," added the Prince, turning to Francis, "give me the diamond."

Without a word the casket was handed over.

"You have done right," said Florizel, "your sentiments have properly inspired you, and you will live to be grateful for the misfortunes of to-night. A man, Mr. Scrymgeour, may fall into a thousand perplexities, but if his heart be upright and his intelligence unclouded, he will issue from them all without dishonour. Let your mind be at rest; your affairs are in my hand; and with the aid of heaven I am strong enough to bring them to a good end. Follow me, if you please, to my carriage."

So saying the Prince arose and, having left a piece of gold for the waiter, conducted the young man from the café and along the Boulevard to where an unpretentious brougham and a couple of servants out of livery awaited his arrival.

"This carriage," said he, "is at your disposal; collect your baggage as rapidly as you can make it convenient, and my servants will conduct you to a villa in the neighbourhood of Paris where you can wait in some degree of comfort until I have had time to arrange your situation. You will find there a pleasant garden, a library of good authors, a cook, a cellar, and some good cigars, which I recommend to your attention. Jerome," he added, turning to one of the servants, "you have heard what I say; I leave Mr. Scrymgeour in your charge; you will, I know, be careful of my friend."

Francis uttered some broken phrases of gratitude.

"It will be time enough to thank me," said the Prince, "when you are acknowledged by your father and married to Miss Vandeleur."

And with that the Prince turned away and strolled leisurely in the direction of Montmartre. He hailed the first passing cab, gave an address, and a quarter of an hour afterwards, having discharged the driver some distance lower, he was knocking at Mr. Vandeleur's garden gate.

It was opened with singular precautions by the Dictator in person.

"Who are you?" he demanded.

"You must pardon me this late visit, Mr. Vandeleur," replied the Prince.

"Your Highness is always welcome," returned Mr. Vandeleur, stepping back.

The Prince profited by the open space, and without waiting for his host walked right into the house and opened the door of the salon. Two people were seated there; one was Miss Vandeleur, who bore the marks of weeping about her eyes, and was still shaken from time to time by a sob; in the other the Prince recognised the young man who had consulted him on literary matters about a month before, in a club smoking-room.

"Good evening, Miss Vandeleur," said Florizel; "you look

fatigued. Mr. Rolles, I believe? I hope you have profited by the study of Gaboriau, Mr. Rolles."

But the young clergyman's temper was too much embittered for speech; and he contented himself with bowing stiffly, and continued to gnaw his lip.

"To what good wind," said Mr. Vandeleur, following his guest, "am I to attribute the honour of your Highness's presence?"

"I am come on business," returned the Prince; "on business with you; as soon as that is settled I shall request Mr. Rolles to accompany me for a walk. Mr. Rolles," he added with severity, "let me remind you that I have not yet sat down."

The clergyman sprang to his feet with an apology; whereupon the Prince took an armchair beside the table, handed his hat to Mr. Vandeleur, his cane to Mr. Rolles, and, leaving them standing and thus menially employed upon his service, spoke as follows:—

"I have come here, as I said, upon business; but, had I come looking for pleasure, I could not have been more displeased with my reception nor more dissatisfied with my company. You, sir," addressing Mr. Rolles, "you have treated your superior in station with discourtesy; you, Vandeleur, receive me with a smile, but you know right well that your hands are not yet cleansed from misconduct. I do not desire to be interrupted, sir," he added imperiously; "I am here to speak, and not to listen; and I have to ask you to hear me with respect, and to obey punctiliously. At the earliest possible date your daughter shall be married at the Embassy to my friend, Francis Scrymgeour, your brother's acknowledged son. You will oblige me by offering not less than ten thousand pounds dowry. For yourself, I will indicate to you in writing a mission of some importance in Siam which I destine to your care. And now, sir, you will answer me in two words whether or not you agree to these conditions."

"Your Highness will pardon me," said Mr. Vandeleur, "and permit me, with all respect, to submit to him two queries?"

"The permission is granted," replied the Prince.

"Your Highness," resumed the Dictator, "has called Mr. Scrymgeour his friend. Believe me, had I known he was thus honoured, I should have treated him with proportional respect."

"You interrogate adroitly," said the Prince; "but it will not serve your turn. You have my commands; if I had never seen that gentleman before to-night, it would not render them less absolute."

"Your Highness interprets my meaning with his usual subtlety," returned Vandeleur. "Once more: I have, unfortunately, put the police upon the track of Mr. Scrymgeour on a charge of theft; am I to withdraw or to uphold the accusation?"

"You will please yourself," replied Florizel. "The question is one between your conscience and the laws of this land. Give me my hat; and you, Mr. Rolles, give me my cane and follow me. Miss Vandeleur, I wish you good evening. I judge," he added to Vandeleur, "that your silence means unqualified assent."

"If I can do no better," replied the old man, "I shall submit; but I warn you openly it shall not be without a struggle."

"You are old," said the Prince; "but years are disgraceful to the wicked. Your age is more unwise than the youth of others. Do not provoke me, or you may find me harder than you dream. This is the first time that I have fallen across your path in anger; take care that it be the last."

With these words, motioning the clergyman to follow, Florizel left the apartment and directed his steps towards the garden gate; and the Dictator, following with a candle, gave them light, and once more undid the elaborate fastenings with which he sought to protect himself from intrusion.

"Your daughter is no longer present," said the Prince, turning on the threshold. "Let me tell you that I understand your threats; and you have only to lift your hand to bring upon yourself sudden and irremediable ruin."

The Dictator made no reply; but as the Prince turned his back upon him in the lamplight he made a gesture full of menace and insane fury; and the next moment, slipping round a corner, he was running at full speed for the nearest cab-stand.

(Here, says my Arabian, the thread of events is finally diverted from the "Story of the House with the Green Blinds." One more adventure, he adds, and we have done with *The Rajah's Diamond*. That last link in the chain is known among the inhabitants of Bagdad by the name of "The Adventure of Prince Florizel and a Detective.")

# The Adventure of Prince Florizel
## and a Detective

Prince Florizel walked with Mr. Rolles to the door of a small hotel where the latter resided. They spoke much together, and the clergyman was more than once affected to tears by the mingled severity and tenderness of Florizel's reproaches.

"I have made ruin of my life," he said at last. "Help me; tell me what I am to do; I have, alas! neither the virtues of a priest nor the dexterity of a rogue."

"Now that you are humbled," said the Prince, "I command no longer; the repentant have to do with God and not with princes. But if you will let me advise you, go to Australia as a colonist, seek menial labour in the open air, and try to forget that you have ever been a clergyman, or that you ever set eyes on that accursed stone."

"Accursed indeed!" replied Mr. Rolles. "Where is it now? What further hurt is it not working for mankind?"

"It will do no more evil," returned the Prince. "It is here in my pocket. And this," he added kindly, "will show that I place some faith in your penitence, young as it is."

"Suffer me to touch your hand," pleaded Mr. Rolles.

"No," replied Prince Florizel, "not yet."

The tone in which he uttered these last words was eloquent in the ears of the young clergyman; and for some minutes after the Prince had turned away he stood on the threshold following with his eyes the retreating figure and invoking the blessing of heaven upon a man so excellent in counsel.

For several hours the Prince walked alone in unfrequented streets. His mind was full of concern; what to do with the diamond, whether to return it to its owner, whom he judged unworthy of this rare possession, or to take some sweeping and courageous measure and put it out of the reach of all mankind at once and for ever, was a problem too grave to be decided in a moment. The manner in which it had come into his hands appeared manifestly providential; and as he took out the jewel and looked at it under the street lamps, its size and surprising brilliancy inclined him more and more to think of it as of an unmixed and dangerous evil for the world.

"God help me!" he thought; "if I look at it much oftener, I shall begin to grow covetous myself."

At last, though still uncertain in his mind, he turned his steps towards the small but elegant mansion on the river-side which had belonged for centuries to his royal family. The arms of Bohemia are deeply graved over the door and upon the tall chimneys; passengers have a look into a green court set with the most costly flowers, and a stork, the only one in Paris, perches on the gable all day long and keeps a crowd before the house. Grave servants are seen passing to and fro within; and from time to time the great gate is thrown open and a carriage rolls below the arch. For many reasons this residence was especially dear to the heart of Prince Florizel; he never drew near to it without enjoying that sentiment of home-coming so rare in the lives of the great; and on the present evening he beheld its tall roof and mildly illuminated windows with unfeigned relief and satisfaction.

As he was approaching the postern door by which he always entered when alone, a man stepped forth from the shadow and presented himself with an obeisance in the Prince's path.

"I have the honour of addressing Prince Florizel of Bohemia?" said he.

"Such is my title," replied the Prince. "What do you want with me?"

"I am," said the man, "a detective, and I have to present your Highness with this billet from the Prefect of Police."

The Prince took the letter and glanced it through by the light of the street lamp. It was highly apologetic, but requested him to follow the bearer to the Prefecture without delay.

"In short," said Florizel, "I am arrested."

"Your Highness," replied the officer, "nothing, I am certain, could be further from the intention of the Prefect. You will observe that he has not granted a warrant. It is mere formality, or call it, if you prefer, an obligation that your Highness lays on the authorities."

"At the same time," asked the Prince, "if I were to refuse to follow you?"

"I will not conceal from your Highness that a considerable discretion has been granted me," replied the detective with a bow.

"Upon my word," cried Florizel, "your effrontery astounds me! Yourself, as an agent, I must pardon; but your superiors shall dearly smart for their misconduct. What, have you any idea, is the cause of this impolitic and unconstitutional act? You will observe that I have as yet neither refused nor consented, and much may depend on your prompt and ingenuous answer. Let me remind you, officer, that this is an affair of some gravity."

"Your Highness," said the detective humbly, "General Vandeleur and his brother have had the incredible presumption to accuse you of theft. The famous diamond, they declare, is in your hands. A word from you in denial will most amply satisfy the Prefect; nay, I go farther: if your Highness would so far honour a subaltern as to declare his ignorance of the matter even to myself, I should ask permission to retire upon the spot."

Florizel, up to the last moment, had regarded his adventure in the light of a trifle, only serious upon international considerations. At the name of Vandeleur the horrible truth broke upon him in a moment; he was not only arrested, but he was guilty. This was not only an annoying incident—it was a peril to his honour. What was he to say? What was he to do? The Rajah's Diamond was indeed an accursed stone; and it seemed as if he were to be the last victim to its influence.

One thing was certain. He could not give the required assurance to the detective. He must gain time.

His hesitation had not lasted a second.

"Be it so," said he, "let us walk together to the Prefecture."

The man once more bowed, and proceeded to follow Florizel at a respectful distance in the rear.

"Approach," said the Prince. "I am in a humour to talk, and, if I mistake not, now I look at you again, this is not the first time that we have met."

"I count it an honour," replied the officer, "that your Highness should recollect my face. It is eight years since I had the pleasure of an interview."

"To remember faces," returned Florizel, "is as much a part of my profession as it is of yours. Indeed, rightly looked upon, a Prince and a detective serve in the same corps. We are both combatants against crime; only mine is the more lucrative and yours the more dangerous rank, and there is a sense in which both may be made equally honourable to a good man. I had rather, strange as you may think it, be a detective of character and parts than a weak and ignoble sovereign."

The officer was overwhelmed.

"Your Highness returns good for evil," said he. "To an act of presumption he replies by the most amiable condescension."

"How do you know," replied Florizel, "that I am not seeking to corrupt you?"

"Heaven preserve me from the temptation!" cried the detective.

"I applaud your answer," returned the Prince. "It is that of a wise and honest man. The world is a great place and stocked with wealth and beauty, and there is no limit to the rewards that may be offered. Such an one who would refuse a million of money may sell his honour for an empire or the love of a woman; and I myself, who speak to you, have seen occasions so tempting, provocations so irresistible to the strength of human virtue, that I have been glad to tread in your steps and recommend myself to the grace of God. It is thus, thanks to that modest and becoming habit alone," he added, "that you and I can walk this town together with untarnished hearts."

"I had always heard that you were brave," replied the officer, "but I was not aware that you were wise and pious. You speak the truth, and you speak it with an accent that moves me to the heart. This world is indeed a place of trial."

"We are now," said Florizel, "in the middle of the bridge. Lean your elbows on the parapet and look over. As the water rushing below, so the passions and complications of life carry away the honesty of weak men. Let me tell you a story."

"I receive your Highness's commands," replied the man.

And, imitating the Prince, he leaned against the parapet, and disposed himself to listen. The city was already sunk in slumber; had it not been for the infinity of lights and the outline of buildings on the starry sky, they might have been alone beside some country river.

"An officer," began Prince Florizel, "a man of courage and

conduct, who had already risen by merit to an eminent rank, and won not only admiration but respect, visited, in an unfortunate hour for his peace of mind, the collections of an Indian Prince. Here he beheld a diamond so extraordinary for size and beauty that from that instant he had only one desire in life: honour, reputation, friendship, the love of country, he was ready to sacrifice all for this lump of sparkling crystal. For three years he served this semi-barbarian potentate as Jacob served Laban; he falsified frontiers, he connived at murders, he unjustly condemned and executed a brother-officer who had the misfortune to displease the Rajah by some honest freedoms; lastly, at a time of great danger to his native land, he betrayed a body of his fellow-soldiers, and suffered them to be defeated and massacred by thousands. In the end, he had amassed a magnificent fortune, and brought home with him the coveted diamond.

"Years passed," continued the Prince, "and at length the diamond is accidentally lost. It falls into the hands of a simple and laborious youth, a student, a minister of God, just entering on a career of usefulness and even distinction. Upon him also the spell is cast; he deserts everything, his holy calling, his studies, and flees with the gem into a foreign country. The officer has a brother, an astute, daring, unscrupulous man, who learns the clergyman's secret. What does he do? Tell his brother, inform the police? No; upon this man also the Satanic charm has fallen; he must have the stone for himself. At the risk of murder, he drugs the young priest and seizes the prey. And now, by an accident which is not important to my moral, the jewel passes out of his custody into that of another, who, terrified at what he sees, gives it into the keeping of a man in high station and above reproach."

"The officer's name is Thomas Vandeleur," continued Florizel. "The stone is called the Rajah's Diamond. And"—suddenly opening his hand—"you behold it here before your eyes."

The officer started back with a cry.

"We have spoken of corruption," said the Prince. "To me this nugget of bright crystal is as loathsome as though it were crawling with the worms of death; it is as shocking as though it were compacted out of innocent blood. I see it here in my hand, and I know it is shining with hell-fire. I have told you but a hundredth part of its story; what passed in former ages, to what crimes and treacheries it incited men of yore, the imagination trembles to conceive; for years and years it has faithfully served the powers of hell; enough, I say, of blood, enough of disgrace, enough of broken lives and friendships; all things come to an end, the evil like the good; pestilence as well as beautiful music; and as for this diamond, God forgive me if I do wrong, but its empire ends to-night."

The Prince made a sudden movement with his hand, and the jewel, describing an arc of light, dived with a splash into the flowing river.

"Amen," said Florizel with gravity. "I have slain a cockatrice!"

"God pardon me!" cried the detective. "What have you done? I am a ruined man."

"I think," returned the Prince with a smile, "that many well-to-do people in this city might envy you your ruin."

"Alas! your Highness!" said the officer, "and you corrupt me after all?"

"It seems there was no help for it," replied Florizel. "And now let us go forward to the Prefecture."

Not long after, the marriage of Francis Scrymgeour and Miss Vandeleur was celebrated in great privacy; and the Prince acted on that occasion as groomsman. The two Vandeleurs surprised some rumour of what had happened to the diamond; and their vast diving operations on the River Seine are the wonder and amusement of the idle. It is true that through some miscalculation they have chosen the wrong branch of the river. As for the Prince, that sublime person, having now served his turn, may go, along with the Arabian author, topsy-turvy into space. But if the reader insists on more specific information, I am happy to say that a recent revolution hurled him from the throne of Bohemia, in consequence of his continued absence and edifying neglect of public business; and that his Highness now keeps a cigar store in Rupert Street, much frequented by other foreign refugees. I go there from time to time to smoke and have a chat, and find him as great a creature as in the days of his prosperity; he has an Olympian air behind the counter; and although a sedentary life is beginning to tell upon his waistcoat, he is probably, take him for all in all, the handsomest tobacconist in London.

# The Pavilion on the Links

# 1. Tells How I Camped in Graden Sea-Wood, and Beheld a Light in the Pavilion

I was a great solitary when I was young. I made it my pride to keep aloof and suffice for my own entertainment; and I may say that I had neither friends nor acquaintances until I met that friend who became my wife and the mother of my children. With one man only was I on private terms; this was R. Northmour, Esquire, of Graden Easter, in Scotland. We had met at college; and though there was not much liking between us, nor even much intimacy, we were so nearly of a humour that we could associate with ease to both. Misanthropes, we believed ourselves to be; but I have thought since that we were only sulky fellows. It was scarcely a companionship, but a coexistence in unsociability. Northmour's exceptional violence of temper made it no easy affair for him to keep the peace with any one but me; and as he respected my silent ways, and let me come and go as I pleased, I could tolerate his presence without concern. I think we called each other friends.

When Northmour took his degree and I decided to leave the university without one, he invited me on a long visit to Graden Easter; and it was thus that I first became acquainted with the scene of my adventures. The mansion-house of Graden stood in a bleak stretch of country some three miles from the shore of the German Ocean. It was as large as a barrack; and as it had been built of a soft stone, liable to consume in the eager air of the seaside, it was damp and draughty within and half ruinous without. It was impossible for two young men to lodge with comfort in such a dwelling. But there stood in the northern part of the estate, in a wilderness of links and blowing sand-hills, and between a plantation and the sea, a small Pavilion or Belvidere, of modern design, which was exactly suited to our wants; and in this hermitage, speaking little, reading much, and rarely associating except at meals, Northmour and I spent four tempestuous winter months. I might have stayed longer; but one March night there sprang up between us a dispute, which rendered my departure necessary. Northmour spoke hotly, I remember, and I suppose I must have made some tart rejoinder. He leaped from his chair and grappled me; I had to fight, without exaggeration, for my life; and it was only with a great effort that I mastered him, for he was near as strong in body as myself, and seemed filled with the devil. The next morning, we met on our usual terms; but I judged it more delicate to withdraw; nor did he attempt to dissuade me.

It was nine years before I revisited the neighbourhood. I travelled at that time with a tilt cart, a tent, and a cooking-stove, tramping all day beside the waggon, and at night, whenever it was possible, gipsying in a cove of the hills, or by the side of a wood. I believe I visited in this manner most of the wild and desolate regions both in England and Scotland; and, as I had neither friends nor relations, I was troubled with no correspondence, and had nothing in the nature of headquarters, unless it was the office of my solicitors, from whom I drew my income twice a year. It was a life in which I delighted; and I fully thought to have grown old upon the march, and at last died in a ditch.

It was my whole business to find desolate corners, where I could camp without the fear of interruption; and hence, being in another part of the same shire, I bethought me suddenly of the Pavilion on the Links. No thoroughfare passed within three miles of it. The nearest town, and that was but a fisher village, was at a distance of six or seven. For ten miles of length, and from a depth varying from three miles to half a mile, this belt of barren country lay along the sea. The beach, which was the natural approach, was full of quicksands. Indeed I may say there is hardly a better place of concealment in the United Kingdom. I determined to pass a week in the Sea-Wood of Graden Easter, and making a long stage, reached it about sundown on a wild September day.

The country, I have said, was mixed sand-hill and links; *links* being a Scottish name for sand which has ceased drifting and become more or less solidly covered with turf. The pavilion stood on an even space; a little behind it, the wood began in a hedge of elders huddled together by the wind; in front, a few tumbled sand-hills stood between it and the sea. An outcropping of rock had formed a bastion for the sand, so that there was here a promontory in the coast-line between two shallow bays; and just beyond the tides, the rock again cropped out and formed an islet of small dimensions but strikingly designed. The quicksands were of great extent at low water, and had an infamous reputation in the country. Close in shore, between the islet and the promontory, it was said they would swallow a man in four minutes and a half; but there may have been little ground for this precision. The district was alive with rabbits, and haunted by gulls which made a continual piping about the pavilion. On summer days the outlook was bright and even gladsome; but at sundown in September, with a high wind, and a heavy surf rolling in close along the links, the place told of nothing but dead mariners and sea disaster. A ship beating to windward on the horizon, and a huge truncheon of wreck half buried in the sands at my feet, completed the innuendo of the scene.

The pavilion—it had been built by the last proprietor, Northmour's uncle, a silly and prodigal virtuoso—presented little signs of age. It was two storeys in height, Italian in design, surrounded by a patch of garden in which nothing had prospered but a few coarse flowers; and looked, with its shuttered windows, not like a house that had been deserted, but like one that had never been tenanted by man. Northmour was plainly from home; whether, as usual, sulking in the cabin of his yacht, or in one of his fitful and extravagant appearances in the world of society, I had, of course, no means of guessing. The place had an air of solitude that daunted even a solitary like myself; the wind cried in the chimneys with a strange and wailing note; and it was with a sense of escape, as if I were going indoors, that I turned away and, driving my cart before me, entered the skirts of the wood.

The Sea-Wood of Graden had been planted to shelter the cultivated fields behind, and check the encroachments of the blowing sand. As you advanced into it from coastward, elders were succeeded by other hardy shrubs; but the timber was all stunted and bushy; it led a life of conflict; the trees were accustomed to swing there all night long in fierce winter tempests; and even in early spring, the leaves were already flying, and autumn was beginning, in this exposed plantation. Inland the ground rose into a little hill, which, along with the islet, served as a sailing mark for seamen. When the hill was open of the islet to the north, vessels must bear well to the eastward to clear Graden Ness and the Graden Bullers. In the lower ground, a streamlet ran among the trees, and, being dammed with dead leaves and clay of its own carrying, spread out every here and there, and lay in stagnant pools. One or two ruined cottages were dotted about the wood; and, according to Northmour, these were ecclesiastical foundations, and in their time had sheltered pious hermits.

I found a den, or small hollow, where there was a spring of pure water; and there, clearing away the brambles, I pitched the tent, and made a fire to cook my supper. My horse I picketed farther in the wood where there was a patch of sward. The banks of the den not only concealed the light of my fire, but sheltered me from the wind, which was cold as well as high.

The life I was leading made me both hardy and frugal. I never drank but water, and rarely ate anything more costly than oatmeal; and I required so little sleep, that, although I rose with the peep of day, I would often lie long awake in the dark or starry watches of the night. Thus in Graden Sea-Wood, although I fell thankfully asleep by eight in the evening I was awake again before eleven with a full possession of my faculties, and no sense of drowsiness or fatigue. I rose and sat by the fire, watching the trees and clouds tumultuously tossing and fleeing overhead, and hearkening to the wind and the rollers along the shore; till at length, growing weary of inaction, I quitted the den, and strolled towards the borders of the wood. A young moon, buried in mist, gave a faint illumination to my steps; and the light grew brighter as I walked forth into the links. At the same moment, the wind, smelling salt of the open ocean and carrying particles of sand, struck me with its full force, so that I had to bow my head.

When I raised it again to look about me, I was aware of a light in the pavilion. It was not stationary; but passed from one window to another, as though some one were reviewing the different apartments with a lamp or candle.

I watched it for some seconds in great surprise. When I had arrived in the afternoon the house had been plainly deserted; now it was as plainly occupied. It was my first idea that a gang of thieves might have broken in and be now ransacking Northmour's cupboards, which were many and not ill supplied. But what should bring thieves to Graden Easter? And, again, all the shutters had been thrown open, and it would have been more in the character of such gentry to close them. I dismissed the notion, and fell back upon another. Northmour himself must have arrived, and was now airing and inspecting the pavilion.

I have said that there was no real affection between this man and me; but, had I loved him like a brother, I was then so much more in love with solitude that I should none the less have shunned his company. As it was, I turned and ran for it; and it was with genuine satisfaction that I found myself safely back beside the fire. I had escaped an acquaintance; I should have one more night in comfort. In the morning, I might either slip away before Northmour was abroad, or pay him as short a visit as I chose.

But when morning came, I thought the situation so diverting that I forgot my shyness. Northmour was at my mercy; I arranged a good practical jest, though I knew well that my neighbour was not the man to jest with in security; and, chuckling beforehand over its success, took my place among the elders at the edge of the wood, whence I could command the door of the pavilion. The shutters were all once more closed, which I remember thinking odd; and the house, with its white walls and green venetians, looked spruce and habitable in the morning light. Hour after hour passed, and still no sign of Northmour. I knew him for a sluggard in the morning; but, as it drew on towards noon, I lost my patience. To say the truth, I had promised myself to break my fast in the pavilion, and hunger began to prick me sharply. It was a pity to let the opportunity go by without some cause for mirth; but the grosser appetite prevailed, and I relinquished my jest with regret, and sallied from the wood.

The appearance of the house affected me, as I drew near, with disquietude. It seemed unchanged since last evening; and I had expected it, I scarce knew why, to wear some external signs of habitation. But no: the windows were all closely shuttered, the chimneys breathed no smoke, and the front door itself was closely padlocked. Northmour, therefore, had entered by the back; this was the natural and, indeed, the necessary conclusion;

and you may judge of my surprise when, on turning the house, I found the back door similarly secured.

My mind at once reverted to the original theory of thieves; and I blamed myself sharply for my last night's inaction. I examined all the windows on the lower storey, but none of them had been tampered with; I tried the padlocks, but they were both secure. It thus became a problem how the thieves, if thieves they were, had managed to enter the house. They must have got, I reasoned, upon the roof of the outhouse where Northmour used to keep his photographic battery; and from thence, either by the window of the study or that of my old bedroom, completed their burglarious entry.

I followed what I supposed was their example; and, getting on the roof, tried the shutters of each room. Both were secure; but I was not to be beaten; and, with a little force, one of them flew open, grazing, as it did so, the back of my hand. I remember, I put the wound to my mouth, and stood for perhaps half a minute licking it like a dog, and mechanically gazing behind me over the waste links and the sea; and, in that space of time, my eye made note of a large schooner yacht some miles to the north-east. Then I threw up the window and climbed in.

I went over the house, and nothing can express my mystification. There was no sign of disorder, but, on the contrary, the rooms were unusually clean and pleasant. I found fires laid, ready for lighting; three bedrooms prepared with a luxury quite foreign to Northmour's habits, and with water in the ewers and the beds turned down; a table set for three in the dining-room; and an ample supply of cold meats, game, and vegetables on the pantry shelves. There were guests expected, that was plain; but why guests, when Northmour hated society? And, above all, why was the house thus stealthily prepared at dead of night? and why were the shutters closed and the doors padlocked?

I effaced all traces of my visit, and came forth from the window feeling sobered and concerned.

The schooner yacht was still in the same place; and it flashed for a moment through my mind that this might be the *Red Earl* bringing the owner of the pavilion and his guests. But the vessel's head was set the other way.

## 2. Tells of the Nocturnal Landing from the Yacht

I returned to the den to cook myself a meal, of which I stood in great need, as well as to care for my horse, whom I had somewhat neglected in the morning. From time to time I went down to the edge of the wood; but there was no change in the pavilion, and not a human creature was seen all day upon the links. The schooner in the offing was the one touch of life within my range of vision. She, apparently with no set object, stood off and on or lay to, hour after hour; but as the evening deepened, she drew steadily nearer. I became more convinced that she carried Northmour and his friends, and that they would probably come ashore after dark; not only because that was of a piece with the secrecy of the preparations, but because the tide would not have flowed sufficiently before eleven to cover Graden Floe and the other sea quags that fortified the shore against invaders.

All day the wind had been going down, and the sea along with it; but there was a return towards sunset of the heavy weather of the day before. The night set in pitch dark. The wind came off the sea in squalls, like the firing of a battery of cannon; now and then there was a flaw of rain, and the surf rolled heavier with the rising tide. I was down at my observatory among the elders, when a light was run up to the masthead of the schooner, and showed she was closer in than when I had last seen her by the dying daylight. I concluded that this must be a signal to Northmour's associates on shore; and, stepping forth into the links, looked around me for something in response.

A small footpath ran along the margin of the wood, and formed the most direct communication between the pavilion and the mansion-house; and, as I cast my eyes to that side, I saw a spark of light, not a quarter of a mile away, and rapidly approaching. From its uneven course it appeared to be the light of a lantern carried by a person who followed the windings of the path, and was often staggered and taken aback by the more violent squalls. I concealed myself once more among the elders, and waited eagerly for the newcomer's advance. It proved to be a woman; and, as she passed within half a rod of my ambush, I was able to recognise the features. The deaf and silent old dame, who had nursed Northmour in his childhood, was his associate in this underhand affair.

I followed her at a little distance, taking advantage of the innumerable heights and hollows, concealed by the darkness, and favoured not only by the nurse's deafness, but by the uproar of the wind and surf. She entered the pavilion, and, going at once to the upper storey, opened and set a light in one of the windows that looked towards the sea. Immediately afterwards the light at the schooner's masthead was run down and extinguished. Its purpose had been attained, and those on board were sure that they were expected. The old woman resumed her preparations; although the other shutters remained closed, I could see a glimmer going to and fro about the house; and a gush of sparks from one chimney after another soon told me that the fires were being kindled.

Northmour and his guests, I was now persuaded, would come ashore as soon as there was water on the floe. It was a wild night for boat service; and I felt some alarm mingle with my curiosity as I reflected on the danger of the landing. My old acquaintance, it was true, was the most eccentric of men; but the present eccentricity was both disquieting and lugubrious to consider. A variety of feelings thus led me towards the beach, where I lay flat on my face in a hollow within six feet of the track that led to the pavilion. Thence, I should have the satisfaction of recognising the arrivals, and, if they should prove to be acquaintances, greeting them as soon as they had landed.

Some time before eleven, while the tide was still dangerously low, a boat's lantern appeared close in shore; and, my attention being thus awakened, I could perceive another still far to seaward, violently tossed, and sometimes hidden by the billows. The weather, which was getting dirtier as the night went on, and the perilous situation of the yacht upon a lee shore, had probably driven them to attempt a landing at the earliest possible moment.

A little afterwards, four yachtsmen carrying a very heavy chest, and guided by a fifth with a lantern, passed close in front of me as I lay, and were admitted to the pavilion by the nurse.

They returned to the beach, and passed me a second time with another chest, larger but apparently not so heavy as the first. A third time they made the transit; and on this occasion one of the yachtsmen carried a leather portmanteau, and the others a lady's trunk and carriage bag. My curiosity was sharply excited. If a woman were among the guests of Northmour, it would show a change in his habits and an apostasy from his pet theories of life, well calculated to fill me with surprise. When he and I dwelt there together, the pavilion had been a temple of misogyny. And now, one of the detested sex was to be installed under its roof. I remembered one or two particulars, a few notes of daintiness and almost of coquetry which had struck me the day before as I surveyed the preparations in the house; their purpose was now clear, and I thought myself dull not to have perceived it from the first.

While I was thus reflecting, a second lantern drew near me from the beach. It was carried by a yachtsman whom I had not yet seen, and who was conducting two other persons to the pavilion. These two persons were unquestionably the guests for whom the house was made ready; and, straining eye and ear, I set myself to watch them as they passed. One was an unusually tall man, in a travelling hat slouched over his eyes, and a highland cape closely buttoned and turned up so as to conceal his face. You could make out no more of him than that he was, as I have said, unusually tall, and walked feebly with a heavy stoop. By his side, and either clinging to him or giving him support—I could not make out which—was a young, tall, and slender figure of a woman. She was extremely pale; but in the light of the lantern her face was so marred by strong and changing shadows, that she might equally well have been as ugly as sin or as beautiful as I afterwards found her to be.

When they were just abreast of me, the girl made some remark which was drowned by the noise of the wind.

"Hush!" said her companion; and there was something in the tone with which the word was uttered that thrilled and rather shook my spirits. It seemed to breathe from a bosom labouring under the deadliest terror; I have never heard another syllable so expressive; and I still hear it again when I am feverish at night, and my mind runs upon old times. The man turned towards the girl as he spoke; I had a glimpse of much red beard and a nose which seemed to have been broken in youth; and his light eyes seemed shining in his face with some strong and unpleasant emotion.

But these two passed on and were admitted in their turn to the pavilion.

One by one, or in groups, the seamen returned to the beach. The wind brought me the sound of a rough voice crying, "Shove off!" Then, after a pause, another lantern drew near. It was Northmour alone.

My wife and I, a man and a woman, have often agreed to wonder how a person could be, at the same time, so handsome and so repulsive as Northmour. He had the appearance of a finished gentleman; his face bore every mark of intelligence and courage; but you had only to look at him, even in his most amiable moment, to see that he had the temper of a slaver captain. I never knew a character that was both explosive and revengeful to the same degree; he combined the vivacity of the south with the sustained and deadly hatreds of the north; and both traits were plainly written on his face, which was a sort of danger signal. In person he was tall, strong, and active; his hair and complexion very dark; his features handsomely designed, but spoiled by a menacing expression.

At that moment he was somewhat paler than by nature; he wore a heavy frown; and his lips worked, and he looked sharply round him as he walked, like a man besieged with apprehensions. And yet I thought he had a look of triumph underlying all, as though he had already done much, and was near the end of an achievement.

Partly from a scruple of delicacy—which I dare say came too late—partly from the pleasure of startling an acquaintance, I desired to make my presence known to him without delay.

I got suddenly to my feet, and stepped forward. "Northmour!" said I.

I have never had so shocking a surprise in all my days. He leaped on me without a word; something shone in his hand; and he struck for my heart with a dagger. At the same moment I knocked him head over heels. Whether it was my quickness, or his own uncertainty, I know not; but the blade only grazed my shoulder, while the hilt and his fist struck me violently on the mouth.

I fled, but not far. I had often and often observed the capabilities of the sand-hills for protracted ambush or stealthy advances and retreats; and, not ten yards from the scene of the scuffle, plumped down again upon the grass. The lantern had fallen and gone out. But what was my astonishment to see Northmour slip at a bound into the pavilion, and hear him bar the door behind him with a clang of iron!

He had not pursued me. He had run away. Northmour, whom I knew for the most implacable and daring of men, had run away! I could scarce believe my reason; and yet in this strange business, where all was incredible, there was nothing to make a work about in an incredibility more or less. For why was the pavilion secretly prepared? Why had Northmour landed with his guests at dead of night, in half a gale of wind, and with the floe scarce covered? Why had he sought to kill me? Had he not recognised my voice? I wondered. And, above all, how had he come to have a dagger ready in his hand? A dagger, or even a sharp knife, seemed out of keeping with the age in which we lived; and a gentleman landing from his yacht on the shore of his own estate, even although it was at night and with some mysterious circumstances, does not usually, as a matter of fact, walk thus prepared for deadly onslaught. The more I reflected, the further I felt at sea. I recapitulated the elements of mystery, counting them on my fingers: the pavilion secretly prepared for guests; the guests landed at the risk of their lives and to the imminent peril of the yacht; the guests, or at least one of them, in undisguised and seemingly causeless terror; Northmour with a naked weapon; Northmour stabbing his most intimate acquaintance at a word; last, and not least strange, Northmour fleeing from the man whom he had sought to murder, and barricading himself, like a hunted creature, behind the door of the pavilion. Here were at least six separate causes for extreme surprise; each part and parcel with the others, and forming all together one consistent story. I felt almost ashamed to believe my own senses.

As I thus stood, transfixed with wonder, I began to grow painfully conscious of the injuries I had received in the scuffle; skulked round among the sand-hills; and, by a devious path, regained the shelter of the wood. On the way, the old nurse passed again within several yards of me, still carrying her lantern, on the return journey to the mansion-house of Graden. This made a seventh suspicious feature in the case—Northmour and his guests, it appeared, were to cook and do the cleaning for themselves, while the old woman continued to inhabit the big empty barrack among the policies. There must surely be great cause for secrecy, when so many inconveniences were confronted to preserve it.

So thinking, I made my way to the den. For greater security, I trod out the embers of the fire, and lit my lantern to examine the wound upon my shoulder. It was a trifling hurt, although it bled somewhat freely, and I dressed it as well as I could (for its position made it difficult to reach) with some rag and cold water from the spring. While I was thus busied, I mentally declared war against Northmour and his mystery. I am not an angry man by nature, and I believe there was more curiosity than resentment in my heart. But war I certainly declared; and, by way of preparation, I got out my revolver, and, having drawn the charges, cleaned and reloaded it with scrupulous care. Next I became preoccupied about my horse. It might break loose, or fall to neighing, and so betray my camp in the Sea-Wood. I determined to rid myself of its neighbourhood; and long before dawn I was leading it over the links in the direction of the fisher village.

## 3. Tells How I Became Acquainted
## with My Wife

For two days I skulked round the pavilion, profiting by the uneven surface of the links. I became an adept in the necessary tactics. These low hillocks and shallow dells, running one into another, became a kind of cloak of darkness for my enthralling, but perhaps dishonourable, pursuit. Yet, in spite of this advantage, I could learn but little of Northmour or his guests.

Fresh provisions were brought under cover of darkness by the old woman from the mansion-house. Northmour, and the young lady, sometimes together, but more often singly, would walk for an hour or two at a time on the beach beside the quicksand. I could not but conclude that this promenade was chosen with an eye to secrecy; for the spot was open only to the seaward. But it suited me not less excellently; the highest and most accidented of the sand-hills immediately adjoined; and from these, lying flat in a hollow, I could overlook Northmour or the young lady as they walked.

The tall man seemed to have disappeared. Not only did he never cross the threshold, but he never so much as showed face at a window; or, at least, not so far as I could see; for I dared not creep forward beyond a certain distance in the day, since the upper floor commanded the bottoms of the links; and at night, when I could venture farther, the lower windows were barricaded as if to stand a siege. Sometimes I thought the tall man must be confined to bed, for I remembered the feebleness of his gait; and sometimes I thought he must have gone clear away, and that Northmour and the young lady remained alone together in the pavilion. The idea, even then, displeased me.

Whether or not this pair were man and wife, I had seen abundant reason to doubt the friendliness of their relation. Although I could hear nothing of what they said, and rarely so much as glean a decided expression on the face of either, there was a distance, almost a stiffness, in their bearing which showed them to be either unfamiliar or at enmity. The girl walked faster when she was with Northmour than when she was alone; and I conceived that any inclination between a man and a woman would rather delay than accelerate the step. Moreover, she kept a good yard free of him, and trailed her umbrella, as if it were a barrier, on the side between them. Northmour kept sidling closer; and, as the girl retired from his advance, their course lay at a sort of diagonal across the beach, and would have landed them in the surf had it been long enough continued. But, when this was imminent, the girl would unostentatiously change sides and put Northmour between her and the sea. I watched these manoeuvres, for my part, with high enjoyment and approval, and chuckled to myself at every move.

On the morning of the third day, she walked alone for some time, and I perceived, to my great concern, that she was more than once in tears. You will see that my heart was already interested more than I supposed. She had a firm yet airy motion of the body, and carried her head with unimaginable grace; every step was a thing to look at, and she seemed in my eyes to breathe sweetness and distinction.

The day was so agreeable, being calm and sunshiny, with a tranquil sea, and yet with a healthful piquancy and vigour in the air, that, contrary to custom, she was tempted forth a second time to walk. On this occasion she was accompanied by Northmour, and they had been but a short while on the beach, when I saw him take forcible possession of her hand. She struggled, and uttered a cry that was almost a scream. I sprang to my feet, unmindful of my strange position; but, ere I had taken a step, I saw Northmour bareheaded and bowing very low, as if to apologise; and dropped again at once into my ambush. A few words were interchanged; and then, with another bow, he left the beach to return to the pavilion. He passed not far from me, and I could see him, flushed and lowering, and cutting savagely with his cane among the grass. It was not without satisfaction that I recognised my own handiwork in a great cut under his right eye, and a considerable discolouration round the socket.

For some time the girl remained where he had left her, looking out past the islet and over the bright sea. Then with a start, as one who throws off preoccupation and puts energy again upon its mettle, she broke into a rapid and decisive walk. She also was much incensed by what had passed. She had forgotten where she was. And I beheld her walk straight into the borders of the quicksand where it is most abrupt and dangerous. Two or three steps farther and her life would have been in serious jeopardy, when I slid down the face of the sand-hill, which is there precipitous, and, running half-way forward, called to her to stop.

She did so, and turned round. There was not a tremor of fear in her behaviour, and she marched directly up to me like a queen. I was barefoot, and clad like a common sailor, save for an Egyptian scarf round my waist; and she probably took me at first for some one from the fisher village, straying after bait. As for her, when I thus saw her face to face, her eyes set steadily and imperiously upon mine, I was filled with admiration and astonishment, and thought her even more beautiful than I had looked to find her. Nor could I think enough of one who, acting with so much boldness, yet preserved a maidenly air that was both quaint and engaging; for my wife kept an old-fashioned precision of manner through all her admirable life—an excellent thing in woman, since it sets another value on her sweet familiarities.

"What does this mean?" she asked.

"You were walking," I told her, "directly into Graden Floe."

"You do not belong to these parts," she said again. "You speak like an educated man."

"I believe I have right to that name," said I, "although in this disguise."

But her woman's eye had already detected the sash. "Oh!" she said; "your sash betrays you."

"You have said the word *betray*," I resumed. "May I ask you not to betray me? I was obliged to disclose myself in your interest; but if Northmour learned my presence it might be worse than disagreeable for me."

"Do you know," she asked, "to whom you are speaking?"

"Not to Mr. Northmour's wife?" I asked, by way of answer.

She shook her head. All this while she was studying my face with an embarrassing intentness. Then she broke out—

"You have an honest face. Be honest like your face, sir, and tell me what you want and what you are afraid of. Do you think I could hurt you? I believe you have far more power to injure me! And yet you do not look unkind. What do you mean—you, a gentleman—by skulking like a spy about this desolate place? Tell me," she said, "who is it you hate?"

"I hate no one," I answered; "and I fear no one face to face. My name is Cassilis—Frank Cassilis. I lead the life of a vagabond for my own good pleasure. I am one of Northmour's oldest friends; and three nights ago, when I addressed him on these links, he stabbed me in the shoulder with a knife."

"It was you!" she said.

"Why he did so," I continued, disregarding the interruption, "is more than I can guess, and more than I care to know. I have not many friends, nor am I very susceptible to friendship; but no man shall drive me from a place by terror. I had camped in Graden Sea-Wood ere he came; I camp in it still. If you think I mean harm to you or yours, madam, the remedy is in your hand. Tell him that my camp is in the Hemlock Den, and to-night he can stab me in safety while I sleep."

With this I doffed my cap to her, and scrambled up once more among the sand-hills. I do not know why, but I felt a prodigious sense of injustice, and felt like a hero and a martyr; while, as a matter of fact, I had not a word to say in my defence, nor so much as one plausible reason to offer for my conduct. I had stayed at Graden out of a curiosity natural enough, but undignified; and though there was another motive growing in along with the first, it was not one which, at that period, I could have properly explained to the lady of my heart.

Certainly, that night, I thought of no one else; and, though her whole conduct and position seemed suspicious, I could not find it in my heart to entertain a doubt of her integrity. I could have staked my life that she was clear of blame, and, though all was dark at the present, that the explanation of the mystery would show her part in these events to be both right and needful. It was true, let me cudgel my imagination as I pleased, that I could invent no theory of her relations to Northmour; but I felt none the less sure of my conclusion because it was founded on instinct in place of reason, and, as I may say, went to sleep that night with the thought of her under my pillow.

Next day she came out about the same hour alone, and, as soon as the sand-hills concealed her from the pavilion, drew nearer to the edge, and called me by name in guarded tones. I was astonished to observe that she was deadly pale, and seemingly under the influence of strong emotion.

"Mr. Cassilis!" she cried; "Mr. Cassilis!"

I appeared at once, and leaped down upon the beach. A remarkable air of relief overspread her countenance as soon as she saw me.

"Oh!" she cried, with a hoarse sound, like one whose bosom has been lightened of a weight. And then, "Thank God you are still safe!" she added; "I knew, if you were, you would be here." (Was not this strange? So swiftly and wisely does Nature prepare our hearts for these great life-long intimacies, that both my wife and I had been given a presentiment on this the second day of our acquaintance. I had even then hoped that she would seek me; she had felt sure that she would find me.) "Do not," she went on swiftly, "do not stay in this place. Promise me that you will sleep no longer in that wood. You do not know how I suffer; all last night I could not sleep for thinking of your peril."

"Peril?" I repeated. "Peril from whom? From Northmour?"

"Not so," she said. "Did you think I would tell him after what you said?"

"Not from Northmour?" I repeated. "Then how? From whom? I see none to be afraid of."

"You must not ask me," was her reply, "for I am not free to tell you. Only believe me, and go hence—believe me, and go away quickly, quickly, for your life!"

An appeal to his alarm is never a good plan to rid oneself of a spirited young man. My obstinacy was but increased by what she said, and I made it a point of honour to remain. And her solicitude for my safety still more confirmed me in the resolve.

"You must not think me inquisitive, madam," I replied; "but, if Graden is so dangerous a place, you yourself perhaps remain here at some risk."

She only looked at me reproachfully.

"You and your father—" I resumed; but she interrupted me almost with a gasp.

"My father! How do you know that?" she cried.

"I saw you together when you landed," was my answer; and I do not know why, but it seemed satisfactory to both of us, as indeed it was the truth. "But," I continued, "you need have no fear from me. I see you have some reason to be secret, and, you may believe me, your secret is as safe with me as if I were in Graden Floe. I have scarce spoken to any one for years; my horse is my only companion, and even he, poor beast, is not beside me. You see, then, you may count on me for silence. So tell me the truth, my dear young lady, are you not in danger?"

"Mr. Northmour says you are an honourable man," she returned, "and I believe it when I see you. I will tell you so much; you are right; we are in dreadful, dreadful danger, and you share it by remaining where you are."

"Ah!" said I; "you have heard of me from Northmour? And he gives me a good character?"

"I asked him about you last night," was her reply. "I pretended," she hesitated, "I pretended to have met you long ago, and spoken to you of him. It was not true; but I could not help myself without betraying you, and you had put me in a difficulty. He praised you highly."

"And—you may permit me one question—does this danger come from Northmour?" I asked.

"From Mr. Northmour?" she cried. "Oh no; he stays with us to share it."

"While you propose that I should run away?" I said. "You do not rate me very high."

"Why should you stay?" she asked. "You are no friend of ours."

I know not what came over me, for I had not been conscious of a similar weakness since I was a child, but I was so mortified by this retort that my eyes pricked and filled with tears, as I continued to gaze upon her face.

"No, no," she said, in a changed voice; "I did not mean the words unkindly."

"It was I who offended," I said; and I held out my hand with a look of appeal that somehow touched her, for she gave me hers at once, and even eagerly. I held it for awhile in mine, and gazed into her eyes. It was she who first tore her hand away, and, forgetting all about her request and the promise she had sought to extort, ran at the top of her speed, and without turning, till she was out of sight.

And then I knew that I loved her, and thought in my glad heart that she—she herself—was not indifferent to my suit. Many a time she has denied it in after days, but it was with a smiling and not a serious denial. For my part, I am sure our hands would not have lain so closely in each other if she had not begun to melt to me already. And, when all is said, it is no great contention, since, by her own avowal, she began to love me on the morrow.

And yet on the morrow very little took place. She came and called me down as on the day before, upbraided me for lingering at Graden, and, when she found I was still obdurate, began to ask me more particularly as to my arrival. I told her by what series of accidents I had come to witness their disembarkation, and how I had determined to remain, partly from the interest which had been wakened in me by Northmour's guests, and partly because of his own murderous attack. As to the former, I fear I was disingenuous, and led her to regard herself as having been an attraction to me from the first moment that I saw her on the links. It relieves my heart to make this confession even now, when my wife is with God, and already knows all things, and the honesty of my purpose even in this; for while she lived, although it often pricked my conscience, I had never the hardihood to undeceive her. Even a little secret, in such a married life as ours, is like the rose-leaf which kept the Princess from her sleep.

From this the talk branched into other subjects, and I told her much about my lonely and wandering existence; she, for her part, giving ear, and saying little. Although we spoke very naturally, and latterly on topics that might seem indifferent, we were both sweetly agitated. Too soon it was time for her to go; and we separated, as if by mutual consent, without shaking hands, for both knew that, between us, it was no idle ceremony.

The next, and that was the fourth day of our acquaintance, we met in the same spot, but early in the morning, with much familiarity and yet much timidity on either side. When she had once more spoken about my danger—and that, I understood, was her excuse for coming—I, who had prepared a great deal of talk during the night, began to tell her how highly I valued her kind interest, and how no one had ever cared to hear about my life, nor had I ever cared to relate it, before yesterday. Suddenly she interrupted me, saying with vehemence—

"And yet, if you knew who I was, you would not so much as speak to me!"

I told her such a thought was madness, and, little as we had met, I counted her already a dear friend; but my protestations seemed only to make her more desperate.

"My father is in hiding!" she cried.

"My dear," I said, forgetting for the first time to add "young lady," "what do I care? If he were in hiding twenty times over, would it make one thought of change in you?"

"Ah, but the cause!" she cried, "the cause! It is—" she faltered for a second—"it is disgraceful to us!"

## 4. Tells in What a Startling Manner
## I Learned That I Was Not Alone
## in Graden Sea-Wood

This was my wife's story, as I drew it from her among tears and sobs. Her name was Clara Huddlestone: it sounded very beautiful in my ears; but not so beautiful as that other name of Clara Cassilis, which she wore during the longer and, I thank God, the happier portion of her life. Her father, Bernard Huddlestone, had been a private banker in a very large way of business. Many years before, his affairs becoming disordered, he had been led to try dangerous, and at last criminal, expedients to retrieve himself from ruin. All was in vain; he became more and more cruelly involved, and found his honour lost at the same moment with his fortune. About this period, Northmour had been courting his daughter with great assiduity, though with small encouragement; and to him, knowing him thus disposed in his favour, Bernard Huddlestone turned for help in his extremity. It was not merely ruin and dishonour, nor merely a legal condemnation, that the unhappy man had brought upon his head. It seems he could have gone to prison with a light heart. What he feared, what kept him awake at night or recalled him from slumber into frenzy, was some secret, sudden, and unlawful attempt upon his life. Hence, he desired to bury his existence and escape to one of the islands in the South Pacific, and it was in Northmour's yacht, the *Red Earl*, that he designed to go. The yacht picked them up clandestinely upon the coast of Wales, and had once more deposited them at Graden, till she could be refitted and provisioned for the longer voyage. Nor could Clara doubt that her hand had been stipulated as the price of passage. For, although Northmour was neither unkind nor even discourteous, he had shown himself in several instances somewhat overbold in speech and manner.

I listened, I need not say, with fixed attention, and put many questions as to the more mysterious part. It was in vain. She had no clear idea of what the blow was, nor of how it was expected to fall. Her father's alarm was unfeigned and physically prostrating, and he had thought more than once of making an unconditional surrender to the police. But the scheme was finally abandoned, for he was convinced that not even the strength of our English prisons could shelter him from his pursuers. He had had many affairs with Italy, and with Italians resident in London, in the later years of his business; and these last, as Clara fancied, were somehow connected with the doom that threatened him. He had shown great terror at the presence of an Italian seaman on board the *Red Earl*, and had bitterly and repeatedly accused Northmour in consequence. The latter had protested that Beppo (that was the seaman's name) was a capital fellow, and could be trusted to the death; but Mr. Huddlestone had continued ever since to declare that all was lost, that it was only a question of days, and that Beppo would be the ruin of him yet.

I regarded the whole story as the hallucination of a mind shaken by calamity. He had suffered heavy loss by his Italian transactions; and hence the sight of an Italian was hateful to him, and the principal part in his nightmare would naturally enough be played by one of that nation.

"What your father wants," I said, "is a good doctor and some calming medicine."

"But Mr. Northmour?" objected your mother. "He is untroubled by losses, and yet he shares in this terror."

I could not help laughing at what I considered her simplicity.

"My dear," said I, "you have told me yourself what reward he has to look for. All is fair in love, you must remember; and if Northmour foments your father's terrors, it is not at all because he is afraid of any Italian man, but simply because he is infatuated with a charming English woman."

She reminded me of his attack upon myself on the night of the disembarkation, and this I was unable to explain. In short, and from one thing to another, it was agreed between us, that I should set out at once for the fisher village, Graden Wester, as it was called, look up all the newspapers I could find, and see for myself if there seemed any basis of fact for these continued alarms. The next morning, at the same hour and place, I was to make my report to Clara. She said no more on that occasion about my departure; nor, indeed, did she make it a secret that she clung to the thought of my proximity as something helpful and pleasant; and, for my part, I could not have left her, if she had gone upon her knees to ask it.

I reached Graden Wester before ten in the forenoon; for in those days I was an excellent pedestrian, and the distance, as I think I have said, was little over seven miles; fine walking all the way upon the springy turf. The village is one of the bleakest on that coast, which is saying much: there is a church in a hollow; a miserable haven in the rocks, where many boats have been lost as they returned from fishing; two or three score of stone houses arranged along the beach and in two streets, one leading from the harbour, and another striking out from it at right angles; and, at the corner of these two, a very dark and cheerless tavern, by way of principal hotel.

I had dressed myself somewhat more suitably to my station in life, and at once called upon the minister in his little manse beside the graveyard. He knew me, although it was more than nine years since we had met; and when I told him that I had been long upon a walking tour, and was behind with the news, readily lent me an armful of newspapers, dating from a month back to the day before. With these I sought the tavern, and, ordering some breakfast, sat down to study the "Huddlestone Failure."

It had been, it appeared, a very flagrant case. Thousands of persons were reduced to poverty; and one in particular had blown out his brains as soon as payment was suspended. It was strange to myself that, while I read these details, I continued rather to sympathise with Mr. Huddlestone than with his victims; so complete already was the empire of my love for my wife. A price was naturally set upon the banker's head; and, as the case was inexcusable and the public indignation thoroughly aroused, the unusual figure of 750 pounds was offered for his capture. He was reported to have large sums of money in his possession. One day, he had been heard of in Spain; the next, there was sure intelligence that he was still lurking between Manchester and Liverpool, or along the border of Wales; and the day after, a telegram would announce his arrival in Cuba or Yucatan. But in all this there was no word of an Italian, nor any sign of mystery.

In the very last paper, however, there was one item not so clear. The accountants who were charged to verify the failure had, it seemed, come upon the traces of a very large number of thousands, which figured for some time in the transactions of the house of Huddlestone; but which came from nowhere, and disappeared in the same mysterious fashion. It was only once referred to by name, and then under the initials "X. X."; but it had plainly been floated for the first time into the business at a period of great depression some six years ago. The name of a distinguished Royal personage had been mentioned by rumour in connection with this sum. "The cowardly desperado"—such, I remember, was the editorial expression—was supposed to have escaped with a large part of this mysterious fund still in his possession.

I was still brooding over the fact, and trying to torture it into some connection with Mr. Huddlestone's danger, when a man entered the tavern and asked for some bread and cheese with a decided foreign accent.

"*Siete Italiano?*" said I.

"*Si, signor,*" was his reply.

I said it was unusually far north to find one of his compatriots; at which he shrugged his shoulders, and replied that a man would go anywhere to find work. What work he could hope to find at Graden Wester, I was totally unable to conceive; and the incident struck so unpleasantly upon my mind, that I asked the landlord, while he was counting me some change, whether he had ever before seen an Italian in the village. He said he had once seen some Norwegians, who had been shipwrecked on the other side of Graden Ness and rescued by the lifeboat from Cauldhaven.

"No!" said I; "but an Italian, like the man who has just had bread and cheese."

"What?" cried he, "yon black-avised fellow wi' the teeth? Was he an I-talian? Weel, yon's the first that ever I saw, an' I dare say he's like to be the last."

Even as he was speaking, I raised my eyes, and, casting a glance into the street, beheld three men in earnest conversation together, and not thirty yards away. One of them was my recent companion in the tavern parlour; the other two, by their handsome, sallow features and soft hats, should evidently belong to the same race. A crowd of village children stood around them, gesticulating and talking gibberish in imitation. The trio looked singularly foreign to the bleak dirty street in which they were standing, and the dark grey heaven that overspread them; and I confess my incredulity received at that moment a shock from which it never recovered. I might reason with myself as I pleased, but I could not argue down the effect of what I had seen, and I began to share in the Italian terror.

It was already drawing towards the close of the day before I had returned the newspapers at the manse, and got well forward on to the links on my way home. I shall never forget that walk. It grew very cold and boisterous; the wind sang in the short grass about my feet; thin rain showers came running on the gusts; and an immense mountain range of clouds began to arise out of the bosom of the sea. It would be hard to imagine a more dismal evening; and whether it was from these external influences, or because my nerves were already affected by what I had heard and seen, my thoughts were as gloomy as the weather.

The upper windows of the pavilion commanded a considerable spread of links in the direction of Graden Wester. To avoid observation, it was necessary to hug the beach until I had gained cover from the higher sand-hills on the little headland, when I might strike across, through the hollows, for the margin of the wood. The sun was about setting; the tide was low, and all the quicksands uncovered; and I was moving along, lost in unpleasant thought, when I was suddenly thunderstruck to perceive the prints of human feet. They ran parallel to my own course, but low down upon the beach instead of along the border of the turf; and, when I examined them, I saw at once, by the size and coarseness of the impression, that it was a stranger to me and to those in the pavilion who had recently passed that way. Not only so; but from the recklessness of the course which he had followed, steering near to the most formidable portions of the sand, he was as evidently a stranger to the country and to the ill-repute of Graden beach.

Step by step I followed the prints; until, a quarter of a mile farther, I beheld them die away into the south-eastern boundary of Graden Floe. There, whoever he was, the miserable man had perished. One or two gulls, who had, perhaps, seen him disappear, wheeled over his sepulchre with their usual melancholy piping. The sun had broken through the clouds by a last effort, and coloured the wide level of quicksands with a dusky purple. I stood for some time gazing at the spot, chilled and disheartened by my own reflections, and with a strong and commanding consciousness of death. I remember wondering how long the tragedy had taken, and whether his screams had been audible at the pavilion. And then, making a strong resolution, I was about to tear myself away, when a gust fiercer than usual fell upon this quarter of the beach, and I saw now, whirling high in air, now skimming lightly across the surface of the sands, a soft, black, felt hat, somewhat conical in shape, such as I had remarked already on the heads of the Italians.

I believe, but I am not sure, that I uttered a cry. The wind was driving the hat shoreward, and I ran round the border of the floe to be ready against its arrival. The gust fell, dropping the hat for a while upon the quicksand, and then, once more freshening, landed it a few yards from where I stood. I seized it with the interest you may imagine. It had seen some service; indeed, it was rustier than either of those I had seen that day upon the street. The lining was red, stamped with the name of the maker, which I have forgotten, and that of the place of manufacture, *Venedig*. This (it is not yet forgotten) was the name given by the Austrians to the beautiful city of Venice, then, and for long after, a part of their dominions.

The shock was complete. I saw imaginary Italians upon every side; and for the first, and, I may say, for the last time in my experience, became overpowered by what is called a panic terror. I knew nothing, that is, to be afraid of, and yet I admit that I was heartily afraid; and it was with a sensible reluctance that I returned to my exposed and solitary camp in the Sea-Wood.

There I ate some cold porridge which had been left over from the night before, for I was disinclined to make a fire; and, feeling strengthened and reassured, dismissed all these fanciful terrors from my mind, and lay down to sleep with composure.

How long I may have slept it is impossible for me to guess;

but I was awakened at last by a sudden, blinding flash of light into my face. It woke me like a blow. In an instant I was upon my knees. But the light had gone as suddenly as it came. The darkness was intense. And, as it was blowing great guns from the sea and pouring with rain, the noises of the storm effectually concealed all others.

It was, I dare say, half a minute before I regained my self-possession. But for two circumstances, I should have thought I had been awakened by some new and vivid form of nightmare. First, the flap of my tent, which I had shut carefully when I retired, was now unfastened; and, second, I could still perceive, with a sharpness that excluded any theory of hallucination, the smell of hot metal and of burning oil. The conclusion was obvious. I had been wakened by some one flashing a bull's-eye lantern in my face. It had been but a flash, and away. He had seen my face, and then gone. I asked myself the object of so strange a proceeding, and the answer came pat. The man, whoever he was, had thought to recognise me, and he had not. There was yet another question unresolved; and to this, I may say, I feared to give an answer; if he had recognised me, what would he have done?

My fears were immediately diverted from myself, for I saw that I had been visited in a mistake; and I became persuaded that some dreadful danger threatened the pavilion. It required some nerve to issue forth into the black and intricate thicket which surrounded and overhung the den; but I groped my way to the links, drenched with rain, beaten upon and deafened by the gusts, and fearing at every step to lay my hand upon some lurking adversary. The darkness was so complete that I might have been surrounded by an army and yet none the wiser, and the uproar of the gale so loud that my hearing was as useless as my sight.

For the rest of that night, which seemed interminably long, I patrolled the vicinity of the pavilion, without seeing a living creature or hearing any noise but the concert of the wind, the sea, and the rain. A light in the upper storey filtered through a cranny of the shutter, and kept me company till the approach of dawn.

## 5. Tells of an Interview Between Northmour, Clara, and Myself

With the first peep of day, I retired from the open to my old lair among the sand-hills, there to await the coming of my wife. The morning was grey, wild, and melancholy; the wind moderated before sunrise, and then went about, and blew in puffs from the shore; the sea began to go down, but the rain still fell without mercy. Over all the wilderness of links there was not a creature to be seen. Yet I felt sure the neighbourhood was alive with skulking foes. The light that had been so suddenly and surprisingly flashed upon my face as I lay sleeping, and the hat that had been blown ashore by the wind from over Graden Floe, were two speaking signals of the peril that environed Clara and the party in the pavilion.

It was, perhaps, half-past seven, or nearer eight, before I saw the door open, and that dear figure come towards me in the rain. I was waiting for her on the beach before she had crossed the sand-hills.

"I have had such trouble to come!" she cried. "They did not wish me to go walking in the rain."

"Clara," I said, "you are not frightened!"

"No," said she, with a simplicity that filled my heart with confidence. For my wife was the bravest as well as the best of women; in my experience, I have not found the two go always together, but with her they did; and she combined the extreme of fortitude with the most endearing and beautiful virtues.

I told her what had happened; and, though her cheek grew visibly paler, she retained perfect control over her senses.

"You see now that I am safe," said I, in conclusion. "They do not mean to harm me; for, had they chosen, I was a dead man last night."

She laid her hand upon my arm.

"And I had no presentiment!" she cried.

Her accent thrilled me with delight. I put my arm about her, and strained her to my side; and, before either of us was aware, her hands were on my shoulders and my lips upon her mouth. Yet up to that moment no word of love had passed between us. To this day I remember the touch of her cheek, which was wet and cold with the rain; and many a time since, when she has been washing her face, I have kissed it again for the sake of that morning on the beach. Now that she is taken from me, and I finish my pilgrimage alone, I recall our old lovingkindnesses and the deep honesty and affection which united us, and my present loss seems but a trifle in comparison.

We may have thus stood for some seconds—for time passes quickly with lovers—before we were startled by a peal of laughter close at hand. It was not natural mirth, but seemed to be affected in order to conceal an angrier feeling. We both turned, though I still kept my left arm about Clara's waist; nor did she seek to withdraw herself; and there, a few paces off upon the beach, stood Northmour, his head lowered, his hands behind his back, his nostrils white with passion.

"Ah! Cassilis!" he said, as I disclosed my face.

"That same," said I; for I was not at all put about.

"And so, Miss Huddlestone," he continued slowly but savagely, "this is how you keep your faith to your father and to me? This is the value you set upon your father's life? And you are so infatuated with this young gentleman that you must brave ruin, and decency, and common human caution—"

"Miss Huddlestone—" I was beginning to interrupt him, when he, in his turn, cut in brutally—

"You hold your tongue," said he; "I am speaking to that girl."

"That girl, as you call her, is my wife," said I; and my wife only leaned a little nearer, so that I knew she had affirmed my words.

"Your what?" he cried. "You lie!"

"Northmour," I said, "we all know you have a bad temper, and I am the last man to be irritated by words. For all that, I propose that you speak lower, for I am convinced that we are not alone."

He looked round him, and it was plain my remark had in some degree sobered his passion. "What do you mean?" he asked.

I only said one word: "Italians."

He swore a round oath, and looked at us, from one to the other.

"Mr. Cassilis knows all that I know," said my wife.

"What I want to know," he broke out, "is where the devil Mr. Cassilis comes from, and what the devil Mr. Cassilis is doing here. You say you are married; that I do not believe. If you were, Graden Floe would soon divorce you; four minutes and a half, Cassilis. I keep my private cemetery for my friends."

"It took somewhat longer," said I, "for that Italian."

He looked at me for a moment half daunted, and then, almost civilly, asked me to tell my story. "You have too much the advantage of me, Cassilis," he added. I complied of course; and he listened, with several ejaculations, while I told him how I had come to Graden: that it was I whom he had tried to murder on the night of landing; and what I had subsequently seen and heard of the Italians.

"Well," said he, when I had done, "it is here at last; there is no mistake about that. And what, may I ask, do you propose to do?"

"I propose to stay with you and lend a hand," said I.

"You are a brave man," he returned, with a peculiar intonation.

"I am not afraid," said I.

"And so," he continued, "I am to understand that you two are married? And you stand up to it before my face, Miss Huddlestone?"

"We are not yet married," said Clara; "but we shall be as soon as we can."

"Bravo!" cried Northmour. "And the bargain? D——n it, you're not a fool, young woman; I may call a spade a spade with you. How about the bargain? You know as well as I do what your father's life depends upon. I have only to put my hands under my coat-tails and walk away, and his throat would he cut before the evening."

"Yes, Mr. Northmour," returned Clara, with great spirit; "but that is what you will never do. You made a bargain that was unworthy of a gentleman; but you are a gentleman for all that, and you will never desert a man whom you have begun to help."

"Aha!" said he. "You think I will give my yacht for nothing? You think I will risk my life and liberty for love of the old gentleman; and then, I suppose, be best man at the wedding, to wind up? Well," he added, with an odd smile, "perhaps you are not altogether wrong. But ask Cassilis here. *He* knows me. Am I a man to trust? Am I safe and scrupulous? Am I kind?"

"I know you talk a great deal, and sometimes, I think, very foolishly," replied Clara, "but I know you are a gentleman, and I am not the least afraid."

He looked at her with a peculiar approval and admiration; then, turning to me, "Do you think I would give her up without a struggle, Frank?" said he. "I tell you plainly, you look out. The next time we come to blows—"

"Will make the third," I interrupted, smiling.

"Aye, true; so it will," he said. "I had forgotten. Well, the third time's lucky."

"The third time, you mean, you will have the crew of the *Red Earl* to help," I said.

"Do you hear him?" he asked, turning to my wife.

"I hear two men speaking like cowards," said she. "I should despise myself either to think or speak like that. And neither of you believe one word that you are saying, which makes it the more wicked and silly."

"She's a trump!" cried Northmour. "But she's not yet Mrs. Cassilis. I say no more. The present is not for me." Then my wife surprised me.

"I leave you here," she said suddenly. "My father has been too long alone. But remember this: you are to be friends, for you are both good friends to me."

She has since told me her reason for this step. As long as she remained, she declares that we two would have continued to quarrel; and I suppose that she was right, for when she was gone we fell at once into a sort of confidentiality.

Northmour stared after her as she went away over the sand-hill.

"She is the only woman in the world!" he exclaimed with an oath. "Look at her action."

I, for my part, leaped at this opportunity for a little further light.

"See here, Northmour," said I; "we are all in a tight place, are we not?"

"I believe you, my boy," he answered, looking me in the eyes, and with great emphasis. "We have all hell upon us, that's the truth. You may believe me or not, but I'm afraid of my life."

"Tell me one thing," said I. "What are they after, these Italians? What do they want with Mr. Huddlestone?"

"Don't you know?" he cried. "The black old scamp had *Carbonaro* funds on a deposit—two hundred and eighty thousand; and of course he gambled it away on stocks. There was to have been a revolution in the Tridentino, or Parma; but the revolution is off, and the whole wasp's nest is after Huddlestone. We shall all be lucky if we can save our skins."

"The *Carbonari!*" I exclaimed; "God help him indeed!"

"Amen!" said Northmour. "And now, look here: I have said that we are in a fix; and, frankly, I shall be glad of your help. If I can't save Huddlestone, I want at least to save the girl. Come and stay in the pavilion; and, there's my hand on it, I shall act as your friend until the old man is either clear or dead. But," he added, "once that is settled, you become my rival once again, and I warn you—mind yourself."

"Done!" said I; and we shook hands.

"And now let us go directly to the fort," said Northmour; and he began to lead the way through the rain.

# 6. Tells of My Introduction
## to the Tall Man

We were admitted to the pavilion by Clara, and I was surprised by the completeness and security of the defences. A barricade of great strength, and yet easy to displace, supported the door against any violence from without; and the shutters of the dining-room, into which I was led directly, and which was feebly illuminated by a lamp, were even more elaborately fortified. The panels were strengthened by bars and cross-bars; and these, in their turn, were kept in position by a system of braces and struts, some abutting on the floor, some on the roof, and others, in fine, against the opposite wall of the apartment. It was at once a solid and well-designed piece of carpentry; and I did not seek to conceal my admiration.

"I am the engineer," said Northmour. "You remember the planks in the garden? Behold them?"

"I did not know you had so many talents," said I.

"Are you armed?" he continued, pointing to an array of guns and pistols, all in admirable order, which stood in line against the wall or were displayed upon the sideboard.

"Thank you," I returned; "I have gone armed since our last encounter. But, to tell you the truth, I have had nothing to eat since early yesterday evening."

Northmour produced some cold meat, to which I eagerly set myself, and a bottle of good Burgundy, by which, wet as I was, I did not scruple to profit. I have always been an extreme temperance man on principle; but it is useless to push principle to excess, and on this occasion I believe that I finished three-quarters of the bottle. As I ate, I still continued to admire the preparations for defence.

"We could stand a siege," I said at length.

"Ye-es," drawled Northmour; "a very little one, perhaps. It is not so much the strength of the pavilion I misdoubt; it is the doubled anger that kills me. If we get to shooting, wild as the country is some one is sure to hear it, and then—why then it's the same thing, only different, as they say: caged by law, or killed by *Carbonari*. There's the choice. It is a devilish bad thing to have the law against you in this world, and so I tell the old gentleman upstairs. He is quite of my way of thinking."

"Speaking of that," said I, "what kind of person is he?"

"Oh, he!" cried the other; "he's a rancid fellow, as far as he goes. I should like to have his neck wrung to-morrow by all the devils in Italy. I am not in this affair for him. You take me? I made a bargain for Missy's hand, and I mean to have it too."

"That by the way," said I. "I understand. But how will Mr. Huddlestone take my intrusion?"

"Leave that to Clara," returned Northmour.

I could have struck him in the face for this coarse familiarity; but I respected the truce, as, I am bound to say, did Northmour, and so long as the danger continued not a cloud arose in our relation. I bear him this testimony with the most unfeigned satisfaction; nor am I without pride when I look back upon my own behaviour. For surely no two men were ever left in a position so invidious and irritating.

As soon as I had done eating, we proceeded to inspect the lower floor. Window by window we tried the different supports, now and then making an inconsiderable change; and the strokes of the hammer sounded with startling loudness through the house. I proposed, I remember, to make loop-holes; but he told me they were already made in the windows of the upper storey. It was an anxious business this inspection, and left me down-hearted. There were two doors and five windows to protect, and, counting Clara, only four of us to defend them against an unknown number of foes. I communicated my doubts to Northmour, who assured me, with unmoved composure, that he entirely shared them.

"Before morning," said he, "we shall all be butchered and buried in Graden Floe. For me, that is written."

I could not help shuddering at the mention of the quicksand, but reminded Northmour that our enemies had spared me in the wood.

"Do not flatter yourself," said he. "Then you were not in the same boat with the old gentleman; now you are. It's the floe for all of us, mark my words."

I trembled for Clara; and just then her dear voice was heard calling us to come upstairs. Northmour showed me the way, and, when he had reached the landing, knocked at the door of what used to be called My Uncle's Bedroom, as the founder of the pavilion had designed it especially for himself.

"Come in, Northmour; come in, dear Mr. Cassilis," said a voice from within.

Pushing open the door, Northmour admitted me before him into the apartment. As I came in I could see the daughter slipping out by the side door into the study, which had been prepared as her bedroom. In the bed, which was drawn back against the wall, instead of standing, as I had last seen it, boldly across the window, sat Bernard Huddlestone, the defaulting banker. Little as I had seen of him by the shifting light of the lantern on the links, I had no difficulty in recognising him for the same. He had a long and sallow countenance, surrounded by a long red beard and side whiskers. His broken nose and high cheekbones gave him somewhat the air of a Kalmuck, and his light eyes shone with the excitement of a high fever. He wore a skull-cap of black silk; a huge Bible lay open before him on the bed, with a pair of gold spectacles in the place, and a pile of other books lay on the stand by his side. The green curtains lent a cadaverous shade to his cheek; and, as he sat propped on pillows, his great stature was painfully hunched, and his head protruded till it overhung his knees. I believe if he had not died otherwise, he must have fallen a victim to consumption in the course of but a very few weeks.

He held out to me a hand, long, thin, and disagreeably hairy.

"Come in, come in, Mr. Cassilis," said he. "Another protector—ahem!—another protector. Always welcome as a friend of my daughter's, Mr. Cassilis. How they have rallied about me, my daughter's friends! May God in heaven bless and reward them for it!"

I gave him my hand, of course, because I could not help it; but the sympathy I had been prepared to feel for Clara's father was immediately soured by his appearance, and the wheedling, unreal tones in which he spoke.

"Cassilis is a good man," said Northmour; "worth ten."

"So I hear," cried Mr. Huddlestone eagerly, "so my girl tells me. Ah, Mr. Cassilis, my sin has found me out, you see! I am very low, very low; but I hope equally penitent. We must all come to the throne of grace at last, Mr. Cassilis. For my part, I come late indeed; but with unfeigned humility, I trust."

"Fiddle-de-dee!" said Northmour roughly.

"No, no, dear Northmour!" cried the banker. "You must not say that; you must not try to shake me. You forget, my dear, good boy, you forget I may be called this very night before my Maker."

His excitement was pitiful to behold; and I felt myself grow indignant with Northmour, whose infidel opinions I well knew, and heartily derided, as he continued to taunt the poor sinner out of his humour of repentance.

"Pooh, my dear Huddlestone!" said he. "You do yourself injustice. You are a man of the world inside and out, and were up to all kinds of mischief before I was born. Your conscience is tanned like South American leather—only you forgot to tan your liver, and that, if you will believe me, is the seat of the annoyance."

"Rogue, rogue! bad boy!" said Mr. Huddlestone, shaking his finger. "I am no precisian, if you come to that; I always hated a precisian; but I never lost hold of something better through it all. I have been a bad boy, Mr. Cassilis; I do not seek to deny that; but it was after my wife's death, and you know, with a widower, it's a different thing: sinful—I won't say no; but there is a gradation, we shall hope. And talking of that—Hark!" he broke out suddenly, his hand raised, his fingers spread, his face racked with interest and terror. "Only the rain, bless God!" he added, after a pause, and with indescribable relief.

For some seconds he lay back among the pillows like a man near to fainting; then he gathered himself together, and, in somewhat tremulous tones, began once more to thank me for the share I was prepared to take in his defence.

"One question, sir," said I, when he had paused. "Is it true that you have money with you?"

He seemed annoyed by the question, but admitted with reluctance that he had a little.

"Well," I continued, "it is their money they are after, is it not? Why not give it up to them?"

"Ah!" replied he, shaking his head, "I have tried that already, Mr. Cassilis; and alas that it should be so! but it is blood they want."

"Huddlestone, that's a little less than fair," said Northmour. "You should mention that what you offered them was upwards of two hundred thousand short. The deficit is worth a reference; it is for what they call a cool sum, Frank. Then, you see, the fellows reason in their clear Italian way; and it seems to them, as indeed it seems to me, that they may just as well have both while they're about it—money and blood together, by George, and no more trouble for the extra pleasure."

"Is it in the pavilion?" I asked.

"It is; and I wish it were in the bottom of the sea instead," said Northmour; and then suddenly—"What are you making faces at me for?" he cried to Mr. Huddlestone, on whom I had unconsciously turned my back. "Do you think Cassilis would sell you?"

Mr. Huddlestone protested that nothing had been further from his mind.

"It is a good thing," retorted Northmour in his ugliest manner. "You might end by wearying us. What were you going to say?" he added, turning to me.

"I was going to propose an occupation for the afternoon," said I. "Let us carry that money out, piece by piece, and lay it down before the pavilion door. If the *Carbonari* come, why, it's theirs at any rate."

"No, no," cried Mr. Huddlestone; "it does not, it cannot belong to them! It should be distributed *pro rata* among all my creditors."

"Come now, Huddlestone," said Northmour, "none of that."

"Well, but my daughter," moaned the wretched man.

"Your daughter will do well enough. Here are two suitors, Cassilis and I, neither of us beggars, between whom she has to choose. And as for yourself, to make an end of arguments, you have no right to a farthing, and, unless I'm much mistaken, you are going to die."

It was certainly very cruelly said; but Mr. Huddlestone was a man who attracted little sympathy; and, although I saw him wince and shudder, I mentally endorsed the rebuke; nay, I added a contribution of my own.

"Northmour and I," I said, "are willing enough to help you to save your life, but not to escape with stolen property."

He struggled for a while with himself, as though he were on the point of giving way to anger, but prudence had the best of the controversy.

"My dear boys," he said, "do with me or my money what you will. I leave all in your hands. Let me compose myself."

And so we left him, gladly enough I am sure. The last that I saw, he had once more taken up his great Bible, and with tremulous hands was adjusting his spectacles to read.

## 7. Tells How a Word Was Cried
## Through the Pavilion Window

The recollection of that afternoon will always be graven on my mind. Northmour and I were persuaded that an attack was imminent; and if it had been in our power to alter in any way the order of events, that power would have been used to precipitate rather than delay the critical moment. The worst was to be anticipated; yet we could conceive no extremity so miserable as the suspense we were now suffering. I have never been an eager, though always a great, reader; but I never knew books so insipid as those which I took up and cast aside that afternoon in the pavilion. Even talk became impossible, as the hours went on. One or other was always listening for some sound, or peering from an upstairs window over the links. And yet not a sign indicated the presence of our foes.

We debated over and over again my proposal with regard to the money; and had we been in complete possession of our faculties, I am sure we should have condemned it as unwise; but we were flustered with alarm, grasped at a straw, and determined, although it was as much as advertising Mr. Huddlestone's presence in the pavilion, to carry my proposal into effect.

The sum was part in specie, part in bank paper, and part in circular notes payable to the name of James Gregory. We took it out, counted it, enclosed it once more in a despatch-box belonging to Northmour, and prepared a letter in Italian which he tied to the handle. It was signed by both of us under oath, and declared that this was all the money which had escaped the failure of the house of Huddlestone. This was, perhaps, the maddest action ever perpetrated by two persons professing to be sane. Had the despatch-box fallen into other hands than those for which it was intended, we stood criminally convicted on our own written testimony; but, as I have said, we were neither of us in a condition to judge soberly, and had a thirst for action that drove us to do something, right or wrong, rather than endure the agony of waiting. Moreover, as we were both convinced that the hollows of the links were alive with hidden spies upon our movements, we hoped that our appearance with the box might lead to a parley, and, perhaps, a compromise.

It was nearly three when we issued from the pavilion. The rain had taken off; the sun shone quite cheerfully.

I have never seen the gulls fly so close about the house or approach so fearlessly to human beings. On the very doorstep one flapped heavily past our heads, and uttered its wild cry in my very ear.

"There is an omen for you," said Northmour, who like all freethinkers was much under the influence of superstition. "They think we are already dead."

I made some light rejoinder, but it was with half my heart; for the circumstance had impressed me.

A yard or two before the gate, on a patch of smooth turf, we set down the despatch-box; and Northmour waved a white handkerchief over his head. Nothing replied. We raised our voices, and cried aloud in Italian that we were there as ambassadors to arrange the quarrel; but the stillness remained unbroken save by the sea-gulls and the surf. I had a weight at my heart when we desisted; and I saw that even Northmour was unusually pale. He looked over his shoulder nervously, as though he feared that some one had crept between him and the pavilion door.

"By God," he said in a whisper, "this is too much for me!"

I replied in the same key: "Suppose there should be none, after all!"

"Look there," he returned, nodding with his head, as though he had been afraid to point.

I glanced in the direction indicated; and there, from the northern quarter of the Sea-Wood, beheld a thin column of smoke rising steadily against the now cloudless sky.

"Northmour," I said (we still continued to talk in whispers), "it is not possible to endure this suspense. I prefer death fifty times over. Stay you here to watch the pavilion; I will go forward and make sure, if I have to walk right into their camp."

He looked once again all round him with puckered eyes, and then nodded assentingly to my proposal.

My heart beat like a sledge-hammer as I set out walking rapidly in the direction of the smoke; and, though up to that moment I had felt chill and shivering, I was suddenly conscious of a glow of heat over all my body. The ground in this direction was very uneven; a hundred men might have lain hidden in as many square yards about my path. But I had not practised the business in vain, chose such routes as cut at the very root of concealment, and, by keeping along the most convenient ridges, commanded several hollows at a time. It was not long before I was rewarded for my caution. Coming suddenly on to a mound somewhat more elevated than the surrounding hummocks, I saw, not thirty yards away, a man bent almost double, and running as fast as his attitude permitted, along the bottom of a gully. I had dislodged one of the spies from his ambush. As soon as I sighted him, I called loudly both in English and Italian; and he, seeing concealment was no longer possible, straightened himself out, leaped from the gully, and made off as straight as an arrow for the borders of the wood.

It was none of my business to pursue; I had learned what I wanted—that we were beleaguered and watched in the pavilion; and I returned at once, and walking as nearly as possible in my old footsteps, to where Northmour awaited me beside the despatch-box. He was even paler than when I had left him, and his voice shook a little.

"Could you see what he was like?" he asked.

"He kept his back turned," I replied.

"Let us get into the house, Frank. I don't think I'm a coward, but I can stand no more of this," he whispered.

All was still and sunshiny about the pavilion as we turned to re-enter it; even the gulls had flown in a wider circuit, and were seen flickering along the beach and sand-hills; and this loneliness terrified me more than a regiment under arms. It was not until the door was barricaded that I could draw a full inspiration and relieve the weight that lay upon my bosom. Northmour and I exchanged a steady glance; and I suppose each made his own reflections on the white and startled aspect of the other.

"You were right," I said. "All is over. Shake hands, old man, for the last time."

"Yes," replied he, "I will shake hands; for, as sure as I am here, I bear no malice. But, remember, if, by some impossible accident, we should give the slip to these blackguards, I'll take the upper hand of you by fair or foul."

"Oh," said I, "you weary me!"

He seemed hurt, and walked away in silence to the foot of the stairs, where he paused.

"You do not understand," said he. "I am not a swindler, and I guard myself; that is all. It may weary you or not, Mr. Cassilis, I do not care a rush; I speak for my own satisfaction, and not for your amusement. You had better go upstairs and court the girl; for my part, I stay here."

"And I stay with you," I returned. "Do you think I would steal a march, even with your permission?"

"Frank," he said, smiling, "it's a pity you are an ass, for you have the makings of a man. I think I must be *fey* to-day; you cannot irritate me even when you try. Do you know," he continued softly, "I think we are the two most miserable men in England, you and I? we have got on to thirty without wife or child, or so much as a shop to look after—poor, pitiful, lost devils, both! And now we clash about a girl! As if there were not several millions in the United Kingdom! Ah, Frank, Frank, the one who loses this throw, be it you or me, he has my pity! It were better for him—how does the Bible say?—that a millstone were hanged about his neck and he were cast into the depth of the sea. Let us take a drink," he concluded suddenly, but without any levity of tone.

I was touched by his words, and consented. He sat down on the table in the dining-room, and held up the glass of sherry to his eye.

"If you beat me, Frank," he said, "I shall take to drink. What will you do, if it goes the other way?"

"God knows," I returned.

"Well," said he, "here is a toast in the meantime: *'Italia irredenta!'*"

The remainder of the day was passed in the same dreadful tedium and suspense. I laid the table for dinner, while Northmour and Clara prepared the meal together in the kitchen. I could hear their talk as I went to and fro, and was surprised to find it ran all the time upon myself. Northmour again bracketed us together, and rallied Clara on a choice of husbands; but he continued to speak of me with some feeling, and uttered nothing to my prejudice unless he included himself in the condemnation. This awakened a sense of gratitude in my heart, which combined with the immediateness of our peril to fill my eyes with tears. After all, I thought—and perhaps the thought was laughably vain— we were here three very noble human beings to perish in defence of a thieving banker.

Before we sat down to table, I looked forth from an upstairs window. The day was beginning to decline; the links were utterly deserted; the despatch-box still lay untouched where we had left it hours before.

Mr. Huddlestone, in a long yellow dressing-gown, took one end of the table, Clara the other; while Northmour and I faced each other from the sides. The lamp was brightly trimmed; the wine was good; the viands, although mostly cold, excellent of their sort. We seemed to have agreed tacitly; all reference to the impending catastrophe was carefully avoided; and, considering our tragic circumstances, we made a merrier party than could have been expected. From time to time, it is true, Northmour or I would rise from table and make a round of the defences; and, on each of these occasions, Mr. Huddlestone was recalled to a sense of his tragic predicament, glanced up with ghastly eyes, and bore for an instant on his countenance the stamp of terror. But he hastened to empty his glass, wiped his forehead with his handkerchief, and joined again in the conversation.

I was astonished at the wit and information he displayed. Mr. Huddlestone's was certainly no ordinary character; he had read and observed for himself; his gifts were sound; and, though I could never have learned to love the man, I began to understand his success in business, and the great respect in which he had been held before his failure. He had, above all, the talent of society; and though I never heard him speak but on this one and most unfavourable occasion, I set him down among the most brilliant conversationalists I ever met.

He was relating with great gusto, and seemingly no feeling of shame, the manoeuvres of a scoundrelly commission merchant whom he had known and studied in his youth, and we were all listening with an odd mixture of mirth and embarrassment when our little party was brought abruptly to an end in the most startling manner.

A noise like that of a wet finger on the window-pane interrupted Mr. Huddlestone's tale; and in an instant we were all four as white as paper, and sat tongue-tied and motionless round the table.

"A snail," I said at last; for I had heard that these animals make a noise somewhat similar in character.

"Snail be d——d!" said Northmour. "Hush!"

The same sound was repeated twice at regular intervals; and then a formidable voice shouted through the shutters the Italian word *"Traditore!"*

Mr. Huddlestone threw his head in the air; his eyelids quivered; next moment he fell insensible below the table. Northmour and I had each run to the armoury and seized a gun. Clara was on her feet with her hand at her throat.

So we stood waiting, for we thought the hour of attack was certainly come; but second passed after second, and all but the surf remained silent in the neighbourhood of the pavilion.

"Quick," said Northmour; "upstairs with him before they come."

## 8. Tells the Last of the Tall Man

Somehow or other, by hook and crook, and between the three of us, we got Bernard Huddlestone bundled upstairs and laid upon the bed in My Uncle's Room. During the whole process, which was rough enough, he gave no sign of consciousness, and he remained, as we had thrown him, without changing the position of a finger. His daughter opened his shirt and began to wet his head and bosom; while Northmour and I ran to the window. The weather continued clear; the moon, which was now about full, had risen and shed a very clear light upon the links; yet, strain our eyes as we might, we could distinguish nothing moving. A few dark spots, more or less, on the uneven expanse were not to be identified; they might be crouching men, they might be shadows; it was impossible to be sure.

"Thank God," said Northmour, "Aggie is not coming to-night."

Aggie was the name of the old nurse; he had not thought of her till now; but that he should think of her at all, was a trait that surprised me in the man.

We were again reduced to waiting. Northmour went to the fireplace and spread his hands before the red embers, as if he were cold. I followed him mechanically with my eyes, and in so doing turned my back upon the window. At that moment a very faint report was audible from without, and a ball shivered a pane of glass, and buried itself in the shutter two inches from my head. I heard Clara scream; and though I whipped instantly out of range and into a corner, she was there, so to speak, before me, beseeching to know if I were hurt. I felt that I could stand to be shot at every day and all day long, with such marks of solicitude for a reward; and I continued to reassure her, with the tenderest caresses and in complete forgetfulness of our situation, till the voice of Northmour recalled me to myself.

"An air-gun," he said. "They wish to make no noise."

I put Clara aside, and looked at him. He was standing with his back to the fire and his hands clasped behind him; and I knew by the black look on his face, that passion was boiling within. I had seen just such a look before he attacked me, that March night, in the adjoining chamber; and, though I could make every allowance for his anger, I confess I trembled for the consequences. He gazed straight before him; but he could see us with the tail of his eye, and his temper kept rising like a gale of wind. With regular battle awaiting us outside, this prospect of an internecine strife within the walls began to daunt me.

Suddenly, as I was thus closely watching his expression and prepared against the worst, I saw a change, a flash, a look of relief, upon his face. He took up the lamp which stood beside him on the table, and turned to us with an air of some excitement.

"There is one point that we must know," said he. "Are they going to butcher the lot of us, or only Huddlestone? Did they take you for him, or fire at you for your own *beaux yeux*?"

"They took me for him, for certain," I replied. "I am near as tall, and my head is fair."

"I am going to make sure," returned Northmour; and he stepped up to the window, holding the lamp above his head, and stood there, quietly affronting death, for half a minute.

Clara sought to rush forward and pull him from the place of danger; but I had the pardonable selfishness to hold her back by force.

"Yes," said Northmour, turning coolly from the window; "it's only Huddlestone they want."

"Oh, Mr. Northmour!" cried Clara; but found no more to add; the temerity she had just witnessed seeming beyond the reach of words.

He, on his part, looked at me, cocking his head, with a fire of triumph in his eyes; and I understood at once that he had thus hazarded his life, merely to attract Clara's notice, and depose me from my position as the hero of the hour. He snapped his fingers.

"The fire is only beginning," said he. "When they warm up to their work, they won't be so particular."

A voice was now heard hailing us from the entrance. From the window we could see the figure of a man in the moonlight; he stood motionless, his face uplifted to ours, and a rag of something white on his extended arm; and as we looked right down upon him, though he was a good many yards distant on the links, we could see the moonlight glitter on his eyes.

He opened his lips again, and spoke for some minutes on end, in a key so loud that he might have been heard in every corner of the pavilion, and as far away as the borders of the wood. It was the same voice that had already shouted *"Traditore!"* through the shutters of the dining-room; this time it made a complete and clear statement. If the traitor "Oddlestone" were given up, all others should be spared; if not, no one should escape to tell the tale.

"Well, Huddlestone, what do you say to that?" asked Northmour, turning to the bed.

Up to that moment the banker had given no sign of life, and I, at least, had supposed him to be still lying in a faint; but he replied at once, and in such tones as I have never heard elsewhere, save from a delirious patient, adjured and besought us not to desert him. It was the most hideous and abject performance that my imagination can conceive.

"Enough," cried Northmour; and then he threw open the window, leaned out into the night, and in a tone of exultation, and with a total forgetfulness of what was due to the presence of a lady, poured out upon the ambassador a string of the most abominable raillery both in English and Italian, and bade him be gone where he had come from. I believe that nothing so delighted Northmour at that moment as the thought that we must all infallibly perish before the night was out.

Meantime the Italian put his flag of truce into his pocket, and disappeared, at a leisurely pace, among the sand-hills.

"They make honourable war," said Northmour. "They are all gentlemen and soldiers. For the credit of the thing, I wish we could change sides—you and I, Frank, and you too, Missy, my darling—and leave that being on the bed to some one else. Tut! Don't look shocked! We are all going post to what they call eternity, and may as well be above-board while there's time. As far as I'm concerned, if I could first strangle Huddlestone and then get Clara in my arms, I could die with some pride and satisfaction. And as it is, by God, I'll have a kiss!"

Before I could do anything to interfere, he had rudely

embraced and repeatedly kissed the resisting girl. Next moment I had pulled him away with fury, and flung him heavily against the wall. He laughed loud and long, and I feared his wits had given way under the strain; for even in the best of days he had been a sparing and a quiet laugher.

"Now, Frank," said he, when his mirth was somewhat appeased, "it's your turn. Here's my hand. Good-bye; farewell!" Then, seeing me stand rigid and indignant, and holding Clara to my side—"Man!" he broke out, "are you angry? Did you think we were going to die with all the airs and graces of society? I took a kiss; I'm glad I had it; and now you can take another if you like, and square accounts."

I turned from him with a feeling of contempt which I did not seek to dissemble.

"As you please," said he. "You've been a prig in life; a prig you'll die."

And with that he sat down in a chair, a rifle over his knee, and amused himself with snapping the lock; but I could see that his ebullition of light spirits (the only one I ever knew him to display) had already come to an end, and was succeeded by a sullen, scowling humour.

All this time our assailants might have been entering the house, and we been none the wiser; we had in truth almost forgotten the danger that so imminently overhung our days. But just then Mr. Huddlestone uttered a cry, and leaped from the bed.

I asked him what was wrong.

"Fire!" he cried. "They have set the house on fire!"

Northmour was on his feet in an instant, and he and I ran through the door of communication with the study. The room was illuminated by a red and angry light. Almost at the moment of our entrance, a tower of flame arose in front of the window, and, with a tingling report, a pane fell inwards on the carpet. They had set fire to the lean-to outhouse, where Northmour used to nurse his negatives.

"Hot work," said Northmour. "Let us try in your old room."

We ran thither in a breath, threw up the casement, and looked forth. Along the whole back wall of the pavilion piles of fuel had been arranged and kindled; and it is probable they had been drenched with mineral oil, for, in spite of the morning's rain, they all burned bravely. The fire had taken a firm hold already on the outhouse, which blazed higher and higher every moment; the back door was in the centre of a red-hot bonfire; the eaves we could see, as we looked upward, were already smouldering, for the roof overhung, and was supported by considerable beams of wood. At the same time, hot, pungent, and choking volumes of smoke began to fill the house. There was not a human being to be seen to right or left.

"Ah, well!" said Northmour, "here's the end, thank God."

And we returned to My Uncle's Room. Mr. Huddlestone was putting on his boots, still violently trembling, but with an air of determination such as I had not hitherto observed. Clara stood close by him, with her cloak in both hands ready to throw about her shoulders, and a strange look in her eyes, as if she were half hopeful, half doubtful of her father.

"Well, boys and girls," said Northmour, "how about a sally? The oven is heating; it is not good to stay here and be baked; and, for my part, I want to come to my hands with them, and be done."

"There is nothing else left," I replied.

And both Clara and Mr. Huddlestone, though with a very different intonation, added, "Nothing."

As we went downstairs the heat was excessive, and the roaring of the fire filled our ears; and we had scarce reached the passage before the stairs window fell in, a branch of flame shot brandishing through the aperture, and the interior of the pavilion became lit up with that dreadful and fluctuating glare. At the same moment we heard the fall of something heavy and inelastic in the upper storey. The whole pavilion, it was plain, had gone alight like a box of matches, and now not only flamed sky-high to land and sea, but threatened with every moment to crumble and fall in about our ears.

Northmour and I cocked our revolvers. Mr. Huddlestone, who had already refused a firearm, put us behind him with a manner of command.

"Let Clara open the door," said he. "So, if they fire a volley, she will be protected. And in the meantime stand behind me. I am the scapegoat; my sins have found me out."

I heard him, as I stood breathless by his shoulder, with my pistol ready, pattering off prayers in a tremulous, rapid whisper; and I confess, horrid as the thought may seem, I despised him for thinking of supplications in a moment so critical and thrilling. In the meantime, Clara, who was dead white but still possessed her faculties, had displaced the barricade from the front door. Another moment, and she had pulled it open. Firelight and moonlight illuminated the links with confused and changeful lustre, and far away against the sky we could see a long trail of glowing smoke.

Mr. Huddlestone, filled for the moment with a strength greater than his own, struck Northmour and myself a back-hander in the chest; and while we were thus for the moment incapacitated from action, lifting his arms above his head like one about to dive, he ran straight forward out of the pavilion.

"Here I am!" he cried—"Huddlestone! Kill me, and spare the others!"

His sudden appearance daunted, I suppose, our hidden enemies; for Northmour and I had time to recover, to seize Clara between us, one by each arm, and to rush forth to his assistance, ere anything further had taken place. But scarce had we passed the threshold when there came near a dozen reports and flashes from every direction among the hollows of the links. Mr. Huddlestone staggered, uttered a weird and freezing cry, threw up his arms over his head, and fell backward on the turf.

*"Traditore! Traditore!"* cried the invisible avengers.

And just then, a part of the roof of the pavilion fell in, so rapid was the progress of the fire. A loud, vague, and horrible noise accompanied the collapse, and a vast volume of flame went soaring up to heaven. It must have been visible at that moment from twenty miles out at sea, from the shore at Graden Wester, and far inland from the peak of Graystiel, the most eastern summit of the Caulder Hills. Bernard Huddlestone, although God knows what were his obsequies, had a fine pyre at the moment of his death.

## 9. Tells How Northmour Carried Out His Threat

Ishould have the greatest difficulty to tell you what followed next after this tragic circumstance. It is all to me, as I look back upon it, mixed, strenuous, and ineffectual, like the struggles of a sleeper in a nightmare. Clara, I remember, uttered a broken sigh and would have fallen forward to earth, had not Northmour and I supported her insensible body. I do not think we were attacked; I do not remember even to have seen an assailant; and I believe we deserted Mr. Huddlestone without a glance. I only remember running like a man in a panic, now carrying Clara altogether in my own arms, now sharing her weight with Northmour, now scuffling confusedly for the possession of that dear burden. Why we should have made for my camp in the Hemlock Den, or how we reached it, are points lost for ever to my recollection. The first moment at which I became definitely sure, Clara had been suffered to fall against the outside of my little tent, Northmour and I were tumbling together on the ground, and he, with contained ferocity, was striking for my head with the butt of his revolver. He had already twice wounded me on the scalp; and it is to the consequent loss of blood that I am tempted to attribute the sudden clearness of my mind.

I caught him by the wrist.

"Northmour," I remember saying, "you can kill me afterwards. Let us first attend to Clara."

He was at that moment uppermost. Scarcely had the words passed my lips, when he had leaped to his feet and ran towards the tent; and the next moment, he was straining Clara to his heart and covering her unconscious hands and face with his caresses.

"Shame!" I cried. "Shame to you, Northmour!"

And, giddy though I still was, I struck him repeatedly upon the head and shoulders.

He relinquished his grasp, and faced me in the broken moonlight.

"I had you under, and I let you go," said he; "and now you strike me! Coward!"

"You are the coward," I retorted. "Did she wish your kisses while she was still sensible of what she wanted? Not she! And now she may be dying; and you waste this precious time, and abuse her helplessness. Stand aside, and let me help her."

He confronted me for a moment, white and menacing; then suddenly he stepped aside.

"Help her then," said he.

I threw myself on my knees beside her, and loosened, as well as I was able, her dress and corset; but while I was thus engaged, a grasp descended on my shoulder.

"Keep your hands of her," said Northmour fiercely. "Do you think I have no blood in my veins?"

"Northmour," I cried, "if you will neither help her yourself, nor let me do so, do you know that I shall have to kill you?"

"That is better!" he cried. "Let her die also, where's the harm? Step aside from that girl! and stand up to fight."

"You will observe," said I, half rising, "that I have not kissed her yet."

"I dare you to," he cried.

I do not know what possessed me; it was one of the things I am most ashamed of in my life, though, as my wife used to say, I knew that my kisses would be always welcome were she dead or living; down I fell again upon my knees, parted the hair from her forehead, and, with the dearest respect, laid my lips for a moment on that cold brow. It was such a caress as a father might have given; it was such a one as was not unbecoming from a man soon to die to a woman already dead.

"And now," said I, "I am at your service, Mr. Northmour."

But I saw, to my surprise, that he had turned his back upon me.

"Do you hear?" I asked.

"Yes," said he, "I do. If you wish to fight, I am ready. If not, go on and save Clara. All is one to me."

I did not wait to be twice bidden; but, stooping again over Clara, continued my efforts to revive her. She still lay white and lifeless; I began to fear that her sweet spirit had indeed fled beyond recall, and horror and a sense of utter desolation seized upon my heart. I called her by name with the most endearing inflections; I chafed and beat her hands; now I laid her head low, now supported it against my knee; but all seemed to be in vain, and the lids still lay heavy on her eyes.

"Northmour," I said, "there is my hat. For God's sake bring some water from the spring."

Almost in a moment he was by my side with the water. "I have brought it in my own," he said. "You do not grudge me the privilege?"

"Northmour," I was beginning to say, as I laved her head and breast; but he interrupted me savagely.

"Oh, you hush up!" he said. "The best thing you can do is to say nothing."

I had certainly no desire to talk, my mind being swallowed up in concern for my dear love and her condition; so I continued in silence to do my best towards her recovery, and, when the hat was empty, returned it to him, with one word—"More." He had, perhaps, gone several times upon this errand, when Clara reopened her eyes.

"Now," said he, "since she is better, you can spare me, can you not? I wish you a good night, Mr. Cassilis."

And with that he was gone among the thicket. I made a fire, for I had now no fear of the Italians, who had even spared all the little possessions left in my encampment; and, broken as she was by the excitement and the hideous catastrophe of the evening, I managed, in one way or another—by persuasion, encouragement, warmth, and such simple remedies as I could lay my hand on—to bring her back to some composure of mind and strength of body.

Day had already come, when a sharp "Hist!" sounded from the thicket. I started from the ground; but the voice of Northmour was heard adding, in the most tranquil tones: "Come here, Cassilis, and alone; I want to show you something."

I consulted Clara with my eyes, and, receiving her tacit permission, left her alone, and clambered out of the den. At some distance off I saw Northmour leaning against an elder; and, as soon as he perceived me, he began walking seaward. I had almost overtaken him as he reached the outskirts of the wood.

"Look," said he, pausing.

A couple of steps more brought me out of the foliage. The

light of the morning lay cold and clear over that well-known scene. The pavilion was but a blackened wreck; the roof had fallen in, one of the gables had fallen out; and, far and near, the face of the links was cicatrised with little patches of burnt furze. Thick smoke still went straight upwards in the windless air of the morning, and a great pile of ardent cinders filled the bare walls of the house, like coals in an open grate. Close by the islet a schooner yacht lay to, and a well-manned boat was pulling vigorously for the shore.

"The *Red Earl!*" I cried. "The *Red Earl* twelve hours too late!"

"Feel in your pocket, Frank. Are you armed?" asked Northmour.

I obeyed him, and I think I must have become deadly pale. My revolver had been taken from me.

"You see I have you in my power," he continued. "I disarmed you last night while you were nursing Clara; but this morning—here—take your pistol. No thanks!" he cried, holding up his hand. "I do not like them; that is the only way you can annoy me now."

He began to walk forward across the links to meet the boat, and I followed a step or two behind. In front of the pavilion I paused to see where Mr. Huddlestone had fallen; but there was no sign of him, nor so much as a trace of blood.

"Graden Floe," said Northmour.

He continued to advance till we had come to the head of the beach.

"No farther, please," said he. "Would you like to take her to Graden House?"

"Thank you," replied I; "I shall try to get her to the minister's at Graden Wester."

The prow of the boat here grated on the beach, and a sailor jumped ashore with a line in his hand.

"Wait a minute, lads!" cried Northmour; and then lower and to my private ear: "You had better say nothing of all this to her," he added.

"On the contrary!" I broke out, "she shall know everything that I can tell."

"You do not understand," he returned, with an air of great

dignity. "It will be nothing to her; she expects it of me. Good-bye!" he added, with a nod.

I offered him my hand.

"Excuse me," said he. "It's small, I know; but I can't push things quite so far as that. I don't wish any sentimental business, to sit by your hearth a white-haired wanderer, and all that. Quite the contrary: I hope to God I shall never again clap eyes on either one of you."

"Well, God bless you, Northmour!" I said heartily.

"Oh, yes," he returned.

He walked down the beach; and the man who was ashore gave him an arm on board, and then shoved off and leaped into the bows himself. Northmour took the tiller; the boat rose to the waves, and the oars between the thole-pins sounded crisp and measured in the morning air.

They were not yet half-way to the *Red Earl*, and I was still watching their progress, when the sun rose out of the sea.

One word more, and my story is done. Years after, Northmour was killed fighting under the colours of Garibaldi for the liberation of the Tyrol.

# A Lodging for the Night:
# A Story of Francis Villon

# A Lodging for the Night:
## A Story of Francis Villon

It was late in November 1456. The snow fell over Paris with rigorous, relentless persistence; sometimes the wind made a sally and scattered it in flying vortices; sometimes there was a lull, and flake after flake descended out of the black night air, silent, circuitous, interminable. To poor people, looking up under moist eyebrows, it seemed a wonder where it all came from. Master Francis Villon had propounded an alternative that afternoon, at a tavern window: was it only Pagan Jupiter plucking geese upon Olympus? or were the holy angels moulting? He was only a poor Master of Arts, he went on; and as the question somewhat touched upon divinity, he durst not venture to conclude. A silly old priest from Montargis, who was among the company, treated the young rascal to a bottle of wine in honour of the jest and the grimaces with which it was accompanied, and swore on his own white beard that he had been just such another irreverent dog when he was Villon's age.

The air was raw and pointed, but not far below freezing; and the flakes were large, damp, and adhesive. The whole city was sheeted up. An army might have marched from end to end and not a footfall given the alarm. If there were any belated birds in heaven, they saw the island like a large white patch, and the bridges like slim white spars, on the black ground of the river. High up overhead the snow settled among the tracery of the cathedral towers. Many a niche was drifted full; many a statue wore a long white bonnet on its grotesque or sainted head. The gargoyles had been transformed into great false noses, drooping towards the point. The crockets were like upright pillows swollen on one side. In the intervals of the wind, there was a dull sound of dripping about the precincts of the church.

The cemetery of St. John had taken its own share of the snow. All the graves were decently covered; tall white housetops stood around in grave array; worthy burghers were long ago in bed, benightcapped like their domiciles; there was no light in all the neighbourhood but a little peep from a lamp that hung swinging in the church choir, and tossed the shadows to and fro in time to its oscillations. The clock was hard on ten when the patrol went by with halberds and a lantern, beating their hands; and they saw nothing suspicious about the cemetery of St. John.

Yet there was a small house, backed up against the cemetery wall, which was still awake, and awake to evil purpose, in that snoring district. There was not much to betray it from without; only a stream of warm vapour from the chimney-top, a patch where the snow melted on the roof, and a few half-obliterated footprints at the door. But within, behind the shuttered windows, Master Francis Villon the poet, and some of the thievish crew with whom he consorted, were keeping the night alive and passing round the bottle.

A great pile of living embers diffused a strong and ruddy glow from the arched chimney. Before this straddled Dom Nicolas, the Picardy monk, with his skirts picked up and his fat legs bared to the comfortable warmth. His dilated shadow cut the room in half; and the firelight only escaped on either side of his broad person, and in a little pool between his outspread feet. His face had the beery, bruised appearance of the continual drinker's; it was covered with a network of congested veins, purple in ordinary circumstances, but now pale violet, for even with his back to the fire the cold pinched him on the other side. His cowl had half fallen back, and made a strange excrescence on either side of his bull neck. So he straddled, grumbling, and cut the room in half with the shadow of his portly frame.

On the right, Villon and Guy Tabary were huddled together over a scrap of parchment; Villon making a ballade which he was to call the "Ballade of Roast Fish," and Tabary spluttering admiration at his shoulder. The poet was a rag of a man, dark, little, and lean, with hollow cheeks and thin black locks. He carried his four-and-twenty years with feverish animation. Greed had made folds about his eyes, evil smiles had puckered his mouth. The wolf and pig struggled together in his face. It was an eloquent, sharp, ugly, earthly countenance. His hands were small and prehensile, with fingers knotted like a cord; and they were continually flickering in front of him in violent and expressive pantomime. As for Tabary, a broad, complacent, admiring imbecility breathed from his squash nose and slobbering lips: he had become a thief, just as he might have become the most decent of burgesses, by the imperious chance that rules the lives of human geese and human donkeys.

At the monk's other hand, Montigny and Thevenin Pensete played a game of chance. About the first there clung some flavour of good birth and training, as about a fallen angel; something long, lithe, and courtly in the person; something aquiline and darkling in the face. Thevenin, poor soul, was in great feather: he had done a good stroke of knavery that afternoon in the Faubourg St. Jacques, and all night he had been gaining from Montigny. A flat smile illuminated his face; his bald head shone rosily in a garland of red curls; his little protuberant stomach shook with silent chucklings as he swept in his gains.

"Doubles or quits?" said Thevenin. Montigny nodded grimly.

"*Some may prefer to dine in state*," wrote Villon, "*On bread and cheese on silver plate*. Or—or—help me out, Guido!"

Tabary giggled.

"*Or parsley on a golden dish*," scribbled the poet.

The wind was freshening without; it drove the snow before it, and sometimes raised its voice in a victorious whoop, and made sepulchral grumblings in the chimney. The cold was growing sharper an the night went on. Villon, protruding his lips, imitated the gust with something between a whistle and a groan. It was an eerie, uncomfortable talent of the poet's, much detested by the Picardy monk.

"Can't you hear it rattle in the gibbet?" said Villon. "They are all dancing the devil's jig on nothing, up there. You may dance, my gallants, you'll be none the warmer! Whew! what a gust! Down went somebody just now! A medlar the fewer on the three-legged medlar-tree!—I say, Dom Nicolas, it'll be cold to-night on the St. Denis Road?" he asked.

Dom Nicolas winked both his big eyes, and seemed to choke upon his Adam's apple. Montfaucon, the great grisly Paris gibbet, stood hard by the St. Denis Road, and the pleasantry touched him on the raw. As for Tabary, he laughed immoderately over the medlars; he had never heard anything more light-hearted; and he held his sides and crowed. Villon fetched him a fillip on the nose, which turned his mirth into an attack of coughing.

"Oh, stop that row," said Villon, "and think of rhymes to 'fish.'"

"Doubles or quits," said Montigny doggedly.

"With all my heart," quoth Thevenin.

"Is there any more in that bottle?" asked the monk.

"Open another," said Villon. "How do you ever hope to fill that big hogshead, your body, with little things like bottles? And how do you expect to get to heaven? How many angels, do you fancy, can be spared to carry up a single monk from Picardy? Or do you think yourself another Elias—and they'll send the coach for you?"

"*Hominibus impossibile,*" replied the monk, as he filled his glass.

Tabary was in ecstasies.

Villon filliped his nose again.

"Laugh at my jokes, if you like," he said.

"It was very good," objected Tabary.

Villon made a face at him. "Think of rhymes to 'fish,'" he said. "What have you to do with Latin? You'll wish you knew none of it at the great assizes, when the devil calls for Guido Tabary, clericus—the devil with the hump-back and red-hot finger-nails. Talking of the devil," he added in a whisper, "look at Montigny!"

All three peered covertly at the gamester. He did not seem to be enjoying his luck. His mouth was a little to a side; one nostril nearly shut, and the other much inflated. The black dog was on his back, as people say, in terrifying nursery metaphor; and he breathed hard under the gruesome burden.

"He looks as if he could knife him," whispered Tabary, with round eyes.

The monk shuddered, and turned his face and spread his open hands to the red embers. It was the cold that thus affected Dom Nicolas, and not any excess of moral sensibility.

"Come now," said Villon—"about this ballade. How does it run so far?" And beating time with his hand, he read it aloud to Tabary.

They were interrupted at the fourth rhyme by a brief and fatal movement among the gamesters. The round was completed, and Thevenin was just opening his mouth to claim another victory, when Montigny leaped up, swift as an adder, and stabbed him to the heart. The blow took effect before he had time to utter a cry, before he had time to move. A tremor or two convulsed his frame; his hands opened and shut, his heels rattled on the floor; then his head rolled backward over one shoulder with the eyes wide open; and Thevenin Pensete's spirit had returned to Him who made it.

Everyone sprang to his feet; but the business was over in two twos. The four living fellows looked at each other in rather a ghastly fashion; the dead man contemplating a corner of the roof with a singular and ugly leer.

"My God!" said Tabary; and he began to pray in Latin.

Villon broke out into hysterical laughter. He came a step forward and ducked a ridiculous bow at Thevenin, and laughed still louder. Then he sat down suddenly, all of a heap, upon a stool, and continued laughing bitterly as though he would shake himself to pieces.

Montigny recovered his composure first.

"Let's see what he has about him," he remarked; and he picked the dead man's pockets with a practised hand, and divided the money into four equal portions on the table. "There's for you," he said.

The monk received his share with a deep sigh, and a single stealthy glance at the dead Thevenin, who was beginning to sink into himself and topple sideways of the chair.

"We're all in for it," cried Villon, swallowing his mirth. "It's a hanging job for every man jack of us that's here—not to speak of those who aren't." He made a shocking gesture in the air with his raised right hand, and put out his tongue and threw his head on one side, so as to counterfeit the appearance of one who has been hanged. Then he pocketed his share of the spoil, and executed a shuffle with his feet as if to restore the circulation.

Tabary was the last to help himself; he made a dash at the money, and retired to the other end of the apartment.

Montigny stuck Thevenin upright in the chair, and drew out the dagger, which was followed by a jet of blood.

"You fellows had better be moving," he said, as he wiped the blade on his victim's doublet.

"I think we had," returned Villon with a gulp. "Damn his fat head!" he broke out. "It sticks in my throat like phlegm. What right has a man to have red hair when he is dead?" And he fell all of a heap again upon the stool, and fairly covered his face with his hands.

Montigny and Dom Nicolas laughed aloud, even Tabary feebly chiming in.

"Cry baby," said the monk.

"I always said he was a woman," added Montigny with a sneer. "Sit up, can't you?" he went on, giving another shake to the murdered body. "Tread out that fire, Nick!"

But Nick was better employed; he was quietly taking Villon's purse, as the poet sat, limp and trembling, on the stool where he had been making a ballade not three minutes before. Montigny and Tabary dumbly demanded a share of the booty, which the monk silently promised as he passed the little bag into the bosom of his gown. In many ways an artistic nature unfits a man for practical existence.

No sooner had the theft been accomplished than Villon shook himself, jumped to his feet, and began helping to scatter and extinguish the embers. Meanwhile Montigny opened the door and cautiously peered into the street. The coast was clear; there was no meddlesome patrol in sight. Still it was judged wiser to slip out severally; and as Villon was himself in a hurry to escape from the neighbourhood of the dead Thevenin, and the rest were in a still greater hurry to get rid of him before he should discover the loss of his money, he was the first by general consent to issue forth into the street.

The wind had triumphed and swept all the clouds from heaven. Only a few vapours, as thin as moonlight, fleeting rapidly across the stars. It was bitter cold; and by a common optical effect, things seemed almost more definite than in the broadest daylight. The sleeping city was absolutely still: a company of white hoods, a field full of little Alps, below the twinkling stars. Villon cursed his fortune. Would it were still snowing! Now, wherever he went, he left an indelible trail behind him on the glittering streets; wherever he went he was still tethered to the house by the cemetery of St. John; wherever he went he must weave, with his own plodding feet, the rope that bound him to the crime and would bind him to the gallows. The leer of the dead man came back to him with a new significance. He snapped his fingers as if to pluck up his own spirits, and choosing a street at random, stepped boldly forward in the snow.

Two things preoccupied him as he went: the aspect of the gallows at Montfaucon in this bright windy phase of the night's existence, for one; and for another, the look of the dead man with his bald head and garland of red curls. Both struck cold upon his heart, and he kept quickening his pace as if he could escape from unpleasant thoughts by mere fleetness of foot. Sometimes he looked back over his shoulder with a sudden nervous jerk; but he was the only moving thing in the white streets, except when the wind swooped round a corner and threw up the snow, which was beginning to freeze, in spouts of glittering dust.

Suddenly he saw, a long way before him, a black clump and a couple of lanterns. The clump was in motion, and the lanterns swung as though carried by men walking. It was a patrol. And though it was merely crossing his line of march, he judged it wiser to get out of eyeshot as speedily as he could. He was not in the humour to be challenged, and he was conscious of making a very conspicuous mark upon the snow. Just on his left hand there stood a great hotel, with some turrets and a large porch before the door; it was half-ruinous, he remembered, and had long stood empty; and so he made three steps of it and jumped into the shelter of the porch. It was pretty dark inside, after the glimmer of the snowy streets, and he was groping forward with outspread hands, when he stumbled over some substance which offered an indescribable mixture of resistances, hard and soft, firm and loose. His heart gave a leap, and he sprang two steps back and stared dreadfully at the obstacle. Then he gave a little laugh of relief. It was only a woman, and she dead. He knelt beside her to make sure upon this latter point. She was freezing cold, and rigid like a stick. A little ragged finery fluttered in the wind about her hair, and her cheeks had been heavily rouged that same afternoon. Her pockets were quite empty; but in her stocking, underneath the garter, Villon found two of the small coins that went by the name of whites. It was little enough; but it was always something; and the poet was moved with a deep sense of pathos that she should have died before she had spent her money. That seemed to him a dark and pitiable mystery; and he looked from the coins in his hand to the dead woman, and back again to the coins, shaking his head over the riddle of man's life. Henry V of England, dying at Vincennes just after he had conquered France, and this poor jade cut off by a cold draught in a great man's doorway, before she had time to spend her couple of whites—it seemed a cruel way to carry on the world. Two whites would have taken such a little while to squander; and yet it would have been one more good taste in the mouth, one more smack of the lips, before the devil got the soul, and the body was left to birds and vermin. He would like to use all his tallow before the light was blown out and the lantern broken.

While these thoughts were passing through his mind, he was feeling, half mechanically, for his purse. Suddenly his heart stopped beating; a feeling of cold scales passed up the back of his legs, and a cold blow seemed to fall upon his scalp. He stood petrified for a moment; then he felt again with one feverish movement; and then his loss burst upon him, and he was covered at once with perspiration. To spendthrifts money is so living and actual—it is such a thin veil between them and their pleasures! There is only one limit to their fortune—that of time; and a spendthrift with only a few crowns is the Emperor of Rome until they are spent. For such a person to lose his money is to suffer the most shocking reverse, and fall from heaven to hell, from all to nothing, in a breath. And all the more if he has put his head in the halter for it; if he may be hanged to-morrow for that same purse, so dearly earned, so foolishly departed! Villon stood and cursed; he threw the two whites into the street; he shook his fist at heaven; he stamped, and was not horrified to find himself trampling the poor corpse. Then he began rapidly to retrace his steps towards the house beside the cemetery. He had forgotten all fear of the patrol, which was long gone by at any rate, and had no idea but that of his lost purse. It was in vain that he looked right and left upon the snow: nothing was to be seen. He had not dropped it in the streets. Had it fallen in the house? He would have liked dearly to go in and see; but the idea of the grisly occupant unmanned him. And he saw besides, as he drew near, that their efforts to put out the fire had been unsuccessful; on the contrary, it had broken into a blaze, and a changeful light played in the chinks of door and window, and revived his terror for the authorities and Paris gibbet.

He returned to the hotel with the porch, and groped about upon the snow for the money he had thrown away in his childish passion. But he could only find one white; the other had probably struck sideways and sunk deeply in. With a single white in his pocket, all his projects for a rousing night in some wild tavern vanished utterly away. And it was not only pleasure that fled laughing from his grasp; positive discomfort, positive pain, attacked him as he stood ruefully before the porch. His perspiration had dried upon him; and though the wind had now fallen, a binding frost was setting in stronger with every hour, and he felt benumbed and sick at heart. What was to be done? Late as was the hour, improbable as was success, he would try the house of his adopted father, the chaplain of St. Benoit.

He ran there all the way, and knocked timidly. There was no answer. He knocked again and again, taking heart with every stroke; and at last steps were heard approaching from within. A barred wicket fell open in the iron-studded door, and emitted a gush of yellow light.

"Hold up your face to the wicket," said the chaplain from within.

"It's only me," whimpered Villon.

"Oh, it's only you, is it?" returned the chaplain; and he cursed him with foul unpriestly oaths for disturbing him at such an hour, and bade him be off to hell, where he came from.

"My hands are blue to the wrist," pleaded Villon; "my feet are dead and full of twinges; my nose aches with the sharp air; the cold lies at my heart. I may be dead before morning. Only this once, father, and before God I will never ask again!"

"You should have come earlier," said the ecclesiastic coolly. "Young men require a lesson now and then." He shut the wicket and retired deliberately into the interior of the house.

Villon was beside himself; he beat upon the door with his hands and feet, and shouted hoarsely after the chaplain.

"Wormy old fox!" he cried. "If I had my hand under your twist, I would send you flying headlong into the bottomless pit."

A door shut in the interior, faintly audible to the poet down long passages. He passed his hand over his mouth with an oath. And then the humour of the situation struck him, and he laughed and looked lightly up to heaven, where the stars seemed to be winking over his discomfiture.

What was to be done? It looked very like a night in the frosty streets. The idea of the dead woman popped into his imagination, and gave him a hearty fright; what had happened to her in the early night might very well happen to him before morning. And he so young! and with such immense possibilities of disorderly amusement before him! He felt quite pathetic over the notion of his own fate, as if it had been some one else's, and made a little imaginative vignette of the scene in the morning when they should find his body.

He passed all his chances under review, turning the white between his thumb and forefinger. Unfortunately he was on bad terms with some old friends who would once have taken pity on him in such a plight. He had lampooned them in verses, he had beaten and cheated them; and yet now, when he was in so close a pinch, he thought there was at least one who might perhaps relent. It was a chance. It was worth trying at least, and he would go and see.

On the way, two little accidents happened to him which coloured his musings in a very different manner. For, first, he fell in with the track of a patrol, and walked in it for some hundred yards, although it lay out of his direction. And this spirited him up; at least he had confused his trail; for he was still possessed with the idea of people tracking him all about Paris over the snow, and collaring him next morning before he was awake. The other matter affected him very differently. He passed a street corner, where, not so long before, a woman and her child had been devoured by wolves. This was just the kind of weather, he reflected, when wolves might take it into their heads to enter Paris again; and a lone man in these deserted streets would run the chance of something worse than a mere scare. He stopped and looked upon the place with an unpleasant interest—it was a centre where several lanes intersected each other; and he looked down them all one after another, and held his breath to listen, lest he should detect some galloping black things on the snow or hear the sound of howling between him and the river. He remembered his mother telling him the story and pointing out the spot, while he was yet a child. His mother! If he only knew where she lived, he might make sure at least of shelter. He determined he would inquire upon the morrow; nay, he would go and see her too, poor old girl! So thinking, he arrived at his destination—his last hope for the night.

The house was quite dark, like its neighbours; and yet after a few taps, he heard a movement overhead, a door opening, and a cautious voice asking who was there. The poet named himself in a loud whisper, and waited, not without some trepidations, the result. Nor had he to wait long. A window was suddenly opened, and a pailful of slops splashed down upon the doorstep. Villon had not been unprepared for something of the sort, and had put himself as much in shelter as the nature of the porch admitted; but for all that, he was deplorably drenched below the waist. His hose began to freeze almost at once. Death from cold and exposure stared him in the face; he remembered he was of phthisical tendency, and began coughing tentatively. But the gravity of the danger steadied his nerves. He stopped a few hundred yards from the door where he had been so rudely used, and reflected with his finger to his nose. He could only see one way of getting a lodging, and that was to take it. He had noticed a house not far away, which looked as if it might be easily broken into, and thither he betook himself promptly, entertaining himself on the way with the idea of a room still hot, with a table still loaded with the remains of supper, where he might pass the rest of the black hours, and whence he should issue, on the morrow, with an armful of valuable plate. He even considered on what viands and what wines he should prefer; and as he was calling the roll of his favourite dainties, roast fish presented itself to his mind with an odd mixture of amusement and horror.

"I shall never finish that ballade," he thought to himself; and then, with another shudder at the recollection, "Oh, damn his fat head!" he repeated fervently, and spat upon the snow.

The house in question looked dark at first sight; but as Villon made a preliminary inspection in search of the handiest point of attack, a little twinkle of light caught his eye from behind a curtained window.

"The devil!" he thought. "People awake! Some student or some saint, confound the crew! Can't they get drunk and lie in bed snoring like their neighbours? What's the good of curfew, and poor devils of bell-ringers jumping at a rope's end in bell-towers? What's the use of day, if people sit up all night? The gripes to them!" He grinned as he saw where his logic was leading him. "Every man to his business, after all," added he, "and if they're awake, by the Lord, I may come by a supper honestly for this once, and cheat the devil."

He went boldly to the door and knocked with an assured hand. On both previous occasions, he had knocked timidly and with some dread of attracting notice; but now when he had just discarded the thought of a burglarious entry, knocking at a door seemed a mighty simple and innocent proceeding. The sound of his blows echoed through the house with thin, phantasmal reverberations, as though it were quite empty; but these had scarcely died away before a measured tread drew near, a couple of bolts were withdrawn, and one wing was opened broadly, as though no guile or fear of guile were known to those within. A tall figure of a man, muscular and spare, but a little bent, confronted Villon. The head was massive in bulk, but finely sculptured; the nose blunt at the bottom, but refining upward to where it joined a pair of strong and honest eyebrows; the mouth and eyes surrounded with delicate markings, and the whole face based upon a thick white beard, boldly and squarely trimmed. Seen as it was by the light of a flickering hand-lamp, it looked perhaps nobler than it had a right to do; but it was a fine face, honourable rather than intelligent, strong, simple, and righteous.

"You knock late, sir," said the old man in resonant, courteous tones.

Villon cringed, and brought up many servile words of

apology; at a crisis of this sort, the beggar was uppermost in him, and the man of genius hid his head with confusion.

"You are cold," repeated the old man, "and hungry? Well, step in." And he ordered him into the house with a noble enough gesture.

"Some great seigneur," thought Villon, as his host, setting down the lamp on the flagged pavement of the entry, shot the bolts once more into their places.

"You will pardon me if I go in front," he said, when this was done; and he preceded the poet upstairs into a large apartment, warmed with a pan of charcoal and lit by a great lamp hanging from the roof. It was very bare of furniture: only some gold plate on a sideboard; some folios; and a stand of armour between the windows. Some smart tapestry hung upon the walls, representing the crucifixion of our Lord in one piece, and in another a scene of shepherds and shepherdesses by a running stream. Over the chimney was a shield of arms.

"Will you seat yourself," said the old man, "and forgive me if I leave you? I am alone in my house to-night, and if you are to eat I must forage for you myself."

No sooner was his host gone than Villon leaped from the chair on which he had just seated himself, and began examining the room, with the stealth and passion of a cat. He weighed the gold flagons in his hand, opened all the folios, and investigated the arms upon the shield, and the stuff with which the seats were lined. He raised the window curtains, and saw that the windows were set with rich stained glass in figures, so far as he could see, of martial import. Then he stood in the middle of the room, drew a long breath, and retaining it with puffed cheeks, looked round and round him, turning on his heels, as if to impress every feature of the apartment on his memory.

"Seven pieces of plate," he said. "If there had been ten, I would have risked it. A fine house, and a fine old master, so help me all the saints!"

And just then, hearing the old man's tread returning along the corridor, he stole back to his chair, and began humbly toasting his wet legs before the charcoal pan.

His entertainer had a plate of meat in one hand and a jug of wine in the other. He set down the plate upon the table, motioning Villon to draw in his chair, and going to the sideboard, brought back two goblets, which he filled.

"I drink to your better fortune," he said, gravely touching Villon's cup with his own.

"To our better acquaintance," said the poet, growing bold. A mere man of the people would have been awed by the courtesy of the old seigneur, but Villon was hardened in that matter; he had made mirth for great lords before now, and found them as black rascals as himself. And so he devoted himself to the viands with a ravenous gusto, while the old man, leaning backward, watched him with steady, curious eyes.

"You have blood on your shoulder, my man," he said. Montigny must have laid his wet right hand upon him as he left the house. He cursed Montigny in his heart.

"It was none of my shedding," he stammered.

"I had not supposed so," returned his host quietly.

"A brawl?"

"Well, something of that sort," Villon admitted with a quaver.

"Perhaps a fellow murdered?"

"Oh no, not murdered," said the poet, more and more confused. "It was all fair play—murdered by accident. I had no hand in it, God strike me dead!" he added fervently.

"One rogue the fewer, I dare say," observed the master of the house.

"You may dare to say that," agreed Villon, infinitely relieved. "As big a rogue as there is between here and Jerusalem. He turned up his toes like a lamb. But it was a nasty thing to look at. I dare say you've seen dead men in your time, my lord?" he added, glancing at the armour.

"Many," said the old man. "I have followed the wars, as you imagine."

Villon laid down his knife and fork, which he had just taken up again.

"Were any of them bald?" he asked.

"Oh yes, and with hair as white as mine."

"I don't think I should mind the white so much," said Villon. "His was red." And he had a return of his shuddering and tendency to laughter, which he drowned with a great draught of wine. "I'm a little put out when I think of it," he went on. "I knew him—damn him! And then the cold gives a man fancies—or the fancies give a man cold, I don't know which."

"Have you any money?" asked the old man.

"I have one white," returned the poet, laughing. "I got it out of a dead jade's stocking in a porch. She was as dead as Caesar, poor wench, and as cold as a church, with bits of ribbon sticking in her hair. This is a hard world in winter for wolves and wenches and poor rogues like me."

"I," said the old man, "am Enguerrand de la Feuillée, seigneur de Brisetout, bailly du Patatrac. Who and what may you be?"

Villon rose and made a suitable reverence. "I am called Francis Villon," he said, "a poor Master of Arts of this university. I know some Latin, and a deal of vice. I can make chansons, ballades, lais, virelais, and roundels, and I am very fond of wine. I was born in a garret, and I shall not improbably die upon the gallows. I may add, my lord, that from this night forward I am your lordship's very obsequious servant to command."

"No servant of mine," said the knight; "my guest for this evening, and no more."

"A very grateful guest," said Villon politely; and he drank in dumb show to his entertainer.

"You are shrewd," began the old man, tapping his forehead, "very shrewd; you have learning; you are a clerk; and yet you take a small piece of money off a dead woman in the street. Is it not a kind of theft?"

"It is a kind of theft much practised in the wars, my lord."

"The wars are the field of honour," returned the old man proudly. "There a man plays his life upon the cast; he fights in the name of his lord the king, his Lord God, and all their lordships the holy saints and angels."

"Put it," said Villon, "that I were really a thief, should I not play my life also, and against heavier odds?"

"For gain, but not for honour."

"Gain?" repeated Villon with a shrug. "Gain! The poor fellow wants supper, and takes it. So does the soldier in a campaign. Why, what are all these requisitions we hear so much about? If they are not gain to those who take them, they are loss enough to the others. The men-at-arms drink by a good fire, while the burgher bites his nails to buy them wine and wood. I have seen a good many ploughmen swinging on trees about the country, ay, I have seen thirty on one elm, and a very poor figure they made; and when I asked some one how all these came to be hanged, I was told it was because they could not scrape together enough crowns to satisfy the men-at-arms."

"These things are a necessity of war, which the low-born must endure with constancy. It is true that some captains drive over hard; there are spirits in every rank not easily moved by pity; and indeed many follow arms who are no better than brigands."

"You see," said the poet, "you cannot separate the soldier from the brigand; and what is a thief but an isolated brigand with circumspect manners? I steal a couple of mutton chops, without so much as disturbing people's sleep; the farmer grumbles a bit, but sups none the less wholesomely on what remains. You come up blowing gloriously on a trumpet, take away the whole sheep, and beat the farmer pitifully into the bargain. I have no trumpet; I am only Tom, Dick, or Harry; I am a rogue and a dog, and hanging's too good for me—with all my heart; but just you ask the farmer which of us he prefers, just find out which of us he lies awake to curse on cold nights."

"Look at us two," said his lordship. "I am old, strong, and honoured. If I were turned from my house to-morrow, hundreds would be proud to shelter me. Poor people would go out and pass the night in the streets with their children, if I merely hinted that I wished to be alone. And I find you up, wandering homeless, and picking farthings off dead women by the wayside! I fear no man and nothing; I have seen you tremble and lose countenance at a word. I wait God's summons contentedly in my own house, or, if it please the king to call me out again, upon the field of battle. You look for the gallows; a rough, swift death, without hope or honour. Is there no difference between these two?"

"As far as to the moon," Villon acquiesced. "But if I had been born lord of Brisetout, and you had been the poor scholar Francis, would the difference have been any the less? Should not I have been warming my knees at this charcoal pan, and would not you have been groping for farthings in the snow? Should not I have been the soldier, and you the thief?"

"A thief!" cried the old man. "I a thief! If you understood your words, you would repent them."

Villon turned out his hands with a gesture of inimitable impudence. "If your lordship had done me the honour to follow my argument!" he said.

"I do you too much honour in submitting to your presence," said the knight. "Learn to curb your tongue when you speak with old and honourable men, or some one hastier than I may reprove you in a sharper fashion." And he rose and paced the lower end of the apartment, struggling with anger and antipathy. Villon surreptitiously refilled his cup, and settled himself more comfortably in the chair, crossing his knees and leaning his head upon one hand and the elbow against the back of the chair. He was now replete and warm; and he was in nowise frightened for his host, having gauged him as justly as was possible between two such different characters. The night was far spent, and in a very comfortable fashion after all; and he felt morally certain of a safe departure on the morrow.

"Tell me one thing," said the old man, pausing in his walk. "Are you really a thief?"

"I claim the sacred rights of hospitality," returned the poet. "My lord, I am."

"You are very young," the knight continued.

"I should never have been so old," replied Villon, showing his fingers, "if I had not helped myself with these ten talents. They have been my nursing mothers and my nursing fathers."

"You may still repent and change."

"I repent daily," said the poet. "There are few people more given to repentance than poor Francis. As for change, let somebody change my circumstances. A man must continue to eat, if it were only that he may continue to repent."

"The change must begin in the heart," returned the old man solemnly.

"My dear lord," answered Villon, "do you really fancy that I steal for pleasure? I hate stealing, like any other piece of work or of danger. My teeth chatter when I see a gallows. But I must eat,

I must drink, I must mix in society of some sort. What the devil! Man is not a solitary animal—*cui Deus faeminam tradit*. Make me king's pantler—make me abbot of St. Denis; make me bailly of the Patatrac; and then I shall be changed indeed. But as long as you leave me the poor scholar Francis Villon, without a farthing, why, of course, I remain the same."

"The grace of God is all-powerful."

"I should be a heretic to question it," said Francis. "It has made you lord of Brisetout and bailly of the Patatrac; it has given me nothing but the quick wits under my hat and these ten toes upon my hands. May I help myself to wine? I thank you respectfully. By God's grace, you have a very superior vintage."

The lord of Brisetout walked to and fro with his hands behind his back. Perhaps he was not yet quite settled in his mind about the parallel between thieves and soldiers; perhaps Villon had interested him by some cross-thread of sympathy; perhaps his wits were simply muddled by so much unfamiliar reasoning; but whatever the cause, he somehow yearned to convert the young man to a better way of thinking, and could not make up his mind to drive him forth again into the street.

"There is something more than I can understand in this," he said at length. "Your mouth is full of subtleties, and the devil has led you very far astray; but the devil is only a very weak spirit before God's truth, and all his subtleties vanish at a word of true honour, like darkness at morning. Listen to me once more. I learned long ago that a gentleman should live chivalrously and lovingly to God, and the king, and his lady; and though I have seen many strange things done, I have still striven to command my ways upon that rule. It is not only written in all noble histories, but in every man's heart, if he will take care to read. You speak of food and wine, and I know very well that hunger is a difficult trial to endure; but you do not speak of other wants; you say nothing of honour, of faith to God and other men, of courtesy, of love without reproach. It may be that I am not very wise— and yet I think I am—but you seem to me like one who has lost his way and made a great error in life. You are attending to the little wants, and you have totally forgotten the great and only real ones, like a man who should be doctoring a toothache on the Judgment Day. For such things as honour and love and faith are not only nobler than food and drink, but indeed I think that we desire them more, and suffer more sharply for their absence. I speak to you as I think you will most easily understand me. Are you not, while careful to fill your belly, disregarding another appetite in your heart, which spoils the pleasure of your life and keeps you continually wretched?"

Villon was sensibly nettled under all this sermonising. "You think I have no sense of honour!" he cried. "I'm poor enough, God knows! It's hard to see rich people with their gloves, and you blowing in your hands. An empty belly is a bitter thing, although you speak so lightly of it. If you had had as many as I, perhaps you would change your tune. Any way I'm a thief—make the most of that—but I'm not a devil from hell, God strike me dead. I would have you to know I've an honour of my own, as good as yours, though I don't prate about it all day long, as if it was a God's miracle to have any. It seems quite natural to me; I keep it in its box till it's wanted. Why now, look you here, how long have I been in this room with you? Did you not tell me you were alone in the house? Look at your gold plate! You're strong, if you like, but you're old and unarmed, and I have my knife. What did I want but a jerk of the elbow and here would have been you with the cold steel in your bowels, and there would have been me, linking in the streets, with an armful of gold cups! Did you suppose I hadn't wit enough to see that? And I scorned the action. There are your damned goblets, as safe as in a church; there are you, with your heart ticking as good as new; and here am I, ready to go out again as poor as I came in, with my one white that you threw in my teeth! And you think I have no sense of honour—God strike me dead!"

The old man stretched out his right arm. "I will tell you what you are," he said. "You are a rogue, my man, an impudent and a black-hearted rogue and vagabond. I have passed an hour with you. Oh! believe me, I feel myself disgraced! And you have eaten and drunk at my table. But now I am sick at your presence; the day has come, and the night-bird should be off to his roost. Will you go before, or after?"

"Which you please," returned the poet, rising. "I believe you to be strictly honourable." He thoughtfully emptied his cup. "I wish I could add you were intelligent," he went on, knocking on his head with his knuckles. "Age, age! the brains stiff and rheumatic."

The old man preceded him from a point of self-respect; Villon followed, whistling, with his thumbs in his girdle.

"God pity you," said the lord of Brisetout at the door.

"Good-bye, papa," returned Villon with a yawn. "Many thanks for the cold mutton."

The door closed behind him. The dawn was breaking over the white roofs. A chill, uncomfortable morning ushered in the day. Villon stood and heartily stretched himself in the middle of the road.

"A very dull old gentleman," he thought. "I wonder what his goblets may be worth."

# Word Cloud Classics

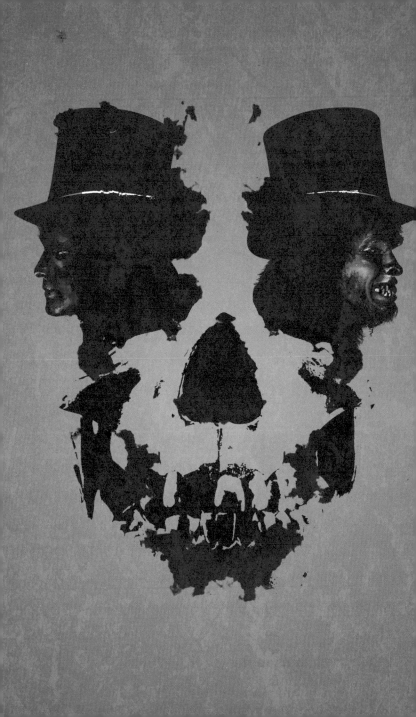